June 1991

To all the Spikers,

   With love and understanding
for openness in all your
communication,

   Barry

perspectives on

ORGANIZATIONAL COMMUNICATION

TOM D. DANIELS
Ohio University

BARRY K. SPIKER
Andersen Consulting

wcb
WM. C. BROWN PUBLISHERS
DUBUQUE, IOWA

Book Team

Editor *Stan Stoga*
Developmental Editor *Jane F. Lambert*
Production Coordinator *Kay Driscoll*

WCB Wm. C. Brown Publishers

President *G. Franklin Lewis*
Vice President, Publisher *George Wm. Bergquist*
Vice President, Publisher *Thomas E. Doran*
Vice President, Operations and Production *Beverly Kolz*
National Sales Manager *Virginia S. Moffat*
Senior Marketing Manager *Kathy Law Laube*
Marketing Manager *Kathleen Nietzke*
Executive Editor *Edgar J. Laube*
Managing Editor, Production *Colleen A. Yonda*
Production Editorial Manager *Julie A. Kennedy*
Production Editorial Manager *Ann Fuerste*
Publishing Services Manager *Karen J. Slaght*
Manager of Visuals and Design *Faye M. Schilling*

Printed in the United States of America by Wm. C. Brown Publishers,
2460 Kerper Boulevard, Dubuque, IA 52001

10 9 8 7 6 5 4 3 2 1

To my parents, Harlin and Doris Daniels, to my wife, Deborah, and to my daughters, Shannon, Erica, Lindsey, and Lauren.   —TDD

To the memory of my father, Bill Spiker, and to the indomitable spirit of my mother, Imogene Spiker.   —BKS

Contents

Preface ix

Part
1
Foundations 1

Chapter 1
An Orientation to Organizational Communication 3

Studying Organizational Communication 4
  Understanding Organizations 4
  Awareness of Skills 5
  Career Opportunities 5
Development of the Field 6
  Relationship to Other Fields 7
  *Perspectives on Organizational
    Communication 8*
Alternative Models of Organizational
  Communication 14
Distinctions Among the Perspectives 15
  *Critical Theory and the Radical
    Perspectives 15*
  *Reality and Order in Contemporary
    Functionalism 16*
  *Other Features of Contemporary
    Functionalism 17*
Acceptance of the Perspectives 19
Approach of the Text 20

Summary 21

**Discussion Questions/Activities
21**

Case Study 22

References 24

Chapter 2
The Concept of Communication 29

What is Communication? 29
  Information and Meaning 30
  Verbal Behavior 30
  Nonverbal Behavior 35
  Other Definitions 41
What Happens When Communication
  Occurs? 42
  Linear Model 43
  Interactional Model 44
  Transactional Model 44

Summary 46

**Discussion Questions/Activities
47**

Case Study 47

References 50

Chapter 3
Theories of Organization and Organizational Effectiveness 53

Scientific and Classical Management 54
  Taylor's Scientific Management 54
  Fayol's General Management 55
  Weber's Bureaucratic Theory 56
Eclectic Theories 60
  Follett's Administrative Theory 60
  Barnard's Executive Functions 61
The Human Relations Movement 62

Dale Carnegie 62
The Hawthorne Studies and Elton Mayo
62
Human Resource Development 65
Maslow's Need Hierarchy 65
McGregor's Theory X and Theory Y 66
Likert's Four Systems 67
A System Theory 70
Wholeness 71
Hierarchy 71
Openness 72
Feedback 74

Summary 75

**Discussion Questions/Activities
76**

Case Study 77

References 79

**Part
2**
Themes 81

Chapter 4

Organizational Communication Function and Structure 83

Two Precautions 83
Function and Structure Relationship 84
Impact of Organizational Politics 84
Communication Functions 85
Traditional Function Categories 85
Uncertainty and Information Adequacy
86
Unanswered Questions About
Communication Functions 89
Communication Structure 91
Formal Communication 92
Informal Communication 99
Limitations of the Traditional View 102
Communication Structure as a Network
104

Summary 110

**Discussion Question/Activities
111**

Case Study 112

References 114

Chapter 5

Communication and Organizational Culture 119

The Concept of Organizational Culture 119
Functionalist Perspective 120
Interpretivist Perspective 121
Studying Organizational Culture 122
Fantasy Theme Analysis 122
Metaphor Analysis 125
Analysis of Reflexive Comments 127
Communication and Cultural Change 129
Forces Influencing Organizational
Culture 130
The Symbolic Manager 130
A Final Caution 132

Summary 133

**Discussion Questions/Activities
134**

Case Study 134

References 136

Chapter 6

Power and Conflict 139

Traditional Views of Status and Power 139
Status Symbols 140
Types of Power 140
Power, Competition, and Cooperation
142
Social Exchange and Power 142
Power in the View of Critical Theory 143
Power and Legitimization 144
Power and Organizational Structure 144
Power, Symbols, and Systematic
Distortion 145
Critical Theory in Organizational
Communication Research 147
Critical Theory vs. Interpretivism 149
Conflict 149
Sources of Conflict 151
Managing Conflict 154
Interpersonal Conflict 155
Coalitions and Intergroup Conflict 157
Bargaining and Negotiation 160

Summary 162

**Discussion Questions/Activities
163**

Case Study 163

References 166

Chapter 7

Information Technology: The New Medium 171

Types of Information Systems 172
  Computerized Accounting 173
  Integrated Data Processing 173
  Integrated Management Information Systems 173
  Real-time MIS 174
  Distributed Processing 174
Technological Consequences for Communication 175
  Changes in Organizational Structure 178
  Effects on Staffing and Job Functions 183
  Communication in the Information Network: LANs and WANs 185

Summary 190

Discussion Questions/Activities 191

Case Study 191

References 193

Part

3

Contexts 197

Chapter 8

Dyadic Communication 199

Theories of Dyadic Communication 200
  Motivational Theory 200
  Personality Theory 202
  Rules Theory 203
Superior-Subordinate Communication 207
  Subordinate Satisfaction 211
  Superior's Compliance-Gaining 217
  Subordinate Behavior 219
  Assimilation Theory 221
  Conclusions from Superior-Subordinate Research 222
Unanswered Questions in Dyadic Communication 223

Summary 225

Discussion Questions/Activities 226

Case Study 226

References 228

Chapter 9

Group Communication 233

Groups as Organizational Subsystems 233
Concepts in Group Communication 235
  Norms and Conformity 236
  Roles and Role Categories in Groups 238
  Leadership Behavior 239
Group Decision Making 245
  Decision Making and Culture 247
  Effective Group Decision Making 248
  Group Decision Development 250
  Prescriptive Models for Decision Making 253
Groups, Values, and Sense-Making 256

Summary 257

Discussion Questions/Activities 257

Case Study 258

References 260

Chapter 10

Public Communication 265

Characteristics of Public Communication 266
  The Source in Organizational Public Communication 266
  Public Communication as Transaction 267
Grunig's Multisystems Theory 268
Internal Public Communication 271
  Orientation and Indoctrination 271
  Safety and Loss Prevention 272
  Compensation and Benefits 273
  Organizational Change and Development 273
  Morale and Satisfaction 274
External Public Communication 275
  Public Relations and Image-Building 276
  Public Affairs and Issues Management 277

Summary 285

Discussion Questions/Activities 286

Case Study 286

References 287

Part

4

Applications 289

Chapter 11

Communication Professionals in Organizations 291

Basic Occupational Roles 292
Consultation Models 294
    Provision Model 294
    Prescription Model 295
    Collaboration Model 296
    Organization Development 297
Professional Politics 300
Professional Ethics 301

Summary 303

Discussion Questions/Activities 304

Case Study 304

References 306

Chapter 12

Organizational Communication Evaluation 309

Purposes of OCE 310
OCE Perspectives: Inner and Outer 311
General OCE Methods 312
    Direct Observation 312
    Interviews 313
    Survey Questionnaire 314
    Documents 315

Specific OCE Tools 315
    Communication Audits and Their
      Limitations 315
    Content Analysis 320
    Interaction Analysis 321
    Episodic Communication Channels in
      Organizations 323

Summary 323

Discussion Questions/Activities 324

Case Study 324

References 326

Chapter 13

Changing Organizational Communication 329

The Concept of Intervention 329
Models of Intervention 330
Organizational Communication Interventions 332
    Agenda Setting 332
    Feedback of Observations 336
    Coaching and Training 338
    Structural Suggestions 340

Summary 342

Discussion Questions/Activities 343

Case Study 343

References 346

Author Index 347

Subject Index 351

Preface

In the preface to the first edition of *Perspectives on Organizational Communication,* we admitted that we probably had fallen short of our goal "to present an artful mosaic which would somehow include every subtle nuance of this phenomenon" (1987, p. xii). Even so, we were confident that we had produced a sound survey text for the study of organizational communication. The wide acceptance of this book in the basic organizational communication course has supported that confidence. Thankfully, those who adopted the first edition of the book also turned out to be enthusiastic and constructive critics, who have offered us many ideas that we have incorporated as improvements in the second edition.

The first edition of *Perspectives* was shaped largely by the instability, flux, and transitions that characterized the academic study of organizational communication in the 1980s. In a sense, the book represented our response to this instability. We anchored the book on a foundation of traditional concepts and themes that had guided the study of organizational communication into the 1980s. At the same time, we wanted to acknowledge and incorporate new themes and orientations to the study of the subject that were beginning to challenge old and established ways of thinking about organizational communication. Consequently, the book was dominated by the conventional socio-behavioral science tradition that has been labeled variously as functionalist, modernist, or rationalist. We included a chapter on newer interpretive orientations to organizational communication along with occasional references to interpretive studies at various points in the book. We reviewed, but also essentially dismissed radical perspectives on organizational communication as relatively unimportant at that time. Well, much has changed in the four years since *Perspectives* originally was published.

As we enter the 1990s, it is fair to say that organizational communication is still a field in transition, but the emerging shape of this particular discipline is now much clearer and much more discernible. The conventional social science approach to the field, while still very prominent, has nonetheless given way to the emergence of a healthy and maturing school of naturalistic, interpretive scholarship on organizational communication. And both of these approaches have been obliged to make room for the arrival of a small, but steadily growing and assertive body of radical scholarship that has been inspired largely by the neo-Marxist influence of the Institute for Social Research at the University of Frankfurt. Neo-Marxism is, by the way, not quite the same thing as the orthodox, economic Marxism that has been crumbling throughout Eastern Europe. Despite the demise of its older cousin, neo-Marxism appears to be alive and well. Indeed, it even may have provided some of the impetus for change in Eastern Europe. Neo-Marxist scholarship, referred to generally as the critical perspective, certainly is beginning to influence the study of organizational communication.

The second edition of *Perspectives on Organizational Communication* is designed to reflect the state of the field as it exists in the 1990s. Consequently, we have retained our reviews of familiar standard topics, but we also have expanded our treatment of new trends and emerging issues in the field. You will still find all of the standard theories of organization and organizational effectiveness (classical, scientific, human relations, human resource development, systems) as well as traditional scholarship on communication structure and function, superior-subordinate relationships, and group decision making, but we have updated the book to include the most recent lines of research in each of these areas. We have expanded our discussion of interpretive research in the chapter on organizational culture. We have added a new chapter on power and conflict. This chapter contrasts the traditional view of power with the radical view and introduces students to scholarship that has developed from the critical perspective. Of course, the very first chapter of the book also has been rewritten to reflect these changes.

We have revised substantially our chapter on information technology. At the time this chapter originally was prepared for the first edition (i.e., in 1985), we were obliged to conclude that there was much more speculation than real research regarding the potential impact of these technologies on organizations. Again, the world has changed in a few short years. We now know that new technologies—or at least the choices that people make when they use these technologies—are changing the form and content of organizations generally, and organizational communication specifically.

The new edition includes a number of minor changes, mostly in the form of updating the content, but there is one more major change. Case studies for the first edition were included in an accompanying instructor's manual prepared by Michael Smilowitz. As a consequence of feedback from numerous users of the book (as well as one fairly uncharitable review of the book!), we located the thirteen case studies in the book for the second edition. Each chapter is accompanied by a specific case study. Three of these cases were written by Michael Smilowitz for the original instructor's manual. Three more were prepared by Tom Daniels. The remaining cases were written by professionals with Andersen Consulting at the Center for Professional Education, Arthur Andersen & Co., S.C., St. Charles, IL. These individuals are Janice Goodman, Bill Hendry, Mark Holt, Jill Peddicord, Grover Ray, Rob Reindle, and Jeanne Russell. Each case study is based on a real incident or an amalgam of two or more real incidents, but the cases have been written with fictitious names, settings, and other elements in order to protect the identities of the persons and the organizations involved in these incidents.

Organization of the Text

The second edition of the book is, like its progenitor, organized in four sections: Orientation, Themes, Contexts, and Applications. Unit I, including the first three chapters, provides some basic *foundations* for understanding the field of organizational communication. In chapter 1, we define organizational communication and discuss some of the history as well as the present status of the field we give special attention to several different perspectives that influence the study of organizational communication, namely, functionalism, interpretivism, radical humanism, and radical structuralism, but we subsume the two radical groups more generally under critical theory in this edition. In chapter 2, we review definitions and models from communication theory that have influenced the study of organizational communication. This chapter is included primarily for students who may be entering the organizational communication course without prior coursework in communication fundamentals. Since organizational communication is influenced not only by communication theory, but also by organization theory, we review the major twentieth century theories of organization and organizational effectiveness in chapter 3, namely, classical, scientific, human relations, human resource development, and systems as well as some ecletic theories that do not fit these categories.

Unit II includes four chapters on important *themes* or general topic areas in organizational communication. In chapter 4, we discuss organizational communication themes from the perspective of structural-functionalism, a central model in the contemporary functionalist view of organizations as living systems. The topics in this chapter include various communication functions, formal and informal systems, and network characteristics. Chapter 5 presents the cultural perspective of organizational communication themes, with special attention to interpretivists' use of this perspective. Again, we have expanded this chapter somewhat to include discussion of recent interpretive scholarship in organizational communication. Chapter 6 on power and conflict is new. We borrowed a few pages from sections on power and conflict that had already been included in the first edition, but most of the content is completely new to the book, including material on critical theory and scholarship, updated research on conflict, and theory and research on bargaining and negotiation. Chapter 7 includes a significant revision of our review of information processing technology and its influence on organizational communication, especially in the case of computer-mediated communication within local and wide area networks. Unit III includes chapters on three major *contexts* in organizational communication, dyadic, group, and public (chapters 8 to 10). These contexts are related closely to the structural-functional concept of levels, but we review both functionalist, interpretivist, and, occasionally, critical scholars' work on organizational communication within these contexts. Chapters 8 and 9 include up-to-date reviews of research on topics such as superior-subordinate communication, mentor-protege relationships, and group decision-making processes. Chapter 10 includes an expanded discussion of public relations, issues management, and corporate advocacy along with a discussion of traditional concepts in internal and external public communication.

Finally, we consider the problem of organizational communication *applications* in Unit IV from the vantage point of communication professionals in organizations. Chapter 11 concerns the roles of communication professionals in organizations. Chapter 12 describes the tools and techniques that they use in order to evaluate organizational communication. Chapter 13 presents some of the major strategies that are employed to improve organizational communication.

We have retained the Unit IV because there is, in fact, a large profession and vocation where people apply the kinds of concepts and principles described in this book in an effort to improve organizational communication. Barry Spiker and most of the people who contributed case studies to this book earn their livings by doing precisely those things that are described in chapters 12 and 13. Nevertheless, students should be made aware of two important points about Unit IV.

First, one need not be a communication professional engaged in evaluation research and intervention activity in order to benefit from organizational communication theory. The concepts and principles can be just as useful to ordinary organization members in making sense of their day-to-day experiences as they are to professionals who apply them in evaluation and intervention. Second, reading a chapter in a basic organizational communication text about the activities of people in the vocation will not prepare one to enter this vocation. One might as well expect to become a biologist simply by reading a chapter on that vocation in a basic biology text. We have tried to be very clear in this text about the realities of the market demand for such professionals and the extensive academic preparation required to enter the profession.

Special Features
The book includes topic outlines and summaries for each chapter. Key terms are displayed in bold face type at or near points where they are first defined or used in a meaningful way. Activities, discussion questions, a case study, and complete references are included at the end of each chapter.

Instructor's Manual
The instructor's manual, prepared by Michael Smilowitz of the University of North Carolina—Charlotte in collaboration with Tom Daniels, is a very useful tool for both experienced and new instructors. It includes a statement of learning objectives, a very detailed full-content outline, and multiple-choice test items for each chapter in the book.

Acknowledgements
We especially wish to thank four scholars who provided very careful reviews of the revision plan for this edition. These individuals are Stephen Banks, Arizona State University; Kevin Lamude, University of New Mexico; Michael

Papa, Ohio University; and Ron Sandwina, Purdue University. We incorporated many of their suggestions in this edition.

The Authors

Tom D. Daniels (Ph.D., Ohio University, 1979) is Professor and Associate Dean of the College of Communication at The Ohio University. He also served as an assistant professor of communication at the University of Wisconsin–Green Bay and at the University of New Mexico. He has held line management positions in both private and public-sector organizations and is an experienced trainer and consultant. He has authored and coauthored articles and book chapters on various topics in organizational communication, communication theory, philosophy of social science, and research methods. Daniels is past secretary of the organizational communication division in the Speech Communication Association, past chair of the organizational communication division in the Central States Communication Association, a member of the organizational communication division of the International Communication Association, and serves on the editorial board of *Communication Education.* When Tom is not writing and teaching, he brews beer, canoes whitewater rivers in West Virginia, and coaches girls' little league softball.

Barry K. Spiker (Ph.D., Ohio University, 1979) is Senior Manager in the Change Management Services unit with Andersen Consulting of Arthur Andersen & Co., S.C., Chicago, IL. Prior to assuming this position, he held positions as Manager of Organization Development and Manager of Automation Planning for Honeywell, Inc. He also was an assistant professor in the Department of Communication at the University of New Mexico and corporate chief of staff for a privately held, midwestern manufacturing corporation. He has authored and coauthored articles and book chapters on topics in organizational communication, technological advancement and integration, and social science research methods. He is a member of the organizational communication divisions of the International Communication Association and the Academy of Management, a member of American Society for Training and Development, a member of the Organization Development Network, and an associate editor for *Management Communication Quarterly.* When Barry is not traveling for Andersen Consulting, he travels for himself, often to New Mexico where he owns land near the Sandia Mountains. Barry flies airplanes and cooks gourmet meals.

We have worked together on research studies and consulting projects in organizational communication since 1976. Between us, we have nearly forty years of management, consulting, and teaching experience. We have tried to incorporate as much of that experience as possible in this text.

Tom D. Daniels, Athens, Ohio
Barry K. Spiker, Chicago, Illinois

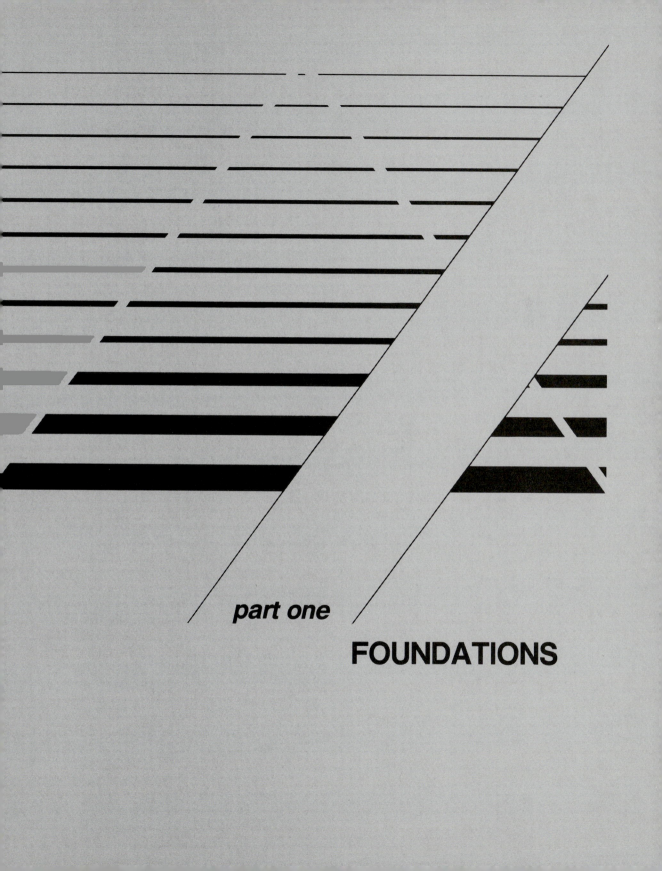

part one

FOUNDATIONS

Outline

Studying Organizational
    Communication
    Understanding Organizations
    Awareness of Skills
    Career Opportunities
Development of the Field
    Relationship to Other Fields
    Perspectives on Organizational
        Communication
    Organizational Order
    Organizational Reality
    Functionalism
    Interpretivism
    Radical Humanism and
        Radical Structuralism
Alternative Models of
    Organizational
    Communication
Distinctions among the Perspectives

Critical Theory and the Radical
    Perspectives
Reality and Order in
    Contemporary
    Functionalism
Other Features of Contemporary
    Functionalism
    Human Communication
    Organizations and
        Organizational
        Effectiveness
    Organizational
        Communication
    Communication Professionals
Acceptance of the Perspectives
Approach of the Text
Summary
Discussion Questions/Activities
Case Study
References

An Orientation to Organizational Communication

1

Organizational life is a major feature of human experience. We are not only social creatures, but also organizational creatures. We work in, play in, cope with, and depend on many types of organizations. They include business, industrial, governmental, educational, professional, religious, social, and political organizations.

You probably have been involved with organizations in one form or another for most of your life. If you ever joined the Boy Scouts or Girl Scouts, became a member of a service club, or worked in some type of company, you were a member of an organization. As a student, you participate in the complex organizational dynamics of your college or university. You must deal with your institution's policies, procedures, expectations, customs, and habits. You may even be caught up in its internal conflicts, territorial rivalries, and power struggles.

Basically, human beings **organize** in order to get things done. When we organize, we define and arrange positions or roles in complex relationships. We engage in concerted action with one another by coordinating these roles in order to accomplish some purpose. Organizations, then, are elaborate and complicated forms of human endeavor.

We often talk about organizations as if they are separate from the people who comprise them. A young engineer speaks of "going to work for IBM," or a news report advises us that "Chrysler has announced a recall," as if IBM and Chrysler are actual places or beings. This is not especially surprising because many organizations do seem to exist apart from individual members. People come and go, but the organization remains. Even so, the image of the organization as an independent object is misleading. It implies that the organization is like the shell of the notorious little jumping bean—a container in which some mysterious activity (in this case, human behavior) is occurring. We need to remember that an organization is not merely a container for behavior. Rather, an organization literally *is* human behavior.

An organization is constituted by interaction among the people who comprise it. In other words, an organization really is defined by its members' joint actions. Since the basis for joint action is communication, the process of human communication is the central feature of an organization. As Daniel Katz and Robert Kahn, two prominent organizational pyschologists, observed, "Communication . . . is the very essence of a social system or organization" (1978, p. 428).

This book is about the communication processes that characterize human organizations, processes referred to collectively as **organizational communication.** We have tried to present our discussion of organizational communication from a comprehensive, contemporary point of view that will provide you with a sound foundation of concepts for understanding and discussing this subject. No one book or course is going to cover everything that you could or should learn about organizational communication. This book is no exception. It is intended only as an introduction to the field of study.

We think that this book will be more useful to you if you understand something about the background for it and for the course in which it is being used. In order to provide that background, we need to answer four basic questions:

1. Why is the study of organizational communication useful to you?
2. How did this field of study develop?
3. What is the status of the field today?
4. What is the authors' approach to the field in light of answers to the first three questions?

The answers to these four questions provide background for this book and for the course in which it is being used. A really good understanding of the field depends on some familiarity with this background.

Studying Organizational Communication

You may have wondered from time to time just why you should enroll in a particular course or of what relevance and importance the course is going to be to you. In the case of organizational communication, we see at least three reasons for studying this topic:

1. You can improve your understanding of organizations and of your own experiences as an organization member.
2. You can develop awareness of the kinds of communication skills that are important in organizations.
3. The course may start you down the path to a career as a communication professional in an organization or as an academic scholar in the field.

Understanding Organizations

"I've seen all of this before, but I never had a way to make sense of it until I took this course." This is a common remark that we hear from students who have just completed their first course in organizational communication. Because communication is such a central feature of life in organizations, the study of organizational communication provides a basis for understanding virtually every *human* process that occurs in organizations. Conflict, cooperation, decision making, the use of power and authority, compliance gaining, resistance, morale and cohesion, and the creation and maintenance of relationships all are reflected in human interaction.

Of course, organizational communication does not provide insights about *every* aspect of human organizations. It is not a study of the technology for creating a product or service or of the methods for producing and marketing these things. It is not a study of cost control and financing or of laws and regulations governing business and employment practices. Such topics often are relevant to organizational communication. Some people in the field spend a lot of time discussing them, but organizational communication primarily is concerned with the content and structure of human interaction in organizations' day-to-day activities. Unless you plan to be a hermit, you are almost certain to participate in and cope with organizational communication throughout most of your life.

Awareness of Skills

There is broad, general agreement that well-developed communication skills are essential to personal effectiveness in organizations or, at least, in managerial, professional, and leadership positions (Huse & Bowditch, 1977). Review any survey of skills that organizations expect of new college graduates upon entry into the job market and you probably will find communication skills placed somewhere in the list (Di Salvo, 1980).

The kinds of communication skills that new college graduates should possess in order to meet organizational expectations can be developed through courses in public speaking, interviewing, group discussion, listening, and writing. Sometimes, a number of these skills are taught in one course with a title such as Business and Professional Communication. The introductory course in organizational communication usually is not concerned with providing training in specific individual communication skills. However, it does focus attention on many of the functional demands in organizations that require good personal communication skills. These demands and the situations in which they arise are reflected in examples throughout this text.

Career Opportunities

The study of organizational communication also is important because many organizations have developed an intense interest in this subject. Leaders and decision makers in such organizations not only want themselves and others to possess good communication skills, but they also want an understanding of the dynamics of organizational communication. Many apparently are convinced that there is a strong connection between communication effectiveness and organizational effectiveness (Williams, 1978). Although organization leaders often understand "organizational effectiveness" only in terms of increased productivity, improved work performance, or higher morale, the belief that effective communication is essential to these conditions has led to a variety of career opportunities in organizational communication.

Today, many organizations employ writers, editors, and media specialists to produce and distribute company magazines, newsletters, films, videos, and even closed-circuit television programs for an audience comprised of the organization membership itself. People in these occupations usually are trained in journalism or media production. Recently, a flourishing training and development industry also has emerged as organizations have hired staff professionals and outside consultants to help them evaluate and change organizational communication practices. This industry includes people who teach communication concepts and skills to organization members (usually to managers and supervisors), evaluate the effectiveness of organizational communication, and help to improve interpersonal, group, and public communication processes in organizational settings (Eich, 1977). The career path into training and development is not restricted to any one academic field, but people who enter this profession often receive their preparation in organizational communication (Redding, 1979).

We should point out that the demand for communication professionals in organizations does not mean that a course or even a major related to organizational communication will lead to a job in the field. In 1988, the Bureau of Labor Statistics (BLS) predicted faster-than-average growth throughout the 1990s for occupations related to organizational communication, but they also noted that most of the job openings will occur through turnover. The abundant supply of trained college graduates and experienced professionals will lead to intense competition for the available jobs. Our own personal experiences are consistent with the BLS prediction. It is not easy to break into this field. Many of the positions in training and development now require a master's degree and, in some cases, even a doctoral degree (Redding, 1979). If you are thinking of a career related to organizational communication, you must obtain a thorough education and be able to apply what you know. Even if you do not pursue such a career, an organizational communication course should be helpful to you in any organizational role that you may assume.

Development of the Field

While scholars in various disciplines have studied communication in organizations for many years, the development of organizational communication as an identifiable field with courses and academic programs in university departments of communication is a relatively recent occurrence. W. Charles Redding traces the origin of the field to a convergence of interest in "business speech" and "industrial communication" that emerged in the wake of World War II (Redding, 1985; Tompkins & Redding, 1988). By the early 1950s, doctoral students in speech departments at Northwestern University, Ohio State University, Purdue University, and the University of Southern California were producing dissertations on industrial communication. In 1952, Purdue's speech department established its Industrial Communication Research Center. Annual conferences that brought together professors of speech and communication with social scientists from other disciplines provided forums for discussion and definition of the emerging field.

Skills-oriented "how to" books on communication for managers began to appear in the late 1950s, but the concerns of the field already were expanding beyond these narrow prescriptive interests to embrace description and explanation of organizational communication processes in general. The nation's first undergraduate major in "organizational communication" was established by Edward Penson and Elizabeth Andersch at Ohio University in 1962 (Boase & Carlson, 1989). According to Redding, general academic acceptance of the field of organizational communication was signaled by several events in 1967 and 1968, which included a NASA-sponsored conference on organizational communication and the creation of the Organizational Communication Division of the International Communication Association. Redding's personal influence on the development of the field is legendary. As Redding's doctoral students graduated from the program at Purdue, they initiated courses in organizational communication at other instititions. Academic programs in organizational communication at many of the nation's colleges and universities today were established by Redding's protégés and colleagues. Even exceptions such as the Ohio University program appear to have been influenced directly by their creators' familiarity with Redding's work at Purdue.

The relatively recent and rapid emergence of organizational communication as an academic field has been accompanied by some healthy, but occasionally troublesome, growing pains. Scholars have found it difficult to create an identity for the field. At first, this difficulty arose from similarities between organizational communication and other fields of study. Later, it involved the development of several different and sometimes competing approaches to the study of organizational communication. While both of these identity problems have been troubling, each in its own way has helped to develop and refine the field. In order to explain the point of view of this book, we must first review some of the history involved in these two identity problems.

Relationship to Other Fields

Communication scholars began to study organizations at a time when other social and behavioral sciences already had a long history of organizational research. The new field of organizational communication borrowed heavily from ideas developed in these more established disciplines. Consequently, it was difficult at times to tell the difference between organizational communication, organizational psychology, organizational sociology, and organizational behavior as fields of study. Sharing ideas between different academic disciplines is both useful and necessary in order to develop a good understanding of our world. However, ideas from one field often have to be adapted to fit the needs of another field. Organizational communication sometimes borrowed ideas without making important adaptations.

When psychologists, sociologists, and social psychologists began to study organizations in the twentieth century, they certainly were concerned with many processes related to human communication. They often encouraged organizations to pay attention to communication and interpersonal relationships, but their explanations of organizational behavior did not focus on human communication.

For example, management theorists such as Paul Hersey and Ken Blanchard (1982) often are interested in the problem of motivating employees to be productive. They rely on theories of motivation in which the behavior of individual human beings is explained as a means of meeting physical, psychological, or social needs. If asked about the role of communication in organizational behavior, these theorists might say that communication is one of several types of motivated behavior in organizations or that it is a means of motivating organization members. From this point of view, communication is only one ingredient among many in a recipe for organizational behavior. The central problem is to understand human motivation in organizations and the role of motivation in **organizational effectiveness,** (i.e., in getting people to work more productively). Communication is merely a peripheral concern.

When the field of organizational communication imported concepts from other disciplines, it also imported their peripheral views of human communication in organizations along with a preoccupation with organizational effectiveness. Communication scholars identified dozens of elements in organizational communication, then studied the relationships of these elements to a veritable grab bag of factors in organizational effectiveness. For example, we asked questions about the relationship between organizational communication and productivity, job satisfaction, turnover, and absenteeism. Most researchers studied "economic" organizations engaged in the creation and delivery of products or services. Communication became "one more variable" that figured into organizational effectiveness.

The field's early emphasis on organizational effectiveness is entirely understandable because effectiveness has been (and generally still is) the principal concern of people in charge of economic organizations. However, attempts to relate many elements in organizational communication to various indicators of organizational effectiveness quickly produced a large body of disjointed and fragmented research (Dennis, Goldhaber, & Yates, 1978). The field consisted of hundreds of individual facts and bits of knowledge like so many pieces of an unassembled jigsaw puzzle. We needed theories of organizational communication, per se, in order to integrate and organize our work.

The need to define the field of organizational communication more clearly led to several new developments in the late 1970s and early 1980s. While many scholars worked to refine the traditional social science themes that already had developed in the field, others began to study organizational communication in ways that differed substantially from the traditional approach. Consequently, several different points of view or perspectives on the study of organizational communication have developed in recent years. The description of these perspectives in the next section provides a map of the organizational communication field as we know it today.

Perspectives on Organizational Communication

Linda L. Putnam (1982) pointed out that various approaches to the study of organizational communication can be classified according to a model developed by Gibson Burrell and Gareth Morgan (1979). This model is displayed in figure 1.1.

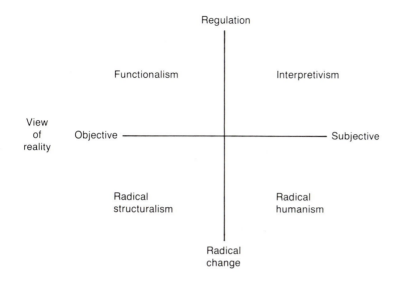

Figure 1.1
View of organizational reality
and order in four perspectives
on organizational
communication.

Burrell and Morgan's model includes four basic perspectives of organizations: functionalism, interpretivism, radical structuralism, and radical humanism. They explain the similarities and differences between the four perspectives on the basis of ideas about reality and organizational order. Figure 1.1 represents views of reality on a horizontal line ranging from objective to subjective. Views of organizational order are placed on a vertical line ranging from regulative to radical change. The two lines intersect in order to form four areas that represent viewpoints on reality and order. According to Burrell and Morgan, each of the four perspectives is located in one of these areas.

Functionalists and radical structuralists adopt an objective view of reality, while interpretivists and radical humanists take a subjective position. Although functionalists and interpretivists have different ideas about reality, both groups adhere to a regulative view of organizational order. Radical structuralists and radical humanists endorse fundamental change in the existing order of organizations. In order to understand how each of the four perspectives approaches organizational communication, we need to explain what is involved in the ideas of organizational order and organizational reality.

Organizational Order

The idea of **organizational order** is fairly easy to understand. In one sense, order is created when we arrange positions in a particular way to perform a task. For example, we create an order in a work group when we assign each member to a particular job and designate a leader to direct the group's activities. However, organizational order also is *political*. The political order of an organization includes at least two important features: (1) a system of allocating and using power and resources and (2) ways of maintaining and protecting this system. Organizational order tells us who has power; who gets certain organizational resources, privileges, and rewards (money, materials, equipment, positions, status symbols); which groups or individuals can control the fate of others; and how the goals of the organization are to be defined and accomplished.

In most Western organizations, order is based on clear distinctions in status, authority, and power at different levels and between different groups in the organization. For example, consider the distinctions between officers and enlisted personnel in the military or the favored treatment given to members of a valued organizational group, such as engineers in a high-technology manufacturing company. As described by Burrell and Morgan, a **regulative point of view** values the existing order and strives to maintain it. A **radical change point of view** seeks to make fundamental changes in the existing order. Since organizational order is political, commitments to support or change this order also are political.

Organizational Reality

The idea of **organizational reality** is not quite so easy to understand. If you take an **objective** point of view, you see organizations as concrete objects with physical features reflected in the process of communication. These physical features exist apart from anybody's personal experience of them. Thus, communicative behavior is tangible stuff that can be observed, measured, and classified. The **subjective** point of view regards an organization as an idea that exists in its members' shared experiences. The "reality" of an organization is not defined by the physical features of behavior but by common interpretations of experience that organization members literally construct by communicating with one another.

The difference between objective and subjective points of view is easier to understand with a simple example. Consider the experience of registering for classes at a college. At many institutions, one registers by filling out forms, moving through lines, obtaining official approvals, and, of course, paying someone some money. Registration can take a full day or more to complete. From an objective viewpoint, "registration" is a physical event made up of observable human behaviors. But what does this event really mean to those who are involved in it? From a subjective viewpoint, the meaning is a personal, private experience for each individual. To a student, registration may mean endless hours of boredom, red tape, and frustration. To an administrator, it is an orderly, necessary set of procedures for efficiently managing the institution's affairs. Which experience is the "real" registration? In a sense, both are.

When students participate in registration, they share and reinforce their private experiences of this event with one another. The common interpretation that emerges is their "registration reality." This interpretation is **socially constructed** through communication. It also provides a basis for enacting the registration event from the students' point of view. For example, students at University X call registration, "The Gauntlet." They report grimly each semester to face the ordeal. They complain to one another about the process. ("Every semester, it's the same &#%$ @! thing. They ought to do something about this!") They see the frustrations when they are closed out of classes. ("Wouldn't you know it. Three semesters in a row I've been shut out of Econ.") They seem to derive great pleasure from telling registration "war stories" to new freshmen who have yet to go through it. ("Better pack your lunch. You'll have to eat it in line.")

The administrators also socially construct and enact a registration reality, although it probably is quite different from the students' reality. For example, they slap one another on the back and comment about how smoothly everything is running. They compliment one another on new innovations that have improved the registration process. They agree at the end of the day that once again, they have managed the unmanageable.

Our registration reality example is not unusual. Organization members socially construct reality through the process of communicating with one another about many day-to-day experiences. Some features of this reality may be widely shared throughout the organization. Other features may vary greatly across different groups in the organization. For instance, when Ford Motor Company tells us that Ford is the place where, "Quality is Job One," is this merely advertising hype, a belief that is firmly held throughout the company, or a management vision of a corporate ideal that employees reject or regard as a joke?

By applying the concepts of organizational order and reality, we can compare and contrast the four perspectives of organizational communication. Each is described below according to its position in figure 1.1.

Functionalism

Functionalism regards organizations as *objects* that can be studied with the concepts and methods of traditional social science. Functionalists believe that organizational communication behavior is an objectively observable activity. It can be measured, labeled, classified, and related to other organizational processes. For example, suppose we want to know whether managers' styles of communication with employees have any effect on employee job satisfaction. We think that employees will be more satisfied when managers adopt an "open" style of communication, but we are not sure. A functionalist might answer this question through the following actions:

1. Observe and measure managers' communicative behaviors in order to classify each manager as high or low in "communication openness."
2. Measure the levels of job satisfaction among each manager's employees.
3. Statistically analyze the measurements to see whether employee job satisfaction is greater under "high-openness" managers than it is under "low-openness" managers.

Functionalists in organizational communication often are concerned with the relationship between communication processes and organizational effectiveness. They study factors in organizational communication such as information flow within organizational networks, distortion of messages, breakdowns in channels of communication, strategies of managers and supervisors in communicating with their subordinates, and the dynamics of group problem solving and decision making. If some of these ideas are unfamiliar to you at this point, there is no need to worry. Much of the second unit in this book is concerned with defining and elaborating on these concepts.

Since functionalism has changed over the years, it is useful to distinguish between its traditional and contemporary forms. Traditional functionalists treat the organization as a *machine*. This machine is an engineered set of interconnected parts that operates by managerial control and depends on well-maintained communication in order to function efficiently and effectively. Managers control the machine through principles and techniques of gaining compliance and cooperation from employees. The various parts of the machine (departments, individuals) are supposed to act in a coordinated manner. Both control and coordination depend on effective communication. Communication is understood primarily as a process of sending and receiving messages. **Communication effectiveness** involves two conditions: (1) the processes of message sending and receiving are accurate and reliable; (2) the message receiver understands and responds to the message in the way that the message sender intends.

While some functionalists continue to hold traditional views of organizations, most have refined their perspective with more contemporary ideas that differ substantially from the traditional viewpoint. We will describe the features of contemporary functionalism later in this chapter.

Interpretivism

The second important perspective is **interpretivism,** which regards organizations as *cultures* (Pacanowsky & O'Donnell-Trujillo, 1984). To the interpretivist, the organization is a subjective rather than objective phenomenon. It literally emerges from the shared experiences of the people who comprise it. This does not mean that the organization is an unreal figment of someone's imagination. It means, instead, that organizational reality is socially constructed through communication (Putnam, 1982).

Interpretive scholars are interested in revealing socially constructed realities. They study communication as the process through which this social construction occurs. Consequently, they are interested in the symbols and meanings involved in various forms of organizational behavior. Interpretivists attempt to describe the ways in which organization members understand their experiences through communication and how they enact "the organization" on the basis of shared meanings.

In our description of functionalism, we illustrated how a functionalist might try to find out about the relationship between management communication style and employee job satisfaction by measuring these two conditions and statistically analyzing the measurements. How would an interpretivist approach the problem of understanding employee experiences of managers' communication styles?

To begin with, the interpretivist probably would neither ask specific questions about concepts like "openness" and "satisfaction" nor attempt to measure these conditions. Instead, the interpretivist is more likely to ask organization members to provide illustrations or stories about their experiences. Then, the interpretivist analyzes and describes the themes that appear in these reports. These themes reveal the ways in which organization members share their experiences and socially construct an understanding of these experiences. If an idea like the importance of openness in managers' communication happens to appear as a theme in the reports, the interpretivist might discuss it as an indication of how organization members use "openness" to understand their relationships with managers. The interpretivist's goal is to reveal those communicative activities that occur in a variety of settings to produce the unique character of an organization (Smilowitz, 1982).

Radical Humanism and Radical Structuralism

Radical humanism is similar to interpretivism in its perspective on organizational reality. Both are concerned with symbols, meanings, and interpretations of experience. **Radical structuralism** is similar to functionalism in its attention to the objective features of organizational communication. Radical humanists and radical structuralists, however, share one belief that distinguishes them from functionalists and interpretivists. The two radical groups regard organizations as systems of oppression (Putnam, 1982), in which some members or groups manipulate, abuse, or otherwise inflict injustice on others.

Radical humanists and radical structuralists begin with the assumption that at least some features of the prevailing order in most organizations are inherently harmful or undesirable. They want to make fundamental changes in these conditions. Some advocates of radical positions believe that communication scholars and professionals should work to eliminate the oppressive features of organizational life. The two groups differ in their ideas about the origin and nature of oppression.

Radical humanists locate the source of organizational oppression in systems of language and meaning. For example, a radical humanist might argue that sexual discrimination and harassment in organizational life arise from a language that demeans and debases women (Bosmajian, 1983). In other words, common ways of *talking* about women influence ways of *thinking* about and *acting* toward women. If asked how to correct these problems, the radical humanist might suggest eliminating sexist language in order to reconstruct symbolic expressions of male dominance.

In contrast, radical structuralists attribute oppression to power differences and inequalities that exist in the design of organizational structure. Discrimination against women, for example, is not merely a problem of language, but it is also a problem of physical segregation and isolation from sources of power and information (Crawford, 1977). A radical structuralist would argue that if a woman is assigned to a "do-nothing" job, or denied promotion and advancement, or cannot get past the boss's secretary in order to get an appointment, she faces *structural* barriers to her goals. If asked how to control such discrimination, the radical structuralist might suggest forcing the male-dominated power structure to integrate women into its ranks and to provide them with all of the information that they require in order to function effectively.

As indicated by the descriptions of these four perspectives, the field of organizational communication is diverse. It includes different points of view on the principles and purposes of organizational communication scholarship and practice. In one sense, the existence of these different perspectives compounds the field's identity problem because no one set of concepts and assumptions fully characterizes the study of organizational communication. The way that you understand organizational communication depends on the perspective that you use. In another sense, however, the development of these perspectives has helped to define the domain of the field. When you consider the perspectives collectively, you get a good idea of what is included in the study of organizational communication.

Putnam presented an accurate and insightful use of Burrell and Morgan's model, but three limitations are associated with its application to organizational communication. First, the Burrell and Morgan model is not the only way of organizing scholarship in organizational communication. Second, distinctions between the four perspectives are not as clear as they might seem to be from a superficial examination of figure 1.1. Third, the four perspectives are not equally accepted within the field. These limitations are revealed in the present status of the field and have influenced many of the choices that we have made in preparing this text.

Alternative Models of Organizational Communication

In addition to Putnam's application of the Burrell and Morgan model, there are at least two other schemes for organizing and discussing scholarship in organizational communication. Krone, Jablin, and Putnam (1988) applied Fisher's (1978) general model of communication perspectives to classify work in organizational communication under *mechanistic, psychological, interactionist,* and *pragmatic* categories. At about the same time, Tompkins and Redding (1988) argued that most of the work in organizational communication can be classified under three orientations that they identify as *modernist, naturalistic,* and *critical.* Now we do not intend to make our discussion of organizational communication perspectives unnecessarily complicated by including detailed descriptions of these alternative models, but we are obligated to at least call them to your attention. The Tompkins and Redding model requires at least some discussion because it represents an important development in the field during the 1980s. We can do this by comparing their model to the Burrell and Morgan model.

To simplify matters somewhat, the **modernist** orientation is essentially the same thing as functionalism, while the **naturalistic** category corresponds to interpretivism. So where is the difference? It occurs in the so-called **critical** orientation. In effect, Tompkins and Redding show that the radical humanist and radical structuralist perspectives have merged into a more general scholarly position that subsumes elements of both. But if these two perspectives have completely different views of organizational reality, how is such a merger possible? This question suggests the second limitation in the Burrell and Morgan model (i.e., that the differences between perspectives are not always clear cut).

Distinctions among the Perspectives

The Burrell and Morgan model oversimplifies the distinctions between the four perspectives. The differences between functionalism, interpretivism, radical humanism, and radical structuralism are not as clean and clear as figure 1.1 suggests. The merger of the two radical orientations in organizational communication under the label, "critical theory," is a case in point.

Critical Theory and the Radical Perspectives

Critical scholars are unified in their view of organizations as instruments of oppression. They focus their attention on members of oppressed organizational classes (i.e., workers, women, minorities, or other groups that fit the critical theorists' definition of an oppressed class). At the risk of oversimplification, we might say that they are concerned at once in the same time with social structure *and* with symbolic processes. Organizational oppression does not reside in structure alone nor in symbols alone. It resides in the *relationship* between structure and symbols.

A good example of the linkage between structure and symbols can be found in Dennis Mumby's (1987) comments about interpretivism. Mumby, a critical theorist, agrees that interpretive research "demonstrates that organizational reality is fundamentally symbolic in nature" (p. 120), but he also believes that interpretive research is naive because "it does little to explicate the *deep structure* process through which certain organizational realities come to hold sway over competing world-views" (p. 113). In other words, it does little to explain the role of symbols in dominance and oppression of some classes over others.

Why does Mumby make this argument and what does he mean by *deep structure*? As he explains it, "Domination involves getting people to organize their behavior around a particular rule system" (p. 115). This rule system is the deep structure of the organization. It defines power relationships. Some of the symbolic forms that we find in organizational communication function to "produce, maintain, and reproduce these power structures" (Mumby, p. 113). This occurs through the **systematic distortion** of communication (Deetz, 1982).

Tompkins and Redding point out that distortion of communication does not mean the same thing to a critical theorist that it might mean to a functionalist. When functionalists talk about distortion, they usually are concerned with inaccuracies or errors in information that lead to inefficiency and ineffectiveness in communication. But critical theorists regard distortion as a systematic and deliberate *symbolic* process through which "the owner/manager's interests are falsely joined with those of the worker in ideological communication" (Tompkins and Redding, p. 27). For example, one can find many instances in organizations of stories that are told about company heroes and heroines—legendary figures in the history of the organization. These legendary figures personify values and beliefs that are important to the success of the organization. The stories are presented with great drama so as to inspire organization members to rally around and embrace the values that they promote. But whose interests do these values really serve? Those of all organization members or only those of an elite group or class?

We will have a lot more to say in chapter 6 about the critical theorists' idea of systematic distortion. For now, however, it is only important to know that critical scholarship, as its label implies, *criticizes* systematic distortion in organizational communication with the goal of consciousness-raising and emancipation for oppressed organizational classes. It does this by examining the way in which systematic distortion occurs through the use of language and symbols.

Firm distinctions between the various perspectives also pose a problem because the perspectives themselves change over time. This is clearly evident in the case of functionalism. It has evolved into a contemporary form that differs in important ways from its traditional version. These differences are reflected in **contemporary functionalist** ideas about reality and order.

Reality and Order in Contemporary Functionalism

The contemporary functionalist view of reality is no longer based strictly on objectivism (i.e., the idea that organizations are concrete objects with physical features that exist apart from anybody's personal experience of them). Contemporary functionalists are concerned not only with studying the concrete features of organizational communication, but also with the ways in which organization members perceive and subjectively experience organizational communication (Falcione & Werner, 1978). But the functionalist's idea of studying subjective experience is still not quite the same as the interpretivist's.

A functionalist researcher usually asks organization members to report their perceptions of organizational experience *in terms that the researcher defines*. If a functionalist wants to know whether employees experience managers as open communicators, he or she probably will identify several characteristics of openness, then ask employees to *rate* on some type of measuring scale the extent to which they perceive managers to exhibit these characteristics. The idea of openness is defined by the kinds of characteristics and items that the *researcher* includes in the rating scale (e.g., To what extent is your boss honest? To what extent does your boss freely share information with you?). The employees merely report their perceptions of managers by responding to the rating scale items.

In contrast, the interpretivist is not interested in measuring organization members' perceptions of predefined characteristics in communication. Since the interpretivist wants to reveal socially constructed reality, he or she asks organization members to describe experience *from their own frame of reference*.

Students often ask, "Which of these two approaches is best?" The answer to this question really depends on what you want to know. Functionalism is best suited for describing and relating variables in organizational communication processes. Interpretivism is more appropriate for questions about the role of communication in members' experiences of organizational life.

It is doubtful that functionalism ever had a complete philosophical commitment to preserving existing organizational order (Strauss, 1963). If it did have such a commitment in its traditional form, this commitment has changed in the contemporary form. Functionalism frequently is concerned with efforts to change organizations (Pace, 1983). Sometimes, the change is intended to improve organizational effectiveness as management defines it. In other cases, the change involves objectives that conflict sharply with management values and beliefs (Beer, 1980). Occasionally, as Strauss pointed out, the functionalist advocates fundamental change directed at reducing the power inequalities that allow one organizational group to dominate another. In this respect, the interests of functionalists sometimes are very close to those of critical theorists, although functionalists do not assume that organizations are inherently oppressive.

The obstacles to organizational change are not found in functionalist philosophy but in the practical and political dynamics of organizational power. Even though organizational communication theorists may work for change, the fact that management hires and fires consultants and staff professionals and also controls the scholar's access to organizations "may mean that little real shift occurs in such matters as power distribution, the conditions of work, or compensation" (Miles, 1979, p. 4). Fundamental change can be made in organizations, but the process that recognized authorities describe is one of regulated change in gradual increments (Beckhard, 1983; Shepard, 1975). Functionalists do attempt to change organizational order, but their approach is evolutionary rather than radical.

Other Features of Contemporary Functionalism

Contemporary functionalism has several distinctive features in addition to those that we already have discussed. Four of these features provide the basis for much of the material in this text. These four features include contemporary functionalist perspectives on (1) the process of human communication, (2) the nature of organizations and organizational effectiveness, (3) the characteristics of organizational communication, and (4) the role of communication professionals in organizations. An introduction to each of these features will provide you with an idea of what to expect in several of our chapters.

Human Communication

Traditional functionalism regarded communication as nothing more than a process of sending and receiving messages. Communication effectiveness meant little more than getting a desired response to one's message. In other words, "communication" was something that Person A did to Person B in order to get B to act in a particular way. This idea certainly has not disappeared, but it has been modified in contemporary functionalism. Instead of defining communication as something that A does *to* B, contemporary functionalists see communication as a process through which A and B influence each other, share experience, and create meanings. Communication also is our means for "making sense out of people, objects, and events" (Pace, 1983, p. 30).

Organizations and Organizational Effectiveness

While traditional functionalism regarded the organization as a machine that managerial design engineers and controls, contemporary functionalism sees the organization as a *living system* (Monge, Farrell, Eisenberg, Miller, & White, 1984). Organizations are more like living systems than machines in two ways. First, the idea of management control over the organizational machine sounds something like a person's running a lawn mower or driving a car. Organizations, like living systems, are a bit more complicated. They have many systems of *self-regulation* and control. Managerial designs and intentions are important factors, but they are not the only factors that regulate an organizational system. Internally, unions, trade and professional groups, and even informal coalitions may exert substantial control over the organization. Externally, local, state, and federal government agencies as well as consumer or community groups also regulate or, at least, influence the system.

Moreover, different organizational subsystems (for example, departments, work groups, and individuals) do not generally work together in machinelike harmony. While they cooperate to accomplish a common purpose, they also are in conflict. They often compete for resources, assert different values, and desire different ways of ordering work and organizational life. Even "management" usually is not an undifferentiated monolith that acts with a single-minded purpose. Vice presidents of different divisions may squabble over territory or middle managers may disagree with their bosses over the best way to accomplish an organization's mission.

Second, organizations, unlike machines, grow and adapt to change. The people who make up organizations process information and make choices based on interpretations of situations and circumstances. They plan in order to accomplish goals. They make decisions to expand or to cut back, to begin new activities, to redefine or stop old activities, and to restructure the order of the organization or to maintain it.

Contemporary functionalism also has changed its ideas about organizational effectiveness. We are still concerned with the relationship between communication and organizational effectiveness, but we have expanded our idea of organizational effectiveness to include more than managerial objectives such as productivity and morale. Organizational effectiveness also includes the welfare of organization members in general and the overall quality of organizational life (Dessler, 1980; French, Bell, & Zawacki, 1983; Pace, 1983). Contemporary functionalists believe that they are obligated to serve the interests of many organizational groups, not just those of management. They also admit that it is not easy to live up to this obligation (Beer, 1980; Miles, 1979).

Organizational Communication

The functionalist perspective of organizational communication has become much more sophisticated over the years. Our knowledge about organizational communication is still based on literally hundreds of isolated studies, but some comprehensive models for making sense of the field have been developed. One widely used model is a conceptual framework developed by Richard Farace, Peter Monge, and Hamish Russell (1977). This model, known as **structural functionalism,** organizes the field according to knowledge about organizational communication *functions* (what communication does), the *structure* of organizational communication systems (who communicates with whom), and the organizational *levels* at which communication occurs (individual, dyad, group, or organization-wide).

Although the integrated model of structural functionalism is a relatively recent development, the basic concepts of communication functions, structure, and levels have been used in the study of organizational communication for many years. These concepts provide the foundation for the functionalist perspective.

Communication Professionals

The field of organizational communication includes professional practitioners as well as academic scholars. Many scholars also are part-time consultants to organizations, and professional practitioners sometimes serve as faculty members in universities. The relationship between scholars and practitioners is not always close because the two groups are faced with different needs and problems. In general, however, the functionalist perspective of organizational communication has influenced both academic scholarship and professional practice (Goldhaber, 1990; Redding, 1979).

Acceptance of the Perspectives

Putnam identified the third limitation in the Burrell and Morgan model when she pointed out that the various perspectives are not equally accepted in the field, but this situation is clearly changing. Functionalism has been and continues to be the dominant orientation to organizational communication. Although interpretive and critical approaches are **relatively** new in organizational communication, they have gained adherents very rapidly. The growing acceptance and influence of these perspectives arise from at least two major sources of dissatisfaction with functionalism.

First, functionalism was responsible for the disorganized state of the field in the 1960s and 1970s. Although several major textbooks and articles attempted to assemble the jigsaw puzzle of organizational communication in the 1970s, questions remained about our ability to make sense of our own work. As recently as 1984, H. Lloyd Goodall, Jr. concluded from a review of organizational communication research that different studies "read like newspapers from different planets" (p. 135).

Second, some scholars objected that functionalism is "managerially biased" because it is concerned primarily with work organizations and with the relationships between communication and organizational effectiveness. This bias is compounded because the organizational communication scholar's audience consists mainly of managers, administrators, professionals, and, of course, college students who plan to enter similar roles. Michael Pacanowsky and Nick O'Donnell-Trujillo summed up this criticism when they argued that functionalists try "to understand organizations better so that organizations can be made to run better. . . . What has come to count as 'better organizational function' are notions with a distinctly managerial flavor" (1982, p. 119).

While attention to managerial perspectives and problems certainly is not wrong, many interpretivists point out that an exclusive preoccupation with these concerns results in a very narrow definition of our field of study. Much of the day-to-day communication in organizations has relatively little to do with managerial definitions of organizational effectiveness. Managerial processes involve only one slice of the organizational communication pie.

Critics of functionalism began to turn to interpretive and critical concepts as a way of at least escaping if not correcting the problems that they saw in the functionalist perspective. Instead of identifying dozens of communication and organizational variables, then explaining their relationships in piecemeal statistical studies, interpretivists concentrate on the communication process of constructing the meanings and frames of reference from which members experience organizational life. Critical theorists concentrate on criticizing oppression and systematic distortion of organizational communication. Interpretivism and critical theory are minority views of organizational communication in the sense that fewer scholars and practitioners work from these perspectives than from the functionalist perspective. Even so, interpretivism and critical theory present serious alternatives to the traditional concepts and methods of functionalist social science.

Approach of the Text

We are faced with three perspectives on organizational communication. Functionalism clearly is dominant. It also has changed through evolution from traditional to contemporary form. Yet, functionalism does not represent the whole field of organizational communication. There are some questions that the concepts of methods of functionalist social science are not equipped to ask, let alone answer. Interpretivism and critical theory have emerged as **serious alternatives** with concepts and methods that differ from those of functionalism. These are the considerations that shape our orientation to organizational communication in this book.

Our approach to organizational communication is based primarily on contemporary functionalism, although some of the ideas that we will review were developed under the traditional functionalist model. We also have included interpretivist and critical ideas about organizational communication at many points in the text, along with a complete chapter on the interpretivist orientation to organizational culture and a chapter on the critical theorists' approach to power in organizations.

Summary

The study of organizational communication can be important to you for at least three reasons. It can improve your understanding of organizational life, provide you with an awareness of important communication skills in organizations, and perhaps start you on a path to a career in the field. In order to really appreciate the field, though, you should also know something about its background and the factors that shaped our approach to this book.

Organizational communication is a relatively new field of study. When it began, it borrowed ideas from other social and behavioral sciences in such a way that its focus on communication was unclear. Many critics felt that the new field was fragmented and disorganized. These problems led to at least four different perspectives of organizational communication: functionalism, interpretivism, radical humanism, and radical structuralism. These perspectives differ according to their views of reality (objective versus subjective) and organizational order (regulative versus radical change). Recently, the two radical perspectives appear to have been subsumed or merged under critical theory.

Functionalism continues to be the dominant perspective in the study of organizational communication, but it has evolved from a traditional form into a different contemporary form. Traditional functionalism understands organizations as machines and regards communication as a machinelike process. Contemporary functionalism sees organizations as living systems and communication as a dynamic, organismic process. Despite these changes in functionalism, interpretivism and critical theory have developed as serious alternatives to the functionalist study of organizations. Interpretivists are concerned with the symbolic processes through which organizational reality is socially constructed. Critical theorists are concerned with the relationship between structure and symbolic processes in the efforts to criticize oppression and the systematic distortion of organizational communication. This text attempts to present the field of study as these positions currently represent it.

Discussion Questions/ Activities

1. What are some common examples of communication in organizations? What do these examples indicate about the importance of communication in organizational life? Try to generate some examples from your own experiences in organizations, then compare them with those of another person.
2. How would you describe the similarities and differences among functionalist, interpretivist, and critical perspectives of organizational communication?
3. What are some of the reasons that might explain the dominance of functionalism in the study of organizational communication?
4. According to the text, there are some questions that functionalism is not equipped to answer. What do you think some of the questions might be? How could they be answered from other perspectives?

It's How You Do the Job

It was almost noon, and Junior had been at her desk since 8:30 A.M. As she left her desk to go to lunch, she thought about her father's statement about how important it was for her to gain experience in the divisions by doing different jobs. That conversation had only been three weeks ago, but she already felt that her assignment as a marketing analyst in the Pickel's Pneumatic Valve Division located in Hampton, Illinois, was an awful way to gain experience. Hampton was a typical midwestern small town, and it had very little to offer, especially in the way of restaurants and entertainment. Nevertheless, she believed that her father had her and the firm's best interests in mind, so she did everything that she could to make the best of it.

As she walked down Main Street to the diner where most of the division's management ate lunch, she thought about how different this Main Street was from the Main Street of her hometown. In Los Angeles, she rarely saw people talking on the street. In Hampton, people frequently stopped each other to say, "hello" and to carry on a conversation. "It must be the local form of entertainment," she thought, yet, she wasn't sure if she wanted to be in Hampton that long to have people stop her for a conversation.

At least Sally's Diner was a clean place. The food was better than the commissary in the plant, but that didn't make Sally's eligible as a four-star restaurant. The service was slow because the waitresses spent a lot of their time chatting with the customers. Nobody seemed to mind, however.

Junior walked past a few rows of booths and looked for a place to sit. She noticed Alice and Becky, who were both Level I systems analysts in the Pickel's data processing section. Both of them smiled and asked Junior to sit down.

"Well Junior, what do you think of Hampton so far? It must be quite a let down for a big city girl like you!" said Alice.

"It certainly is different, Alice," replied Junior.

"I bet," responded Alice, "but you get used to it after a while. In fact, I even sort of like it now. I might as well, I'm going to be here for a long time."

"How long have you both been here?"

"I've been here since I graduated from college," Becky answered. "This is my hometown. I knew I'd come back to work at Pickel's. Alice has been here for three years. She's from Cleveland."

"Cleveland? Cleveland's a big city," Junior said. "Aren't you going crazy in a small town?"

Alice looked at Becky for a moment and then back at Junior. "It doesn't pay to go crazy. It is unlikely that I'm going to move out of here unless, of course, I go to work for another company."

"Why not move and work for another company?" After she had asked the question, Junior sensed that she might be getting into a place in the conversation where she didn't want to be.

"Look back there . . . that's why not," said Alice.

Junior glanced to the back of the restaurant. She saw a few long tables. Seated around them were groups of men. At one of the tables she saw Bob

Watson, division manager. Seated with Bob was Fred Allan, the manager of data processing. Also seated at the table were several of the senior analysts and men from other departments.

"So?" Junior asked.

Alice hesitated. "Junior, you just happen to be the boss's daughter. It's different for Becky and me. If we're going to get ahead, we gotta first get past those guys. And we're not part of the club."

Junior was now sure that she didn't like where this conversation was going. "What club?" she asked.

Becky was quick to answer. "The 'bunch for lunch' club. Those are the guys that run this place. They go back there everyday and make the decisions. If you're not one of them, then you don't have any say. And with no say, it's no go."

Alice added, "You see, we're not one of the guys; we can't be, and furthermore we don't want to be."

Junior knew what Alice and Becky were saying. In college she was one of seven women in the engineering department. When she first began the program, the undergraduate men looked down at her and the other women. There was very little interaction. By the time, however, that she had finished, the men and women in the program were spending a lot of time together working on projects and getting to know each other. At the time she hadn't thought that she had become one of the guys; it was just that she had learned to be friends with them. She remembered the first time that she had decided to eat lunch with the men. At first she was uncomfortable, but eventually she was glad to be there. "Why don't you two go back there and eat with them?"

"Are you kidding, Junior? They would chase us out. They've got a good thing for themselves and they're not about to share it."

Alice agreed. "Becky's right," replied Alice, "those guys don't want us back there, and we know it. That's not the way. We don't want to be like them. The women in this company have to stick together in order to be our own support. That's the only way we're going to get ahead in this company. That's why we're glad you're here. You're a woman, and you understand. Things might be different when you take over. We want you to be part of our group."

Junior didn't like hearing that. She wanted to say that Alice and Becky could do something about it, but she wasn't quite sure what. She felt that she was being "set-up" by Alice and Becky. Besides, she wasn't in any hurry to take over the company from her father, and she didn't like the implication that her father wasn't running the company in the right way. However, she didn't want to offend Alice and Becky so she changed the subject to the possibilities for entertainment in Hampton.

When Junior got back to her office, she sat down and thought about the conversation that she had with Alice and Becky. Junior knew that they were somewhat right. She believed that it was hard for women to succeed in business. While Junior wouldn't call herself a feminist, she knew that much more had to be done to give women a fair chance in Pickel's Pneumatic Valve Division. But she also knew that her company had always been an outstanding performer because of the good relations between management and employees. The employees had never seriously considered a union because there had always been excellent relations between employees and management. What Alice and Becky were talking about sounded to Junior like a "women's union" and that wasn't something Junior wanted in her company. She was also afraid that her own gender might cause dissension, especially if both the men and women of the company used her gender as justification for their own purposes. If she promoted a woman, the men would say that it was because Junior was a woman. If she promoted a man, the women would say that she had "sold out."

There was a lot to learn, thought Junior. She decided that she needed to talk to Alice and Becky again to give them advice. But first, she wanted to talk to her father. Red, her father, cared about the employees, and he would have something to say. She got ready to make the telephone call to her father, then stopped to decide what to say. As she was thinking about her father, she thought about Gramps. For a moment she thought that Gramps was in the room with her and that he was whispering in her ear, "It's how you do the job that counts."

1. Is the situation described in the case a "management problem," an "organizational behavior problem," or an "organizational communication problem?" Explain your answer.
2. Let's suppose that Junior wants to think about and to analyze this situation from the vantage point of the major perspectives presented in chapter 1. How should she interpret this case from a functionalist point of view? Interpretive? Radical or critical?
3. What can you infer from this case about the importance of communication in other organizational processes, such as conflict, the use of authority, decision making, control and coordination, and maintaining relationships with superiors, subordinates, and peers?

References

Beckhard, R. (1983). Strategies for large system change. In W. L. French, C. H. Bell, Jr., & R. A. Zawacki (Eds.), *Organization development: Theory, practice, and research* (2nd ed.). Plano, TX: Business Publications.

Beer, M. (1980). *Organization changes and development: A systems view.* Santa Monica, CA: Goodyear Publishing.

Boase, P. H., & Carlson, C. V. (1989). *The School of Interpersonal Communication: An historical perspective.* Unpublished manuscript, School of Interpersonal Communication, Ohio University.

Bosmajian, H. A. (1983). *The language of oppression* (2nd ed.). Lanham, MD: University Press of America.

Bureau of Labor Statistics (1988). *Occupational outlook handbook* (1988–89 ed.). Washington, DC: U.S. Department of Labor. (Bulletin 2300).

Burrell, G., & Morgan G. (1979). *Sociological paradigms and organizational analysis.* London: Heinemann Press.

Crawford, J. S. (1977). *Women in middle management: Selection, training, advancement, performance.* Ridgewood, NJ: Forkner.

Deetz, S. A. (1982). Critical interpretive research in organizational communication. *Western Journal of Speech Communication, 46,* 131–149.

Dennis, H. S., III, Goldhaber, G. M., & Yates, M. P. (1978). Organizational communication theory and research: An overview of research methods. In B. D. Ruben (Ed.), *Communication yearbook 2*. New Brunswick, NJ: Transaction Books.

Dessler, G. (1980). *Organization theory: Integrating structure and behavior*. Englewood Cliffs, NJ: Prentice-Hall.

Di Salvo, V. (1980). A summary of current research identifying communication skills in various organization contexts. *Communication Education, 29*, 283–290.

Eich, R. K. (1977). *Organizational communication consulting: A descriptive study of consulting practices and prescriptions*. Unpublished doctoral dissertation, Michigan State University, East Lansing.

Falcione, R. L., & Werner, E. (1978). *Organizational climate and communication climate: A state of the art*. Paper presented at the annual meeting of the International Communication Association, Chicago.

Farace, R. V., Monge, P. R., & Russell, H. M. (1977). *Communicating and organizing*. Reading, MA: Addison-Wesley.

Fisher, B. A. (1978). *Perspectives on human communication*. New York: Macmillan.

French, W. L., Bell, C. H., Jr., & Zawacki, R. A. (Eds.). (1983). *Organization development: Theory, practice, and research* (2nd ed.). Plano, TX: Business Publications.

Goldhaber, G. M. (1990). *Organizational communication* (5th ed.). Dubuque, IA: Wm. C. Brown Company Publishers.

Goodall, H. L., Jr. (1984). The status of communication studies in organizational contexts: One rhetorician's lament after a year-long odyssey. *Communication Quarterly, 32*, 133–147.

Hersey, P., & Blanchard, K. (1982). *Management of organizational behavior: Utilizing human resources* (4th ed.). Englewood Cliffs, NJ: Prentice-Hall.

Huse, E. F., & Bowditch, J. L. (1977). *Behavior in organizations: A systems approach to managing* (2nd ed.). Reading, MA: Addison-Wesley.

Katz, D., & Kahn, R. L. (1978). *The social psychology of organizations* (2nd ed.). New York: John Wiley & Sons.

Krone, K. J., Jablin, F. M., & Putnam, L. L. (1987). Communication theory and organizational communication: multiple perspectives. In F. M. Jablin, L. L. Putnam, K. H. Roberts, & L. W. Porter (Eds.), *Handbook of Organizational Communication* (pp. 18–40). Newsbury Park, CA: Sage.

Miles, M. B. (1979, October). Ethical issues in OD intervention. *OD Practitioner*, pp. 1–10.

Monge, P. R., Farace, R. V., Eisenberg, E. M., Miller, K. I., and White, L. L. (1984). The process of studying process in organizational communication. *Journal of Communication, 34*, 22–43.

Mumby, D. K. (1987). The political function of narrative in organizations. *Communication Monographs, 54*, 113–127.

Pacanowsky, M. E., & O'Donnell-Trujillo, N. (1982). Communication and organizational cultures. *Western Journal of Speech Communication, 46*, 115–130.

Pacanowsky, M. E., & O'Donnell-Trujillo, N. (1984). Organizational communication as cultural performance. *Communication Monographs, 50*, 126–147.

Pace, R. W. (1983). *Organizational communication: Foundations for human resource development*. Englewood Cliffs, NJ: Prentice-Hall.

Putnam, L. L. (1982). Paradigms for organizational communication research: An overview and synthesis. *Western Journal of Speech Communication, 46*, 192–206.

Redding, W. C. (1979). Graduate education and the communication consultant: Playing God for a fee. *Communication Education, 28,* 346–352.

Redding, W. C. (1985). Stumbling toward identify: The emergence of organizational communication as a field of study. In R. D. McPhee & P. Tompkins (Eds.), *Organizational communication: Traditional themes and new directions* (pp. 15–54). Newbury Park, CA: Sage.

Shepard, H. A. (1975, November). Rules of thumb for change agents. *OD Practitioner,* pp. 1–5.

Smilowitz, M. (1982). *Ought as was in organizational reality.* Paper presented at the Second Conference on Interpretive Research in Organizational Communication, Alta, UT.

Strauss, G. (1963). Some notes on power equalization. In H. J. Leavitt (Ed.), *The social science of organizations.* Englewood Cliffs, NJ: Prentice-Hall.

Tompkins, P. K., & Redding, W. C. (1988). Organizational communication—past and present tenses. In G. M. Goldhaber & G. A. Barnett (Eds.), *Handbook of organizational communication* (pp. 5–33). Norwood, NJ: Ablex.

Williams, L. C., Jr. (1978). What 50 presidents and CEO's think about employee communications. *Public Relations Quarterly, 23,* 6–11.

Outline

What Is Communication?
  Information and Meaning
  Verbal Behavior
    Ambiguity
    Group-Restricted Codes
  Nonverbal Behavior
    Paralanguage
    Body Movement
    Space
  Other Definitions
    Source Experience

    Receiver Experience
    Bilateral Experience
What Happens When
Communication Occurs?
  Linear Model
  Interactional Model
  Transactional Model
Summary
Discussion Questions/Activities
Case Study
References

The Concept of Communication

2

Each of us has an intuitive understanding of what is involved in human communication. After all, we communicate with others virtually every day of our lives. Yet, it is not easy to develop a precise definition and description of the communication process. The term *communication,* has become such a buzzword in modern society that one can use it to mean just about anything. A well-meaning friend tells a troubled married couple that they need to communicate more (i.e., they need to fight with each other less). A business executive complains about a communication breakdown (i.e., some important mail was delivered late). A governor explains that a major city cannot get state funds to repair its decaying sewage system because it has not properly communicated its needs to the legislature (i.e., the city voted for the wrong political party in the last election).

The people in these examples are a little like Lewis Carroll's Humpty-Dumpty, who insisted that whenever he uses a word, the word means exactly what he wants it to mean—nothing more, nothing less. Since we all have a bit of Humpty-Dumpty in us, it is not surprising that we use the term *communication* in so many different ways. Our task in this chapter is to make some sense of the concept of communication by answering two questions: What is communication and what happens when the process of communication occurs? The first question usually is answered with a definition, while the second is answered with a model of the process. We are going to review several definitions and models of communication that have influenced the study of organizational communication.

What Is Communication?

We regard **communication** as *shared meaning created among two or more people through verbal and nonverbal transaction.* The basic raw material of communication is verbal and nonverbal information. When two or more human beings engage in verbal and nonverbal transaction, they are involved in generating, perceiving, and interpreting such information. To the extent that **shared meaning** or a *common* interpretation among them results from this process, communication has occurred.

This definition of communication is not unusual. Others have offered similar definitions (Goyer, 1970; Tubbs & Moss, 1980), but not everyone agrees with this approach. The idea of "shared meaning" is only one way to define communication. Before we consider some alternate definitions that you are likely to encounter in the study of communication, we will elaborate on our own definition because the key terms, at least, are common in many definitions of communication.

Information and Meaning

In a simple sense, **information** includes any kind of pattern that a person can observe or sense in the environment. The significance or meaning attached to the pattern may range from negligible to very substantial. **Meaning** occurs when information is placed within a context. The context may be as simple as pattern recognition or as complex as reflective interpretation, in which one piece of information is related to and understood with reference to many others. For example, consider the following markings:

ЭЮЯ

While a very small child may perceive little more than the contrast between the color of the page and the color of the markings, a normal adult will see patterns or definite characteristics such as linear and curvilinear features. Beyond these features, the English-speaking reader may assign very little meaning to these markings. If you know something about the structure of languages, you may realize that the markings represent letters or even a word in some language. If you understand Russian, you are almost certain to recognize the markings as the last three letters of the Russian alphabet. In addition to this denotative meaning, the connection between the markings and "Russian" may also evoke other feelings for you. The level of significance or meaning in each case is different, depending on the frame of reference that your experience has given you.

Information provides the basis for communication. Although any perceivable aspect of one's environment is potentially informative, we are concerned with information in the forms of human verbal and nonverbal behavior.

Verbal Behavior

Verbal behavior includes speaking and writing in the code of a language system. The words in a vocabulary and the grammatical rules for arranging them in expressions are the basic features of a language system. Grammar does not necessarily mean an eighth grade English teacher's *prescriptive* rules for how one is supposed to use language. It also includes all of the regularities that occur in the verbal behavior of a group of language users. Any mode of expression that occurs as a common usage within a particular language community represents a rule for that community. A lawyer representing a client who intends to sue you as well as some other people may say, "To protect my client's interests, I have concluded that it will be necessary to join you as a party defendant in the above styled action, to wit steps to effect this joinder have been undertaken." You may find the rules of this language to be odd and even ungrammatical from a prescriptive standpoint, but the phrase will make perfect sense to another lawyer who uses this same language.

All of the words in a language are **symbols.** All symbols have three basic characteristics. They are representational, freely created, and culturally transmitted (Pollio, 1974).

A symbol is **representational** because it stands for something other than itself. Word symbols provide labels for objects, actions, and experiences. They also permit us to talk about and share conceptions of the things that they label. A word symbol is a substitute that represents an object by providing a link to the idea or concept of this object (Langer, 1942).

Symbols also are **freely created.** The relationship between a symbol and its referent (the thing the symbol represents) is arbitrary because the users of a particular language make up and choose the symbols. The founders of International Business Machines could just as easily have named the company Acme Typewriters. The referent would have been the same (although "IBM" admittedly has more flare). Human beings are continually inventing new symbols to refer to new conditions. Today, we talk about storing files on "floppy disks," "microwaving" our food, and "keyboarding" on "word processors," with meanings for these terms that were virtually nonexistent a decade ago.

Finally, symbols are **culturally transmitted.** This means that symbols are taught and learned, carried on from one generation to another within a language system. Although symbols are freely created and languages do change over time, much of the basic form and content of a language remains stable through cultural transmission. Others created most of our symbols and the rules for using them a long time before we arrived in the world. We are born into a system of symbols and language rules that imposes a particular order on our world. As we acquire the language, we acquire the order that comes along with it.

Some scholars have argued that language exerts a very powerful influence on the way we experience the world. For example, Benjamin Whorf (1957) found that Hopi Indian and English languages handle time in very different ways. The Hopi has no means for marking time that corresponds to the English use of past, present, and future tense. Whorf reasoned that the Hopi experience of time must be quite different from the experience of someone whose language affords convenient ways of carving up time according to verb tense. If Whorf is right, language is much more than a mere tool for expressing thought. Thought itself depends on language, and our notions about "reality" are products of that language. It is even possible that something that is "think-able" in one language may be "unthinkable" in another. Avis Rent-A-Car encountered this problem some years ago when the company attempted to translate its famous "We Try Harder" slogan into the languages of other countries where Avis did business. The closest approximation in German translates roughly as "We give of ourselves more effort." Somehow, the essence of "We Try Harder" seems to be lost in the German equivalent (Pollio, 1974).

Is language an important factor in structuring our experience of organizational life? Interpretivists and critical theorists certainly seem to think so. In part, this is the point that they are making when they argue that organizational reality is socially constructed. Studies by Koch and Deetz and by Wood and Conrad provide some evidence for this point of view.

Koch and Deetz (1981) reported that language systems in organizations revealed "root metaphors" that members use to order and to make sense of their experiences. For example, members might talk about and understand their organization as an efficient, well-oiled machine (mechanical metaphor), a winning team (sports metaphor), a combat group (military metaphor), or even "a big, happy family."

Wood and Conrad (1983) found that organizational languages often contain paradoxes that create double binds for members. A double bind arises from inconsistent messages that result in a "hanged if you do, hanged if you do not" outcome. Consider the manner in which members of a male-dominated management group sometimes solicit ideas from female colleagues:

The invitation often takes the form of soliciting "a woman's perspective" or the "female viewpoint," a form which both subordinates [her] professional expertise and peer status to gender and emphasizes the woman's difference from other [male] members of the group. The woman confronted with such a request is caught in a paradox. If she protests the focus on gender, she runs the risk of being labeled overly sensitive. . . . If she accepts the focus on gender, she collaborates in diminishing her image as a professional. Of course, her colleagues are caught within the same paradox of recognizing her uniqueness, yet being enjoined not to recognize it and to regard her as no different from anyone . . . of equivalent rank in the institution. (pp. 309–310)

Language and symbols systems have two other characteristics that also are important in the study of organizational communication. First, language is ambiguous in the sense that most words and expressions can have more than one meaning. Several scholars state that much of the communication in organizations occurs in an effort to reduce uncertainty associated with ambiguity (Goldhaber, 1990; Weick, 1979). Second, organizational communication often involves the use of group-restricted codes (Baird & Weinberg, 1981). A group-restricted code involves a specialized usage of a language. The vocabulary and rules are unique to a particular group.

Ambiguity

Ambiguity occurs as a consequence of abstract terminology, lack of sufficient detail in messages, and inappropriate or confusing use of modifiers and qualifying phrases (Johnson, 1977). Sometimes, ambiguity is accidental and unintentional, as reflected in the case of a publishing company executive who became angry when someone failed to notify the printing department about a major change in an order. The executive complained to a group of middle managers, "We've got to have better communications around here," then promptly left for a two-week vacation, thinking that the middle managers would lay down the law with employees on the importance of relaying information about any change in a project. When he returned, the middle managers could hardly wait to show him the marketing brochure describing the state-of-the-art office communications system that they had ordered (at a cost of several thousand dollars) during his absence. It was obvious that the middle managers' concept of "better communications" was quite a bit different from the idea that the executive had in mind.

Ambiguity is a common, day-to-day problem in organizational communication, and many organizations expend a great deal of energy in attempting to cope with it. Experts on oral and written expression are quick to advise people that simple, concrete language is the key to reducing ambiguity. But ambiguity in organizational communication involves more than accidental misuse of language or failure to be clear. Ambiguity occurs simply because a symbol or expression has different meanings for different people. There is no guarantee that two people will share the same meaning for a term or expression, even when it is simple and concrete. As Eric Eisenberg (1984) pointed out, ambiguity and clarity are not really embedded in messages but in the *relationship* between source, message, and receiver. Clarity exists only to the extent that "a source has narrowed the possible interpretations of a message and succeeded in achieving a correspondence between his or her intentions and the interpretation of the receiver" (p. 23).

Eisenberg also makes a convincing case that much of the ambiguity in organizational communication is quite deliberate rather than accidental. **Strategic ambiguity,** according to Eisenberg, is not necessarily bad. In fact, it is often very useful and even essential to the organization. Strategic ambiguity helps to promote cohesion by highlighting organization members' agreement on abstract, general ideas and by obscuring their disagreements over specific details. For example, the faculty at University X is "strongly committed to excellence in teaching, research, and service." The university president likes to mention this in public speeches but never attempts to define "excellence" in these areas because different groups of faculty disagree over the specific standards.

Strategic ambiguity in organizational policies and procedures also allows organizations to adapt more readily to change. In 1979–80, Chrysler Corporation used this form of ambiguity to cope with the public perception that the company produced low-quality automobiles. Foss (1984) noted that Chrysler quickly associated itself with Japanese products (generally regarded as high-quality) by marketing the Japanese-made Dodge Colt. The little Colt was advertised as "The Most Technologically Advanced Japanese Import You Can Buy." At the *same* time, according to Foss, Chrysler *denied* its linkage to Japan in the K car campaign: "K cars are proof . . . you don't have to be Japanese to build quality cars." The strategy allowed Chrysler to capitalize on its Japanese connection as a short-term response to its quality problem until a time came when the corporation "no longer had to rely on its Japanese imports for an image of quality and desirability" (p. 82). In effect, Chrysler used strategic ambiguity to play both ends against the middle.

Finally, Eisenberg argues that strategic ambiguity is an important means for supporting status distinctions and maintaining interpersonal relationships in organizations. Consider, for example, the relationship between physicians and nurses in hospital settings. Suppose that a physician gives a nurse an erroneous or inappropriate order for a patient's treatment. If the nurse knows that the order is inappropriate, he or she is legally obligated to confront the situation. But such a confrontation challenges the physician's supreme authority over patient care and nursing actions. The nurse's only way out of this bind "is to use the doctor-nurse game and communicate . . . without appearing to" (Stein, 1967, p. 703). In other words, the nurse uses an *indirect* rather than direct means of communicating with the physician about the problem. Instead of making an unambiguous statement that the order is inappropriate or that it should be changed (statements that would challenge or threaten the physician's authority), the nurse might say, "Doctor, I'm concerned about this order. Could you explain it to me?" This is a face-saving strategy that allows the physician to discover the problem and correct it. However, Cunningham and Wilcox (1984) noted that nurses will take stronger, less ambiguous actions if the risk to the patient is serious and if indirect strategies are ineffective in getting the physician to change the order.

The idea of anyone's being obliged to engage in these kinds of interpersonal gymnastics merely to avoid embarrassment to an authority figure is unpalatable and typical of the kind of paradox that Wood and Conrad describe. But the politics of organizational life are filled with such paradoxes. Ambiguity, as Eisenberg suggests, can be a very effective tool for managing one's way through a paradox.

Group-Restricted Codes

Whether or not ambiguity in organizational communication is accidental or strategically deliberate, it can be reduced only to the extent that people share the same meaning for a code. Groups and organizations often try to ensure that shared meaning will occur by adopting a **group-restricted code** that is highly specialized (Baird & Weinberg, 1981). Many professions and technical occupations use such codes in the form of "jargon"—terms and modes of expression that are known primarily to members of these groups. One's success as a member of such a group depends in part on the ability to master the group's restricted code. We know of one high-technology corporation (Intel) in which the restricted code has become so elaborate that the company issues a comprehensive dictionary of terms and expressions to new employees.

Group-restricted codes are paradoxical. They help to minimize ambiguity and promote a common identity among group members, yet they can be quite confusing to nonmembers. For example, the lawyer's jargon that we used earlier in this chapter may seem like a maze of abstractions to an outsider, but group members (other attorneys) share relatively precise meanings for the code. Even restricted codes that seem to be simple and precise to a nonmember may have "hidden" meanings that are known only within the group itself.

The influence of a restricted code in professional situations is illustrated well by the compelling case of William Borham, who became chief administrator of a large mental hospital in Wisconsin. Borham had no formal education in mental health. In fact, William Borham was not even William Borham. He was really Raymond Metzgar, a former inmate in a psychiatric institution. Metzgar's familiarity with mental hospitals and his ability to speak the language of the mental health profession enabled him to deceive his employer into believing that he was William Borham, a trained clinical psychologist. The fact that Metzgar, alias Borham, became a prominent advocate for mental health programs in Wisconsin brought great embarrassment to state officials when his deception was uncovered by Chicago police after they arrested him for child molestation.

The influence of language on our interpretations of experience, on the nature of ambiguity in organizational communication, and on the characteristics of group-restricted codes should make it clear that verbal behavior and symbolic processes in organizational communication are quite complicated. This complexity increases when we consider nonverbal behavior as the second source of information in human communication.

Nonverbal Behavior

Much of the information involved in human communication is **nonverbal behavior** that occurs in forms other than the word symbols of a language. Harrison (1970) estimated that 65 percent of the information in day-to-day interaction is nonverbal, but the role of nonverbal behavior in communication is not as clear as the role of verbal behavior. Ekman and Friesen (1972) regarded nonverbal behavior as "communicative" only when the person who exhibits the behavior intends it as a message for someone else. In contrast, Watzlawick, Beavin, and Jackson (1967) argued that any behavior, whether intentional or unintentional, is communicative if another person perceives and interprets it.

Nonverbal behavior may be symbolic or signalic. While symbolic behavior clearly is communicative, scholars do not agree that all signalic nonverbal behavior is communicative. Some nonverbal behaviors serve as substitutes for verbal behavior. These nonverbal substitutes have all of the characteristics of symbols. Other nonverbal behaviors are not symbols, but may be **signs.** While a symbol represents its referent, a sign *indicates* a related event (Pollio, 1974). Just as smoke is a physical sign of fire, crying is a sign of an intense emotional state and drooping eyelids usually indicate drowsiness. These nonverbal behaviors signify related conditions. They are not substitutes for these conditions.

The distinction between symbols and signs can be a bit confusing at times. Common nonverbal symbols include behaviors such as the hitchhiker's uplifted thumb, which is a representative, freely created, and culturally transmitted symbol for requesting a ride in a situation in which verbal behavior would be useless. The system of hand gestures that the deaf use and the nonverbal cues that athletic coaches employ to relay plays also have symbolic properties, even though they are called "sign language" or "signals." Many nonverbal behaviors do not have these properties.

A nonverbal sign may be a consistent indicator of some condition. In this case, the sign "means" the condition that it indicates. But nonverbal signs, like symbols, often are ambiguous. They can indicate any one of several potential conditions. Moreover, nonverbal behavior sometimes signifies nothing more than random nervous system activity that has no meaning beyond its own occurrence. It is not always easy to tell whether a nonverbal behavior is a symbol, a sign, or a random activity. A senior manager's finger-drumming during critical negotiations with a labor union could be a random nervous system impulse, a sign of annoyance, or a deliberate message to a junior partner that the union negotiator has just made a major blunder.

The communicative value of ambiguous nonverbal signs and random behaviors is subject to a problem that does not occur with symbolic behavior. Symbolic behavior depends on high-level mental processes. Such behaviors are purposive and intentional. The actual behavior does not always correspond with the intention (for example, a slip of the tongue in speech or an accidental transposition of letters in typing), but an intention is present, the symbol user is aware of the behavior, and the user could, on reflection, indicate the intention (Dance & Larson, 1976). Nonverbal behaviors, on the other hand, often occur unintentionally and without any awareness on the part of the person who exhibits them (Burgoon, 1978). Hence, much of what is called "nonverbal communication" occurs in situations in which a receiver assigns meaning to ambiguous nonverbal signs or random behaviors that have no meaning for the source of the behaviors.

Some popular treatments of nonverbal communication imply that any nonverbal behavior communicates a precise meaning and that we can reliably attribute these behaviors to certain causes or conditions if we simply understand the rules (Fast, 1970). Thus, folded arms indicate withdrawal, a certain posture suggests one's sexual availability, and the placement of a desk between an office occupant and a visitor signifies the occupant's attempt to communicate power, authority, or formality. In fact, any of these examples could involve ambiguous or random activity that occurs without intent or awareness on the part of the person who generates the behavior.

If communication is defined as shared meaning, one's behavior in the presence of another is communicative only to the extent that *both* parties are aware of the behavior, attach some meaning to it, and achieve some commonality in this meaning. Communication occurs when Person A is aware of and assigns meaning to his or her own behavior and Person B perceives and assigns a similar meaning to this behavior even though A may not specifically intend the behavior as a message for B. It does not occur when one party or the other is unaware of or assigns no meaning to the behavior.

Does our rather restrictive definition of nonverbal communication mean that we can ignore nonverbal behaviors when they occur without intent, awareness, or meaning? Probably not. Even when we are unaware of our own behaviors in the presence of others, they may be interpreting these behaviors and acting toward us on the basis of the interpretation. The behavior itself may not be "communicative," but it can certainly influence the communication process. We should all be aware of the possibility that others assign meaning to our behavior even when it has no meaning for us. We also should exercise caution in attaching meanings to others' nonverbal behaviors when these behaviors may be ambiguous or even random. Even Sigmund Freud, who was fond of reading hidden meanings in virtually any human behavior, had to admit, "Sometimes a cigar is just a cigar." With this caution in mind, we will describe three forms of nonverbal behavior that are important in organizational communication: paralanguage, body movement, and the use of space.

Paralanguage

Paralanguage consists of nonverbal speech sounds. Tone, pitch, volume, inflection, rhythm, and rate are elements of paralanguage. Paralanguage is important because the meaning of spoken expression often depends on the paralanguage cues that accompany verbal sounds. We know, for example, that feelings and emotions in spoken expression are indicated primarily by paralanguage cues (Davitz, 1964). Although there is little research on the association between specific paralanguage cues and emotions, it is intuitively obvious that we infer others' attitudes and feelings from paralanguage cues in their speech. The phrase, "What a day," spoken quickly, in a bright tone, and with emphasis, may lead us to infer that the speaker is in a jovial mood. The same phrase in a grumbling, colorless drawl suggests that the speaker is miserable.

Paralanguage also provides cues to meaning in less obvious ways. For example, distinctions between statement types often are provided in paralanguage cues. The difference between a declarative statement and a question often is indicated by the sentence structure, but sometimes can be detected only through paralanguage. Suppose that you take a work-related problem to your boss. The boss listens, then replies, "You know what to do. . . ." A downward inflection from beginning to end may suggest a declarative statement. The boss has heard the problem and is *telling* you that you know how to handle it. An upward inflection at the end could be a question. The boss is *asking* whether you know how to proceed. Some authorities believe that women often use paralanguage cues in ways that undermine their authority as managers and professionals, e.g., by making declarative statements sound like questions that suggest that the speaker is tentative or uncertain (Lakoff, 1975).

Paralanguage also regulates spoken expression. A pause can indicate the end of a thought or provide a cue that another party can take a turn at speaking. In this sense, paralanguage cues are like punctuation marks in written expression.

Written expression also has other characteristics that correspond to paralanguage in speech. Italics and boldface type may be used for emphasis. Readers use clarity, crispness, and overall appearance of writing in making inferences about writers in much the same way that listeners use paralanguage to make inferences about speakers. The potential cues in writing may be much more limited than those available in speech because many of the devices that one might use are regarded as inappropriate in formal writing (Perrin, 1965).

One of the most important functions of paralanguage in both written and spoken expression in organizational communication may be its role in influencing person perception. Several studies show that employment interviewers' hiring decisions and judgments of an applicant's suitability for a particular type of job are influenced by accent and dialect. De La Zerda and Hopper (1979) found that Hispanic Americans who speak "standard," unaccented English are more likely to be regarded as appropriate candidates for supervisory or managerial jobs than those who speak accented English. Schenck-Hamlin (1978) also found that perceptions of a person's competence, coherence, and character appeal are influenced by dialect, but the effect depends on the content of the message. Midwesterners judged "midwestern" and "southern" dialect speakers about equally on neutral topics, but a topic that evoked midwestern stereotypes of southerners led to much lower ratings for the southern dialect speaker. A "midwesterner" opposing racial desegregation was perceived as more competent, coherent, and appealing than a "southerner" presenting the same message.

Body Movement

Much of the information available in face-to-face communication is provided through **body movement.** Ray Birdwhistell (1952), a leading theorist in this area, has claimed for many years that all body movement is meaningful within the context in which it occurs. Birdwhistell believes that body movement can be subjected to systematic analysis and that the characteristics of body movement correspond to the characteristics of language. He based his concepts for the study of body movement, which he called **kinesics,** on the same ideas used in linguistics, the study of language. The idea that body movement is a kind of language has been popularized through work in kinesics, but some scholars have questioned this notion (Littlejohn, 1989).

Is body movement like a language in the sense that it has a vocabulary, grammar, and syntax? Not really, but there is no doubt that body movement has some important functions in human communication. One very useful description of these functions is a system of categories devised by Paul Ekman and Wallace Friesen (1972). Their categories include emblems, illustrators, regulators, affect displays, and adaptors.

Emblems are kinesics substitutes for verbal behavior. An emblem usually is intended to transmit a particular message, but the meaning may depend on the group that uses it and the context in which it occurs. The two-fingered "V" traditionally is an emblem for victory. During the 1960s, young people also adopted it as an emblem for peace.

Illustrators are kinesic cues that directly support speech behavior. These cues are not substitutes for the spoken word, but they help to emphasize what is being said. Illustrators include behaviors to point out, outline a form, or depict motion. In one sense, an illustrator is a kind of kinesic "visual aid." People who use many illustrators when speaking are likely to be perceived as more animated and energetic than those who use few or no illustrators (Norton, 1978).

Regulators help to control and coordinate face-to-face interaction. These behaviors include eye movements, head positions, and postures that signal taking turns in conversations. Eye contact in particular is important as a signal for seeking feedback, initiating interaction, or terminating conversations (McCroskey, Larson, & Knapp, 1971).

Affect displays are cues to feelings and emotional states. These behaviors may include facial movements such as smiles, frowns, and sneers, as well as certain postures. Facial expression seems to be a good indicator of at least six emotions: happiness, anger, sadness, surprise, disgust, and fear (Knapp, 1978).

Adaptors involve release of physical tension. These behaviors may be either the means for or the results of tension release. For instance, scratching your head may be an instrumental behavior to relieve an itch. In contrast, moment-to-moment wiggles and jiggles of various body parts may result merely from random nervous system activity.

Space

The use of **space** is a subtle but powerful factor in human social and organizational behavior that appears to vary greatly across different cultures. In general, we humans seem to be territorial creatures who define and defend the boundaries of our space. We also arrange objects in space to either suit ourselves or to accomplish various purposes. Finally, we use space to define appropriate distance between people in interpersonal settings.

The formal study of the use of space is called **proxemics.** Edward Hall (1959), who developed the field of proxemics along the lines of Birdwhistell's kinesics, identified three basic types of space: fixed-feature, semifixed-feature, and informal. **Fixed-feature space** involves either concrete or imaginary but stable boundaries that define territory. Goldhaber (1990) points out that there often is a close relationship between status and territory in organizations. He has identified three principles in this relationship that have the potential to influence organizational communication:

1. The higher up you are in the organization, the more and better space you have [sic].
2. The higher up you are in the organization, the better protected your territory is [sic].
3. The higher up you are in the organization, the easier it is to invade the territory of lower-status personnel. (pp. 188–190)

Whether or not the amount of space in one's territory, the ability to protect it, or the ability to invade someone else's territory are directly communicative, these conditions certainly can influence organizational communication. The allocation of space itself signifies status, and status gives one more control over initiating, structuring, and terminating interaction with others.

Offices and work areas in organizations contain many objects and fixtures that must somehow be positioned in space—desks, chairs, files, equipment, decorations. The arrangement of these objects involves the use of **semifixed-feature space.** Such arrangements may or may not be intended to transmit a particular message, but the idea of communication through placement of objects has become so popular that *any* arrangement is almost certain to provoke an interpretation.

If you can penetrate the well-protected territory of a high-level executive, you may find that this person's space is furnished more like a living room than an office. Presumably, such an arrangement "communicates" an atmosphere of openness and accessibility. The lower-level manager with a cast-off military surplus desk, stacked with volumes of reports and positioned as a barrier behind a door to a cramped office, may be telling visitors, "Go away. I really don't have time for you." Such interpretations may be perfectly valid, but one should exercise them with caution because they presume that the person who occupies the space has a specific intent and purpose for the arrangement of objects within it. In fact, the use of semifixed-feature space may be more dependent on organizational customs and allocation of resources than on any conscious personal choice that the office occupant makes.

The final category, **informal space,** refers to the physical proximity of one person to another in interpersonal settings. Hall identified four distinct informal zones in American culture: intimate (one to eighteen inches), personal (eighteen inches to four feet), social (four to twelve feet), public (over twelve feet). Most interpersonal conversations occur in the personal zone of informal space, but cultures vary in the use of this space. The Chinese seem to require more personal distance for interaction than Americans require. In turn, Americans require more than Arabs require. Most interaction in American business organizations occurs in the social zone of informal space. A Chinese visitor might find this practice to be appropriate and tasteful. An Arabic visitor might be most uncomfortable under similar conditions.

While paralanguage, body movement, and use of space are three important forms of nonverbal behavior in human communication, researchers have identified other behaviors and characteristics of human demeanor that may also be relevant to our discussion. These include use of time, touch, clothing, and overall physical appearance (body type). Whether these behaviors and personal characteristics are communicative in the sense that we have defined communication will depend on many factors in any given situation. In any case, such behaviors certainly will influence the day-to-day process of communication.

Other Definitions

While everyone agrees that verbal information, nonverbal information, and meaning are central features of human communication, not everyone is prepared to define communication as shared meaning. Three other definitions of communication are applied frequently in the organizational setting: source experience, receiver experience, bilateral experience.

Source Experience

Communication sometimes is regarded as a **source experience.** Berelson and Steiner (1964) adopted this view when they defined communication as "the transmission of information, ideas, emotions, skills, etc., by the use of symbols. . . . It is the act or process of transmission that is usually called communication" (p. 527). In other words, communication is something that a person does by sending messages. It is an act of message transmission performed by a source. The message usually is regarded as symbolic content in spoken or written form.

Source experience definitions of communication say nothing about the processes that occur when messages and information are *received*. For example, is the information understood? Is the receiver's interpretation the same as the source's? The events that occur when a message is received may determine the *effectiveness* of communication, but they are not a part of the definition of communication. The fact that a person (source) has engaged in an act of message transmission means that communication has occurred.

Receiver Experience

Receiver experience definitions of communication take a viewpoint that is exactly opposite of the position in source experience definitions. The receiver approach regards communication either as a behavioral response or as an interpretive act on the part of a person who receives information. S. S. Stevens (1950) adopted a behavioral view by defining communication as "the discriminatory response of an organism to a stimulus" (p. 689).

Behavioral views such as Stevens' often are held in disfavor because they imply that humans are merely reactive creatures who respond passively to stimuli. By definition, a stimulus is anything that incites or causes behavior. Communication theorists usually are more inclined to see human beings as the originators of their own behavior—active agents rather than passive respondents (Miller, 1983). The "active agent" version of the receiver experience view suggests that communication occurs whenever a person actively interprets another person's verbal and nonverbal behaviors by selecting information, assigning meanings, and making inferences and choices (Littlejohn, 1989).

Whether receiver experience definitions imply that humans are passive respondents or active agents, they share the view that communication is the interpretation of or response to information rather than the transmission of information. As Jurgen Ruesch and Gregory Bateson explained, "All actions and events have communicative aspects as soon as they are perceived by a human being" (1961, pp. 5–6). This viewpoint is reflected in the popular notion that "one cannot *not* communicate" (Watzlawick, Beavin, & Jackson, 1967, p. 51). In other words, everything that a person does in the presence of another is communication. Obviously, advocates of this view would not accept Ekman and Friesen's restriction of communicative behavior to intentional acts, nor would they require that shared meaning occur in order to classify behavior as communicative.

Bilateral Experience

A final way of defining communication falls between the extremes of the source experience and receiver experience views. This approach treats communication as a **bilateral** or two-sided process that involves both source and receiver experiences. G. A. Sanborn, who worked with Redding to develop the study of organizational communication, typified this approach by defining communication as "the process of sending and receiving messages" (1964, p. 3).

Neither message transmission nor receiver interpretation of information is sufficient by itself to constitute communication in the bilateral view. As explained by Shamo and Bittner, "Communication requires both a source and a destination" (1972, p. 181). The source must transmit "meaningful signals" in a message, and a receiver must perceive and assign meaning to the message. The concept of a "message" in such definitions may be limited to symbolic content or defined broadly to include any behavior that is meaningful to both source and receiver. This does not imply, however, that meaning must be shared for communication to occur. Shared meaning is one measure of communication effectiveness. Communication effectiveness also means that the source gets a desired response from the receiver.

There is no consensus in the field on the "correct" definition of communication. All four of the approaches that we have reviewed—shared meaning, source experience, receiver experience, and bilateral experience—have been used in the study of organizational communication. Since the bilateral approach treats messages as concrete objects and effectiveness as a problem of getting a desired response, this approach has been the most commonly used in organizational communication, especially in the traditional functionalist perspective (e.g., see Koehler, Anatol, & Applbaum, 1981).

What Happens When Communication Occurs?

Just as there are several ways of defining communication, there also are different ways of modeling the process in order to describe what happens when communication occurs. Three basic models of communication that provide different descriptions of the process have been developed. These models are referred to as linear, interactional, and transactional (Tubbs & Moss, 1980).

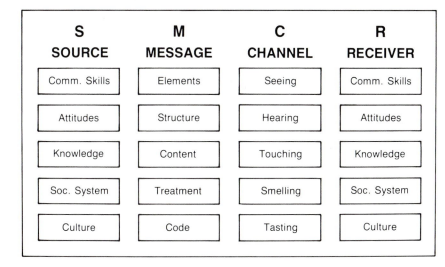

Figure 2.1
Berlo's S-M-C-R model of communication. From THE PROCESS OF COMMUNICATION: AN INTRODUCTION TO THEORY AND PRACTICE, by David K. Berlo. Copyright © 1960 by Holt, Rinehart & Winston, Inc. Adapted by permission of CBS College Publishing.

Linear Model

Linear models provide the simplest description of the communication process. These models represent communication as the one-way flow of a message from a source to a receiver. David K. Berlo (1960) developed a model of communication that reflects the linear view. Berlo's S-M-C-R model is displayed in figure 2.1.

In Berlo's model, a source (S) transmits a message (M) through a channel (C) to a receiver (R). Both the source and receiver are affected by their own attitudes, prior knowledge, sociocultural background, and other factors in this process. The source must *encode* the message; the receiver must *decode* it. Encoding refers to the process of changing ideas into symbols—verbal and nonverbal stimuli that are assumed to have common referents for the source and receiver. Decoding involves assignment of meaning to symbols.

The message is transmitted through a channel. The channel might involve speech, writing, or some system of nonverbal gestures. Fidelity of the message may be affected by *noise*—anything that interferes with or distorts the message as it is transmitted through the channel.

Message fidelity, according to Berlo, refers to more than the simple clarity or quality of transmission. Berlo linked fidelity with the idea of obtaining a desired response and expanded the definition of noise to include anything that interferes with the process of obtaining this response. A receiver's communication skills, attitudes, knowledge, cultural background, and social position are potential sources of noise, since these factors "affect the ways in which he [or she] receives and interprets the message" (p. 52).

Figure 2.2
An interaction model of communication.

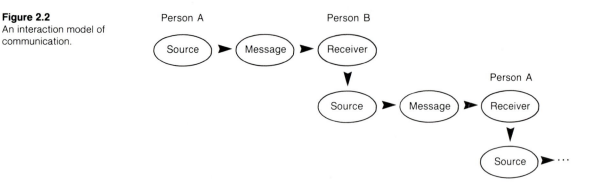

Interactional Model

Berlo's model is not entirely linear because he did provide for a *feedback loop* from the receiver to the source. Feedback is a response from the receiver that may influence the source to modify further messages. Although the addition of feedback is the first step in the transition from a linear to an **interactional model** of communication, Burgoon and Ruffner (1978) claimed that Berlo's model underestimates the importance of feedback and "fails to account fully for the dynamic nature of human communication" (p. 22). An interactional model improves our understanding of these dynamics because it emphasizes a *two-way* perspective of communication. Such a model is displayed in figure 2.2.

The interactional model portrays communication as a process of message exchange. Person A (source) sends a message to Person B (receiver). Then B becomes a source by responding with a message to A, who is now the receiver. The participants in communication exchange roles during the process.

Transactional Model

The most recent perspective of the communication process is represented in **transactional models.** While the interactional model describes communication as a two-way, reciprocal process of message exchange, a transactional model emphasizes the idea that communication is mutual as well as reciprocal. As described by Wenburg and Wilmot (1973), "All persons are engaged in sending (encoding) and receiving (decoding) messages simultaneously. Each person is constantly *sharing* in the encoding and decoding process and each person is *affecting* the other" (p. 6). Figure 2.3 represents a transactional model of communication.

In the transactional view, communication occurs without sharp distinctions between source and receiver roles. A person occupies both roles at the same time. Suppose that you have just begun your first professional job. You are having a conversation at work with a new friend (Yuppie, another young professional who has been with the company for about one year). You mention that you have just been assigned to a new project. Yuppie, who has taken you

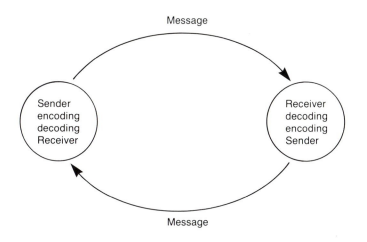

Figure 2.3
A transactional model of
communication.

under wing and provided you with a lot of good information about the company, appears to be interested in hearing more. But as you describe the project, Yuppie begins to frown. You continue, "I did a dozen projects like this as a college student." Yuppie's face is getting red. This does not seem right to you, but you press on with your story. "This job," you say, "will be piece of cake." Yuppie is now steaming and you are really concerned, but you continue, "Working on this project is going to get me a sure fire promotion." Even as you say this, you are thinking that maybe you should not. Sure enough, Yuppie explodes and tells you to drop dead. Later, you discover from another source that Yuppie has been campaigning to work on the same project for more than six months, but management refused to give the job to Yuppie. Instead, they gave it to you.

Now who is the "source" and who is the "receiver" in this conversation? You are doing all of the talking until Yuppie blows up, but you also are receiving and processing information about Yuppie's emotional state throughout the episode. Unfortunately, you do not sort out a clear interpretation of the information until after you have alienated Yuppie.

Linear, interactional, and transactional models all can be applied as accurate descriptions of the communication process, but their ranges of application differ. A linear model is very limited because few instances of human communication truly occur in a one-way fashion. Episodes of superiors giving orders to subordinates and some forms of public communication, such as issuing policy pronouncements through memorandums or newsletters with no expectation of feedback, appear to be linear, but most instances of organizational communication are interactional and transactional.

An interactional model does a good job of describing *mediated* forms of communication. Interaction through an electronic or paper medium (e.g., letters, memorandums, or computer terminals) separates the communicators and often structures communication as a process of message exchange. A sends a message to B, then must wait for B to follow up with a reply. Of course, telemediated interaction is an exception if the channel allows for simultaneous, bidirectional message flow (e.g., in teleconferences where you can see and hear others on visual and voice channels even as you are speaking to them).

The transactional model usually serves as the most appropriate model for face-to-face encounters in which communication occurs through speech and various nonverbal behaviors. To the extent that each participant in such an encounter has an awareness of self and others in the situation, the source and receiver aspects of human communication are enacted simultaneously. Again, some forms of telemediated interaction may be characterized accurately as transactional.

Summary

The term *communication* is something of a buzzword in modern society. People use the word to refer to many different human activities and conditions. Even academic scholars who specialize in the study of human communication define this concept in various ways.

We define communication as *shared meaning created among two or more people through verbal and nonverbal transaction.* The basic raw material of communication is information, which includes any aspect of the environment in which one can discern a pattern. Meaning occurs when information is placed within a context. Human communication is concerned with the meaning of verbal and nonverbal information.

Verbal information occurs in the spoken and written forms of a language code. This code involves a system of symbols as well as rules for how symbols are used. Symbols are representative, freely created, and culturally transmitted. Some experts regard symbols as tools for expressing thought. Others argue that thought as we understand it depends on symbols, that our knowledge and sense of reality are products of our language system. The influence of language in organizational communication is suggested by the use of root metaphors to make sense of organizational experiences, certain types of language paradoxes in organizational behavior, strategic use of ambiguity, and the prevalence of group-restricted codes.

Nonverbal information also is important in organizational communication, but the concept of nonverbal communication is troublesome because many nonverbal behaviors may be ambiguous and unreliable signs of emotional states or even random activities that occur without awareness or intent on the part of a source. Although an observer is likely to interpret such behaviors, they lead to no shared meaning. Popular notions that nonverbal behaviors are consistent indicators of specific messages and conditions that can be interpreted reliably if one knows the rules are misleading. One should exercise caution when attaching interpretations to nonverbal behavior.

Three important forms of nonverbal information are paralanguage, body movement (kinesics), and space (proxemics). Paralanguage cues such as volume, rate, rhythm, inflection, tone, and pitch help us to interpret verbal behavior. These cues also influence our perceptions of a speaker. Kinesic behaviors can be organized in five functional categories: emblems, illustrators, regulators, affect displays, and adaptors. Proxemics involves fixed-feature space, semifixed-feature space, and informal space. Fixed-feature space is essentially a territory. Territory and status are highly connected in many organizations. Arrangement of objects in semifixed-feature space can be used to convey a variety of messages. Informal space, the area in which interaction occurs, has four basic zones—intimate, personal, social, and public—that appear to vary widely across cultures.

Three other approaches to defining communication are source experience, receiver experience, and bilateral experience. All three have been employed in the study of organizational communication, but the bilateral approach has been the most common, especially in traditional functionalism.

Communication also may be modeled in various ways. The simplest models are linear. Such models portray communication as a one-way process of message flow from a source to a receiver. Such a model is highly limited because most episodes of organizational communication do not fit this characterization. Organizational communication is better described by interactional models, which stress two-way communication in which participants exchange source and receiver roles, or by transactional models, which emphasize simultaneous conduct of source and receiver activity by all participants in the process.

Discussion Questions/ Activities

1. Which of the four definitions of communication presented in this chapter (shared meaning, source experience, receiver experience, bilateral experience) makes the most sense to you when it is applied to organizations? Why?
2. Apply the three models of communication in this chapter to several different episodes of human interaction. Are there appropriate applications for each model or does one generally work better than the other two? Why?
3. Try to identify some instances of ambiguous communication. How do people in these situations try to cope with ambiguity? What is the final result of these coping efforts? Is ambiguity used strategically in any of these situations?
4. Observe the nonverbal behaviors of others in public settings. What information can you reliably infer from these behaviors? Under what circumstances would you consider the behaviors to be communicative?
5. Try to observe a group that uses a restricted code, then describe this code in as much detail as you can. What functions does the code seem to serve for this group?

Case Study

The Circle of Misunderstanding

John Andriate likes to boast that he got his education in the "college of hard knocks." Andriate quit high school during his junior year to enlist in the military during the Korean conflict. After his discharge in 1953, he spent five years holding odd jobs in grocery stores before he persuaded his two brothers to join him in a produce business (supplying fresh fruits and vegetables to supermarkets).

Although you would never have guessed it from the condition of the company's facility (a run-down, ramshackle warehouse), Andriate Brothers Produce had become, over the years, a very successful company with massive amounts of reserve cash. Everybody in town knew the Andriates, so when John contacted Kanarick & Associates Accounting about the possibility of assuming full-charge bookkeeping for Andriate Brothers, it seemed that Kanarick & Associates was routinely taking on just one more well-established client.

Andriate met with Kate Malone, the supervisor for accounting services at Kanarick. He told her that he and his brothers had "handled the books during spare time" for many years but that the size of the company had begun to make this task impossible. Andriate wanted an accounting firm to take over the job. Malone, a CPA and an experienced supervisor, questioned Andriate about the condition of his company's accounting system. Andriate said, "We've got a basic ledger and complete tax and payroll records. Everything is up-to-date, so you should be able to just take it over."

Normally, Kate would personally examine a company's set of books before quoting a fee for providing a monthly bookkeeping service. Sometimes, Kanarick & Associates would have to set up a completely new system because the client's books had been poorly maintained or had not complied with the law. But Kate was preoccupied today. She was leaving town late that afternoon for a week-long workshop, and she knew that John Andriate was not the sort of fellow who waited for answers. Kate said, "Okay, the basic service charge will be $250 per month, assuming that the condition of your system is as you describe it. We'll set up a service contract as soon as I get back from my trip."

Malone introduced Andriate to Bob Plax, a 25–year-old bookkeeper at Kanarick. Plax worked part-time at Kanarick while pursuing an accounting degree at the local college. Malone instructed Plax to arrange an on-site meeting at Andriate Brothers for the next day. Bob was instructed to review the condition of the books and to take possession of all records required to set up the service.

When Plax arrived at Andriate Brothers the next day, he was visibly dismayed at the conditions he found. There was no general ledger. The only "accounting system" was the transaction record in the company checkbook. All income and expenses went through the same account. Tax records, payroll records, invoices, bills, and receipts were piled in old produce boxes along the walls of John Andriate's office. The boxes were labeled by year, but the material in each box was in complete disarray. Plax looked at the boxes, hung his head, and sighed in disgust. Andriate saw his reaction and started the following exchange:

"What's the matter, kid? You got a problem?"

"Well, Mr. Andriate, it is not a problem for me, but *you've* got a mess here."

"What do you mean, I got a mess? It's all here, just like I said. The ledger's in the checkbook and the records are in the boxes. Look, everything for this year is right here in this box."

"Mr. Andriate, a lot of small businesses just don't understand these things. We're going to have to do a lot to sort this out."

"Sort out what? What's to sort out?"

"Well," Plax replied, "let me give you some examples of things you probably don't know about. You'll need a double-entry accounting system, a complete reorganization of your records by function, and a P & L statement. The worst of it is that you're in the middle of the FY, so we'll have to completely reconstruct your records for the past six months."

"The only thing getting reconstructed here is how much all this is gonna cost. Nobody mentioned this stuff when I talked to your boss," Andriate replied.

"Mr. Andriate, we didn't know how disorganized you were when you talked to my boss."

"Look, kid," said Andriate sharply, "I got no time for this. You want the business or not? If you do, then pack up what you need, get back to your office, and do what needs to be done."

Plax assembled everything that he needed and returned to his office. He figured that he would check with somebody. Since Kate Malone was out of town, Plax went to the supervisor of the auditing department (a separate unit from the accounting department) and explained that he had run into problems at Andriate Brothers. The auditing supervisor asked whether Andriate understood the situation . . . that the cost of setting up the system was going to be much higher than anticipated and that the additional cost would be added to the service contract. Plax replied, "Yeah, I guess so. He told me to take the records and do whatever needs to be done." The auditing supervisor barely looked up from a report that he had been reading during the conversation and said, "Well, go ahead with it and check in with Kate as soon as she gets back."

Plax worked diligently day and night for the rest of the week—more than 70 hours altogether—to organize an up-to-date set of books for the Andriate account. He hoped that Kate Malone would be impressed and that Andriate would be easier to deal with if Kanarick gave him quick and efficient service. Besides, this was a good chance for Plax to show Kanarick & Associates why the firm should hire him as a full-time accountant after his graduation.

On the day Malone returned to the office, Plax proudly displayed his work on the Andriate account. Malone responded, "This really looks great, Bob, but I'm a little surprised to see it. Does Andriate know that we had to do all of this?"

Plax replied, "Well, he hasn't seen it, but he told me to do it and the auditing supervisor told me to go ahead."

Malone seemed satisfied. She prepared and mailed the service contract that she had promised to Andriate. The contract included the $250–per-month service charge, plus a $900 setup fee for the work that Plax had done.

Two days later, Kate Malone received a phone call from an angry Andriate. He was in no mood for explanations. He insisted that the $900 setup fee was totally unexpected and way out of line. "I'm gonna pay this setup cost so I can feel like I'm doin' right, but I'm gonna spread the word on you people. I want that kid of yours to bring back the new books *and* my records, then I don't wanna hear from you people ever again!"

1. At what points are there problems with ambiguous communication in this case?
2. What factors contribute to the ambiguity?
3. Do Plax and Andriate use different "codes"? How does this contribute to the problem?
4. What (if anything) could Plax have done to minimize or prevent the problem that developed in this situation?

References

Baird, J. E., Jr., & Weinberg, S. B. (1981). *Group communication: The essence of synergy* (2nd ed.). Dubuque, IA: Wm. C. Brown Company Publishers.

Berelson, B., & Steiner, G. (1964). *Human behavior.* New York: Harcourt Brace Jovanovich.

Berlo, D. K. (1960). *The process of communication.* New York: Holt, Rinehart & Winston.

Birdwhistell, R. (1952). *Introduction to kinesics.* Louisville, KY: University of Louisville Press.

Burgoon, J. K. (1978). Nonverbal communication. In M. Burgoon & M. Ruffner, *Human communication.* New York: Holt, Rinehart & Winston.

Burgoon, M., & Ruffner, M. (1978). *Human communication.* New York: Holt, Rinehart & Winston.

Cunningham, M. A., & Wilcox, J. R. (1984). *Modifying a bind: The effects of patient harm and physician interpersonal risk on nurse communication in the inappropriate-order situation.* Paper presented at the annual meeting of the International Communication Association, San Francisco.

Dance, F. E. X., & Larson, C. E. (1976). *The functions of human communication: A theoretical approach.* New York: Holt, Rinehart & Winston.

Davitz, J. R. (1964). *The communication of emotional meaning.* New York: McGraw-Hill.

De La Zerda, N., & Hopper, R. (1979). Employment interviewers' reactions to Mexican American speech. *Communication Monographs, 46,* 126–134.

Eisenberg, E. M. (1984). Ambiguity as a strategy in organizational communication. *Communication Monographs, 51,* 227–242.

Ekman, P., & Friesen, W. V. (1972). Hand movements. *Journal of Communication, 22,* 353–374.

Fast, J. (1970). *Body language.* New York: Pocket Books.

Foss, S. K. (1984). Retooling and image: Chrysler Corporation's rhetoric of redemption. *Western Journal of Speech Communication, 48,* 75–91.

Goldhaber, G. M. (1990). *Organizational communication* (5th ed.). Dubuque, IA: Wm. C. Brown Company Publishers.

Goyer, R. S. (1970). Communication, communication process, meaning: Toward a unified theory. *Journal of Communication, 20,* 6–7.

Hall, E. (1959). *Silent language.* Greenwich, CT: Fawcett.

Harrison, R. (1970). Nonverbal communication: Explorations into time, space, action, and object. In J. Campbell & H. Helper (Eds.), *Dimensions in communication.* Belmont, CA: Wadsworth.

Johnson, B. M. (1977). *Communication: The process of organizing.* Boston: Allyn and Bacon.

Knapp, M. (1978). *Nonverbal communication in human interaction* (2nd ed.). New York: Holt, Rinehart & Winston.

Koch, S., & Deetz, S. A. (1981). *Metaphor analysis of social reality in organizations.* Journal of Applied Communication Research, *9,* 1–15.

Koehler, J. W., Anatol, K. W. E., & Applbaum, R. L. (1981). *Organizational communication: Behavioral perspectives* (2nd ed.). New York: Holt, Rinehart & Winston.

Lakoff, R. (1975). *Language and woman's place.* New York: Harper & Row.

Langer, S. (1942). *Philosophy in a new key.* Cambridge, MA: Harvard University Press.

Littlejohn, S. W. (1983). *Theories of human communication* (2nd ed.). Belmont, CA: Wadsworth.

McCroskey, J. C., Larson, C., & Knapp M. (1971). *An introduction to interpersonal communication.* Englewood Cliffs, NJ: Prentice-Hall.

Miller, G. R. (1983). Taking stock of a discipline. *Journal of Communication, 33,* 31–41.

Norton, R. (1978). Foundation of a communicator style construct. *Human Communication Research, 4,* 99–112.

Perrin, P. G. (1965). *Writer's guide and index to English* (4th ed.). Glenview, IL: Scott, Foresman.

Pollio, H. R. (1974). *The psychology of symbolic activity.* Reading, MA: Addison-Wesley.

Ruesch, J., & Bateson, G. (1961). *The social matrix of psychiatry.* New York: Norton.

Sanborn, G. A. (1964). Communication in business: An overview. In W. C. Redding & G. A. Sanborn (Eds.), *Business and industrial communication.* New York: Harper & Row.

Schenck-Hamlin, W. J. (1978). The effects of dialectical similarity, stereotyping, and message agreement on interpersonal perception. *Human Communication Research, 5,* 15–26.

Shamo, G. W., & Bittner, J. R. (1972). Recall as a function of language style. *Southern Speech Communication Journal, 38,* 181.

Stein, L. I. (1967). The doctor-nurse game. *Archives of General Psychiatry, 16,* 699–703.

Stevens, S. S. (1950). A definition of communication. *Journal of the Acoustical Society of America, 22,* 689.

Tubbs, S. L., & Moss, S. (1980). *Human Communication* (3rd ed.). New York: Random House.

Watzlawick, P., Beavin, J., & Jackson, D. (1967). *Pragmatics of human communication: A study of interactional patterns, pathologies, and paradoxes.* New York: Norton.

Weick, K. (1979). *The social psychology of organizing* (2nd ed.). Reading, MA: Addison-Wesley.

Wenberg, J., & Wilmot, W. (1973). *The personal communication process.* New York: John Wiley & Sons.

Whorf, B. L. (1957). *Language, thought, and reality.* New York: John Wiley & Sons.

Wood, J. T., and Conrad, C. (1983). Paradox in the experiences of professional women. *Western Journal of Speech Communication, 47,* 305–322.

Outline

Scientific and Classical
Management
   Taylor's Scientific Management
   Fayol's General Management
   Weber's Bureaucratic Theory
Eclectic Theories
   Follett's Administrative Theory
   Barnard's Executive Functions
The Human Relations Movement
   Dale Carnegie
   The Hawthorne Studies and
      Elton Mayo
     The Illumination Studies
     Relay Assembly-Room Studies
     The Interview Program
     Bank-Wiring Studies
     Implications of the Studies

Human Resource Development
   Maslow's Need Hierarchy
   McGregor's Theory X and
     Theory Y
   Likert's Four Systems
A System Theory
   Wholeness
   Hierarchy
   Openness
   Feedback
Summary
Discussion Questions/Activities
Case Study
References

Theories of Organization and Organizational Effectiveness

3

Organizational behavior is as old as the human social experience. We know from historical accounts that early civilizations sometimes had elaborate organizational systems for governmental, military, religious, and economic purposes. The ancient peoples who created these organizations had "theories" of organizational behavior—concepts, principles, and prescriptions for organizational structure and function. These theories were fitted to the needs of agricultural societies only a few generations removed from their tribal origins.

During the Middle Ages of Western civilization, the dominance of institutionalized religion and ordering of society into localized feudal economies produced principles of divine right and social class systems of authority and labor as guidelines for organizing. Feudal serfs (average citizens), as well as their lords, had tradition to tell them what to do in an era when the patterns of life and society were virtually unchanged for centuries (Dessler, 1980).

The Renaissance and, later, the Industrial Revolution effectively removed the basic foundations of feudal life. As a consequence, organizations in the developed nations of today's world function within a complex and sometimes rapidly changing economic, legal, political, and social environment. This environment has evolved from four centuries of commercialization and industrialization, international trade, secularization of social and governmental institutions, and compression of time and distance through technological advances in transportation and communications.

When the industrialized world entered the twentieth century, it was apparent that new and clearer concepts of organizational behavior would be required to deal with the complexities of modern society (Dessler, 1980). The first modern perspectives on organizational behavior were developed in the early 1900s when several prominent theorists advanced the basic principles of scientific and classical management. Scientific and classical theories envisioned organizations as machinelike objects driven by management plan and control. Individual organization members often were regarded as simple parts in the machine.

Scientific and classical theories were followed quickly by eclectic theories of organization and by the emergence of the human relations movement. The eclectic theories, which cut across several different schools of thought about organizations, were much broader than scientific and classical theories. The human relations movement actually challenged scientific and classical notions by arguing that organizational effectiveness depends more on the social processes of organization than on management design. These principles never really replaced classical and scientific views. Instead, many assumptions about organizational behavior drawn from human relations theory simply were grafted onto classical and scientific management ideas about organizational structure.

Later, the development of new concepts in human motivation and the emergence of system theory led to further refinements in organizational theory. Human resource development theory, based on motivational principles of the human need for self-fulfillment, began to compete with earlier human relations and classical/scientific perspectives of organizational behavior. System theories treated organizations as adaptive organisms rather than as machines operated solely by management control. They attempted to describe and to explain organizations with some general principles that were presumed to apply to all systems.

Most of these theories are concerned not only with the characteristics of organizations, but also with the problems of managerial and organizational effectiveness. With the exception of some versions of system theory, they are *prescriptive* theories that indicate how organizational processes (including communication) should function. Whether or not prescriptions for organizational structure, managerial strategy, and communication always work, the pursuit of reliable methods for attaining organizational effectiveness has been a traditional concern in organizational theory. This concern carries over into the field of organizational communication.

Scientific and Classical Management

Scientific and classical theories of management represented the earliest attempts to cope with the complexities of twentieth-century organizations. Three of the most influential theorists during the early 1900s were Frederick Taylor, an American engineer; Henri Fayol, a French industrialist; and Max Weber, a German university professor. Taylor published his system of "Scientific Management" in 1919. Fayol and Weber wrote classical treatises on the principles of organization and management at about the same time, although their works were not available in English translations for an American market until the 1940s. These three theorists differed from one another in many of the principles that they advocated, but they shared a common idea that effective organizational performance is determined by efficient design of work and organizational structure.

Taylor's Scientific Management

Frederick Taylor was concerned primarily with the scientific study and design of work processes. Most of his principles addressed problems of work efficiency, but he also offered recommendations regarding organizational structure and processes. Essentially, Taylor (1919) advanced four ideas:

1. There is "one best way" to perform any job. The best way can be determined through scientific analysis. For example, a time and motion

study can reveal the fewest number of steps and shortest amount of time required to perform a task efficiently. Experiments can determine the physical working conditions under which productivity will be highest.

2. Personnel should be selected scientifically. One should choose and assign people to tasks according to their skills or potential for developing skills.

3. Workers should be compensated on an incentive plan that pays them in direct proportion to the work that they produce. An hourly wage is inappropriate, not so much because of differences in individual productivity but because economic need is the principal factor that motivates people to work. Workers will produce more if they realize that they will be paid acccordingly.

4. Labor should be divided so that managers plan the work and workers follow the plan. In Taylor's scheme, each aspect of any task is supervised by a different "functional foreman." A given worker takes orders from any one or all of these foremen, depending on the characteristics of the task.

Taylor believed that the central problem in organizational effectiveness involved management's inability to obtain compliance from workers. He argued that if organizations followed his principles, then managers and workers would realize that they can cooperate to increase the organization's wealth and resources "until the surplus becomes so large that it is unnecessary to quarrel over how it shall be divided." In other words, everybody would benefit under scientific management.

Taylor applied his principles at Bethlehem Steel Company in order to improve the work efficiency of coal and iron ore shovelers. The volume of material moved each day jumped by more than 30 percent, the cost of moving the material was cut in half, and the average pay for shovelers increased by 60 percent (Koehler, Anatol, & Applbaum, 1981). The results were fantastic, but this particular silver lining surrounded an ominous cloud. Given the improved efficiency, Bethlehem Steel officials decided that the necessary labor could be done with a much smaller work force. They laid off more than 260 employees. Taylor's principles of scientific work analysis caught on quickly in American industry with results that Taylor himself may not have intended.

Fayol's General Management

While Taylor focused on the technical details of production work, Henri Fayol was concerned primarily with the basic principles of organizational structure and management practice. Fayol (1949) offered 14 fundamental principles. Most are prescriptions for organizational structure and design.

1. *Division of work.* Each member has one and only one job to do.
2. *Authority and responsibility.* Authority includes the right to give orders and the power to exact compliance. Official authority depends on one's position. Personal authority depends on ability and experience.

3. *Discipline.* Good discipline depends on good superiors, clear and fair policies, and judiciously applied sanctions.
4. *Unity of command.* An employee receives orders from one and only one superior for any action.
5. *Unity of direction.* A group of activities with the same objective should have "one head with one plan."
6. *Subordination of individual interests.* The interests of the organization must prevail over those of any given group or person.
7. *Remuneration.* Employees should be paid fairly, in a manner that satisfies them and the firm.
8. *Centralization.* Whether decision making is centralized (restricted to higher-level management) or decentralized (allocated to subordinates) depends on the organization's circumstances.
9. *Scalar chain.* The system of authority is structured as a hierarchy with clear lines of command from one level to the next, but the system must allow for departure from the chain of command when necessary.
10. *Order.* There is a place for each employee and each employee is to be in his or her place.
11. *Equity.* Personnel should be treated with kindness and justice, but this does not exclude forcefulness and sternness.
12. *Stability in tenure.* Assuming that an employee has the ability to do a job, he or she must still have time to learn and to succeed in performing it.
13. *Initiative.* The ability to think out and execute a plan is a valuable organizational resource.
14. *Esprit de corps.* Management should strive to promote a sense of unity, harmony, and cohesion.

Fayol's ideas were based on his experience during a 58–year career with a large mining company. He spent twelve of those years as a mining engineer, sixteen years as a middle-level manager, and thirty years as the company's managing director. The company was nearly bankrupt when Fayol assumed the directorship in 1888, but it gradually became a profitable model of effective management and organizational practices. The company's success helped Fayol to popularize his management theory after his retirement in 1918.

Weber's Bureaucratic Theory

Max Weber borrowed the French term, **bureaucracy,** as a label for his concept of the ideal modern organization. Weber believed that complex organizations in an industrial age required speed, precision, certainty, and continuity. These conditions could be realized most effectively if organizational designs were as machinelike as possible. According to Weber (1947), the bureaucratic machine should have six basic features:

1. A clear hierarchical system of authority.
2. Division of labor according to specialization.

3. A complete system of rules regarding the rights, responsibilities, and duties of personnel.
4. Exhaustive procedures for work performance.
5. Impersonality in human organizational relationships.
6. Selection and promotion of personnel solely on the basis of technical competence.

Weber intended for bureaucracy to eliminate ambiguity and capriciousness in organizational life. Formalized rules, clear descriptions of authority and responsibilty at all organizational levels, and predictability in human relationships should lead to several desirable outcomes. In particular, decision making should be faster, efficiency in task performance should improve, and treatment of personnel should be more equitable (fair and impartial). According to Weber, all actions in a bureaucracy are derived mechanically from rules in a rational system based on military discipline. The individual organization member "is only a single cog in an ever-moving mechanism which prescribes to him an essentially fixed route of march" (1969, p. 34).

The theories that Taylor, Fayol, and Weber developed certainly were not identical. Taylor's concept of functional foremanship in which any worker might receive orders at various points from several different superiors ran counter to the idea of unity of command that Fayol and Weber both advocated. Moreover, Fayol's attitudes toward flexibility in organizational structure, centralizing or decentralizing decision making to fit the organization's circumstances, and encouragement of esprit de corps were quite inconsistent with Weber's prescriptions for fixed, constant rules and impersonal relationships. Yet, several clear themes are common to scientific and classical management theory.

First, the organization is driven by management authority. Employees are simply the instruments for carrying out the management plan. This implies that organizational communication is merely a tool for managerial **control** and **coordination** of organizational processes. Communication involving planning and decision making is **centralized** (concentrated) near the top of the organizational hierarchy (although Fayol allowed for some flexibility on this point). Organizational policies and task-oriented messages regarding the execution of orders flow from the top down. Upward communication from subordinates to superiors serves only a reporting function to verify compliance with orders or to indicate any work-related problems.

Second, scientific and classical theorists believed that people behave according to rational, economic models. The primary motivation for work is money. If people are compensated in a fair manner, they will be more productive and more compliant with authority. Social and political motivations in organizational behavior were regarded as irrelevant or detrimental to organizational effectiveness. A rationally specified system of organization structure and functions would reduce the ill effects of group conflicts, personal rivalries, vindictiveness, power struggles, and petty egoism.

Finally, each theorist advanced a machinelike prescription for organizational design. The analogy between the human organization and the well-maintained machine performing at peak efficiency is most obvious in Weber's

Table 3.1   Principles in Scientific and Classical Management.

Summary of Principles in Scientific and Classical Management

Scientific Management (Taylor)	Classical Management	
Theme: Effectiveness is a function of work design.	*Theme: Effectiveness is a function of organizational design.*	
1. Find the "one best way" to perform each job. 2. Scientifically select and train workers. 3. Reward workers in direct proportion to productivity. 4. Use "functional foremanship"; managers plan, workers produce, expert supervisors (potentially several) direct various aspects of a given worker's job.	*Fayol* (flexible hierarchy) 1. Order based on divison of labor, unity of command and direction, but centralization must "vary according to different cases." 2. Managerial authority is derived from both official and personal bases. 3. Equity through kindness and justice, but does not exclude "forcefulness and sternness." 4. Esprit de corps.	*Weber* (bureaucracy) 1. Order based on division of labor, clear authority structure, and a complete system of technical rules for conduct and procedure. 2. Authority derived from a rational-legal system where a person is "only a single cog in an ever-moving mechanism." 3. Justice "mechanically derived from a code." 4. Impersonality in interpersonal relations.

work, but Taylor's concept of scientific management envisioned exactly the same ideal for work processes. Even Fayol, who argued that his principles of organizational structure and management should be applied flexibly, still insisted that order, discipline, hierarchical authority, and fixed division of labor were the basic elements in a tried and true formula for organizational effectiveness. A summary for easier comparison of the central principles in each theory is presented in table 3.1.

Scientific and classical management theories have been very influential in the design of modern organizations. Time and motion studies of the type that Taylor's followers introduced are used as basic tools to determine the most efficient procedures for task performance in large organizations. Organization charts, detailed job descriptions, and elaborate policy manuals spelling out lines of authority, work procedures, and individual rights and responsibilities are quite common in American organizations. Such documents often define channels of message flow and appropriate communicative behavior for organization members as well. For example, the U.S. Postal Service makes it clear that all official communication in the organization must conform to Fayol's principles of unity of command, unity of direction, and scalar authority:

Any communication on matters requiring discretion or policy determination shall proceed through each successive level of authority upward and downward without bypassing any. . . . An administrative reporting relationship establishes a clear line of authority between positions or units in the organizational hierarchy. . . . Subordinate positions never report administratively to more than one higher-level supervisor. (1979, sec. 153)

In other organizations, the influence of classical organizational theory is more subtle. The principles are intuitively understood rules for defining relationships among organization members—rules that generally are taken for granted. Consider the case of a large grocery store that we will call Supervalue Market. The owner, who is also the general manager, insists that Supervalue does not have organization charts and policy manuals: "We're all just one big happy family here." But the people who work at Supervalue understand that their organization has a specific structure. The store is arranged in departments. Each department has a supervisor. Every employee has a job title (checker, sacker, stocker, etc.) and a specific assignment in a designated department.

The employees at Supervalue communicate with their department supervisors on all work-related matters. In turn, the supervisors report to designated assistant managers, and the assistant managers report to the general manager. Although managers occasionally carry on casual conversations and light banter with most of the employees, they rarely speak officially with anyone except department supervisors. Supervisors relay any official information from managers to the employees. In general, different supervisors (and employees) stay out of one another's departments unless they are assigned to help out or cover for someone else. Unlike the U.S. Postal Service, Supervalue has no written policies that specify these rules. But when you go to work at Supervalue, you find out quickly from observing and listening to others that "This is the way we do it here." Even though nobody has ever published an organization chart for Supervalue, all of the members understand and use the rules to enact this organizational structure.

If we translate the implicit operating rules of Supervalue Market into an explicit organization chart, it might look something like the diagram in figure 3.1.

Figure 3.1 illustrates a functional **division of labor** with different departments and job classifications for different types of work. The organization chart also specifies a **scalar chain of command** with lines of authority and reporting relationships from the general manager to the assistant managers, from these assistants to department supervisors, and from supervisors to employees. This type of **hierarchical structure** provides the basic framework for many different types of organizations, both private and public, profit and nonprofit.

Despite the influence of scientific and classical principles in contemporary organizations, these theories have been criticized extensively. Most of the critics point out that classical and scientific assumptions about human motivation are naive. Human organizational behavior depends on many complex factors besides the desire for economic reward or blind obedience to authority. The theories also are criticized for producing rigid, unadaptive organizational structures. Hierarchies with centralized decision making, many levels of authority, and highly specialized divisions of labor can function reasonably well

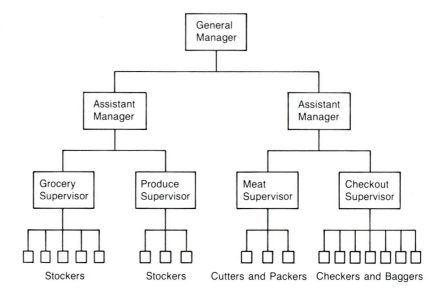

Figure 3.1
Fictitious organization chart for Supervalue Market.

in a stable environment, but they lack the flexibility to adapt to change. The very fact that "bureaucracy" conjures up images of red tape, inefficiency, and indifference (features quite the opposite of those that Weber extolled) suggests that classical and scientific theorists failed to understand the social and psychological dynamics of organizational behavior and human communication.

During the 1920s and 1930s, two developments in theories of organization and human relationships began to point to shortcomings in scientific and classical theory. One of these developments involved the appearance of two eclectic theories of organization. The second development was the emergence of the human relations movement.

Eclectic Theories

While scientific and classical theories focused rather narrowly on questions of organizational structure and work design, at least two **eclectic theories** addressed broader concerns, including the use of power, the psychology of compliance, variability in the behavior of individual organization members, and the importance of communication in organizational processes. Mary Parker Follett introduced the first in the 1920s. Chester Barnard developed the second in the 1930s.

Follett's Administrative Theory

Follett was an administrative theorist and political scientist who was trained in philosophy and had interests in social psychology. She was concerned primarily with ways of building and sustaining democracy through integration of different, competing interests. In order to achieve integration of interests as Follett understood it, traditional ideas about power and authority had to be redefined. Integration of interests depends on shared power. One exercises power *with* others rather than *over* others. As she explained it, "One person should not give orders to another person, but both should agree to take their orders from the situation" (1924, p. 59). Dessler (1980) pointed out that Follett's theory would abolish many of the distinctions between the roles of superiors and subordinates. There is some evidence that Follett's work exerted direct influence on Chester Barnard's thinking (Richetto, 1977).

Barnard's Executive Functions

Barnard, who was president of New Jersey Bell Telephone and at one time chaired the National Science Foundation, apparently felt that classical theories of organization failed to provide adequate explanations of organizational behavior as he had experienced it. In his 1938 book, *The Functions of the Executive,* Barnard attempted to correct these shortcomings in three areas: *individual behavior, compliance,* and *communication.*

In Barnard's view, classical theorists had underestimated both the variability of individual behavior in organizations and the impact of this behavior on organizational effectiveness. Organization members are not simply so many cogs in a machine who behave predictably out of rational, economic interests. Members are individuals who differ from one another in many respects. Barnard believed that the individual is the "basic strategic factor" in all organizations and that organizational effectiveness depends on the individual's willingness to cooperate. This assumption led directly to Barnard's ideas about compliance.

Barnard regarded compliance as willingness to cooperate. Compliance in this sense requires individuals to surrender their personal preferences. An order has authority to the extent that a person is willing to surrender personal preference to carry out the order. Orders must fall within a person's *zone of indifference,* meaning that orders must be perceived in neutral terms so that they are carried out without conscious questioning of their authority. Incentives, inducements, and rewards can be used to expand a person's zone of indifference, but material incentives alone are limited in their power to effect compliance. Inducements such as status, prestige, and personal power also are necessary.

Finally, Barnard made communication an indispensable concept in the analysis of organizational structure. He pointed out that decision-making processes hinge on communication and described the characteristics and importance of communication in the informal organization. (i.e., the interaction in a social, political, and unofficial world that is not specified on the formal organization chart). Barnard's strong belief in the centrality of communication for organizational processes is indicated in his argument that "the first function of an executive" is to establish and maintain a system of communication. According to Dessler, Barnard "presented a new theory of organization structure, one that focused on the organization as a communication system" (1980, p. 38).

The Human Relations Movement

The **human relations movement** emerged from various currents of thought during the 1930s. At least two of these currents influenced the field of organizational communication. One of these currents was the work of Dale Carnegie. The other was the Harvard-affiliated human relations school of management that emerged in the wake of a complex series of industrial investigations known as the Hawthorne Studies.

Dale Carnegie

Dale Carnegie was the first writer to link communication skill explicitly with managerial effectiveness through his ideas about the social and psychological aspects of "winning friends and influencing people" (Richetto, 1977). Carnegie (1936) argued that gaining compliance from other people depends on interpersonal dynamics of attraction and influence. He offered his own prescriptions for influencing others by listening, showing an interest in their concerns, and gaining their confidence. Carnegie's message to managers was clear. Compliance does not depend solely on economic motivators or the authority of a manager's position. Compliance is gained through skill in interpersonal communication.

By the time of Carnegie's death in 1955, nearly 5 million people had purchased his book and thousands of managers and administrators had flocked to Dale Carnegie seminars for training in his methods. Although Carnegie's work never exerted much influence among academic scholars, it had broad appeal within the business community. Carnegie seminars are still very popular today in many areas of the United States.

The Hawthorne Studies and Elton Mayo

The second and more influential current in the human relations movement began in 1924 with a series of studies at Western Electric Company's Hawthorne Plant in Illinois. The **Hawthorne Studies** were conducted over a period of several years in four phases: the illumination studies, the relay assembly-room studies, the interviewing program, and the bank wiring-room studies (Roethlisberger & Dickson, 1939). The results challenged scientific management principles by suggesting that interpersonal communication, group dynamics, and organization members' attitudes and values are more important than work structure and organizational design in determining organizational effectiveness. These studies provided the foundation for the Harvard-affiliated human relations school of management.

The Illumination Studies

The Hawthorne Studies began because an industrial engineering research group wanted to determine the relationship between lighting (illumination) conditions in a work area and worker productivity. In line with scientific management theory, the researchers believed that productivity would be greatest under some optimum or ideal level of lighting. (i.e., neither too little nor too much light). They set out to find this optimum condition by experimenting with the lighting levels, but the results of the study defied explanation. Productivity increased regardless of what the researchers did to the lighting. When the light was increased, productivity went up. When the light was held constant, productivity still went up. Even when the level of light was decreased, productivity continued to increase until workers literally could no longer see what they were doing.

Relay Assembly-Room Studies

The results of the illumination studies were disturbing to engineers schooled in the principles of scientific management. In order to understand why these principles apparently failed in the illumination studies, researchers decided to isolate a small group of telephone relay assembly workers in order to study systematically the relationships between various working conditions and productivity. The studies included changes in compensation, rest periods, work schedules, and work methods. In general, productivity increased during the studies regardless of changes in the work conditions. The researchers finally concluded that the *relationship* between the researchers and the workers accounted for the results. The test-room observer had shown a personal interest in the workers, consulted with and kept them informed about changes that were being made during the experiments, and listened sympathetically to their concerns and opinions. This relationship was quite different from the task-oriented, rule-bound, impersonal manner of supervision that characterized the rest of the plant (Roethlisberger & Dickson, 1939).

The Interview Program

The results of the relay assembly-room studies led researchers to conduct interviews with thousands of employees in order to discover their attitudes toward working conditions, supervisors, and work in general. The interviews soon indicated that *people who worked under similar conditions experienced these conditions in different ways and assigned different meanings to their experiences.* For example, a given style of supervision could be satisfying to some people and dissatisfying to others.

When researchers tried to account for different reactions to similar conditions, they found that personal background and expectations contributed to satisfaction. In particular, "the meaning a person assigns to his [her] position depends on whether or not that position is allowing him [her] to fulfill the social demands he [she] is making of his [her] work" (Roethlisberger & Dickson, 1939). They concluded that *employee's attitudes depend on the social organization of the groups in which they work and their positions in these groups.*

Bank-Wiring Studies

The interview program was followed by another intensive study with a small group of employees who wired circuit banks. The purpose was to observe the effects of the work group's social processes on productivity. The results of the study indicated that work group norms exert substantial influence over performance standards.

Employees in the bank-wiring study shared a clear idea of the "right" amount of output for a day's work. Production from day to day should be constant—neither too much nor too little. Even though they were paid on an incentive plan, group members pressured faster workers to slow down. Production reports were falsified to reflect either more or less output in order to maintain the appearance of a constant rate of production. The group developed an informal system that controlled and regulated the members' behavior and, at the same time, protected them from outside interference (for example, from higher-level managers). The findings puzzled industrial engineers, but the workers who lost their jobs in the wake of Taylor's studies at Bethlehem Steel easily would have understood the norms in the bank-wiring group against producing "too much."

Implications of the Studies

The Hawthorne Studies occupy such a prominent place in the history of organizational research that questions about the appropriateness of the methods used in these studies and the validity of the conclusions drawn from the results have been debated for many years. For example, Carey (1967) argued that several serious flaws in the research methods prevent any reliable interpretation of results from these studies. More recently, Franke and Kaul (1978) developed a statistically based reinterpretation of the results that led them to conclusions that differed dramatically from those drawn by Roethlisberger & Dickson. According to Franke and Kaul, "It is not release from oppressive supervision but its reassertion that explains higher rates of productivity [in the Hawthorne Studies]" (p. 636).

Whatever the weaknesses that may have afflicted the Hawthorne Studies, these studies were significant because they led to the emergence of the human relations school of management under the leadership of Elton Mayo and his colleagues at the Harvard Business School. Mayo, who intensely disliked conflict and competition, tried to promote a concept of worker-management harmony (Landsberger, 1958). He was involved in the Hawthorne Studies almost from their beginning and interpreted the results as support for a "people-oriented" approach to management.

According to Mayo (1947), managers should be friendly in their relationships with workers, listen to worker concerns, and give workers a sense of participation in decisions in order to meet their *social* needs. In many respects, Mayo's advice was much like Dale Carnegie's. In fact, both Mayo and Carnegie have been criticized for promoting highly manipulative, managerial communication strategies intended only to gain compliance from workers and to promote acceptance of managerial authority (Redding, 1979). It is important to note that human relations principles *did not change* the classical features of organizations. Instead, human relations ideas simply provided a tool for management relationships with employees under traditional systems of authority and hierarchy.

While classical and scientific management theories offer prescriptions for organizational structure and communication, they are theories of worker motivation and compliance, not theories of organizational communication. Miles (1965) pointed out that this also is true of human relations. Classical and scientific theorists believed that workers are motivated by economic need. If this need is satisfied and the organization is properly designed, compliance with managerial authority will follow. Human relations advocates stressed the importance of social rather than economic needs and urged managers to adopt communication strategies that give workers a sense of participation. According to Miles, the heart of the human relations model is the idea that participation improves morale and morale leads to greater compliance with managerial authority. Consequently, all of these theories see communication only as a managerial tool for motivating workers and controlling organizational processes.

Human Resource Development

Just as human relations challenged some of the key assumptions in classical and scientific management, the development of new theories of human motivation led to concepts of **human resource development** that challenged human relations. These new theories pointed out that motivation is not merely economic or social, but also tied to one's sense of self-worth or **self-actualization.** Abraham Maslow's need hierarchy is a commonly cited example of this change in ideas about motivation.

Maslow's Need Hierarchy

Maslow (1954) argued that motivational needs can be hierarchically organized. His hierarchy includes five needs:

1. *Physiological needs* for food, oxygen, and other basic requirements to sustain life. These are fundamental needs at the lowest level of the hierarchy.
2. *Safety needs* for security, protection from danger, and freedom from threat.
3. *Social needs* for love, affection, affiliation, and acceptance.
4. *Esteem needs* for a sense of status, recognition, and self-respect.
5. *Self-actualization needs* to realize one's full potential as a human being. Self-actualization is the most abstract and highest-level need in the hierarchy.

Maslow believed that lower-level needs are stronger than higher-level needs. In general, any need at a given level of the hierarchy must be relatively satisfied before the need at the next higher level is activated. Thus, a person who has reliable and stable means of meeting physiological and safety needs will become motivated to fulfill social needs, while a starving, homeless individual is preoccupied only with finding food and shelter.

More importantly, Maslow believed that self-actualization differs fundamentally from the other needs. Physiological, safety, social, and esteem needs are **deficiency needs.** They involve physical or psychological conditions that a person strives to maintain within an acceptable range—a kind of balance in which there is neither "too much" nor "too little." If you are deprived of a need such as food, the need becomes a **drive** (hunger) that causes behavior to satisfy the need (foraging for food). Once the need is fulfilled, the drive (motivation) is reduced and the behavior stops. In contrast, self-actualization is a **growth need.** The process of satisfying this need actually increases rather than decreases motivation.

McGregor's Theory X and Theory Y

As management theorists became familiar with Maslow's work, they soon realized the possibility of connecting higher-level needs to worker motivation. If organizational goals and individual needs could be *integrated* so that people would acquire self-esteem and, ultimately, self-actualization through work, then motivation would be self-sustaining. According to Douglas McGregor (1960), the key to linking self-actualization with work lies in managerial trust of subordinates. McGregor identified two sets of underlying assumptions about human nature that affects managers' trust of subordinates. He called these sets of assumptions **Theory X** and **Theory Y.**

Many managers subscribe to Theory X. They believe that employees dislike work and will attempt to avoid it if possible. Employees value security above everything else, dislike responsibility, and want someone else to control and direct them. If organizational goals are to be accomplished, managers must rely on threat and coercion to gain employee compliance. Theory X beliefs lead to mistrust, highly restrictive supervision, and a punitive atmosphere.

Theory Y managers believe that work is as natural as play. Employees want to work. They have the ability for creative problem solving, but their talents are underutilized in most organizations. Given proper conditions, employees will learn to seek out and accept responsibility and to exercise self-control and self-direction in accomplishing objectives to which they are committed. According to McGregor, Theory Y managers are more likely than Theory X managers to develop the climate of trust with employees that is required for human resource development.

In order for human resource development to occur, managers must communicate openly with subordinates, minimize status distinctions in superior-subordinate relationships, solicit subordinates' ideas and opinions, and create a climate in which subordinates can develop and use their abilities. This climate would include decentralization of decision making, delegation of authority to subordinates, variety in work tasks to make jobs more interesting, and **participative management** in which subordinates have influence in decisions that affect them.

As described by Miles (1965), the human resource development concept is based on a model that differs greatly from human relations. Here, participation leads to better performance, better performance improves morale, and morale feeds even more improvement in performance. The end result of human resource development is not so much compliance with managerial authority as it is a form of self-development through fulfillment of organizational goals. Participation in the process presumably provides even greater motivation to accomplish these goals.

As human resource development concepts emerged, it became clear that these concepts not only involved managerial communication with employees, but they also included many aspects of organizational communication in general. If an organization is to implement the principles of participative management and decentralized decision making, those who participate must have effective interpersonal and group communication skills, open and flexible channels of communication, and adequate information for a variety of organizational functions. The importance of these conditions for human resource development was stressed in the results of studies by Rensis Likert.

Likert's Four Systems

Likert (1961) argued that there are four basic types of management orientations or systems: **exploitative-authoritative** (system 1); **benevolent-authoritative** (system 2); **consultative** (system 3); and **participative** (system 4). Although Likert and McGregor worked independently, their ideas are quite similar. Likert's system 1 corresponds to McGregor's Theory X, while system 4 is similar to Theory Y. Systems 2 and 3 are located in between the other two positions. Likert's research indicated that organizations with system 4 participative characteristics were more effective than organizations based on other systems. The characteristics of system 4 include the following:

1. Communication between superiors and subordinates is open and extensive. Superiors solicit ideas and opinions, and subordinates feel free to discuss problems with superiors.
2. Decision making is decentralized. Decisions are made at all levels of the organization through group processes. Both superiors and subordinates are able to influence performance goals, work methods, and organizational activities.
3. Information flows freely through flexible channels of communication and in all directions—upward, downward, and laterally. Information is relatively accurate and undistorted.
4. Performance goals are developed through participative management. The goals are high but realistic. Goals are supported by favorable attitudes and motivation of organization members and by organizational commitment to development of human resources.
5. Control processes also are decentralized. Organization members seek and use feedback in order to exercise self-control.

In contrast, the characteristics of system 1 are as follows:

1. Superior-subordinate communication is minimal and characterized by mutual mistrust.
2. Decision making is centralized. Input from lower levels is neither solicited nor desired.
3. Flow of information is restricted to specified channels. Information usually moves downward in the form of orders, policies, procedures, and directions.
4. Employees do not support managerial goals. The organizational climate is characterized by fear, intimidation, and dissatisfaction.
5. Control processes are exercised by management, but an active informal organization usually develops among lower-level personnel in order to resist or oppose managerial control.

We are not overstating the case when we say that much of the scholarship and practice in organizational communication rests on the belief that Likert's participative system 4 represents the ideal climate for which organizations should strive. Characteristics such as those in system 4 have been advocated extensively as prescriptions for effective organizational communication. The **structure of communication** (channels and networks), **communication functions** (purposes, content, and adequacy), and the quality of communication at interpersonal and group **levels** (e.g., superior-subordinate communication, the dynamics of group decision making, and social processes) are regarded as indicators of **organizational communication climate.** Scholars and practitioners (e.g., Goldhaber, 1990; Pace & Faules, 1989) generally have equated the following characteristics of organizational communication climate with organizational effectiveness:

1. Flexible networks with open channels of communication and multidirectional message flow (upward, downward, and lateral).
2. Availability of accurate, adequate information on matters such as work procedures, evaluation of job performance, organizational policies, decisions, and problems.
3. Mutual trust, openness, and supportiveness in superior-subordinate communication.
4. Participation and cohesiveness in group decision making, problem solving, and other task-related processes under "team-oriented" or democratic leadership.

Despite the influence of human resource development concepts in the field of organizational communication, the theory is essentially a managerial approach to employee motivation. It happens to have clear implications for organizational communication, but its primary concern does not differ from earlier scientific, classical, and human relations theories: *the promotion of organizational effectiveness through prescriptions for organizational structure and/or managerial practice.* A complete comparison of traditional, human relations, and human resource development assumptions is presented in table 3.2.

Table 3.2 Comparison of Traditional, Human Relations, and Human Resource Development Assumptions about People. From "Leadership Attitudes Among Public Health Officers," by R. E. Miles, L. W. Porter, and J. A. Craft, 1966, *American Journal of Public Health, 56*, pp. 1990–2005.

Traditional Model	Human Relations Model	Human Resources Model
Assumptions	*Assumptions*	*Assumptions*
1. Work is inherently distasteful to most people.	1. People want to feel useful and important.	1. Work is not inherently distasteful. People want to contribute to meaningful goals which they have helped establish.
2. What they do is less important than what they earn for doing it.	2. People desire to belong and to be recognized as individuals.	2. Most people can exercise far more creative, responsible self-direction and self-control than their present jobs demand.
3. Few want or can handle work which requires creativity, self-direction, or self-control.	3. These needs are more important than money in motivating people to work.	
Policies	*Policies*	*Policies*
1. The manager's basic task is to closely supervise and control his subordinates.	1. The manager's basic task is to make each worker feel useful and important.	1. The manager's basic task is to make use of his "untapped" human resources.
2. He must break tasks down into simple, repetitive, easily learned operations.	2. He should keep his subordinates informed and listen to their objections to his plans.	2. He must create an environment in which all members may contribute to the limits of their ability.
3. He must establish detailed work routines and procedures, and enforce these firmly but fairly.	3. The manager should allow his subordinates to exercise some self-direction and self-control on routine matters.	3. He must encourage full participation on important matters, continually broadening subordinate self-direction and control.
Expectations	*Expectations*	*Expectations*
1. People can tolerate work if the pay is decent and the boss is fair.	1. Sharing information with subordinates and involving them in routine decisions will satisfy their basic needs to belong and to feel important.	1. Expanding subordinate influence, self-direction, and self-control will lead to direct improvement in operating efficiency.
2. If tasks are simple enough and people are closely controlled, they will produce up to standard.	2. Satisfying these needs will improve morale and reduce resistance to formal authority: subordinates will "willingly cooperate."	2. Work satisfaction may improve as a "by-product" of subordinates making full use of their resources.

Like the theories that preceded it, human resource development has been criticized for placing too much faith in the power of its prescriptions for virtually any organizational setting. One of the earliest critics was Abraham Maslow himself, who expressed concerns that his need hierarchy could not be applied to organizational behavior in the way that McGregor wanted to use it. Maslow confessed, "I'm a little worried about this stuff which I consider tentative being swallowed whole by all sorts of enthusiastic people" (1965, p. 55).

Other critics such as Lawrence and Lorsch (1970) pointed out that no one formula for organizational effectiveness will work in all situations. The conditions of effective organizational performance vary from one situation to another. This position is known as the contingency theory. Those who embrace it argue that we should be less concerned with "searching for the panacea of the one best way to organize" and focus more attention on "situational factors that influence organizational performance" (p. 1).

Although much research in organizational communication supports McGregor and Likert's positions, some studies suggest that Lawrence and Lorsch's advice may be well founded. Investigations conducted in Europe indicate that employee dissatisfaction may result from a highly open communication climate as a consequence of information overload and unrealistic expectations for the results of participative decision making (Wiio, 1978). One study of data from eighteen American organizations found that some organization members who were very well informed were also dissatisfied with their immediate superiors (Daniels & Spiker, 1983). Finally, Pettegrew (1982) presented what he has termed, "The S.O.B. Theory of Management," based on a study of a large medical facility where differences in administrators' styles of communication had no apparent impact on their subordinates. Whether the administrators were authoritative or participative, subordinates generally regarded them as S.O.B.'s. Pettegrew thought that this might occur because the administrators had to make win-lose decisions in which one group would be helped while another would be hurt. Even though the relationship between adequate or open communication and satisfaction generally is positive, there apparently are important exceptions to this rule.

A System Theory

System theory is the product of work begun in the field of philosophy during the nineteenth century and expanded by many scholars in various fields during the twentieth century. Much of the formal elaboration of system theory was presented in Ludwig von Bertalanffy's *General System Theory* (1968), first published in the 1950s. Bertalanffy, a Canadian biologist, wanted to develop a set of concepts and principles that would apply generally to any type of system (hence, the label, general system theory).

The perspective that Bertalanffy and other early system theorists developed soon was adapted to the study of organizations in works by March and Simon (1958), Katz and Kahn (1966), and Huse and Bowditch (1973). The influence of system theory in the study of organizational communication also has been substantial. For example, Karl Weick's theory (1979) that organizing processes arise in order to cope with equivocal information and Farace, Monge, and Russell's 1977 structural-functional model of organizational communication are based on systems principles. Gary Kreps (1990) has adapted Weick's work along with other systems principles to provide the foundation for an entire text on organizational communication. Similarly, Farace, Monge, and Russell developed a complete text around their structural-functional model of organizational communication. Even before publication of Bertalanffy's major works, Chester Barnard had presented some systems principles in his theory of organizational structure (Dessler, 1980; Littlejohn, 1989). As Monge pointed out, "Organizational communication has predominantly been studied from the viewpoint of system theory" (1982, p. 245).

System theory provided a new analogy for the study of organizations and organizational communication—the living organism. While scientific and classical scholars regarded the organization as a machinelike object operated by management control, system theorists stressed the point that organizations are more like living creatures than machines. Organizations experience birth, development, and death. They are dynamic entities that act in purposeful ways. System theory relies on several important concepts in order to explain the organismic characteristics of organizations. These concepts include wholeness, hierarchy, openness, and feedback.

Wholeness

A system is a set of elements bound together in interdependent relationships. Elements in a system are interdependent in the sense that they affect one another. If the relationships are highly interdependent, a change in one part of the system can lead to changes throughout the entire system. This interdependence among parts or elements results in an integrated whole.

Wholeness means that the effect of elements working in relationship to one another differs from the effect of their isolated, individual actions taken collectively. This effect is sometimes referred to as synergy—a condition in which the whole is greater than the sum of its parts. Perhaps you have experienced synergy as a participant in group problem solving.

For example, a group of advertising professionals might "brainstorm" in order to generate a novel, creative idea for promoting a product. As they interact, they build on and modify one anothers' ideas until they arrive at a workable concept. Suppose that we ask these same professionals to generate ideas by working in isolation from one another, then we collect and list the ideas that they produce. We might see many of the same ideas that would appear in a group brainstorming session, but the list would not include ideas that emerged as a result of interaction within the group and it probably would provide barely a hint of the final solution that the group developed. The individuals working as an integrated group (system) produced something greater than they would have produced in a simple collection of isolated, individual efforts. We cannot simply "add up" their individual actions in order to understand how they function as a system.

Hierarchy

The relationships among elements in a system are specified by rules. One of the more important rules is the principle of **hierarchy.** Elements are organized into subsystems. Subsystems are related to one another to form the system.

The system itself operates within a larger environment. In an organization, we might think of the elements as individual human beings, subsystems as work groups, departments, or divisions, and the system as the entire organization.

As we already have seen in this chapter, the principle of hierarchy applies readily to most Western organizations. Even organizations that depart from traditional ideas about division of labor, unity of command, and unity of direction can still be characterized by a basic system hierarchy—elements, subsystems, system, and environment. This type of hierarchy occurs in new contemporary structures such as matrixed organizations.

Matrix structures are intended to give organizations great flexibility in responding to specialized, temporary needs. Consider the case of Universal Products Company (UPC) as described by Mee (1964). UPC has four product divisions (automotive, electrical, chemical, and aerospace). Each division consists of five basic departments (production, engineering, materials, personnel, and accounting). In this form, UPC is a traditionally structured organization, but a major departure from this concept occurs in the aerospace division, as illustrated in figure 3.2.

Aerospace has three major but temporary projects underway (Venus, Mars, and Saturn). Each of the three projects is directed by a manager who has full authority and responsibility for its completion. Each project manager has been assigned personnel from the five departments in the aerospace division. Until completion of the project, the manager decides on tasks, work schedules, promotions, and salary increases for those personnel who are assigned to the project. A purchasing agent who normally would report to the manager of the materials department now reports to a project manager as well. Sometimes, the project manager has total control over personnel assigned to a project, but a project manager's control in many matrixed organizations is shared with functional department heads in the regular line organization. In this case, any individual organization member literally participates in two subsystems at once, fulfilling functions as a regular department member and as a project team member, while reporting to two different superiors. The use of such matrix structures handily illustrates the power of organizational systems to adapt to changing circumstances.

Openness

Systems may be regarded as relatively open or closed. **Open systems** are characterized by active exchange with their outside environment. Organizations are open systems. They take in energy and materials (input), transform these input in some way (throughput), then return products and by-products of throughput to the environment (output).

When the environment is stable, it is tempting to ignore the fact that organizations are open systems. Given a stable environment, an organization is able to operate in a steady, machinelike state. Its performance is regular and routine because nothing in the environment demands anything else. Under such

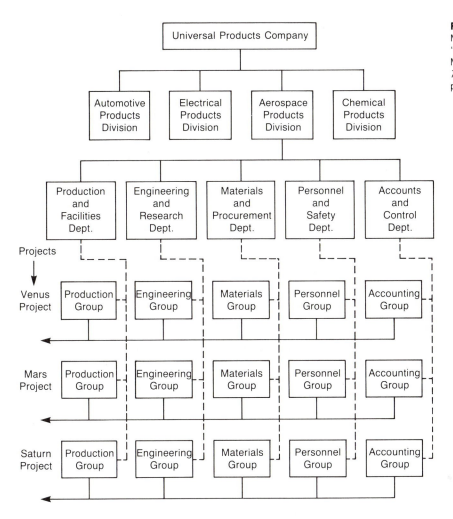

Figure 3.2
Matrix Organization. From "Matrix organizations," by J. Mee, 1964, *Business Horizons, 7,* pp. 92–95. Adapted by permission.

conditions, the organization seems to be a closed, static system that is unaffected by its environment. This view is deceptively simple and can be hazardous when the environment changes in some dramatic way.

During the 1960s, executives in the automobile industry seemed to see their corporations in much the same way as their cars—well-engineered machines continually getting bigger and better through managerial design. The rise of foreign competition and the energy crisis of the 1970s quickly taught auto companies that they are, indeed, open systems faced with a demand to adapt to a changing and sometimes turbulent environment. General Motors and Ford made fundamental changes to respond to unanticipated consumer demand for smaller, more efficient cars. Chrysler was saved from bankruptcy only by government-backed loans. American Motors barely clung to life by creating linkages with Jeep and Renault. When the corporations recovered, they were smaller and leaner. Thousands of workers were laid off with no hope of ever recovering their old jobs, and many auto dealers went out of business.

Feedback

Open systems are characterized by two basic processes: maintenance and adaptation. **Maintenance processes** are regulatory. They are intended to keep certain system conditions within acceptable ranges. **Adaptive processes** bring about change and growth. Both of these processes depend on **feedback**—responses to system actions that provide information for use in adjusting system conditions.

Feedback may be negative or positive. **Negative feedback** indicates deviations from desired conditions. The system adjusts by correcting the deviation. Maintenance processes depend on negative feedback. These processes involve the same principle of dynamic balance associated with deficiency needs in motivation. Suppose that a small manufacturing company wants to maintain a product inventory of 175 to 225 finished units at all times, with an ideal inventory of 200 units. If the inventory rises above 225 because sales slow down, someone sends negative feedback to the production department to ease back on production until the inventory is reduced. If the inventory falls below 175, production receives negative feedback to speed up until the shortage is corrected.

In contrast to negative feedback, **positive feedback** reinforces deviations rather than signaling for a correction. Positive feedback is used to create new system conditions rather than to maintain old ones. This form of feedback is the basis for change and adaptation. For example, government willingness to guarantee loans for Chrysler only if the corporation would adapt to its environment provided an incentive that led to many fundamental changes in the corporate structure, leadership, and products. If Chrysler people wanted to survive as a corporation, they were going to have to act in entirely new ways. As the changes were initiated, public acceptance provided positive reinforcement for Chrysler to continue the adaptation process.

Of course, feedback in living, open systems is not simply a mechanical process of automatic response to deviation-correcting or reinforcing messages. Roger D'Aprix (1982) tells a story about an employee-communications department in a large corporation that decided to publish an article in the corporate magazine about the company's employee-compensation system. When the article was submitted to the personnel department for review, the employee-compensation manager, who feared that the story revealed too much, rejected it. The personnel department proposed a "revision" in the article that would have made it unintelligible to most readers. The employee-communications department appeared to have two options: run the revised version or drop the story. The department manager chose a third path—convincing the compensation manager that most of the personnel department's fears were unfounded. The article that finally appeared in print was based on a compromise between the two managers.

D'Aprix's story is an excellent illustration of informal negotiations in management ranks, the politics of organizational decision making, and even Eisenberg's (1984) principles of strategic ambiguity. It also demonstrates several important points about feedback in episodes of communication that are acted out every day in thousands of organizations. First, deviations from desired conditions often are defined by human values instead of physical circumstances. The compensation manager's desire to conceal information about compensation decisions provided the standard for judging the acceptability of the article. Second, the recipient of feedback may choose to act on it in various ways or even ignore it. The communications manager did not simply make the changes that the compensation manager wanted but chose another action instead. Finally, organizational subsystems and individuals influence each other through *reciprocal* feedback and may employ different standards for evaluating and responding to feedback. The personnel and employee communications departments differed in their assessments of the article's acceptability. The personnel department's rejection was negative feedback. The communications department's response to rejection also was, in effect, a form of feedback. The solution to the conflict emerged from an interaction between the two departments, not from one unit's mechanical acquiescence to feedback from another.

Taken collectively, the basic concepts of system theory—wholeness, hierarchy, openness, and feedback—provide a dynamic view of organizations in action. System theory has been influential in the study of organizational communication because it places the organizing role of communication in a new light (Littlejohn, 1989). Communication is not merely an activity that occurs "within" an organization, nor is communication merely a tool for managerial control. Rather, all of the human processes that define an organization arise from communication. Relationships among individual organization members are defined through communication. The linkages and interactions among subsystems depend on communication and information flow. All feedback processes involve communication.

Despite the popularity of system theory in the field of organizational communication, its impact on research actually has been very limited. What does one do after declaring the newfound revelation that organizations are open systems? So far, this question has received only partial and incomplete answers (Monge, Farace, Eisenberg, Miller, & White, 1984). We have been much more successful in talking about organizational communication with the vocabulary of system theory than we have been in using system theory as a basis for our research. At the very least, however, system theory has provided us with a different and potentially powerful set of ideas and assumptions to frame our thinking about organizational communication.

Summary

When the industrialized world entered the twentieth century, it was apparent that new and clearer concepts of organizational behavior would be required to deal with the complexities of modern society. The first modern perspectives on organizational behavior were developed in the early 1900s when theorists such as Taylor, Fayol, and Weber advanced the basic principles of scientific and classical management. Although the theories of Taylor, Fayol, and Weber differed from one another in some important ways, they generally envisioned organizations as machinelike objects driven by management plan and control. They assumed that individual organization members behave on the basis of rational, economic motivation.

Scientific and classical theories were followed quickly by eclectic theories, such as those developed by Follett and Barnard, and by the human relations movement. Follett redefined traditional ideas about the exercise of power in order to achieve integration of different interests. Barnard pointed out oversights in scientific and classical theory regarding the variability of individual behavior in organizations. He argued that compliance depends on individual willingness to cooperate—cooperation that must be induced through incentives such as status and prestige as well as economic motives. His theory of organization structure treated the organization as a communication system.

The human relations movement evolved from various sources of influence, but the basic ideas are typified in the work of Dale Carnegie and Elton Mayo. Both encouraged managers to adopt a "people-oriented" approach to influence and gaining compliance. Mayo's theory was based primarily on results of the controversial Hawthorne Studies, which challenged scientific and classical notions by concluding that organizational effectiveness depends more on the social processes of organizations than on management design.

Later, the development of system theory and new concepts in human motivation led to further refinements in organizational theory. Human resource development theory, based on motivational principles of the human need for self-fulfillment, began to compete with earlier human relations and classical/ scientific perspectives of organizational behavior. McGregor distinguished between Theory X and Theory Y managerial assumptions, arguing that the Theory Y orientation would lead to effectiveness through development of human resources. Similarly, Likert argued that organizational effectiveness is linked to system 4 participative management. System 4 emphasizes flexible, open communication, relatively accurate, undistorted information, and use of group decision making. Much of the scholarship and practice in the field of organizational communication assumes that system 4 represents the ideal climate for which organizations should strive.

System theories, which view organizations as adaptive organisms rather than machines, gained wide acceptance during the 1960s in the wake of Bertalanffy's general system theory. System theories attempt to describe and explain how organizations function from the standpoint of some very general principles that are presumed to apply to all systems. These general principles include wholeness, hierarchy, openness, and feedback.

Discussion Questions/ Activities

1. Observe some samples of organizational communication. On the basis of these observations, would you say that the characteristics of the organization are closer to Likert's system 4 or system 1? Do these characteristics seem to have any relationship to organizational effectiveness?
2. Barnard argued that organization structure should be understood as a communication system. How does this argument differ from earlier classical management ideas about organizational structure?

3. A bureaucratic theorist assumes that an organization is like a machine. A system theorist assumes that an organization is like a living organism. If these two theorists observe the same organization and then report on what they saw, in what ways would the two reports most likely differ?
4. Compare and contrast human relations theory with human resource development theory. Which of these theories do you think is most consistent with the actual behavior of contemporary managers?

Prophecy Fulfilled

Case Study

Mary Ann Stevens recently was promoted to senior auditor at Jones, Smith & Co.—a major accounting and consulting firm. Mary Ann has worked for Jones, Smith & Co.'s audit practice since joining the firm three years ago. So far, she is pleased with her work experience. She has had the good fortune of working on audits in a variety of industries—from health care to manufacturing. However, recently she has become frustrated. The local economy has taken a turn for the better, resulting in several new clients for Jones, Smith & Co. This, coupled with an increase in staff turnover, has resulted in an enormous increase in Mary Ann's workload. Therefore, when her manager, Beth Williams, called her to say that she had been assigned two staff members for an audit of a new client, Acme Biscuit Company, Mary Ann was relieved.

However, the relief was short-lived. The next day she had lunch with Mark Dillon, also a senior at Jones, Smith & Co. When Mary Ann told Mark her good news, he said, "Actually, that is both good news and bad news. One of your staff, Mike, worked for me on the XYZ engagement. Boy did he screw it up." When Mary Ann pressed Mark for more details, he replied, "Every time the Controller walked by, Mike was on the phone. He was late to meetings; and when he did show up, it looked like he had slept in his suit. The guy is a total slouch. I'd say he won't be around for long. The good news is that Jeanine is supposed to be a real star."

That night, Mary Ann tried to figure out what to do. The Acme engagement had a short time frame so she needed two staff people. On the other hand, she did not have the time to "babysit" a staff person who did not care about his job. She was also concerned because of Acme's status as a new client. She was under a lot of pressure to keep clients and to obtain follow-on work whenever possible. One bad encounter could ruin her chances of a successful selling engagement, let alone additional work.

The next morning, Mary Ann thought she had a solution. Today she would break down the work steps involved in the completion of the engagement. When she assigned work steps to her staff people, she would give Mike the tasks that were easy and required no interaction with the client. Since she knew that Jeanine was a good performer, based on information from Jeanine's last senior, she knew that she would have no problem completing the higher-visibility, more difficult tasks. When she called Mike and Jeanine to announce their engagement planning meeting, she felt relieved and satisfied with her decision.

Mary Ann, Mike, and Jeanine met the next morning to discuss ABC Co. and review the work schedule and assignments. At the conclusion of the meeting, Mary Ann asked Mike and Jeanine if they had any questions. They said, "no." However both had a look on their face that Mary Ann could not interpret. After the meeting, Mary Ann was puzzled. She was not sure what, if anything, had gone wrong. A phone call interrupted her thoughts and soon the meeting was forgotten.

Jeanine and Mike walked back to their work area in silence. Both were thinking about the meeting and the Acme engagement.

"Once again," Mike thought, "someone else gets all the challenging stuff and I get the grunt work. I can't believe that I have to live through another three months of this garbage."

"Why did she have to play favorites?" Jeanine thought. "Why was she so obvious about the assignments? Mike and I have both been here a year. They aren't even giving him a chance. Why doesn't he tell them why he had problems with the XYZ engagement? Should I say something to Mary Ann?"

Overall, Mary Ann was pleased with the results of the Acme engagement. While she did not sell any follow-on work, the client was pleased and committed to bringing Jones, Smith & Co. back for the next year's audit. When it came time to complete Jeanine and Mike's performance evaluations, she retrieved her drop files and reviewed the following facts:

Mike:

Date	Comment
10/1	Complained about working overtime.
10/4	Directed questions from the Controller to Jeanine or me.
10/13	Completed compilation of assets data on schedule.
10/15	Chose not to attend client picnic with Jeanine and me.
11/14	Missed lunch with the engagement Partner.
12/1	Controller made comment about Mike not being a team player.

Jeanine:

Date	Comment
10/5	Completed inventory review two days ahead of schedule.
10/7	Controller made comment about being pleased with Jeanine's work. Also said he would like to have her back next year.

10/29	Jeanine impressed the Partner with her understanding of Acme and the manufacturing industry.
11/15	Jeanine came to me to ask what additional tasks she could complete.
11/22	Wrote an engagement status memo to Beth Williams without being asked.

After reviewing her files, Mary Ann determined that Jeanine was an outstanding performer and that Mike was a satisfactory performer. Then she thought back to her conversations with Mark Dillon and said, "Mark's assessment of Mike was right on target."

1. Does Mary seem to operate from any particular "theory" of management? If so, what is it?
2. What would a human relations theorist say about Mary's approach to this situation? What would a human resource development theorist say?
3. What principles from system theory are illustrated in this case?

References

Barnard, C. (1938). *The functions of the executive.* Cambridge, MA: Harvard University Press.

Bertalanffy, L. V. (1956). General system theory. *General Systems, 1,* 1.

Bertalanffy, L. V. (1968). *General system theory.* New York: George Braziller.

Carey, A. (1967). The Hawthorne Studies: A radical criticism. *American Sociological Review, 30,* 403–416.

Carnegie, D. (1936). *How to win friends and influence people.* New York: Simon & Schuster.

Daniels, T. D., & Spiker, B. K. (1983). Social exchange and the relationship between information adequacy and relational satisfaction. *Western Journal of Speech Communication, 47,* 118–137.

D'Aprix, R. (1982). *Communicating for productivity.* New York: Harper & Row.

Dessler, G. (1980). *Organization theory: Integrating structure and behavior.* Englewood Cliffs, NJ: Prentice-Hall.

Eisenberg, E. M. (1984). Ambiguity as a strategy in organizational communication. *Communciation Monographs, 51,* 227–242.

Farace, R. V., Monge, P. R., & Russell, H. M. (1977). *Communicating and organizing.* Reading, MA: Addison-Wesley.

Fayol, H. (1949). *General and industrial management* (Constance Storrs, Trans.). London: Sir Isaac Putnam.

Follett, M. P. (1924). *Creative experience.* London: Longman, Green.

Franke, R. H., & Kaul, J. D. (1978). The Hawthorne experiments: First statistical reinterpretation. *American Sociological Review, 43,* 623–643.

Goldhaber, G. M. (1990). *Organizational communication* (5th ed.). Dubuque, IA: Wm. C. Brown.

Huse, E. F., & Bowditch, J. L. (1973). *Behavior in organizations: A systems approach to managing.* Reading, MA: Addison-Wesley.

Katz, D., & Kahn, R. (1966). *The social psychology of organizations.* New York: John Wiley & Sons.

Koehler, J. W., Anatol, K. W. E., & Applbaum, R. L. (1981). *Organizational communication: Behavioral perspectives* (2nd ed.). New York: Holt, Rinehart & Winston.

Kreps, G. L. (1990). *Organizational communication: Theory and practice* (2nd ed.). New York: Longman.

Landsberger, H. (1958). *Hawthorne revisited.* Ithaca, NY: Cornell University Press.

Lawrence, P., & Lorsch, J. (1967). *Organization and environment: Managing differentiation and integration.* Boston: Harvard Business School.

Likert, R. (1961). *New patterns of management.* New York: McGraw-Hill.

Littlejohn, S. W. (1989). *Theories of human communication* (3rd ed.). Belmont, CA: Wadsworth.

March, J., & Simon, H. (1958). *Organizations.* New York: John Wiley & Sons.

Maslow, A. H. (1954). *Motivation and personality.* New York: Harper & Row.

Maslow, A. H. (1965). *Eupsychian management.* Homewood, IL: Richard D. Irwin.

Mayo, E. (1947). *The human problems of an industrial civilization.* Boston: Harvard Business School.

McGregor, D. (1960). *The human side of enterprise.* New York: McGraw-Hill.

Mee, J. (1965). Matrix organizations. *Business Horizons, 7,* 70–72.

Miles, R. (1965). Keeping informed: Human relations or human resources. *Harvard Business Review, 43,* 148–163.

Monge, P. R. (1982). System theory and research in the study of organizational communications: The correspondence problem. *Human Communication Research, 8,* 245–261.

Monge, P. R., Farace, R. L., Eisenberg, E. M., Miller, K. I., & White, L. L. (1984). The process of studying process in organizational communication. *Journal of Communication, 34,* 22–43.

Pace, R. W., & Faules, D. F. (1989). *Organizational communication* (2nd ed.). Englewood Cliffs, NJ: Prentice-Hall.

Pettegrew, L. S. (1982). Organizational communication and the S.O.B. theory of management. *Western Journal of Speech Communication, 46,* 179–191.

Redding, W. C. (1979). Organizational communication theory and ideology: An overview. In D. Nimmo (Ed.), *Communication yearbook 3.* New Brunswick, NJ: Transaction Books.

Richetto, G. M. (1977). Organizational communication theory and research: An overview. In B. D. Ruben (Ed.), *Communication yearbook 1.* New Brunswick, NJ: Transaction Books.

Roethlisberger, F. L., & Dickson, W. (1939). *Management and the worker.* New York: John Wiley & Sons.

Taylor, F. W. (1919). *Principles of scientific management.* New York: Harper & Row.

United States Postal Service (1979). *Organization structures manual.* Chapter 1, part 130, sec. 153.21.

Weber, M. (1947). *The theory of social and economic organizations* (A. M. Henderson & T. Parsons, Trans.; T. Parsons, Ed.). New York: Oxford University Press.

Weber, M. (1969). Bureaucracy. In J. A. Litterer (Ed.), *Organizations: Structure and behavior.* New York: John Wiley & Sons.

Weick, K. (1979). *The social psychology of organizing* (2nd ed.). Reading, MA: Addison-Wesley.

Wiio, O. A. (1978). *Contingencies of organizational communication: Studies in organization and organizational communication* (Research Rep. No. 1A771218). Helsinki: Institute for Human Communication.

part two

THEMES

Outline

Two Precautions
   Function and Structure
      Relationship
   Impact of Organizational Politics
Communication Functions
   Traditional Function Categories
   Uncertainty and Information
      Adequacy
   Unanswered Questions About
      Communication Functions
Communication Structure
   Formal Communication
     Downward Communication
     Upward Communication
     Horizontal Communication

Informal Communication
Limitations of the Traditional
   View
   Structure as a Social
     Construction
   Muddled Distinctions
   Loose versus Tight Coupling
Communication Structure as a
   Network
   Network Analysis
   Network Structure and Roles
   Uses of Network Analysis
   Limitations of Network
     Analysis
Summary
Discussion Questions/Activities
Case Study
References

Organizational Communication Function and Structure

4

Functionalists generally have understood the organization either as a machine or as an organism. One of the most useful and convenient ways of describing either machines or organisms is to characterize them according to their functions and structure. **Functions** are activities of a system that serve some purpose or objective. **Structure** is reflected in the linkages or relationships between elements in a system—linkages used to carry out functional activity. Since a systems perspective treats organizations as hierarchical structures, it also examines functions at various **levels** of a system.

Farace, Monge, and Russell (1977) devised a model known as *structural functionalism,* which applies these concepts to organizational communication. In the structural-functional model, the word *functions* refers generally to the content, goals, and effects of communication. *Structure* refers to channels of communication or, literally, the patterns of interaction among organization members. The *levels* of communication include the individual, the dyad, the group, and the organization as a whole. These three concepts—function, structure, and level—lie at the heart of the functionalist perspective on organizational communication.

Although Farace et al. developed what probably is the most comprehensive model of structural functionalism, other scholars employ the concepts of function, structure, and levels in their analysis of organizational communication (e.g., Goldhaber, 1990; Koehler, Anatol, & Applbaum, 1981). The types of functions considered, the descriptions of structure, and the definitions of levels vary from one treatment to another, but the use of the basic concepts themselves pervades the field of study. Since the third unit of this text is organized around three contexts of communication (dyadic, group, and public), which may be regarded as levels of organizational communication, our discussion in this chapter is limited to functions and structure.

Two Precautions

Before we begin our description of organizational communication functions and structure, we need to discuss two precautions that you should keep in mind: (1) communication functions and structure are highly interrelated; (2) any notion that the welfare of the organization as a whole is directly linked to efficiency and effectiveness in communication structure and function is misleading because different groups within an organization may pursue conflicting political objectives.

Function and Structure Relationship

We will treat function and structure as *separate* ideas for the sake of simplicity, but these two concepts are, in fact, highly related. In particular, the communication structure of an organization is developed and elaborated in ways that serve particular purposes. For example, a traditional distinction between formal and informal communication that we will develop later in this chapter implies that the two structures often involve different communication functions. As Farace et al. (1977) pointed out, "Both function and structure are intimately linked together, and major breakdowns in either can render the communication system of an organization inoperative" (p. 59).

Impact of Organizational Politics

The comment of Farace et al. about the relationship between "breakdowns" in function and structure and organizational communication effectiveness reflects a familiar theme in functionalism—treatment of communication as a tool for managerial control of a rationally ordered system. Functionalists often assume that an obvious connection exists between the welfare of the organization as a whole and effectiveness in communication structure and function. This assumption presumes that organizational goals are clearly established. In fact, organizations often pursue "multiple, possibly conflicting, and ambiguous goals" (Stevenson, Pearce, & Porter, 1985, p. 257). Consequently, functionalist discussions of organizational communication may leave the reader with a troubled feeling that something has been left out, that some pieces of the functionalist puzzle are missing. Abraham Zaleznik (1970) provided a clue about the location of these missing pieces when he reminded us:

Whatever else organizations may be (problem-solving instruments, sociotechnical systems, reward systems, and so on), they are political structures [that] provide platforms for the expression of individual interests and motives. (p. 48)

We pointed out in chapter 1 that organizations are political in the sense that they have systems for allocating and using power and resources as well as ways of maintaining and protecting these systems. Political battles over resources and power often emerge when different groups or coalitions (people who act temporarily as a group to advance a common interest) pursue conflicting objectives within the same organization (Cyert & March, 1963). We will have more to say about organizational politics in chapter 6 on power and conflict. For now, you merely need to keep in mind that many functions and corresponding structures of organizational communication are intended to serve the special interests of particular groups and coalitions. While the various groups that comprise an organization are bound together by some kind of common purpose, their specific interests often are in conflict.

Aside from some of the more obvious examples of different organizational groups that can come into political conflict (management versus labor, headquarters versus field offices, staff managers versus line managers, or even one work group versus another), consider a hypothetical clash between two temporary coalitions. The first coalition arises when organization members who have small children band together to pressure top management for a company-supported, day-care center. Suppose that management decides to get the money for a day-care center by reducing the amount that the company pays for employee health insurance. This decision gives rise to a second coalition that resists reduction of health benefits (e.g., older organization members who are more likely to suffer costly catastrophic illnesses).

The two coalitions not only argue with management (which is now a victim of Pettegrew's S.O.B. theory), but they also actively oppose each other. One of the older members happens to supervise the leader of the parents' coalition and makes sure that this person has to work on the same night of the week that the parents' group meets to plan strategy. Younger parents are saying openly that the day-care center could be funded easily if management would reduce labor costs by persuading some "deadwood" older workers to take early retirement.

As our examples of conflicting groups indicate, what is "functional" to one group may be "dysfunctional" to another. The communication structure evolved by one coalition to serve its interests may be resisted or countered by another coalition. The problem of understanding organizational communication structure and function is not as neat and simple as our models may appear to make it.

Communication Functions

The functions of organizational communication may be described in various ways, but most descriptions are tied to three basic processes that occur in an open system: transformation of energy and materials via input, throughput, and output; regulation of system processes; and system growth or adaptation. Farace et al. (1977) describe three communication functions that are traditionally associated with these processes: production, maintenance, and innovation.

Traditional Function Categories

The **production function** includes any communication that controls and coordinates the activities required to produce system outputs. This means communication involved in activities that yield an organization's products or services. Such communication is "work-connected." It includes instructions for the amount and type of output to be produced, job procedures, information about work group organization, and reports on work group activity or problems in the work itself.

The **maintenance function** includes communication that regulates system processes. Regulation implies that system conditions are maintained within certain desirable or acceptable limits. Maintenance communication is concerned with keeping the organization intact and in a steady state of operation. Organizational policies or rules and various forms of deviation-correcting negative feedback serve the maintenance function, but Farace et al. suggested that there is more to maintenance communication than policies, rules, and negative feedback:

Maintenance communication is that which (a) affects the member's feelings of personal worth and significance, (b) changes the "value" placed on interaction with co-workers, supervisors, and subordinates, and (c) alters the perceived importance of continuing to meet the organization's production and innovation needs. (p. 59)

Given such a broad definition, maintenance communication could include events ranging from the employee-of-the-month column in a company newsletter to many of the informal, day-to-day conversations that affect human relationships in the organization. In fact, some writers such as Goldhaber (1990) prefer to include any communication affecting members' feelings of self-worth and quality of organizational relationships in a fourth functional category called **human.** This approach restricts the maintenance function only to regulatory processes.

The **innovation function** includes communication concerned with change in the organization. Communication in this category may involve the development of new ideas and practices as well as the means for implementing and securing acceptance of change. The changes may involve organizational mission, philosophy, structure, and functions. Generally, change implies some alteration in organizational values as well as in organizational behavior. Suggestions from organization members for changes in products, services, or work procedures; recommendations from studies of organizational needs; and long-range planning activities all involve the innovation function.

Uncertainty and Information Adequacy

Several authorities argue that the various functions of organizational communication are all related to a single, more general purpose—the reduction of **uncertainty** (e.g., Weick, 1979). Rosabeth Moss Kanter (1977) claimed that organizations, especially large, bureaucratically structured ones, thrive on predictability. Uncertainty, or the absence of predictability, is an unnerving experience to be avoided whenever possible. Hence, communication is used to reduce or at least cope with uncertainty.

Despite frequent claims that communication serves an uncertainty reduction function, we should not simply assume that this always is true. As we pointed out in chapter 2, Eric Eisenberg (1984) makes a convincing case that many of the messages in day-to-day organizational communication are deliberately and strategically ambiguous because *creating* uncertainty serves the purposes of particular individuals, groups, or even the entire organization. We need only recall some of the earlier examples in the text to realize that organizational communication sometimes is more concerned with creating uncertainty than with reducing it. For example, consider the university president's speeches about commitments to excellence, Chrysler's advertising strategy to promote an image of quality, the doctor-nurse game, and the compensation manager who wanted to revise the communication department's magazine story on employee wage structure so that employees would not understand it.

Even though different individuals and groups within an organization may try to create uncertainty for one another or even to use strategic ambiguity in ways that benefit the organization as a whole, it is probably safe to say that any given individual or group desires certainty for itself. Since information is the key to reduction of uncertainty, organization members usually are concerned with the **adequacy** of this information. Is there enough, too much, or too little information to serve organizational purposes? As Farace et al. (1977) contended, "*What* is known in an organization and *who* knows it are obviously very important in determining the overall functioning of the organization" (p. 27).

Farace et al. explained problems associated with information adequacy by employing Brillouin's (1962) distinction between **absolute** and **distributed information.** Absolute information refers to the total body of information that exists within an organization at any time. This information is distributed to the extent that it is **diffused** (spread) throughout the organization. Information adequacy problems may arise because a piece of information simply does not exist in the organization's pool of absolute information or because existing information is not properly distributed.

Although researchers in organizational communication have been interested in the problem of information adequacy for many years, they have made little effort to study adequacy by systematically matching an organization's information needs against *both* absolute and distributed information in order to identify the sources of adequacy problems. Many like Farace et al. simply assume that inadequate information usually results from distribution problems. Hence, most studies of information adequacy focus on *individual* organization members as *receivers* of distributed information.

Some researchers have evaluated information adequacy by measuring individual members' knowledge about the organization and its functions (Level, 1959; Tompkins, 1962). More commonly, researchers examine the difference between the amount of information that individual members think they *need* and the amount that they think they *actually receive* (Daly, Falcione, & Damhorst, 1979; Daniels & Spiker, 1983; Goldhaber, Yates, Porter, & Lesniak, 1978; Spiker & Daniels, 1981). In these studies, "adequacy" is defined by organization members' *perceptions* of the difference between what is received and what is desired.

Since most research on information adequacy studies the perceptions of individual organization members, it is not surprising that the kinds of information topics examined in these studies involve individual information needs rather than the information needs of the organization as a whole. Several studies have measured information adequacy with a scale developed by the International Communication Association (ICA). This scale asks organization members to report the extent to which they are adequately informed on the following topics:

1. How well I am doing my job.
2. My job duties.
3. Organizational policies.
4. Pay and benefits.
5. How technological changes affect my job.
6. Mistakes and failures of the organization.
7. How I am being judged.
8. How job-related problems are being handled.
9. How organization decisions are made that affect my job.
10. Promotion and advancement opportunities in my organization.
11. Important new product, service, or program developments in my organization.
12. How my job relates to the total organization.
13. Specific problems faced by management.

While studies of these topics may yield valuable knowledge about the extent to which organization members as individuals feel adequately informed, this scale covers only three basic individual needs for information: task and performance issues, compensation and benefits, and problems and progress of the organization (Daniels & Spiker, 1983). Even studies of information adequacy that do not use this particular scale are still based on information topics very much like those in the ICA scale. They also adopt the same focus on organization members as individuals (e.g., Penley, 1982).

Despite the limitations of the focus on individual rather than organizational information needs, studies of information adequacy do indicate that surprisingly large percentages of organization members consider themselves to be inadequately informed on many important topics that directly concern them. The ICA-sponsored studies of eighteen large organizations found that nearly half of the members generally received less information than they wanted (Spiker & Daniels, 1981). Penley (1982), who classified all of the information topics in his study as task- or performance-related, found that 48 percent of the participants in his study were inadequately informed on performance topics and 8 percent were inadequately informed in both task and performance areas.

Penley also found that information adequacy is closely related to the members' sense of identification with and commitment to the organization. This finding was repeated in a study by Smith and DeWine (1987). Spiker and Daniels' (1981) analysis of data from the eighteen ICA studies revealed that information adequacy is related to members' feelings of personal influence in the organization, satisfaction with their immediate superiors, satisfaction with top management, and, to a lesser extent, satisfaction with coworkers.

Even though organization members who consider themselves to be adequately informed generally are more committed, more satisfied, and identify more closely with the organization than those who see themselves as inadequately informed, information adequacy does not always produce such positive outcomes. In a later study, Daniels and Spiker (1983) found that information adequacy on sensitive topics such as management problems, organizational failures, and organizational decision-making processes is *negatively* related to satisfaction with superiors for some organization members. That is, the more some people know about sensitive organizational issues, the less they like their bosses. Daniels and Spiker argued that this may occur because people who develop their own sources of such information become less dependent on their superiors and eventually see themselves as more knowledgeable and competent than those superiors.

While studies of information adequacy generally have been concerned with the potential impact of adequacy on variables such as satisfaction, the most recent work has attempted to identify the conditions under which organization members perceive themselves to be adequately informed. Alexander, Helms, and Curran (1987) found that levels of communication with supervisors, administrative sources, and peers are greater for members who perceive themselves to be adequately informed than for those who perceive themselves to be inadequately informed. Inadequately informed members also were younger than more adequately informed members, and they had been employed with the organization for less time. These results may not be especially surprising, but they do suggest that information adequacy does not occur in a haphazard and unpredictable manner.

Unanswered Questions About Communication Functions

Our present state of knowledge about organizational communication functions and adequacy of information that supports these functions is somewhat limited. While production, maintenance, innovation, and human functions certainly are important in organizational communication and the information needs of individual organization members are now well understood, the purposes and outcomes of organizational communication are more complicated than current models of functions and information adequacy suggest.

Some forms of organizational communication are difficult to assign to conventional categories of functions. A few simple examples illustrate the point.

- A manufacturing division of a large corporation discovers that a new product has potential safety hazards. The division falsifies safety test reports to its own corporate headquarters and to government agencies in order to obtain approval to market the product.
- A publicly egotistical but privately insecure middle manager spends several hours each week trying to impress subordinates by recounting "heroic" stories of his career accomplishments (e.g., the time that he "single-handedly" saved the company from bankruptcy). The stories are greatly exaggerated, but he

has told them so many times that he actually believes them. The subordinates know better. They like to say behind his back, "He's a legend in his own mind."

- Another middle manager verbally abuses subordinates whenever the opportunity presents itself. During a recent meeting of all company employees, she publicly chastised a salesclerk for leaving work too early and failing to put enough merchandise on a display table. At the next employee meeting, she chewed out the same clerk for putting too much on a display table and causing unauthorized overtime by leaving work too late. This manager seems to obtain a perverse form of personal gratification from publicly humiliating subordinates.
- Top managers in a genetic engineering company instruct their research and development group to begin a highly controversial gene-splicing project that may produce some very dangerous bacteria. The research group also is told to write ambiguous reports to top management about its work. The company president tells the research and development director, "We want to know what's going on, but we don't want to know what's going on—if you get my meaning."

The point of these examples is simple. Every day, human communication in organizations occurs for many purposes, including building empires, self-aggrandizement, acting out sadomasochistic rituals, initiating romantic relationships, accomplishing the political objectives of coalitions, and simply keeping one another entertained. Although such acts may have some connection with production, maintenance, human, or innovation communication functions, they also seem to involve several functions simultaneously and to include functions that do not fit into the traditional categories.

The abusing middle manager who attacked the salesclerk did so over a work problem (production) as well as a policy violation (maintenance), and she did so in a way that degraded the employee (a negative form of the human function). If asked to explain her actions, the manager might say that she was enforcing policy, protecting work standards, and sending a message to other employees by making a public example of this errant clerk. However, she also may have acted out a sadistic ritual that fulfilled her own need to derive pleasure from hurting others. Sadism seems to lie beyond our traditional ideas about communication functions.

Some of the research methods and concepts associated with the interpretivist perspective may help us to develop a better understanding of communication functions because interpretivists do not assume that any observed episode of communication should fit somewhere in a predetermined set of functional categories. Rather, communicative acts are observed in a specific situation, and the functions served in that situation are derived from these acts.

For example, Harris and Sutton (1986) studied the functions of communication in the parting rituals of eight dying organizations (going out of business, closing down). Since there was nothing to produce, no organizational conditions to maintain (except the status of certain employee benefits and friendships formed during the life of the organization), and certainly no new innovations to discuss (except the demise of the organization), there was no reason to presume that communication would fit into production, maintenance, and innovation categories. Yet, Harris and Sutton's interpretive investigation suggested that several functions are served by such rituals, including motivation of members to move on, information about benefits and personnel dispositions, gaining external stakeholders' acceptance of the loss, managing impressions about the situation, and assuaging guilt over the organization's failure.

Generally, functionalism itself might benefit from more research on communication functions and from reformulation of the models used to classify functions. It would also be useful to extend the study of information adequacy beyond the needs of individuals as information receivers. We need to know more about the ways in which system and subsystem information needs are defined and how these needs are fulfilled through organizational communication.

Communication Structure

The concept of communication structure is one of the most central ideas in functionalist perspectives on organizational communication. There are at least two different ways to think about the structure of organizational communication. One way is to define structure as a system of pathways through which messages flow—the so-called lines of communication in an organization (Goldhaber, 1990; Koehler, Anatol, & Applbaum, 1981). This is the traditional definition of communication structure. If you think about this definition for a moment, it is easy to see just what it implies. Messages are regarded as concrete objects that are passed back and forth through literal channels of communication. As we noted in chapter 2, many scholars are uneasy about this idea because it misrepresents the dynamics of interpersonal communication.

The second approach defines communication structure as the patterns of interaction among people who comprise the organization. In this sense, structure depends on who communicates with whom. Since these patterns can be observed, the second definition also is consistent with the functionalist focus on objective features of organizational communication. Of course, interpretivists are quick to argue that structure is not really an objective property of communication but an idea that is shared by organization members (Trujillo, 1985).

Is structure an objective property or a subjective idea? Curiously, it seems to be both. On the one hand, when organization members interact, they are engaging in behavior with objective features. These features include discernible patterns that someone else can observe. Yet, the way in which we understand these patterns depends on our ideas about structure. The fact that we can devise at least two different definitions of communication structure (system of channels versus patterns of interaction) means that the concept of structure can be understood in different ways.

The idea that communication structure is a system of pathways or channels of message flow goes hand in hand with a common distinction between formal and informal systems of organizational communication. This distinction is very useful, but it has some limitations. Some of these limitations can be overcome by viewing communication structure as a network that arises from the patterns of interaction among organization members. Since each of these ideas provides a particular way of understanding communication structure, we will review both in some detail.

Formal Communication

Formal communication refers to communication through officially designated channels of message flow between organizational positions. In many organizations, the formal system of communication is specified in policy manuals and organization charts. In other organizations, the formal system is implicit, yet organization members understand it well. The examples of the U.S. Postal Service (USPS) and Supervalue Market in chapter 3 illustrate this point. The USPS has explicit, written policies that define the channels of formal communication, while Supervalue has a system of conventions and rules learned through day-to-day experience.

The USPS and Supervalue examples also involved hierarchical structures based on functional divisions of labor and scalar authority chains. The concept of hierarchy is so ingrained in organizational life that formal communication usually is described in terms of the three directions of message flow within a hierarchical system: downward, upward, and horizontal.

Downward Communication

Downward communication involves the transmission of messages from upper levels to lower levels of the organization hierarchy (i.e., from manager to employee, superior to subordinate). Smith, Richetto, and Zima (1972) claimed that downward communication has been the most frequently studied aspect of formal communication. Twenty years ago, there also was a great deal of evidence that most of the message flow in formal systems was downward (Tompkins, 1967).

Classical and scientific approaches to organizations considered communication primarily as a tool for managerial control and coordination. Consequently, these approaches focused on downward communication of orders and regulations from superiors to subordinates—messages concerned with production and maintenance functions.

Classical theorists assumed that subordinates would accept and comply with downward communication on the basis of superiors' legitimate authority. As the Hawthorne Studies illustrated, compliance with managerial authority is not such a simple matter. The human relations movement stressed the use of downward-communication strategies that would promote morale in the belief that satisfaction would lead to compliance with authority (Miles, 1965). Much of the research that followed human relations assumptions has attempted to determine the conditions under which subordinates comply with messages received from superiors (Smith et al., 1972).

More recently, contemporary theorists have argued that organization members have a "need to know" for their own purposes. Satisfaction of this need is important to the successful assimilation of members into an organization. As Koehler et al. argued, "The best integrated employees are those who are told what goals and objectives are, how their jobs fit into the total picture, and the progress they are making on the job" (1981, p. 10). This idea is the basis for some of the more recent studies on information adequacy that we described earlier. For example, Penley's (1982) work focused on the role of information adequacy in bringing about members' involvement in and identification with organization goals rather than on downward-communication strategies for producing compliance with authority.

Katz and Kahn (1978) identified five types of messages that usually are reflected in downward communication:

1. *Job instructions* involving the work to be done and directions for doing that work.
2. *Job rationales* explaining the purpose of a job or task and its relationship to other organizational activities or objectives.
3. *Procedures and practices information* pertaining to organizational policies, rules, and benefits.
4. *Feedback* providing subordinates with appraisals of their performance.
5. *Indoctrination* of organizational ideology that attempts to foster member commitment to the organization's values, goals, and objectives.

Effective Downward Communication. Despite the attention that downward communication has received in management and communication research, this dimension of formal communication is ineffective in many organizations (Chase, 1970). Problems with downward communication include inadequacy of information, inappropriate means of diffusing information, filtering of information, and a general climate of dominance and submission that pervades downward communication.

Adequacy of information obtained from downward messages presents a puzzling paradox. On the one hand, downward-directed messages frequently create overload in organizations (Davis, 1972). Advances in information technology (the mechanical and electronic ability not only to manipulate information more efficiently but also to send more messages to more people) and, ironically, the importance attached to the idea of effective organizational communication have led to floods of memorandums, bulletins, newsletters, technical reports, and data in reams of computer printouts. Federal Express, a company specializing in overnight delivery of letters and packages, gleefully refers to this condition as "The Paper Blob." On the other hand, organization members consistently report in studies of information adequacy that they do not receive sufficient information on topics that are important to them (Goldhaber, 1990; Penley, 1982; Spiker & Daniels, 1981).

The apparent paradox is difficult to explain. One possible conclusion is that organization members receive too much of the wrong information. This does not mean that the information itself is in error. It means that much of the information that members receive may not be relevant to their personal job and organizational concerns. Farace et al. argued that problems in information-diffusion policies most commonly *"are due to failures by managers to identify which groups of personnel need to know certain things, or to establish where these groups are supposed to be able to obtain the information they need"* (1977, p. 28). Of course, this claim, along with the Koehler et al. argument that the best integrated employees are those who are "told" about goals, the big picture, and their progress, presumes that managers are the ones who should define everybody's information needs. This assumption poses another problem: How much input should employees or subordinates have in deciding what they need and how they will obtain it? Reserving for management the exclusive right to decide who gets what information is an idea that may be unacceptable to many members of modern organizations.

The methods of information diffusion that are used for downward communication also can create problems. According to Goldhaber (1990), organizations often rely too heavily on mediated (written, mechanical, and electronic) methods of transmitting messages rather than on personal, face-to-face contact. Goldhaber, Yates, Porter, and Lesniak (1978) concluded from a review of sixteen ICA-sponsored studies that organization members generally desire more face-to-face interaction. This finding also poses another paradox. How do we cope with the human need for direct, interpersonal contact when today's pressure to get more information to more people more rapidly requires us to rely on the most efficient means of communication available (i.e., paper and electronic media)?

Downward communication also is subjected to filtering. As messages are relayed from superior to subordinate through levels of the organizational hierarchy, they may be changed in various ways. Information may be left out, added, combined, or otherwise modified as it passes through a chain of serial reproduction (Pace & Boren, 1973). **Serial reproduction** is the same effect that occurs in the children's game Telephone when messages are passed from one person to the next. Distortions occur as each person in the transmission series attempts to reproduce the message received for relay to the next person. While oral messages are most easily subjected to such distortions, written messages are not immune if they are in any way relayed from level to level of the organization.

In part, distortions occur because different people have different interpretations of the same information (i.e., as a result of ambiguity) or because human beings simply have a limited capacity to process information. When attempting to reproduce a message in serial transmission, people may simply forget some of the information or "chunk" certain details together in order to handle the information more efficiently.

Downward messages also may be filtered deliberately. Information power is a valuable commodity in many organizations. Culbert and Eden (1970) pointed out that managers often "base their power on withholding, rather than sharing, information" (p. 140), because ability to control situations and outcomes may depend on having knowledge that others do not possess. When managers do choose to share information, their subordinates may prevent it from being relayed to lower levels of the organization. Mellinger (1956) found that subordinates who do not trust a superior often choose to block that superior's messages from others.

In general, the greater the number of steps or linkages in a serial reproduction chain and the greater the perceptual differences among participants in that chain, the more likely it is that some form of message distortion or filtering will occur. The type of information also has a bearing on the extent to which it will even be distributed. In a case study of one large organization, Davis (1968) found that important information was more likely than insignificant information to be relayed by superiors to subordinates, but even the important information often was not relayed by superiors to subordinates despite the fact that the superiors had explicit instructions to pass on this information.

Upward Communication

Upward communication involves transmission of messages from lower to higher levels of the organization; namely, communication initiated by subordinates with their superiors. The role of upward communication in classical theories of organization was limited primarily to basic reporting functions concerning task-related matters. The human relations movement expanded the role of upward communication by emphasizing "two-way" communication between superiors and subordinates as a means of promoting morale. Later, human resource development theories emphasized the necessity of upward communication for integration of organization members and improved decision-making processes. Upward communication is a prerequisite for employee involvement in decision making, problem solving, and development of policies and procedures (Smith, Richetto, & Zima, 1972).

Katz and Kahn (1978) point out that upward communication can provide superiors with information in the following areas:

1. Performance on the job and job-related problems.
2. Fellow employees and their problems.
3. Subordinates' perceptions of organizational policies and practices.
4. Tasks and procedures for accomplishing them.

In addition to those uses noted by Katz and Kahn, Planty and Machaver (1952) stated that upward communication can (1) provide valuable ideas from subordinates, (2) facilitate acceptance of downward messages, and (3) generally facilitate decision making by fostering subordinates' participation and by providing a better picture of performance, perceptions, and possible problems at all levels of the organization.

Effective Upward Communication. Although contemporary managers and executives praise the virtues of upward communication, actual use of upward communication appears to be limited in many organizations (Goldhaber, 1990; Tompkins, 1967). Management often does not establish effective means for upward communication. Moreover, when upward communication does occur, it may be subject to the same filtering problems that affect downward communication.

While upward communication can be encouraged through means such as suggestion systems, systematic reporting methods, grievance procedures, attitude surveys, and employee meetings, the presence of such systems may be only a token gesture in many organizations. A story that a student told us about her first encounter with a suggestion box during a summer job at a factory is not unusual. The little wooden box hung from a supervisor's office door. When the student asked a coworker (a veteran of several years in the factory) about the box, she was told, "Don't pay any attention to that, kid. They never open it and we never put anything in it."

Suggestion systems can be very effective when managers actively encourage their use and employees take them seriously, but our example of the "suggestion box syndrome" typifies two common research findings about upward communication. First, most organization members would rather receive information than provide information to others (Goldhaber, 1990). Second, even when subordinates make attempts at upward communication, their superiors may not be receptive to these attempts. Koehler and Huber (1974) found that managers tend to be more receptive to upward communication when the information is positive (good news rather than bad news), is in line with current policy (criticism and boat rocking are unwelcome), and has intuitive appeal (fits the managers' own biases).

Subordinates are likely to become quite dissatisfied in organizations in which superiors endorse the idea of upward communication but, in practice, actually ignore it. When subordinates develop the impression that superiors only want to hear good news and support for their own ideas, it should not be surprising that upward communication with those superiors is filtered extensively. Krivonos (1976) reported that subordinates tend to tell their superiors what they think the superiors want to hear or only what they want their superiors to hear. Information is distorted so that it will please superiors and reflect positively on subordinates.

While several factors seem to affect accuracy of upward communication, the most important ingredient may be trust. Studies by Read (1962), Maier, Hoffman, and Read (1963), and Roberts and O'Reilly (1974) indicated that accuracy of upward communication is greater when subordinates trust their superiors. The studies by Read and by Maier, Hoffman, and Read also found that subordinates' upward mobility aspirations are negatively related to accuracy. As subordinates' mobility aspirations increase, accuracy in upward communication decreases. This finding is somewhat suspect because the method that Read used to index accuracy was rather crude. Even so, Read's research reminds us that some people who want to move up may distort information to make themselves look good or to protect their chances of promotion.

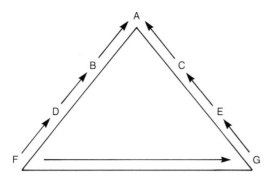

Figure 4.1
Fayol's bridge where F
communicates with G.

Horizontal Communication

Horizontal communication refers to the flow of messages *across* functional areas at a given level of an organization. Although classical approaches to organizing made little provision for horizontal communication, Fayol recognized that emergencies and unforeseen day-to-day contingencies require flexibility in formal channels. Strict adherence to the chain of command would be too time-consuming in emergencies, so some provision has to be made for horizontal bridges that permit people at the same level to communicate directly without going through several levels of organization. Fayol's concept (1949) is illustrated in figure 4.1.

Horizontal communication introduces flexibility in organizational structure. It facilitates problem solving, information sharing across different work groups, and task coordination between departments or project teams. It may also enhance morale and afford a means for resolving conflicts (Koehler et al., 1981). Human resource development theorists regard horizontal communication as an essential feature of participative decision making and organizational adaptiveness (French, Bell, & Zawacki, 1983).

Reliance on horizontal communication for decision making and problem solving does not mean that the process is more *efficient* than simple downward communication of decisions made at top levels of the organization, but horizontal communication may be more *effective*. For example, decision making and problem solving in Japanese organizations usually occur through horizontal communication at lower levels. The results of this process are transmitted to top management for review and approval. Ryutard Nomura (1981), chairman of the board of Japan's Triyo Industries, observed that decision making under this system can be a lengthy and difficult process, but once a decision has been made, its implementation is swift and certain. Organization members are committed to the decision because difficulties have been resolved and opposing points of view reconciled through horizontal communication before plans are presented to top management.

In the conventional Western organization, decisions are made at the top, then orders for compliance and implementation flow downward. According to Nomura, Western-style decision making is fast because it is centralized near the top of the organization. However, acceptance and implementation of top management decisions at lower levels is slow to develop. Lack of commitment to decisions and conflicts over implementation arise at lower levels where members have been excluded from the decision-making process.

There is some evidence that Japanese and American organizations are attempting to adapt the best features of each others' traditional organizational models by mixing Japanese-style participation with Western-style centralization in a way that modifies both. The objective is to produce a new type of organization that can thrive in a complex and turbulent environment in which decisions must be made efficiently and effectively. Ouchi and Jaeger (1978) referred to this new model as the "Type Z" organization. Rehder (1981) simply called such organizations "nontraditional." Regardless of the label, many American organizations are attempting to promote more horizontal communication, but this change is difficult to bring about.

Effective Horizontal Communication. American organizations generally are unaccustomed to high levels of horizontal communication. Albaum (1964) found that any given department in an organization typically will not relay information directly to another, even when it is understood that the information is vitally important to the other department. Although Albaum's research occurred many years ago, there is little reason to suspect that conditions today are much different.

Horizontal-communication problems occur because of territoriality, rivalry, specialization, and simple lack of motivation. Organizations that traditionally have functioned under rigid authority structures with fixed lines of communication may find that the values and expectations that members have acquired under such systems inhibit attempts at horizontal communication.

One inhibiting value is territoriality. Organization members who control task-related activity within a defined and fixed jurisdictional area often regard others' involvement in that area as territorial encroachment. Departments value their turf and strive to protect it. This problem may be compounded through interdepartmental rivalries that arise from win/lose competition for rewards and resources.

Some years ago, corporate executives in a national department store chain encountered territorial rivalry when they discovered that local stores within each of the company's major sales districts refused to cooperate with one another on sales promotions. For example, if Store X ran out of a sale item, it might call Store Y in the same district to obtain more. Even though Store Y would have an ample supply of the item, it would claim to be out. The explanation was simple. Local managers were rewarded only for the sales performance of their individual stores. Consequently, stores within the same sales region literally were in competition with one another as well as with other department store chains. When the company decided to provide managers with bonuses based on district-wide sales, stores within any given district suddenly began to cooperate with one another on all sorts of projects and promotions.

Specialization also may hamper horizontal communication. During the 1960s, for example, a team of experts from various fields was assembled to work on a NASA-sponsored project. The team hardly had begun its work before its members realized that they were having great difficulty in communicating. The main reason seemed to be that different specialties used the same terms in different ways. The problem was so persistent that the group finally appointed a "vocabulary committee" to develop standard definitions for all of the troublesome terms.

Horizontal communication often fails simply because organization members are unwilling to expend the additional effort that it requires. When we engage in upward or downward communication, those with whom we communicate are easy to reach because of proximity or clearly designated channels. Immediate superiors and immediate subordinates may be just across the office. We know them by name and we have well-established rules for initiating and conducting interaction with them. In contrast, horizontal communication may require contact with people in units that are well removed from our own. The channels and rules of interaction may be unclear. We do not really know these people. The need to communicate with them makes us uneasy or takes too much time, so we avoid or ignore it.

Informal Communication

The **informal system** involves episodes of interaction that do not reflect officially designated channels of communication. As defined by Tompkins (1967), the informal system is "not rationally specified." Classical and scientific theorists made no attempt to account for the role of informal communication in organizational functions and its influence on organizational life. Many classical and scientific principles of management were turned upside down when Barnard's work and the Hawthorne Studies suggested that a great deal of organizational communication is informal communication. In fact, one of the most important findings in the Hawthorne Studies concerned the influence of informal communication in developing and reinforcing performance standards, member expectations, and values at the work group level.

Some scholars have argued that informal communication is a substitute for an inadequate formal system. Walton (1961) concluded that informal communication systems arise when information transmitted through the formal system is either insufficient or ambiguous. Other scholars claim that the informal system is much more than a simple substitute for an ineffective formal system. Barnard (1938) and Davis (1953) argued that informal communication is an inherent and even necessary aspect of organizational life. Generally, organizational communication theorists agree that at least some informal communication is inevitable in any organization. Management efforts to stamp it out are misguided at best, although some experts urge managers to control the informal system (Hellweg, 1983).

Much of the research on informal communication is concerned with the study of **grapevine** communication. The terms *informal system* and *grapevine* often are used interchangeably as if they refer to the same thing (Davis, 1953;

Hellweg, 1983). The use of the word *grapevine* as a metaphor for a communication system began during the American Civil War in the 1860s as a description for telegraph lines that were strung through trees in such a way that they looked like grapevines. The system was not very reliable, so the term was soon applied to any form of unofficial communication.

Nearly a century later, organizational communication research indicated that patterns of grapevine communication even look something like a cluster of grapes. Consider the pattern of message flow in figure 4.2. Person A initiates and transmits a message to B and C. B relays the message to D, while C relays it to E and F. The clustering continues as the message is diffused throughout the organization. Some participants in the grapevine act only as receivers. They do not relay information to anyone else. Others relay it to several different people.

Grapevine communication has many other important features. Susan Hellweg (1987) summarized these features in a list of thirty-three general conclusions that she based on a review of nineteen research studies. The conclusions are somewhat cumbersome because the studies themselves are very difficult to relate to one another. Even so, Hellweg presented a comprehensive analysis of what we know about the grapevine. We have reorganized her conclusions under five topic areas for more clarity:

Function and Relationship to Formal System

1. The grapevine emerges from the social and personal interests of employees rather than formal requirements of the organization.
2. The grapevine is people-oriented rather than issue-oriented.
3. The grapevine often carries information that would be inappropriate in formal channels (e.g., social information).
4. Five out of every six messages in the organization are transmitted through the grapevine.
5. While the formal system provides a "blueprint" for the ways employees are supposed to communicate, the informal system reflects the ways in which they actually do communicate.
6. Formal and informal systems tend to be jointly active or inactive.

Participants in Grapevine Communication

7. While the grapevine typically is associated with employee communication, it is just as prevalent among managers.
8. Employee sex is not a predictor of participation in grapevine communication.
9. Secretaries play a key role in grapevine communication.
10. Liaisons play a key role in grapevine communication.
11. Grapevine communication occurs mainly at the work site.

Patterns and Media of Grapevine Communication

12. Grapevine transmission flows in all directions in an organization.
13. Grapevine communication generally occurs in a cluster transmission pattern, although it can take other forms.

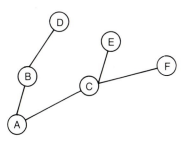

Figure 4.2
A grapevine communication cluster.

14. Most grapevine communication is oral.
15. Grapevine communication can begin and end anywhere in an organization.
16. As the size of the organization increases, grapevine activity increases.
17. Of those who receive grapevine information, relatively few transmit it to others.
18. Only a small percentage of organization members act as liaisons in grapevine communication.

Volume, Speed, and Reliability of Information

19. The grapevine carries more accurate than inaccurate information.
20. Grapevine information generally is incomplete.
21. Grapevine communication is fast.
22. Use of the grapevine as a source for a particular piece of information diminishes over time.
23. People are selective and discriminating in the information that they choose to transmit through the grapevine.
24. Information is handled more loosely and freely in grapevine communication than in formal communication because members are not held responsible for grapevine distortions in the way that they would be for distortions in formal communication.
25. Grapevine activity is associated with "news" events. It may include information that concerns specific individuals.

Role in Rumor Transmission

26. Three types of rumors are diffused (spread) through the grapevine: anxiety rumors, wish-fulfillment rumors, and wedge-driving rumors.
27. Only a small portion of grapevine information consists of rumors.
28. Rumors are more prevalent in organizations that foster secrecy.
29. Diffusion of rumors depends on the importance and ambiguity of the information involved.
30. Rumors move more quickly among organization members who are in close proximity.
31. Rumors are distorted through sharpening, leveling, and assimilation.
32. Rumors are diffused easily over the grapevine because it offers no reliable source for confirmation of facts.
33. Once a rumor is assigned credibility, other events in the organization are altered to fit in with and support the rumor.

In general, Hellweg's review of research on grapevine communication suggests that a great deal of organizational communication occurs through the grapevine. Communication in this system is fast and more often accurate than inaccurate, though much of the information is incomplete. Grapevine communication usually is concerned with people-oriented, social information, although other forms of information are diffused through the grapevine. The grapevine serves as a rumor mill, but rumors comprise only a small proportion of grapevine communication. Participants in grapevine communication include managers as well as employees and men as well as women.

Limitations of the Traditional View

The traditional distinction between formal and informal communication is useful in describing and understanding many aspects of organizational communication, but it is subject to at least three major limitations. First, the concept of organizational structure itself may be regarded as a socially constructed reality. Second, there is no universal agreement on the distinction between formal and informal communication. Finally, it may be easier to understand some features of organizational communication by distinguishing between "tightly coupled" and "loosely coupled" systems rather than between formal and informal communication.

Structure as a Social Construction

The concepts of formal "hierarchy" and informal "grapevine" are good examples of interpretivist notions about the social construction of reality. We often speak of formal messages "flowing upward and downward" and of rumors being "transmitted by the grapevine" as if hierarchy and grapevines are tangible things with a physical, concrete existence. Interpretivists point out that these concepts are metaphors that we use to make sense of organizational communication. After all, messages do not literally flow "up" or "down" and organizations and grapevines do not spring to life in order to "transmit" rumors.

Concepts such as hierarchy and grapevine are rich in implications about power, authority, motives, intentions, and patterns of organizational communication. These terms also are embedded in the language that members of most organizations use to understand their own experiences. But these concepts are not the only ones available for describing and explaining organizational communication.

Muddled Distinctions

The distinction between formal and informal communication also is somewhat muddled. Most scholars make formal communication synonymous with the organization chart and informal communication synonymous with the grapevine. As Hellweg pointed out, grapevine communication usually occurs in cluster-transmission patterns. Since many daily episodes of organizational communication ranging from ritual greetings to coffee-break socializing do not fit this pattern, some scholars prefer a broader definition of informal communication that includes such episodes (Koontz & O'Donnel, 1955). Still others define the formal system as *expected* communication patterns and the informal system as *actual* patterns (Jacoby, 1968). Some even argue that formal communication is written, centralized (vertical), and planned, while informal communication is oral, decentralized (horizontal), and unplanned (Stech, 1983). None of these approaches has proven to be especially workable, so there is no one means of distinguishing between formal and informal communication that scholars uniformly accept.

Loose versus Tight Coupling

Finally, it may make more sense to distinguish between **tightly coupled** and **loosely coupled systems.** As Glassman (1973) explained, two loosely coupled systems either have few common ties or the ties that join them are very weak. In system theory terms, highly interdependent organizational subsystems are tightly coupled. Subsystems that are related but less interdependent are loosely coupled. When an organization is based on tightly coupled subsystems, changes in one subsystem quickly ripple through others. In loosely coupled subsystems, the ripple effect of change is limited, dampened, or gradual. Any given organization might be described generally as either loosely or tightly coupled, but loose and tight coupling are two sides of the same coin. According to Karl Weick (1976), if tight coupling occurs in some areas of an organization, loose coupling must occur in others.

The distinction between tight and loose coupling is important because an organization that appears to be rigidly structured and formal may contain many loosely coupled subsystems, while one that appears to be informal may be tightly coupled. Weick (1976) demonstrated that educational institutions, usually regarded as bureaucracies, are very durable, loosely coupled systems. *Coupling does not depend so much on the degree of formalization in organizational structure as it does on the level of interdependence that actually exists among subsystems.*

Weick believes that the durability of successful organizations is attributable to loose coupling. Loose coupling allows for localized adaptation. When a new situation or problem arises, one area of the organization can respond without requiring organization-wide adaptation every time a change occurs in the environment. The effects of errors and failures are restricted primarily to the subsystems in which they occur.

Loosely coupled systems and the individuals within them have more autonomy and discretion than those in tightly coupled organizations. From an organizational communication standpoint, however, some of the characteristics of loosely coupled systems may surprise you. According to Weick, such organizations are relatively uncoordinated. No single member of the organization knows exactly what is happening throughout the organization as a whole, yet things get done and the organization more or less accomplishes its mission.

Loose coupling does have some potential disadvantages. It reduces benefits of standardization. It promotes diversity rather than selectivity in organizational values and practices. In other words, different groups may be doing things in very different ways. This condition may help to promote adaptation and innovation, but it also allows isolated subsystems to preserve archaic, outmoded traditions. At the same time, "loosely coupled systems should be conspicuous for their cultural lags," yet they also are "vulnerable to producing faddish responses" because so many independent subsystems have the ability to make ad hoc, isolated changes (Weick, 1976, p. 8).

If the concept of coupling is as important as Glassman and Weick suggest, the study of organizational communication *should be less concerned with traditional distinctions between formal and informal communication and more concerned about identifying and understanding the coupling characteristics of organizational communication networks.* These characteristics may be richer and more complex than the traditional distinction between formal and informal communication leads us to believe. We begin to get a better sense of this richness when we change our definition of communication structure from a "system of channels" to "patterns of interaction" in a network of relationships.

Communication Structure as a Network

While the problems in the traditional concepts of formal and informal communication have not been resolved, they can be avoided to some extent by focusing on the patterns of interaction that actually occur among organization members, or the **communication network.** This can be done with a technique known as **network analysis.**

Network Analysis

The basic purpose of network analysis is to provide a picture of the patterns of interaction that define organizational communication structure. Terrance Albrecht and Vikie Ropp (1982) described several ways in which this picture can be developed:

1. Ask organization members to report the interactions that they have with one another (self-report surveys).
2. Make direct, firsthand observations of interaction patterns (naturalistic observation).
3. Unobtrusively "capture" interaction episodes on audiotape or videotape or from other records in the organization (constitutive ethnography).
4. Conduct nondirective interviews with members to obtain information that may help to explain and interpret interaction patterns.

Albrecht and Ropp argued for the use of various methods in any given network analysis because each method has specific advantages and disadvantages. Self-report surveys and interviews allow the researcher to obtain data from the organization members' perspective and to examine network structure

Table 4.1 Albrecht and Ropp's Strategies for Studying Network Relationships. From "The Study of Network Structuring in Organizations Through the Use of Method Triangulation," by T. L. Albrecht and V. A. Ropp, 1982, *Western Journal of Speech Communication, 46*, p. 171.

Method	Viewpoint	Time Perspective	Predominant Level	Amount of Structure Imposed
Self-report surveys	Respondents	Retrospective reporting of static structures	Multilevel (micro-macro)	High
Nondirective interviews	Respondents	Retrospective accounting for actions	Multilevel (micro-macro)	Minimal
Naturalistic structured observations	Researcher	Current tracking of observed actions	Dyad-small unit (micro)	Low
Constitutive ethnography	Researcher	Current taping of interactions as they occur for later analysis	Dyad (micro)	Moderate

of dyadic, group, and organization-wide levels, but the analysis usually is based on members' recollections of past behavior. What they remember doing may not correspond with what actually occurred. Naturalistic observation and constitutive ethnography rely on records of current actual interaction rather than members' potentially faulty reconstructions of past events, but the scope of the analysis is restricted to dyadic and small group levels. Unless you have an army of observers and recording devices, you just cannot be everywhere at once. The various methods also differ in the degree of structure that they impose on the situation and the kind of data that they provide for analysis. Albrecht and Ropp have summarized the methods according to the scheme presented in table 4.1.

Network Structure and Roles

Diagrams of network structure reveal network roles and relationships. Self-report surveys provide the easiest means for developing such diagrams. A self-report analysis is conducted by asking organization members to estimate the frequency of interaction that they have with one another over a specified time frame. These estimates usually are memory-based. If you are asked to report the number of times that you communicate with several other specific people during a typical workweek, you probably reflect back on past experiences in order to arrive at your estimates. These estimates are used to assemble graphic displays of network structure.

Although the resulting structure is derived from memory-based self-reports, it generally is assumed to be a good approximation of the actual structure. To some extent, the accuracy of the self-reports can be validated through the network analysis procedure itself. Your report of interaction frequency

Figure 4.3
A communication network.

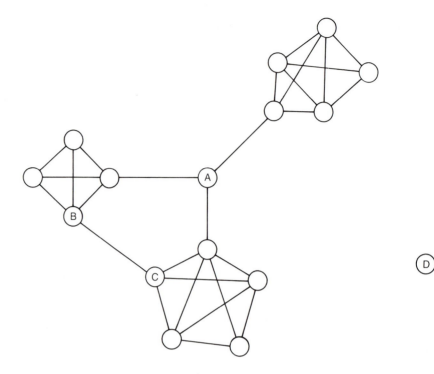

with Person B can be checked against Person B's report of interaction frequency with you. The two reports probably will not be identical, but they should at least be similar. If they are not similar, validity of the self-reports is in question. Figure 4.3 provides an example of the kind of network structure diagram that can be produced from self-report data.

The circles in figure 4.3 represent people. The lines connecting the circles are linkages that show who communicates with whom. This particular diagram shows several distinct **network roles** that members of this organization assume. Assuming that the diagram represents a small organization, the communication network is comprised of three groups. Basically, a **group** is defined by members who interact more frequently with one another than with members of other groups. Most of the people in this network are **group members.** Person A is a **liaison.** A liaison links different groups but is not a member of any of the groups in that link. Individuals B and C form a **bridge link** between two groups. Unlike liaisons, people in a bridge link are group members. Person D is an **isolate** who is not linked to anyone else in the network. This does not mean that D never communicates with anyone else in the organization. It does mean that D has relatively little contact with others (i.e., the amount of interaction that D has with others is negligible in comparison to the amount that occurs among other organization members).

Network analysis techniques applied to large organizations are quite sophisticated. They derive structure not only from simple frequency of interaction, but they also derive structure from its importance. They also require computer programs with complex criteria for defining groups and various network roles. Some of these techniques are described in works by William D. Richards (1971; 1974) and by Farace, Monge, and Russell (1977). Noel Tichy (1981) presents a model of network properties and questions that these properties answer about organizational communication that illustrates just how sophisticated network analysis can be. This model is included in table 4.2.

Table 4.2 Network Properties. From "Networks in Organizations," by N. M. Tichy, 1981, P. C. Nystrom and W. H. Starbuck (Eds.). *Handbook of Organizational Design*. London: Oxford University Press.

Network Properties	Explanations	Characteristics of: Coalitions	Cliques
Transactional Content	The four media of exchange are: (a) expressions of affect, (b) influence, (c) information, and (d) goods and services.	Influence Information	Affect Information
Characteristics of Links			
Reciprocity	To what degree are relationships symmetric rather than asymmetric or nonsymmetrical?	High	High
Clarity of norms	How clear are the ways participants should behave in relationships?	Very	Moderately
Intensity	To what degree will one participant disregard personal costs in order to fulfill obligations?	Low	Moderate
Multiplexity	In how many ways are one pair of participants related?	Few	Many
Structural Characteristics			
Organizational density	What portion of the organizational members participate in this network?	Moderate	Small to moderate
Clustering	How many dense regions, such as coalitions or cliques, does this network contain?	Moderate	One
Size	How many people participate in this network?	Moderate	Few
Visibility	Can uninvolved observers tell who participates in this network, and can participants themselves map their network?	Easily	Moderately well
Membership criteria	How clear are the criteria for recruitment or membership?	Very	Very
Openness		Moderate	Few
	How many relationships does this network have with other networks? Are the participants cosmopolitans or locals?	Both	Locals
Stability	How long is this network expected to survive?	Short	Long
Connectedness	Of all possible relationships among participants, what portion actually exist?	Moderate	Most

Table 4.2 Continued

Reachability	What is the average number of links separating two participants?	Moderate	Few
Occupational density	What portion of all the occupations in the organization are included in this network?	Large	Moderate
Vertical density	What portion of all hierarchical levels does this network encompass?	Moderate	Small
Centrality	Does this network include many sociometric stars or only a few?	Centralized	Moderately decentralized
Key Participants			
Star	A participant who has many relationships with other participants.		
Liaison	A participant who links two or more clusters that would be separate otherwise.		
Bridge or linking pin	A participant who belongs to multiple clusters.		
Gatekeeper	A participant who controls the flow from one section of the network to another.		
Isolate	A person who has no relationship to others.		

Uses of Network Analysis

Why go through complex procedures just to obtain a diagram of network structure? What is the utility of this information? At least three different uses of network analysis have been demonstrated in organizational communication research.

First, a network analysis makes it possible to determine whether the actual communication structure corresponds with expected channels of communication, group structures, and member roles. Second, network analysis can identify individuals in specific network roles (e.g., liaisons and bridge links that seldom appear on formal organization charts). The presence of these linkages reveals patterns of horizontal communication between different groups and organizational units. Network analysis may also identify isolates. This may help to determine how well members are integrated into the organization.

Indentification of network roles can have other important theoretical and practical implications. For example, Albrecht (1984) has reported several important differences between persons in bridge or liaison roles (linkers) and ordinary group members or isolates (nonlinkers). Her research indicates that linkers identify more closely with the organization, have a stronger connection between their jobs and self-concepts, think of their jobs in terms of teamwork and effectiveness, see a closer connection between their jobs and their salaries, and are less frustrated than nonlinkers. However, Albrecht also reported, "They (linkers) also saw their jobs more in terms of problems and pressures than did nonlinkers" (p. 545).

In addition to Albrecht's findings, other studies suggest that isolates do not contribute to organizational functions, tend to withhold information from others, and are relatively dissatisfied (Goldhaber, 1990). An organization committed to a philosophy of participation very likely would want to integrate isolates into the communication network, although there may be situations in which the presence of isolates is welcome news to an organization. For example, some universities and research institutes actively encourage a certain amount of isolation for professors and scientists in order for them to pursue research and scholarly writing.

The final use of network analysis lies in the study of new or "hidden" network structures in organizations. As Tichy (1981) noted, "All organizations consist of multiple networks. . . . These networks may overlap considerably or be quite separate" (p. 227). Some of these multiple networks may involve interest groups or political coalitions that are in no way identified in the rationally ordered world of the organization chart. An information network might differ greatly from an influence network and any given member's network role may change from one type of network to another. If we really want to understand how organizational communication influences virtually every other aspect of organizational life, we need to uncover and compare all of the different networks that comprise any given system of organizational communication.

Although functionalist scholars have not been completely oblivious to such shadowy networks as coalitions, Stevenson, et al. (1985) pointed out that early organizational theorists ignored these structures by assuming that all organizations have simple and well-defined goals. March and Simon (1958) were the first to call attention to conflict over organizational goals. Cyert and March (1963) extended this idea by discussing competition between conflicting coalitions that might arise in an organization, but functionalist scholars never really explored the political implications of such coalitions. Given their traditional objectives of explaining organizational effectiveness and goal-setting, functionalists found it more convenient to simply treat management as a "normally dominant" coalition in order to focus on managerial control and coordination of organizational processes (Stevenson, et al.).

In addition to coalitions, other interest groups may provide the basis for special types of organizational networks. For example, John Van Maanen and Stephen Barley (1984) have shown that "occupational communities" can exert substantial influence over organizational dynamics. An occupational community is a group of people defined by membership in a particular profession or craft (e.g., lawyers, physicians, engineers, police, nurses). These groups develop their own networks—networks that cut across work group, hierarchical, and even organizational lines. Occupational communities develop and reinforce powerful values, vocabularies, and identities among their members. Since individuals' loyalties may be tied much more strongly to their membership in an occupational community than to membership in the work organization, such communities "possess a potentially useful resource to both support and oppose specific organizational policies" (Van Maanen & Barley, p. 334).

Limitations of Network Analysis

Despite the apparent utility of network analysis, Weick (1976) warned researchers to exercise caution when using such techniques. He believes that any technique based on interaction data (who talks to whom) is best suited for revealing tight couplings—"the most visible and obvious couplings . . . the least crucial to understanding what is going on in an organization" (p. 9). In fact, the risks of network analysis may not be as great as Weick claims because the technique allows one to define linkages based on strength and importance as well as frequency of interaction. When these criteria are used, networks that include few liaisons or bridge links or that reveal isolated groups may indicate the loose coupling characteristic with which Weick is concerned. Use of nondirective interviews with methods designed to produce graphic displays of networks also may help in deciding which areas of a network are tightly or loosely coupled.

In addition to the concerns voiced by Weick, there is a second practical but often overlooked limitation in network analysis. Because network data are very difficult to obtain and to analyze, network analysis frequently is conducted with a "snap-shot" approach that provides a picture of the organization at a fixed point in time. However, a study conducted by Stork (1988) on a new research division in a large corporation provides evidence that network structures change over time. It is important to remember that a network is defined by the patterns of interaction that occur among organization members. While some of these patterns may be relatively stable, others are not. It could be very misleading to assume that the results of a network analysis in the present will accurately reflect the structure of the network in the future.

Finally, as we noted earlier, network analysis often depends on memory-based reports of organization members' interaction with one another. This technique is limited not only by the accuracy of members' recollections, but also limited by the need for most if not all of the members in the network to respond to the survey. If an analysis is based on data that does not include reports from many of the members in the network, it will provide an inadequate picture of the communication network.

Summary The concepts of communication structure and function are central ideas in the functionalist perspective of organizational communication. Functions are activities of a system that serve some purpose or objective. Structure is reflected in the linkages or relationships between elements in a system. Function and structure are closely related concepts in organizational communication. Although functionalists usually assume a direct connection between effective organizational performance and effective communication functions and structure, functions and structures of different groups and political coalitions within the same organization may clash when they pursue multiple and conflicting goals.

Communication functions often are classified as production, maintenance, and innovation, although some scholars like to add a fourth category, the human function. This classification scheme is useful, but many instances of organizational communication do not fit easily into these categories.

The concept of communication structure can be defined in at least two different ways. The traditional way treats structure as a system of pathways or channels through which messages flow. This point of view is associated with a basic distinction between formal and informal systems of communication.

Formal communication usually is associated with the use of officially designated channels. Since these channels generally are specified by a hierarchical system of authority, formal communication is described according to the directions of message flow in a hierarchy (i.e., downward, upward, and horizontal). Informal communication usually is associated with the grapevine. Grapevine communication involves a great deal of information (only a portion of which consists of rumors), usually occurs in cluster transmission patterns, is fast, and is more often accurate than inaccurate.

Although the concepts of formal and informal communication are very useful, there is no uniformly accepted distinction between the two systems. Communication structure can be understood in other ways. In particular, structure can be defined as the actual patterns of interaction that occur among members within a network of relationships. These patterns can be studied with a technique known as network analysis, which reveals the linkages between organization members, including group structures, bridge links, liaisons, isolates, and other network roles. Network analysis can indicate the correspondence between expected and actual networks, identify patterns of horizontal communication, provide clues about the extent to which members are integrated in the organization, and reveal multiple or hidden network structures. The technique may also be useful for inferring tight and loose coupling characteristics in an organization.

Discussion Questions/ Activities

1. Observe some episodes of communication in an organization and attempt to classify them according to production, maintenance, innovation, and human functions. How well does the classification system work?
2. Does it really make any difference whether we define communication structure as a system of channels for messages or as patterns of interaction? Why or why not?
3. Consider the theories presented in chapter 3. How would each of these theories view communication functions and structure?
4. Suppose that we have asked each member of a five-person "organization" to estimate the number of times that he or she interacts with each of the other members during a specified time frame. We have entered each person's report in the matrix below by finding the row with that person's name, then recording the estimates of interaction frequency under the columns associated with the other four. For simplicity, the reports of each pair in our example are identical or very similar. For example, Doaks reports eighteen contacts with Marley, and Marley reports twenty with Doaks.

	Doaks	Monte	Smith	Ching	Marley
1 Doaks		5	10	5	18
2 Monte	5		10	20	5
3 Smith	10	10		10	10
4 Ching	5	18	10		5
5 Marley	20	5	10	3	

Draw a diagram that places those who interact more frequently close together and those who interact less frequently further apart from each other. Connect the individuals with lines to represent linkages. Compare your diagram to those of others in the class.

Case Study   Chain of Command

Paul Ward had wanted to work in advertising since high school. When he was promoted to assistant director of O'Toole Oil and Tool's advertising department, he was a very happy man. The pay was great, and his boss encouraged Paul to be creative. It was the sort of job that suited Paul very well. He was amiable, outgoing, and soon made new friends all over the company, particularly with a group of employees who got together every Thursday night to play poker.

Paul's interests went beyond advertising and poker. He particularly enjoyed working with personal computers. Although he had never taken any computer classes in college, he found working with computers to be fun and easy. At work, he had implemented a number of programs to keep track of the department's budget and advertising plans, as well as had implemented a thorough system to file information about the various media in which O'Toole bought advertising space.

At home, Paul also enjoyed working with the computer he had bought for his personal use. One night, he got the idea that he could write a program that could help the warehousing department keep better control of the ordering of supplies. His friend, Harry Liu, a warehouse supervisor, had been complaining at the regular Thursday night poker game about his problems in monitoring orders. He said that he had repeatedly reported the problems to his boss, but hadn't received any response. So, each night for a week, Paul finished dinner and then went to work writing the program. He even skipped that week's poker game in order to finish the program. When the program was ready, he took it to Harry. He showed Harry how to use it, and Harry seemed to think that the program would work very effectively! Paul was pleased with himself and left the program with Harry so that Harry could show it to the director of warehousing.

Two weeks later, the director of advertising, Jane Bales, called Paul into her office. Jane asked Paul to sit down, and then sat down on a chair next to him.

"You know Paul, I'm not mad about this at all. I think you're a bright person and a real asset to the company. But you have ruffled a lot of feathers over in manufacturing, and I'm afraid you're due for a real chewing out."

"What's up Jane? What are you talking about?" asked Paul.

"It's that computer program you conjured up," Jane replied. "Ralph Ames, the vice president of manufacturing, is real upset that you skipped him over when you gave the program directly to your friend in warehousing. Ames thinks that nothing new should happen unless he personally approves it. He runs a tight ship over there and he doesn't like any interference."

"I wasn't interfering," Paul said, "I was just playing with my computer and thought I could make the jobs in warehousing a little easier."

Jane waited for Paul to calm down. She really wasn't upset with Paul, but she knew that Ames wasn't going to let the matter drop without making sure that Paul had been reprimanded for his actions. Jane didn't want to hurt Paul's feelings, but Ames was, after all, an important vice president. Jane began Paul's lesson.

"You see Paul, Ames is from the old school. He'll sit in a staff meeting and talk about his days in the Korean War, when a lot of Americans died because too many guys were giving orders they weren't supposed to give. He really believes that there should be one boss for each person and that things need a tight rein if quality is to stay up and costs to stay down. You skipped him when you went to warehousing, and Ames doesn't like to be skipped on any matter, let alone matters that he feels are his to control."

"I wonder why Harry took the program without saying anything about how Ames might react?"

Jane responded, "You mean the warehouse supervisor? Well, that's how Ames found out. When Harry went to him for approval to install the program."

"Well, I'm sorry. It's just that I thought it was a good idea, and I really wanted to let Harry evaluate the program for me by putting it to a real test."

"I know Paul, and I'm not blaming you. But Ames is upset, and he'll stay upset till you go over and apologize for what you've done."

"You want me to see Ames?" asked Paul.

"Yes, Paul, he's waiting for you now. Go on over and take your medicine. I'll buy your lunch today when you get back."

Paul sat outside Ames office for a half hour, waiting for Ames. Paul rehearsed what he was going to say again and again, and then Ames' secretary told Paul to go in. Inside the office, Ames sat behind his desk and pointed at the chair across from it. Paul sat down.

"So you're the new kid who likes to cut corners, huh? Well, young man, let me tell you that kind of behavior killed a lot of young fellows back in Korea. . . ."

1. What can you infer from this case about the "rules" of formal as well as informal communication in this company? How do the two systems seem to work in this company?
2. Why do Paul and Ames have very different understandings of the rules of communication in this company?
3. What communication functions are accomplished in Paul's interactions with Harry, with Jane, and with Ames?

References

Albaum, G. (1964). Horizontal information flow: An exploratory study. *Academy of Management Journal, 7,* 21–33.

Albrecht, T. L., & Ropp, V. A. (1982). The study of network structuring in organizations through use of method triangulation. *Western Journal of Speech Communication, 46,* 162–178.

Albrecht, T. L. (1984). Managerial communication and work perception. In R. N. Bostrom (Ed.), *Communication yearbook 8* (pp. 538–557). Beverly Hills, CA: Sage.

Alexander, E. R., III, Helms, M. M., & Curran, K. E. (1987). An information processing analysis of organization information adequacy/abundance. *Management Communication Quarterly, 1,* 150–172.

Barnard, C. (1938). *The functions of the executive.* Cambridge, MA: Harvard University Press.

Brillouin, L. (1962). *Science and information theory.* New York: Academic Press.

Chase, A. B. (1970). How to make downward communication work. *Personnel Journal, 49,* 478–483.

Culbert, S. A., & Eden, J. M. (1970). An anatomy of activism for executives. *Harvard Business Review, 48,* 140.

Cyert, R. M., & March, J. G. (1963). *A behavioral theory of the firm.* Englewood Cliffs, NJ: Prentice-Hall.

Daly, J. A., Falcione, R. L., & Damhorst, M. L. (1979). *Communication correlates of relational and organizational satisfaction.* Paper presented at the annual meeting of the International Communication Association, Philadelphia.

Daniels, T. D., & Spiker, B. K. (1983). Social exchange and the relationship between information adequacy and relational satisfaction. *Western Journal of Speech Communication, 47,* 118–137.

Davis, K. (1953). Management communication and the grapevine. *Harvard Business Review, 31,* 43–49.

Davis, K. (1968). Success of chain-of-command oral communication in a manufacturing management group. *Academy of Management Journal, 11,* 379–387.

Davis, K. (1972). *Human behavior at work.* New York: McGraw-Hill.

Eisenberg, E. M. (1984). Ambiguity as a strategy in organizational communication. *Communication Monographs, 51,* 227–242.

Farace, R. V., Monge, P. R., & Russell, H. M. (1977). *Communicating and organizing.* Reading, MA: Addison-Wesley.

Fayol, H. (1949). *General and industrial management* (Constance Storrs, Trans.). London: Sir Isaac Pitman.

French, W. L., Bell, C. H., Jr., & Zawacki, R. A. (1983). *Organization development: Theory, practice, and research* (2nd ed.). Plano, TX: Business Publications.

Glassman, R. B. (1973). Persistence and loose coupling in living systems. *Behavioral Science, 18,* 83–98.

Goldhaber, G. M. (1990). *Organizational communication* (5th ed.). Dubuque, IA: Wm. C. Brown.

Goldhaber, G. M., Yates, M. P., Porter, D. T., & Lesniak, R. (1978). Organizational communication: 1978. *Human Communication Research, 5,* 76–96.

Harris, S. G., & Sutton, R. I. (1986). Functions of parting ceremonies in dying organizations. *Academy of Management Journal, 29,* 5–37.

Hellweg, S. (1987). *Organizational grapevines: A state of the art review.* In B. Dervin & M. Voight (Eds.), *Progress in the Communication Sciences,* vol. 8. Norwood, NJ: Ablex.

Jacoby, J. (1968). Examining the other organization. *Personnel Administration, 31,* 36–42.

Kanter, R. M. (1977). *Men and women of the corporation.* New York: Basic Books.

Katz, D., & Kahn, R. L. (1978). *The social psychology of organizations* (2nd ed.). New York: John Wiley & Sons.

Koehler, J. W., Anatol, K. W. E., & Applbaum, R. L. (1981). *Organizational communication: Behavioral perspectives* (2nd ed.). Holt, Rinehart & Winston.

Koehler, J. W., & Huber, G. (1974). *Effects of upward communication on managerial decision making.* Paper presented at the annual meeting of the International Communication Association, New Orleans.

Koontz, H., & O'Donnel, C. (1955). *Principles of management.* New York: McGraw-Hill.

Krivonos, P. (1976). *Distortion of subordinate to superior communication.* Paper presented at the annual meeting of the International Communication Association, Portland.

Level, D. A. (1959). *A case study of human communication in an urban bank.* Unpublished doctoral dissertation, Purdue University, West Lafayette, IN.

Maier, N., Hoffman, L., & Read, W. (1963). Superior-subordinate communication: The relative effectiveness of managers who held their subordinates' positions. *Personnel Psychology, 26,* 1–11.

March, J. G., & Simon, H. A. (1958). *Organizations.* New York: Wiley.

Mellinger, G. D. (1956). Interpersonal trust as a factor in communication. *Journal of Abnormal and Social Psychology, 52,* 304–309.

Miles, R. (1965). Keeping informed: Human relations or human resources? *Harvard Business Review.*

Nomura, R. (1981). West learns Japanese ways: Executives wear work clothes. *Neihon Keizai Shimbum.* Translation Service Center, The Asia Foundation.

Ouchi, W., & Jaeger, A. (1978, April). Type Z: Organizational stability in the midst of mobility. *Academy of Management Review,* 305–314.

Pace, R. W., & Boren, R. (1972). *The human transaction.* Glenview, IL: Scott, Foresman.

Penley, L. E. (1982). An investigation of the information processing framework of organizational communication. *Human Communication Research, 8,* 348–365.

Planty, E., & Machaver, W. (1952). Upward communication: A project in executive development. *Personnel, 28,* 304–318.

Read, W. H. (1962). Upward communication in industrial hierarchies. *Human Relations, 15,* 3–15.

Rehder, R. (1981, April). Newly emerging nontraditional organizations: What American and Japanese managers are learning from one another in the productivity race. *Business Horizons,* 63–70.

Richards, W. D. (1971). *An improved, conceptually based method for analysis of communication network structure of large complex organizations.* Paper presented at the annual meeting of the International Communication Association, Phoenix. (ERIC Document Reproduction No. ED 064876)

Richards, W. D. (1974). *Network analysis in large complex organizations: Techniques and methods.* Paper presented at the annual meeting of the International Communication Association, New Orleans. (ERIC Document Reproduction No. 098626)

Roberts, K. H., & O'Reilly, Ill, C. A. (1974). Failure in upward communication: Three possible culprits. *Academy of Management Journal, 17,* 205–215.

Smith, R. L., Richetto, G. M., & Zima, J. P. (1972). Organizational behavior: An approach to human communication. In R. Budd & B. Ruben (Eds.), *Approaches to human communication.* Rochelle Park, NJ: Hayden Books.

Smith, G. L., & DeWine, S. (1987). *An investigation of the relationship between organizational commitment and information overload/underload.* Paper presented at the annual meeting of the Central States Speech Association, St. Louis.

Spiker, B. K., & Daniels, T. D. (1981). Information adequacy and communication relationships: An empirical examination of 18 organizations. *Western Journal of Speech Communication, 45,* 342–354.

Stech, E. L. (1983). *An empirically derived model of formal and informal communication in work units.* Paper presented at the annual meeting of the International Communication Association, Dallas.

Stevenson, W. B., Pearce, J. L., & Porter, L. W. (1985). The concept of "coalition" in organization theory and research. *Academy of Management Review, 10,* 256–268.

Stork, D. (1988). *Work and social communication networks: Their development in a young organization.* Paper presented at the annual meeting of the International Communication Association, New Orleans.

Tichy, N. M. (1981). Networks in organizations. In P. C. Nystrom & W. H. Starbuck (Eds.), *Handbook of organizational design* (Vol. 2). London: Oxford University Press.

Tompkins, P. H. (1962). *An analysis of communication between headquarters and selected units of a national union.* Unpublished doctoral dissertation, Purdue University, West Lafayette, IN.

Tompkins, P. H. (1967). Organizational communication: A state of the art review. In G. Richetto (Ed.), *Conference on organizational communication.* Huntsville, AL: NASA, George C. Marshall Space Flight Center.

Trujillo, N. (1985). Organizational communication as cultural performance: Some managerial considerations. *Southern Journal of Speech Communication, 50,* 201–224.

Van Maanen, J. W., & Barley, S. R. (1984). Occupational communities: Culture and control in organizations. In B. M. Staw & L. L. Cummings, (Eds.), *Research in organizational behavior,* vol. 6. Greenwich, CT: Jai Press.

Walton, E. (1961). How efficient is the grapevine? *Personnel, 28,* 45–49.

Weick, K. E. (1976). Educational organizations as loosely coupled systems. *Administrative Science Quarterly, 21,* 1–16.

Weick, K. E. (1979). *The social psychology of organizing* (2nd ed.). Reading, MA: Addison-Wesley.

Zaleznik, A. (1970). Power and politics in organizational life. *Harvard Business Review, 48,* 47–60.

Outline

The Concept of Organizational
  Culture
    Functionalist Perspective
    Interpretivist Perspective
Studying Organizational Culture
    Fantasy Theme Analysis
    Metaphor Analysis
    Analysis of Reflexive Comments

Communication and Cultural
    Change
    Forces Influencing
        Organizational Culture
    The Symbolic Manager
    A Final Caution
Summary
Discussion Questions/Activities
Case Study
References

Communication and Organizational Culture

5

In chapter 4, we concentrated on the idea that organizational communication can be understood by examining its functions, structure, and the levels at which it occurs in an organization. These concepts have been employed for many years in the study of organizational communication (even though Farace, Monge, and Russell's version of structural functionalism was not published until 1977). More recently, an entirely different way of studying organizations has provoked a great deal of interest. The basic idea in this new approach is that organizations can be studied with the same concepts and methods that are used to study cultures.

While the study of culture is a long-standing tradition in the field of anthropology, the concept of **organizational culture** is a relatively recent development. Within the past few years, many scholars and practitioners have become intrigued with the idea that organizations have cultural features. Some even assert that an organization literally *is* a culture and that organizational communication is a *performance* of this culture (Pacanowsky & O'Donnell-Trujillo, 1984). One recent and very popular cultural perspective of organizations is presented in Deal and Kennedy's *Corporate Cultures* (1982). Wright's (1979) *On a Clear Day, You Can See General Motors,* Maccoby's (1976) *The Gamesmen,* and Kanter's (1977) *Men and Women of the Corporation* also have been called studies of organizational culture.

What comes to mind when you think about the word *culture?* Do you think of the history, values, beliefs, language, and modes of expression as part of the culture of a particular people or nation? Or do you think of culture as their customs, folklore, and artifacts? If you associate any of these elements with culture, you have at least some sense of the concepts that have been used to study and understand cultures. In this chapter, we will describe the concept of organizational culture, functionalist and interpretivist perspectives of culture, some communication-based methods of studying organizational culture, and the process of change in organizational culture.

The Concept of Organizational Culture

In a fundamental sense, a culture exists when people come to share a common frame of reference for interpreting and acting toward one another and the world in which they live. This common frame of reference includes language, values, beliefs, and interpretations of experience. It is reflected in customs,

Table 5.1 Comparison of Functionalist and Interpretionist Orientations to Organizational Culture.

	Functionalism	Interpretivism
Goals	Develop and change organizational culture to produce organizational effectiveness	Describe and criticize organizational culture according to the meanings that it makes possible to members
Definition of Culture	Artifacts of organizational life such as stories, myths, legends, and rituals	Common interpretive frame of reference; a network of shared meanings
Activities	Promote managerial control over cultural artifacts through management of symbolism	Study meanings and themes in members' organizational sense making, as revealed in symbolic discourse

folkways, communication, and other observable features of the community, including rites, rituals, celebrations, legends, myths, and heroic sagas (Bormann, Howell, Nichols, & Shapiro, 1982).

For many years, anthropologists have used the concept of culture to study nations, communities, and even tribal groups, but the discipline of anthropology has never settled on a uniform definition of culture. The term is used in several different ways. The same problem occurs in organizational studies. Although there is consensus among scholars in various fields that the concept of culture can be applied to organizations, there are different ways of defining organizational culture.

Smircich (1981) pointed out that both functionalist and interpretivist scholars have written about and produced studies of organizational culture, but she argues that these two groups understand organizational culture in entirely different ways. To the functionalist, a culture is something that an organization *has*—a set of characteristics that the organization possesses. The interpretivist sees culture as what the organization *is*—the essence of organizational life. The basic differences between the two approaches to organizational culture are summarized in table 5.1.

Functionalist Perspective

According to Smircich, functionalism always has been concerned with the actions that organizations can take to ensure their "continued survival in an essentially competitive situation" (p. 3). This translates into discovering the right combinations of organizational variables that promote effectiveness. Consequently, functionalist research is characterized by studies of variables such as structure, size, technology, leadership, and communication. Eventually, functionalists added cultural variables to those that they typically study in recognition that organizations not only produce goods and services, but they also produce "cultural artifacts, e.g., stories, myths, legends, rituals, that are distinctive" (p. 3).

The kinds of artifacts that Smircich identified are, in effect, the concrete, objective features of a culture. Functionalists study these artifacts in much the same way that they would study any other observable feature or organizational behavior. In line with their traditional concern for regulation of organizational processes, functionalists usually want to know how to develop and change an organizational culture in order to make the organization more effective. Strategies for change usually emphasize managerial control over the observable features of culture (e.g., goals, practices, language, rites, rituals, sagas, and the content of orientation and indoctrination programs).

Deal and Kennedy's *Corporate Cultures,* a very popular book in business circles during the early 1980s, provides an interesting example of the traditional functionalist viewpoint. Deal and Kennedy regard organizational culture as a kind of identity for a corporation. Management is supposed to develop and foster commitment to this identity by propagating desired beliefs and informal rules that influence behavior, by celebrating desired organizational values through rites and rituals, and by creating legends through sagas that glorify the adventures, exploits, and successes of organizational heroes and heroines.

According to Deal and Kennedy, corporate executives should try to build a "strong" culture for two reasons. First, organizational effectiveness can be increased simply by letting employees know what is expected of them. A strong culture provides this information both formally and informally. Second, a strong culture "enables people to feel better about what they do, so they are more likely to work harder" (p. 16). For example, the use of rites, rituals, and sagas helps to legitimize and justify various forms of organizational behavior by answering such questions as: Who are we? What do we do? Why are we here? (Bormann et al., 1982).

What is a strong culture? For Deal and Kennedy, strong culture means a highly cohesive organization in which members are fully committed to organizational goals. In their words, a strong culture exists only when "everyone knows the goals . . . and they are working for them" (1982, p. 4). It follows, then, that organizations characterized by competing values and divided loyalties have "weak" and fragmented cultures.

Interpretivist Perspective

Like the functionalist, the interpretivist also is concerned with uncovering the frame of reference shared by organization members, but the interpretivist understands this frame of reference in a different way. Smircich (1981) describes the difference between functionalist and interpretivist ideas about organizational culture:

Social action becomes possible because of consensually determined meanings for experiences which to an external observer may have the appearance of an independent rulelike existence. What looks like an objective and real world to the Functionalist researcher is seen by the Interpretivist researcher to be a product of interaction processes whereby meanings for experience are negotiated and then continually sustained through the course of interaction. (pp. 5–6)

In other words, the observable, tangible world of social action (i.e., behavior) is based on organization members' sharing of subjective meanings. To the interpretivist, organizational culture is understood only as a network of shared meanings. Consequently, the interpretivist describes organizational culture according to the meanings that it makes possible for its members and the ways in which the culture itself is enacted or "performed" through communication (Pacanowsky & O'Donnel-Trujillo, 1982).

Interpretive studies of organizational culture are characterized by an explicit focus on symbols and themes that are revealed in symbolic discourse (communication). According to Smircich, these themes "show the ways the symbols are linked into meaningful relationships . . . they specify the links between values, beliefs, and actions" (p. 7). Presumably, the interpretive research is primarily concerned with revealing these linkages rather than with connecting organizational culture with traditional functionalist concerns for organizational efficiency and effectiveness.

Studying Organizational Culture

While some scholars argue that the methods of functionalism and interpretivism can be combined in studying organizational communication (e.g., Faules, 1982), many of the ideas associated with the study of organizational culture are new to functionalism. Functionalism usually is concerned with developing general knowledge about relationships among organizational communication variables with data drawn from many types of organizations (e.g., the relationship between openness and job satisfaction in superior-subordinate communication or the effects of different problem-solving methods on group effectiveness). The methods usually are quantitative and statistical. There are some *qualitative* functionalist studies of organizational culture, but these studies are scientific classifications of observable cultural variables.

If the study of organizational culture is intended to reveal the meanings and interpretations of organizational life made possible by a cultural frame of reference or to understand the process by which culture is created, transmitted, and changed through communication, then interpretivist methods are the most appropriate for this purpose. In order to show how interpretive scholars study organizational culture, we will describe three methods that rely on analysis of organizational communication: fantasy theme analysis, work on metaphor analysis, and analysis of reflexive comments.

Fantasy Theme Analysis

Each of us tries to make sense of and give meaning to objects, events, and the things that other people do and say. We do so from our own frames of reference. According to Ernest Bormann (1981), one's frame of reference is a private symbolic world. Symbolic convergence occurs when the private worlds of two or more people meet or come closer together.

Bormann believes that symbolic convergence occurs within a group of people (e.g., an organization) primarily through a process of sharing **fantasies.** Most of us think of fantasies as nothing more than figments of someone's imagination—illusions or daydreams that have no connection with reality. This is not quite what Bormann has in mind. He defines a fantasy as a "creative and imaginative interpretation of events" that includes both real and imagined elements. In this context, a fantasy is something like a "fish story"—the tale about the big one that got away.

We continually create fantasies in our interactions with others. For example, perhaps you and your friends have shared stories about particular professors at your college. A favorite professor might be portrayed in these stories as almost godlike—benevolent, dynamic, and wise beyond any possible description. A less-favored professor might be characterized as a dull-witted sluggard who can barely find the classroom, let alone stumble through a lecture, or as a slave-driving ogre who imposes outrageous demands and expectations on students.

These stories are based on facts—on real events—but they also are dramatized in the telling. They are embellished, exaggerated, and made more colorful. After awhile, the dramatized image becomes a part of the reality for the group. For example, "I can tell you for a fact that Professor Doaks always flunks at least 25 percent of the class." Or, "Everybody knows that Professor Smith is one of the top ten people in her field of study."

Group fantasies serve a very important purpose. They provide the basis for or they reinforce common beliefs, goals, values, and wishes within a group. Fantasies often are reflected in stories, anecdotes, and inside jokes that are told within the cultural community. Sometimes, a story has several different variations, but all versions reflect a common theme (e.g., the ones about professors who give unexpected assignments just when you are already buried in work). This common theme is called a **fantasy type.** Shared fantasies and fantasy types may be organized in a unified **rhetorical vision** in which organization members share "a broader view of the organization and its relationship to the external environment, of the various subdivisions and units of the organization, and of their place in the scheme of things" (Bormann, p. 6).

Earlier, we mentioned that an "us-them" orientation characterizes the management-labor relationship in many organizations. Such an orientation involves a rhetorical vision about the character of the relationship, the meanings that the two groups have for each other, and the meaning of the relationship for the organization. Suppose an organization is characterized by Theory X values. In this type of organization, managers might believe that employees are lazy, unproductive, irresponsible, and untrustworthy. The managers are most likely to share various stories that reinforce this belief. There may be stories about employees who steal *half the company,* who sleep on the job *at least three times a week,* who call in sick, then *go fishing,* and who are *always late for work.*

Employees in this organization probably regard management as profiteering, exploitive, abusive, and also untrustworthy. Stories may abound in work groups and union meetings about the times that management has tried to *take away everything* from workers, fired people for *no reason at all,* or *deliberately covered up management blunders.*

The italicized portions of these examples represent elements that, as Bormann puts it, may be creatively interpreted. The stories themselves are grounded on factual events, but they are highlighted with superlatives, hyperbole, and metaphors. Each group shares stories with fantasies and fantasy types that not only express but also reinforce and proliferate its beliefs about the other group. The fantasies are grouped under broader metaphors that anchor the rhetorical vision. A **metaphor** is a means of understanding one thing by relating it to another.

Robert Blake, the television actor who has played Father Hardstep on the series *Hell Town,* Baretta, and Joe Dancer, illustrates the use of metaphors. Blake, who is infamous for his battles with television executives, likes to refer to them as "The Suits" in a voice that almost drips with contempt. In two short words, he successfully conjures up an image of managers as tight, stuffy, insincere, and arrogant.

How does one identify fantasies and rhetorical visions in an organization's life? Bormann, Howell, Nichols, and Shapiro said, "A good way to discover the symbolic world of a group is by collecting dramatic messages, stories, histories, and anecdotes that they tell and retell" (1982, p. 83). This may be done by observing and listening to members interact with one another, by interviewing organization members, by examining the organization's official written record (mission statements, official memos, reports, and newsletters), and even by using the unofficial written record (underground newsletter, songs, or graffiti).

Once the materials are gathered, they are subjected to a **script analysis** in which organizational life is treated as a drama with characters acting in scenes. The messages, stories, and other materials are examined to identify the following features:

1. heroes, heroines, villains, and their goals and values;
2. the action line, including the things that characters do to achieve their goals;
3. the scene where the action takes place and the forces that are presumed to control the action.

After analyzing a number of stories and messages in this way, the researcher should be able to identify common themes that, like the moral of a story, reflect shared fantasies and rhetorical visions within the organization. One may then be able to understand the values that prevail within the organization or within its various groups and the realities of organizational life as members construct and understand them.

Metaphor Analysis

Susan Koch and Stan Deetz (1981) believe that metaphors are at the heart of an interpretive process "that continually structures the organization's reality" (p. 16). Familiar phrases such as "the game of life," "hard as a rock," "working at a snail's pace," and "running like a well-oiled machine" are all metaphorical statements. The game, the rock, the snail's pace, and the machine are metaphors for other things.

Koch and Deetz argue that metaphors literally anchor our understandings of experience. When we speak metaphorically of life as a game and organizations as machines, these metaphors reflect our interpretations of life and of organizations. Since interpretation not only depends on language but many other factors as well, metaphors may not be as powerful as Koch and Deetz suggest. Cohen (1977) summarized a number of studies suggesting that some forms of interpretation and thinking can occur without any particular reference to language. If this is the case, the metaphors that people use sometimes may be little more than convenient figures of speech. Nevertheless, common metaphors that occur in organizational communication could provide important clues to the meanings that members hold for their experiences.

Metaphor analysis begins by recording the talk of organization members in interviews and discussions. Data also may be obtained from written records. Interview questions should be free of any metaphors that might bias results. For example, "Tell me how the organization *operates*" might prompt the interviewee to answer with "machine" metaphors.

The next step is to isolate metaphors by examining all of the statements in the data. This process is complicated and depends on the researcher's familiarity with different types of metaphors and on the researcher's ability to recognize them in statements. Metaphors may be created in several ways, but four of the most common rely on **spatial orientation, activities, substances,** or **entities.** For example, "I have authority *over* this matter" relates the idea of authority to a spatial orientation, *over*. "We're breathing new life into the company" relates an organizational process to a well-known biblical metaphor for the activity of creation *and* it relates the organization to the substance of a living organism. "We're just one big, happy *family* at Burger Queen" relates the organization to the entity, *family*.

After metaphors are identified, they are worked through progressively until it is possible to identify all of the main or "root" metaphors used in the organization. In many cases, subcultural divisions yield more than one main metaphor. We observed this condition firsthand in a large research laboratory in which conflicts between a technical training department and a human resource development department seemed to be related to differences in root metaphors. The technical training group understood itself as a family, while the human resource development group characterized itself as a small business. The technical trainers spoke in terms of being a good neighbor to others in the laboratory "community." The supervisor was regarded literally as the head of a household. The human resource group described its function as "marketing services" to "client" groups in the laboratory. The supervisor was "the boss," who controlled and coordinated the business. The business group regarded the family group as unprofessional. The family group regarded the business group as rigid, competitive, and cold. Simply identifying these metaphors did not resolve the conflicts between the two departments, but it did seem to help members to make more sense of the conflicts.

One good example of the scholarly application of metaphor analysis is a study by Smith and Eisenberg (1987) of labor-management conflict at Disneyland. Late in 1984, the conflict culminated in a twenty-two day strike by unionized employees. This is an interesting work because, as Smith and Eisenberg put it, "Disneyland occupies a special place in the American psyche" (p. 367). Moreover, the Disney corporation has used its success and strong public image as a foundation for becoming a consultant to other companies on management methods and employee relations. Yet, the study by Smith and Eisenberg revealed a somewhat troubled state of affairs in fantasyland.

Smith and Eisenberg began their study in 1983 through eight interviews with Disneyland managers. Later, in 1985, they conducted intensive audiotaped interviews of thirty-five hourly employees, who were men and women of various ages and lengths of employment, and who represented six different divisions of Disneyland operations. In order to analyze the interviews, they applied what they describe as a "semantic sorting process in which coherent patterns or clusters of meaning emerged around specific metaphorical expressions" (p. 371). In effect, this means that they examined all of the metaphorical expressions in the interview transcripts for shared understandings that could be characterized with a root metaphor. Smith and Eisenberg provide an example of this process:

Expressions
[used by interviewees]: "The cast members"
"The show"
"Our costumes"
"The Disney image"
"The Disney role"

Shared understanding:
Disneyland has actors, costumes, stories to be enacted on stage and an audience to be entertained.

Organizational entailment:
Disneyland puts on a show.

Root metaphor:
Disneyland is a drama.

Smith and Eisenberg found two root metaphors, namely, *drama* and *family* that characterized employees' experiences at Disneyland. They applied both of these metaphors to interpret various aspects of the labor-management conflict. Disney himself played a primary role in shaping the drama metaphor and supporting it with the image of Disneyland as an oasis for friendly family entertainment. This vision was adopted thoroughly by employees. After his death, the management philosophy began to shift, at least as it was perceived by employees. In response, employees cast themselves as defenders and care-takers of Disney's founding vision, but they revised their interpretation of that vision by *extending* the concept of family to Disney employees. Friendliness not only referred to employee-customer relationships (the original intention), but it also referred to relationships among employees themselves (the new interpretation). In short, Disneyland not only provided family entertainment; it *was* a family itself. This new interpretation was one that even Disney himself "may not have fully endorsed [and it] led ultimately to conflict with management" (p. 373).

As explained by Smith and Eisenberg, the family metaphor was accepted uncritically by most employees and by many managers. It was believed to characterize employee relationships and the management-employee relationship. But with increasing competition from other theme parks, take-over attempts, high-level corporate resignations, and greater operating costs, management gradually placed a rather unfamily-like emphasis on the bottom-line, including a wage freeze and elimination of benefits in its efforts to operate at a profit. Management tried to redefine the family metaphor (e.g., family life sometimes is hard and families sometimes have to make sacrifices), but employees rejected management's new idea of family. Management's bottom-line view "was perceived by many as constituting a breach of Disney's caring philosophy" (p. 374).

Another very important feature of this particular study occurs in the way in which Smith and Eisenberg draw conclusions from their analysis. You may recall from chapter 1 that interpretive approaches to organizational communication regard the organization as a negotiated order composed of pluralistic interests. These approaches generally attempt to avoid the managerial bias of functionalism and the worker-oriented bias of critical theory. The interpretive point of view clearly is reflected in Smith and Eisenberg's efforts to find a way for management and labor groups at Disneyland to share a common understanding of their organization:

A conscious reconsideration of the drama metaphor might help reconcile management with employees, and past with present. An appeal of the drama metaphor lies in its ability to subsume some of the interpretations of both management and employees; it simultaneously retains the image of the park as *family* entertainment and permits a *business* orientation. (p. 378)

Analysis of Reflexive Comments

Analysis of reflexive comments is a technique originally described by Harre and Secord (1972). It has been applied in organizational communication studies by Tompkins and Cheney (1983), Cheney (1983), and, more recently, by Geist and Chandler (1984). Like other interpretive methods, this technique focuses on language and discourse in order to reveal meanings and understand human behavior.

What is a **reflexive comment?** To begin with, we human beings generally are not only aware of our actions in social situations, but we also *know* that we are aware. We are both actors and observers of our own actions. This is reflexiveness. It allows us to make comments in the form of explanations, justifications, criticisms, and so forth about our own behavior. If we make a comment about an anticipated action, it is a **plan.** If it is about ongoing action in the present, it is a **commentary.** If it is a statement made after the occurrence of an event or action in a way that justifies or gives reasons for the occurrence, it is an **account.** According to Tompkins and Cheney, these comments reveal "the meanings and interpretations actors assign to items in their environment and the rules . . . that they follow in monitoring their social behavior" (p. 129).

Analysis of reflexive comments may be conducted in various ways. Cheney used analysis of accounts (after-the-fact comments) in a study of the relationship between identification and decision-making processes. He began with the assumption that identification as "the process by which individuals link themselves to elements in the social scene" (p. 342) is acted out in organizational decision making. For example, decisions or evaluations of alternatives might be based on identification with the entire organization, a department, or even a specific individual. Cheney's procedures were developed to explore the extent to which identification helps to explain decision making.

Cheney collected accounts through moderately scheduled interviews (i.e., interviews in which major questions are preplanned, but follow-up questions intended to probe interviewee answers are generated spontaneously in the interview). Questioning proceeded through five steps:

1. the employee's role(s) in the organization (i.e., duties, decision making, responsibilities);
2. "accounts" for specific decisions;
3. "accounts" for decision-making practice (especially useful when an employee does not isolate specific episodes);
4. the employee's identifications;
5. actions by the company that either foster or discourage identification with the organization. (p. 349)

The accounts obtained from interviews were analyzed in order to identify decision premises (the reasons or factors taken into account that influence a decision), the sources of decision premises (person, group, or other authority from which premises are acquired), and targets of identification (people, groups, or organizational units with which an employee identifies). Cheney used this information to answer questions about the relevance of organizational values and goals in employees' evaluations of decision alternatives, about overlap between identification targets and sources of decision premises, about changes in identification and decision making as length of employment increases, and about the influence of organizational policy on identification and decision making.

Geist and Chandler (1984) used reflexive comments to study the exercise of influence in group decision making, although the major purpose of their investigation involved a test of five claims made by Tompkins and Cheney regarding the value of account analysis:

1. Accounts express decisional premises or rules.
2. Accounts point to the sources of rules.
3. Accounts enumerate social units for whom the decision maker was prepared to give accounts at the time of making the decision.
4. Accounts reveal identification targets.
5. Accounts help to explain the nature of the identification process. (pp. 136–139)

In their investigation, Geist and Chandler videotaped weekly staff meetings of a psychiatric health-care team, then transcribed the tapes in order to analyze decisions related to the care and treatment of patients. Instead of soliciting accounts through interviews with organization members, Geist and Chandler attempted to locate reflexive comments in a record of *ongoing group interaction*. They did this by examining any statement that a group member made that revealed the member's values or targets of identification. Consequently, their data appeared to include not only accounts but also plans and commentaries. They concluded that analysis of reflexive comments will serve all five of the functions that Tompkins and Cheney claimed.

Communication and Cultural Change

Our primary purposes in this chapter have been to define the concept of organizational culture and to consider how it is studied in the field of organizational communication, particularly from an interpretivist viewpoint. Nevertheless, we want to conclude the chapter by returning to the concept of cultural change that is associated with the functionalist perspective of organizations because this concept has received a great deal of attention in the American business community.

When the functionalist concept of organizational culture was first popularized, it was so novel and attractive that it quickly became the newest cure-all in corporate America's search for excellence. Many management and communication consultants began to talk to their clients about "changing corporate culture" with an emphasis on managerial control of the culture's objective features. However well-intentioned this idea may be, the concept of cultural change through management direction has been questioned. For example, the October 17, 1983, issue of *Fortune* magazine carried this revealing cover headline: "The Culture Vultures: Can They Help Your Company?" The cover story inside pointed out that change in organizational culture involves many factors that are *not* controlled by unilateral management decisions. As the uncharitable metaphor "vulture" implies, the article took a myopic view of consultants who are telling executives to attempt large-scale change in organizational culture.

Forces Influencing Organizational Culture

Deal and Kennedy's ideal (1982) of a strong culture certainly has intuitive appeal, but it is important to realize that the culture of an organization arises from many forces, interests, and organizational constituencies. These forces include not only top management, but they also include middle- and lower-level managers, various labor groups, the divisions and departments of the organization, occupational groups, the community, and the environment in which the organization functions. Such forces sometimes work in harmony, sometimes conflict sharply, and generally coexist in a dynamic tension and interplay that shape the culture of the organization.

To say that the culture of an organization is based on a commonly held frame of reference for interpreting and acting toward one another does not mean that everyone in the organization is the same or that members have the same values and commitments. As we noted earlier, many large organizations are characterized by an "us-them" frame of reference in management-labor relations. The frame of reference is shared by the two groups as a central feature of organizational culture, but it has different implications for each. An organizational culture can be very "strong" in the sense that it virtually institutionalizes differences, conflicts, and bitter rivalries between groups or even promotes inefficient or ineffective practices in ways that are extremely resistant to change.

We do not mean to imply that organizational cultures are unchanging or that they cannot be changed. We do mean to make it clear that attempts at cultural change through unilateral control by any particular segment of an organization probably are futile. Even Allan Kennedy, Deal's coauthor, admits that cultural change "costs a fortune and takes forever" (Uttal, 1983, p. 70).

The Symbolic Manager

Despite the obvious difficulties in attempting management-directed change of organizational culture, the concept of the **symbolic manager** who directs planned cultural change has gained great popularity. The symbolic manager not only controls and coordinates the technical organization, but the symbolic manager also shapes the symbolic world of organizational values, beliefs, and commitments through the power of rhetoric.

An example of the importance of rhetoric in symbolic management is reflected in a statement that ABC television correspondent Jeff Greenfield once made about Ronald Reagan. When asked by Ted Koeppel to explain Reagan's ability to bring public pressure on the Congress, Greenfield said, "Ronald Reagan knows how to mobilize the power of the spoken word." What did Greenfield mean? Basically, he meant that Reagan could gain public acceptance of his positions and public *commitment* to his plans of action by rhetorically identifying his goals and values with the needs, desires, and hopes of his constituency. This ability prompted many politicians and journalists to refer to Reagan as "the Great Communicator."

The symbolic manager in an organization faces the task of a U.S. president on a smaller scale but uses similar tools in order to accomplish the task. According to the experts, the manager who wants to shape organizational culture must personify these values and communicate this persona to others. The manager must be able to rhetorically dramatize the rites and rituals of organizational life. He or she must also be able to glorify the forces of good through heroic sagas and to villify the forces of evil that work against the good, true, and right purposes of the organization.

Deal and Kennedy suggest that symbolic managers must have the courage and conviction either to remain within or to step outside the prevailing culture of the organization as circumstances require. Good symbolic managers recognize that change is slow and often painful, but they will focus their energies on the change process and on sending messages about change to others in the organization. They will plan for change, monitor the progress of change, and be prepared to repeat the process if necessary.

Can symbolic management profoundly change an organizational culture? There is evidence of some dramatic success stories. One of the best-known cases of large-scale cultural change is reflected in the efforts of Giant Foods Corporation during the 1960s. With the guidance of Paul Forbes, the company began to recognize alarming conditions in central-city areas where many of its stores were located—conditions including urban unrest, high unemployment, and lack of job skills among the people who comprised the majority of Giant Food's customers. Under the direction of the management, Giant literally reconstructed its corporate philosophy and supporting values to meet the needs of citizens in the communities that it served. The company changed the composition of its work force, gave skills and jobs to the unemployed, and became an active partner with communities in economic development. Giant implemented on-the-job training and equal opportunity employment long before federal legislation supported either concept. The programs established the company firmly as a valued member of the communities that it served. Of course, the success of Giant's program can be attributed not only to management perseverance, but also can be attributed to substantial support and reinforcement from the communities that benefited from this cultural change.

Above and beyond the managers' action to symbolically direct or shape organizational culture, many advocates of change also point out that building culture depends on recruitment, selection, and indoctrination of new organization members. Either stability or change can be introduced through this process. Many organizations seem to concentrate on stability and maintenance by selecting new members whose values already fit the existing culture (Kanter, 1977). Sometimes, a deliberate effort is made to bring in "mavericks"—people who have different values and beliefs and will try to move the organization in new directions (Ugbah, Brammer, Compton, Ray, & DeWine, 1985).

Once new members are selected, orientation, indoctrination, and training become important vehicles for socializing and acculturating them. Such programs must be constructed carefully to introduce and encourage commitment to important values. Involvement in the system of informal communication also plays a key role in the new members' acquisition of values.

A Final Caution

Despite the appeal of various strategies for promoting cultural change, the safest attitude toward the concept probably is one of healthy skepticism, particularly where the strategies rely on unilateral management direction. Given the economic, political, and social forces that affect contemporary organizations, it is possible that managers and even entire organizations will end up on the caboose of the train of events that leads to cultural change.

One of the most important forces in organizational change today is the composition of the work force. The walls of the "all white, all male" management and professional fortress have at least been breached, if not broken down, and the new players (women and minorities) appear to want some new rules (Wood & Conrad, 1983). For example, in the twenty-five years between 1960 and 1985, the number of women in the work force more than doubled, increasing from 22 million to 47 million, while the number of men in the work force increased by less than one-third (Bureau of Labor Statistics, 1985b). During the same period, the number of women in management and administrative positions more than quadrupled, giving women a 32 percent share of the management and administrative job market. In some specific professional occupations, the number of women increased anywhere from 500 percent to 1,100 percent (Bureau of Labor Statistics, 1985a). By 1989, women comprised 45 percent of the total work force and held over 40 percent of all management and administrative positions (Bureau of Labor Statistics, 1989).

Changes in gender, ethnic, and racial composition of organizations are not the only factors at work. Age also is playing a more critical role in the dynamics of organizational life. The awesomely enormous post-World War II "baby boom" generation has swelled the ranks of middle management and the professions. Boomers compete intensely with one another for the few available chances at promotion, while blocking the mobility of those who arrive later. At the same time, senior citizens—the most rapidly growing age-group—are expressing less willingness to simply be put out to pasture, while younger people, especially those who are partners in dual-career marriages and/or have families, are struggling to balance their own needs with demands of the workplace. All of these factors may add up to change in organizational cultures whether or not top managers want this change.

Many theorists in organizational change and development have argued for years that organizations and their managers must begin to think in terms of "change management," since change in our era of history is inevitable (French, Bell, & Zawacki, 1983). Although some of these theorists share the managerial control orientation of functionalism, they generally have emphasized that the planned change process cannot be based on unilateral control. Planned organizational and cultural change requires *multilateral* participation and cooperation among all of the organization's constituents.

One good example of the multilateral approach occurred in Chrysler Corporation's recovery from near bankruptcy in the early 1980s. While Lee Iacocca assumed the role of the symbolic leader, even in Chrysler's advertising messages, his initiative would have faltered and perhaps failed completely without the support of the United Auto Workers (UAW) and an organization-wide effort. Labor and management both made major concessions, giving up compensation and status. The UAW president joined the corporate board of directors. The assembly-line workers themselves coined the slogans that symbolized "the New Chrysler Corporation" and its recovery.

But even cooperative change provides no assurance of lasting effects. Cultural change is easy when the alternative is losing your job. Once Chrysler recovered from its woes and paid off its federally guaranteed loans, the spirit of cooperation during the crisis gave way somewhat to the old forces of divisiveness and mistrust.

Summary

In a fundamental sense, a culture exists when people come to share a common frame of reference for interpreting and acting toward one another and the world in which they live. This common frame of reference includes language, values, beliefs, and interpretations of experience. It is reflected in customs, folkways, artifacts, communication, and other observable features of the community, including rites, rituals, celebrations, legends, myths, and heroic sagas.

Although there is consensus among scholars in various fields that the concept of culture can be applied to organizations, there are different ways of understanding organizational culture. Functionalists study cultural artifacts in much the same way that they would study any other observable feature of organizational behavior. In line with their traditional concern for regulation of organizational processes, functionalists usually want to know how to develop and change an organizational culture in order to make the organization more effective.

To the interpretivist, organizational culture is understood only as a network of shared meanings. Consequently, the interpretivist describes organizational culture according to the meanings that it makes possible for its members and the ways in which the culture itself is enacted or "performed" through communication. Interpretive methods such as fantasy theme analysis, metaphor analysis, and analysis of reflexive comments are intended to serve this purpose.

Bormann defines a fantasy as a "creative and imaginative interpretation of events" that includes both real and imagined elements. He believes that symbolic convergence occurs through sharing of fantasies within groups. Group fantasies provide the basis for and reinforce common beliefs, goals, values, and wishes within a group.

Fantasy themes are identified through a script analysis in which organizational life is treated as a drama with characters acting in scenes. Messages, stories, and other materials including written records, jokes, songs, and even graffiti are examined to identify heroes, heroines, villains; the action line, including the things that characters do to achieve their goals; the scene where the action takes place and the forces that are presumed to control the action.

Metaphor analysis assumes that metaphors literally anchor our understandings of experience. Metaphor analysis begins by recording the talk of organization members in interviews and discussions. The next step is to isolate metaphors by examining all of the statements in the data. Three of the most common types of metaphors rely on spatial orientation, activities, or substances and entities.

Reflexive comments are statements of explanation, justification, criticism, and so forth, that we make about our own action. According to Tompkins and Cheney (1983), these comments reveal "the meanings and interpretations actors assign to items in their environment and the rules . . . that they follow in monitoring their social behavior" (p. 129). Organizational communication researchers have gathered reflexive comments through use of moderately scheduled interviews with organization members and by taping and transcribing comments from group meetings.

While interpretive methods appear to be best suited for the study of organizational culture, the functionalist concept of the symbolic manager who directs planned cultural change has gained great popularity. The symbolic manager not only controls and coordinates the technical organization, but the symbolic manager also shapes the symbolic world of organizational values, beliefs, and commitments through the power of rhetoric.

The idea of controlling and changing organizational culture through unilateral management direction is controversial because an organizational culture is influenced by many different forces. This is one of the reasons why organizational change and development theorists have argued that organizations and their managers must begin to think in terms of "change management," based on collaboration through multilateral participation of all organizational constituencies.

Discussion Questions/ Activities

1. Write a brief characterization of the culture at your college. Identify some of the major rites, rituals, myths, legends, and other symbolic artifacts of this culture. What do these artifacts reveal about the meaning that members of the college community have for their experiences?
2. What are some of the essential differences between functionalist and interpretivist perspectives of organizational culture? Are the goals of the two perspectives compatible or incompatible?
3. Studying culture sounds like a problem for an anthropologist. Why should the field of organizational communication be interested in organizational culture?
4. What do you think about the concept of the symbolic manager? What is a symbolic manager, exactly? How much influence do you think such a person can exert to either change or reinforce an organizational culture?

Case Study "Doing Anything Always Does Something"

O'Toole Oil and Tool has a long and profitable history. The company was started three generations ago by an enterprising emigrant whose temper was as red as his hair. "Gramps" taught his son the business; "Pops" taught his son "Red"; Red, the current executive director and chair of the board, is teaching Junior. Each generation has led the business into new and profitable ventures so that now the company is diversified into manufacturing oil drilling equipment, pneumatic valves, air compressors, plastics, and insulating materials.

Although Gramps hasn't much to say nowadays, he still attends the board meetings in what Pop calls the "nurse-operated" wheel chair. Pops likes saying that Gramps still appreciates a "pretty sight." Pops takes an active role with the firm's major clients and maintains an office in the firm's corporate headquarters, but after Pops' retirement fifteen years ago, Red has led the company.

Red received his education when it wasn't fashionable to be a human relations manager. Yet, Red ran O'Toole Oil and Tool in an almost textbook version of the best of human relations theory. Long-range corporate decisions were still made by him, but the bulk of the firm's planning and coordination was left to an executive board comprised of the divisional vice presidents. Each division was organized so that its decision making involved each of the division's managers, right down to the department level. Red set a good model for the rest of the firm; he was always supportive of his employees and genuinely concerned for their well-being. The employees of O'Toole were proud of their firm and its accomplishments. The pay was good, the benefits were excellent, and the work environment was ideal. Employee turnover was never a problem. The employees knew that advancements were granted from within the company and that the advancements depended on their abilities. This advancement policy went all the way up to the executive level. However, everyone also knew that an O'Toole would always be the chief, at least for the next generation.

Junior was a quick learner. Right after receiving an engineering degree, Junior started working in the same machine shop where Gramps began the business. After learning how to run the equipment, Junior went to engineering and then to marketing. Now she was being brought into the corporate office. For the first time, she was attending the board meetings by sitting in a chair instead of sitting on her grandfather's knee.

Pops was beating his hands on the mahogany table of the executive conference suite, swearing and bellowing in the fashion he had learned from his father. Red was storming, too, something he had learned from Pops. The board members were watching Junior intently, trying to hide their embarrassment, for the language of the O'Toole's wasn't the best. Junior didn't mind the language as much as the board members. After all, Junior had grown up with Pops and Red swearing at everything. Junior's mother had explained a long time ago that the O'Toole temper was "just a way of talking, nothing to ever be afraid of." Red stared right at Goldbloom, the firm's corporate lawyer.

"Al, do you mean that woman is going to court and we could lose a $100,000?"

"Yes Red, she's going to court. But, I don't think a judgment would be that high. She might get $25,000 or maybe $50,000 tops. But, it's bad press, especially if we're after more federal contracts."

"DAMMMMN!" Pops screamed. "You mean we're gonna pay $50,000 cause some dumb SOB got the hots for a typist?"

"Actually Pops, there's more to this sexual harassment case than just having the hots. After she turned the guy down, he got pretty upset. The woman has witnesses who will testify that her manager was abusive."

"You mean I have guys who are beating their secretaries?" asked Red. Goldbloom replied, "No Red, they're verbally abusing them."

"Verbally? What did the guy say?"

Goldbloom shuffled through his notes. "According to the report, the guy said 'Get your fat ass behind your machine; I'm going to have you typing crap till your fingers fall off.' "

Pops was even more enraged. "Well, what's wrong with that? That ain't no damn $50,000 dollar sentence."

Korzybski, vice president of employee relations, knew the time had come for a corporate policy on sexual harassment. "No Red, it isn't, but we need to do something to prevent this from happening in the future. Goldbloom's people will take care of this matter without it costing us too much, but we can't afford to have this sort of thing tarnish our reputation or cause our people to think this is a problem we're not doing anything about."

Red recognized that Korzybski was a man of few words. Korzybski asked for something only when he thought it necessary. "Alright," Red replied, "but I don't want our managers afraid of opening their mouths when somebody needs a chewing out. We're a family here, and family ought to be able to say what they want to say. We've been around for fifty years doing business and working with people the same way since Gramps. No one has ever sued us till now, and I don't want it happening again."

Korzybski nodded. "You're right Red, but sexual harrassment isn't something you want happening in your family, is it? And if we take care of the problem, we won't have to worry about being sued. Let's form a task force to formulate a policy."

Pops looked at Junior, "You do it Junior, you know what these people want. You head the task force and write a policy we can all live with." Red nodded his head, and Junior knew the assignment had been made.

Gramps started muttering, "Junior, Junior, Junior" until Junior got up and went over to his wheelchair. Gramps smiled at Junior and leaned his head as if to share a secret. Junior knew the routine and moved in closer to Gramps' mouth. Gramps whispered, "Doing anything always does something."

1. How would you describe the "culture" of O'Toole Company based on the information in this case?
2. What does the use of symbols and language by the participants in the case reveal about their shared meanings and socially constructed reality?
3. How does the interpretive concept of negotiated order apply to this case?

References

Bormann, E. G. (1981). *The application of symbolic convergence communication theory to organizations.* Paper presented at the SCA/ICA Conference on Interpretive Approaches to the Study of Organizational Communication, Alta, UT.

Bormann, E. G., Howell, W. S., Nichols, R. G., & Shapiro, G. L. (1982). *Interpersonal communication in the modern organization* (2nd ed.). Englewood Cliffs, NJ: Prentice-Hall.

Bureau of Labor Statistics (1985a, June). *Handbook of labor statistics.* Washington, DC: U.S. Department of Labor.

Bureau of Labor Statistics (1985b, July). *Employment and earnings.* Washington, DC: U.S. Department of Labor.

Bureau of Labor Statistics (1989, December). *Employment and earnings.* Washington, DC: U.S. Department of Labor.

Cheney, G. (1983). On the various and changing meanings of organizational membership: A field study of organizational identification. *Communication Monographs, 50,* 342–362.

Cohen, G. (1977). *The psychology of cognition.* London: Press.

Deal, T. E., & Kennedy, A. A. (1982). *Corporate cultures: The rites and rituals of corporate life.* Reading, MA: Addison-Wesley.

Deetz, S. A. (1982). Critical interpretive research in organizational communication. *Western Journal of Speech Communication, 46,* 131–149.

Faules, D. (1982). The use of multi-methods in the organizational setting. *Western Journal of Speech Communication, 46,* 150–161.

French, W. L., Bell, C. H., Jr., & Zawacki, R. A. (1983). *Organization development: Theory, research, and practice* (2nd ed.). Plano, TX: Business Publications.

Geist, P., & Chandler, T. (1984). Account analysis of influence in group decision making. *Communication Monographs, 51,* 67–78.

Harre, R., & Secord, P. F. (1972). *The explanation of social behavior.* Totawa, NJ: Littlefield, Adams.

Kanter, R. M. (1977). *Men and women of the corporation.* New York: Basic Books.

Koch, S., & Deetz, S. A. (1981). *Metaphor analysis of social reality in organizations.* Paper presented at the SCA/ICA Conference on Interpretive Approaches to Organizational Communication, Alta, UT.

Maccoby, M. (1976). *The gamesmen: The new corporate leaders.* New York: Simon & Schuster.

Pacanowsky, M. E., & O'Donnell-Trujillo, N. (1982). Communication and organizational cultures. *Western Journal of Speech Communication, 46,* 115–130.

Pacanowsky, M. E., & O'Donnell-Trujillo, N. (1984). Organizational communication as cultural performance. *Communication Monographs, 50,* 126–147.

Smircich, L. (1981). *The concept of culture and organizational analysis.* Paper presented at the SCA/ICA Conference on Interpretive Approaches to Organizational Communication, Alta, UT.

Smith, R. C., & Eisenberg, E. M. (1987). Conflict at Disneyland: A root-metaphor analysis. *Communication Monographs, 54,* 367–380.

Tompkins, P. K., & Cheney, G. (1983). The uses of account analysis: A study of organizational decision making and identification. In L. L. Putnam & M. E. Pacanowsky (Eds.), *Communication and organizations: An interpretive approach* (pp. 123–146). Beverly Hills, CA: Sage.

Ugbah, S., Brammer, C., Compton, C., Ray, G., & DeWine, S. (1985). *Organizational mavericks and innovation: A triangulation study of culture.* Paper presented at the annual meeting of the Speech Communication Association, Denver.

Uttal, B. (1983, October 17). The corporate culture vultures. *Fortune,* pp. 66–72.

Wood, J. T., & Conrad, C. (1983). Paradox in the experiences of professional women. *Western Journal of Speech Communication, 47,* 305–322.

Wright, J. P. (1979). *On a clear day, you can see General Motors.* Grosse Pointe, MI: Wright Enterprises.

Outline

Traditional Views of Status and
     Power
   Status Symbols
   Types of Power
   Power, Competition, and
     Cooperation
   Social Exchange and Power
Power in the View of Critical
     Theory
   Power and Legitimation
   Power and Organizational
     Structure
   Power, Symbols, and Systematic
     Distortion
   Critical Theory in Organizational
     Communication Research
   Critical Theory versus
     Interpretivism

Conflict
   Sources of Conflict
     Role Conflict
     Value and Goal Differences
     Competition for Resources
     Structural Ambiguity
   Managing Conflict
     Superordinate Goals
     Structural Intervention
     Conflict-Resolution Activities
   Interpersonal Conflict
   Coalitions and Intergroup
     Conflict
   Bargaining and Negotiation
Summary
Discussion Questions/Activities
Case Study
References

Power and Conflict

6

We began this text with the simple observation that organizations are constituted through communication. The constitutive function of communication, however, depends upon the manner in which it is used to exercise two of the most pervasive phenomena in organizational life. These two phenomena are **power** and **conflict.** Russell (1983) claims that power is *the* fundamental concept in the social sciences, analogous to the place of energy in physics. The importance of power in organizational life was once expressed quite neatly, though somewhat grimly by W. Charles Redding during some informal comments to members of the International Communication Association's organizational communication division. "We must not forget," said Redding, "that organizations run on subservience." In effect, subservience means being submissive or acting as a servant. Consequently, organizational power is tied to **status.**

Conflict, as Putnam and Poole pointed out, is "an instrinsic part of organizational life" (1987, p. 550). The conflict and power are inextricably related. While organizational action depends on the exercise of power, the exercise of power often leads to conflict. In turn, conflict situations, by definition, involve interdependent actors who have the power to constrain or interfere with each other's goals. In a sense, conflict entails the exercise of power.

Traditional Views of Status and Power

In hierarchically structured organizations, differences in members' status and power are a simple fact of life. These differences, in large part, create the "top to bottom" character of contemporary organizations. Even within groups, different members are accorded varying degrees of power and status. Just as some members of a group have more power and status than others, some groups within an organization have more prestige and are better able to exert influence than other groups.

Status refers essentially to the rank or importance of one's position in a group. Traditionally, power has been regarded as any means or resource that one person may employ to gain compliance and cooperation from others (Secord & Backman, 1964). As Dahl (1957) expressed it, power is the capacity of actor A to get actor B to do what actor B would not otherwise do. Traditional views of power also recognize that it involves the ability to control the agenda or plan of action in a situation, to suppress issues in discussions and decision making that would pose a challenge or create controversy (Bachrach & Baratz, 1962).

Status and power should not be regarded as traits that are inherent in a particular position. Generally, it is more appropriate to think of status and power as conditions that other members of the group accord to a person in a given position. The two conditions are closely related. The ability to exercise power enhances status; status enhances the ability to exercise power.

Status Symbols

Koehler, Anatol, and Applbaum (1981) noted that members of organizations often "strive as much for the symbols of status as for the factors which underlie status" (p. 203). Status symbols that signify the rank of a position may include titles, money, office space and furnishings, privileges, secretarial and clerical support, location of parking places, and more. Randolph Quick, a sociology professor at a small liberal arts college, tells a story about one organization in which he consulted that went to great lengths to maintain status distinctions with symbols. Offices of vice presidents in the company had wall-to-wall carpets, while those of lower-level executives had area carpets. On one occasion, an office once assigned to a vice president was reassigned to a lower-level manager. Before the new occupant was permitted to move in, top management ordered the maintenance department to cut a 12–inch strip from each side of the carpet.

Types of Power

Status distinctions facilitate the use of power by people in higher positions to secure compliance from those in lower positions. In part, the power that actor A has over actor B is determined by B's dependence on A (Emerson, 1962). Status distinctions create barriers that reduce the dependency of those in higher positions upon those in lower positions. Such barriers help to maintain a power difference that favors the higher position.

French and Raven (1959) provided an analysis of social power that has become a classic model for classifying the forms of power applied in organizational relationships. They described five basic types of power: reward, coercive, referent, expert, and legitimate.

Reward and **coercive power** are closely related. The former involves the ability to control and apply rewards, either directly or indirectly, whereas the latter is based on the ability to control and apply punishments. One's reward or coercive power over others depends on at least two factors. First, those things that can be controlled or mediated (e.g., salary increases, promotions, work assignments, demotions, suspensions, terminations) must be perceived as rewards or punishments by others. Second, a person has these forms of power only to the extent that he or she is perceived as being willing and able to apply or at least mediate rewards and punishments. As Secord and Backman (1964) pointed out, "If a supervisor has seldom rewarded or punished an employee, either directly or indirectly, his reward and coercive power is likely to be weak" (p. 275).

Referent power depends on identification. Identification sometimes is defined as the desire to be like another person. In this sense, actor A has referent power with actor B to the extent that B wishes to be like A. The concepts of identification and referent power, however, are somewhat more complex. According to Kelman (1961), identification involves a desirable, satisfying, and self-defining relationship with another person or group. Consequently, a given individual or group has referent power with a person to the extent that this person engages in certain behaviors because these behaviors maintain the relationship or the definition of self that is anchored in the relationship.

One form of identification occurs when one person literally models another's behavior. A second form involves different but complementary behaviors. Identification also occurs when a person adopts the attitudes and values of a self-defining group.

Expert power is based on the perception that a person possesses some special knowledge that is required to solve a problem, perform a task, or decide on a course of action. A person wields expert power with others if they follow his or her course of action in the belief that the individual "knows more" than they do about what should be done in the situation.

Legitimate power is based on acceptance of internal norms and values regarding authority and the right to exercise authority. People accept influence from someone in a certain position because they believe this person has the right to exercise the authority accorded to that position. For example, a company president might create a team leader position for a project group and decree that the position has certain status and powers. Functionally, however, status and power depend on group members' acceptance. In other words, the team leader exercises legitimate power only to the extent that team members accept the leader's authority to exercise controls over the members' behavior.

We are not certain that the five types of power that French and Raven describe exhaust all of the possible sources of power in organizational groups. At the very least, some types of power that do not fit clearly within the traditional definitions of these five categories seem to exist. One important type to communication theorists is **information power.** The fact that a superior has information that may be of use to a subordinate, for example, can provide power over the subordinate through the superior's choice to share or withhold the information.

Suppose the supervisor of a work group has personal knowledge of plans for company expansion that would affect the number and type of internal promotion possibilities during the next two to three years. Members of the work group do not have direct access to this information because it has not been announced officially, but they know that the supervisor has been fully informed. The supervisor capitalizes on the situation by sharing the information only with those group members who are cooperative and compliant. This is not a case of expert power in which the subordinates follow a course of action in the belief that the supervisor has special knowledge about that course of action. Rather, the subordinates comply with the supervisor in an effort to obtain information. The situation is not quite the same as reward power because the information in this case is merely a means for the possibility of attaining a reward.

Power, Competition, and Cooperation

The existence of power differences in organizational relationships generally is regarded as a factor that inhibits cooperation and effective communication. We assume that a certain tension and incompatibility must always exist between high-power and low-power parties in any relationship. Recent research by Tjosvold (1985) suggested that this assumption is not necessarily true. In particular, Tjosvold found that social context influences "how superiors use their power to interact with subordinates" (p. 281). Specifically, both high- and low-power superiors interacted more constructively and supportively with subordinates in a cooperative context rather than in either an individualistic or competitive context. In other words, defining a task context as cooperative, competitive, or individualistic had more of an effect on the superior's mode of interaction with subordinates than did the superior's level of power in the relationship. Moreover, high-power superiors in a cooperative context actually used their power to aid subordinates.

Social Exchange and Power

Social psychologists have claimed for many years that every exercise of power involves some form of exchange (Secord & Backman, 1964). One does not exact compliance from another without incurring some kind of cost—giving up something in return for compliance (Harsanyi, 1962). How often, for instance, have you done something for another person with the implicit understanding that the other person owes you a favor? This is an example of how the exchange process works. In many cases, the cost incurred for the exercise of power is a reduction in its effectiveness. You can use reward just so many times before its recipient is satisfied and no longer desires the reward. Referent power may be exhausted by asking for one favor too many. The receiver of information or expert knowledge becomes less dependent on the provider.

The ability to exercise power over another also is dependent on choices that the other person makes. Power depends on a person's perceptions of the alternatives available in a given situation. Some studies indicate that people who are asked to act in a particular way are less likely to comply as their alternatives increase. When they are asked to *avoid* acting in a particular way, they are more likely to comply as alternatives increase (Meyers, 1944; Tannenbaum, 1962).

Suppose, as a member of a project team, that you are asked by the team leader to endorse plan A as a solution to a project problem. You do not especially like plan A, but the only alternative is a very poor plan B, so you are likely to comply with the team leader. On the other hand, if there are some attractive alternatives to plan A such as plans C, D, and E, it may be much less likely that you will comply with a request to endorse plan A. Now suppose you are asked to *reject* plan A. If plans C, D, and E are good alternatives, the cost of compliance is small. You can reject plan A and still have some options. Should an inferior plan B provide the only alternative to plan A, you may be very unlikely to comply by rejecting plan A. If you do choose to comply with the team leader, the cost to the leader may be a loss or reduction of the power base used to gain the compliance.

Power in the View of Critical Theory

Traditional theories of power have tried to describe the forms of power that occur in social processes and have emphasized social exchange explanations for the operation of power. The result is an appealing—but somewhat sterile— account power that fails to account for the connection between power and communication, while ignoring the dark side of the subservience to which Redding called attention.

Peter J. Frost, a prominent professor of industrial relations at the University of British Columbia, has advanced four propositions about power that are not explicit in traditional treatments of the concept:

1. Organizational life is significantly influenced by the quest for and exercise of power by organizational actors, which constitute the political activity of organization.
2. Power exists both on the surface level of organizational activity and deep within the very structure of organizations.
3. Communication plays a vital role in the development of power relations and the exercise of power.
4. The manipulation and exercise of power is expressed, in the sense both of actions and relations, as organizational games. (1987, p. 504)

Particularly with respect to communication, Frost points out that communication provides the means for the development and exercise of power. In turn, power creates and shapes communication structure and rules. With respect to power and politics, "the communication medium is never neutral" (Frost, p. 507).

In chapter 1, we provided an introduction to critical theory as a perspective of organizational communication that differs from both functionalism and interpretivism. Critical theory is the perspective that focuses explicitly on a communicative and symbolic approach to power.

For the critical theorist, power is confounded with domination and oppression—conditions in the structure of society and in organizations that scholars should reveal and criticize. But critical theory does something that goes beyond mere complaining about societal oppression. As Dennis Mumby explained, it attempts to show how symbolism can "potentially legitimate dominant forms of organizational reality . . . restricting the interpretations and meanings that can be attached to organizational activity" (1987, p. 113).

Power and Legitimation

Critical theory has its roots in the works of Marx, but real development and articulation of modern critical theory began in Germany during the 1930s at the University of Frankfurt's Institute for Social Research, known more simply as "The Frankfurt School" (Farrell & Aune, 1979). Whatever Marx's original notions about history and society, Soviet-style communism had refined Marxist theory into a purely materialistic philosophy. Like the early machine metaphor of functionalism, materialism reduced explanations for social process to machinelike causal relations that were divorced from questions of human consciousness and values. The Frankfurt School aimed at creating a form of neo-Marxism that addressed dominance and oppression in terms of values and morals (McGaan, 1983). Since the 1960s, this effort has been best reflected in the works of Jurgen Habermas (1968; 1979). The difference between traditional Marxism and Habermas's brand of neo-Marxism is explained clearly by Lee McGaan:

The traditional Marxist argument is that the West will fall as a result of economic collapse brought on by an uncontrollable cycle of inflation and recession. This will lead to class consciousness by workers and bring the revolution. Habermas has shown that . . . the real source of difficulty for capitalistic societies involves problems of **legitimation** [emphasis added] . . . the crisis faced by institutions in the West comes from challenges to the legitimacy of power and function of capitalistic structures . . . .

What Habermas did in developing the concept of a legitimation crisis was to shift the traditional Marxist critique of society from the positivistic and material to the conceptual and moral. Critical theory in this light looks not at the economic relations undergirding social institutions. Instead, it focuses on the conceptual structures which justify the existence of institutions and the relation of those legitimations to real human interests. (p. 5)

In fact, since Western capitalism has managed to remain more or less intact despite the doomsaying of traditional Marxist theory, one of the more interesting issues addressed in modern critical theory concerns why this has happened. While dominance can be achieved through force and coercion, and force and coercion are not unusual in organizations, the maintenance of power in capitalist organizations depends in large part on its legitimation (i.e., the manner in which its use is justified and accepted). Thus, as Robert McPhee (1985, p. 1) pointed out, some of the most prominent examples of modern critical research "concentrate on a single question: how is it, given the alienated and exploitative nature of work in capitalist organizations, that workers cooperate with management, labor at their jobs, and forego resistant stances, without the constant presence of coercion and threat?"

Power and Organizational Structure

In an effort to answer this question, critical theory focuses on the intricate relationships between power and organizational structure. The idea of organizational structure in critical theory is not quite the same thing as the functionalist concepts that we presented in chapter 4. There, we considered structure in terms of formally designated lines of authority and divisions of labor and in terms of communication networks. But you may also remember the basic definition of a *system* that we presented in chapter 3; namely, it is a set of elements and the *rules* that define the relationships among those elements. Structure is realized through these rules, and this is the concept of structure with which critical theory is concerned.

What is the relationship between structure and power? As explained by Stewart Clegg (1975), power arises from the **deep structure rules** of organization and is achieved by controlling those rules. Deep structure rules include shared, unquestioned assumptions that guide our social actions. The organizational rule system provides what Clegg characterizes as a "mode of rationality" by shaping and directing the ways in which we think and act. In this sense, power resides in the "socially structured and culturally patterned behavior of groups and practices of institution" (Lukes, 1974, p. 22). From the traditional viewpoint, power may be the ability of actor A to get actor B to do what B otherwise would not do, but, from the vantage point of critical theory, there is nothing quite so powerful as the assumption within a group that things are or should be a particular way.

Power, Symbols, and Systematic Distortion

Obviously, different rule systems provide us with different ways of organizing our behavior. Thus, Dennis Mumby noted, "Domination involves getting people to organize their behavior around a particular rule system" (1987, p. 115). Borrowing from Gramsci (1971), Mumby says, "The process of hegemony [dominance by one class or group over another] works most effectively when the world-view articulated by the ruling elite is actively taken up and pursued by subordinate groups" (p. 123). How does this occur? How is it that people are induced to adopt and, perhaps more importantly, *maintain* a rule system or mode of rationality that actually disadvantages them? This is where symbols and discourse come into play, particularly in a condition that critical theorists refer to as **systematically distorted communication.**

Systematically distorted communication is a bit like magic. It is illusory. It distorts the reality of a situation. In effect, systematically distorted communication legitimizes hegemony *by making it appear to be something other than what it really is.* In developing the concept of systematic distortion, Habermas (1979) distinguished between communicative action and strategic action. Communicative action is intended to achieve mutual understanding and agreement as a basis for consensual action. Communicative action is joint action. Strategic action is a unilateral attempt at achieving one's own goals and aims. Strategic action may be open. Let's suppose that you are presenting a new policy proposal to a management group. You expect some opposition and you want one of your friends in the group to be very vocal in supporting your proposal. If you say this to your friend in an "upfront," nondeceptive manner, you have been openly strategic. But let's suppose, in an effort to get your friend's support, you say something like this instead:

I really dread this meeting today. I think Bill and June are going to give me some trouble about this proposal. You remember how those two really tried to stab you in the back last year. You know, they actually went around outside of meetings trying to line up support to torpedo that new marketing plan you introduced. I remember how most of us in the group supported it and you got it approved, but those two sure tried to kill it.

In this case, your strategic action is *latent*. While all of the information in your statements may be factual, your real intentions are obscured. There is a "hidden agenda" in the action. If you have deliberately tried to deceive your friend about your intentions, you have engaged in manipulation. Systematically distorted communication also arises from latent stategic action, but it is more complicated than manipulation. In manipulation, one person deceives the other. In systematically distorted communication, "at least one of the participants deceives *himself* about the fact that the basis of consensual action is only apparently being maintained" (Habermas, 1979, p. 208).

In organizations, hegemony may be legitimized through systematically distorted communication in various ways, but systematic distortion in its most basic form can be found in the political functions of organizational **ideology.** An ideology is a set of assumptions and beliefs that comprise a system of thought. Ideology provides the structure for an organization's mode of rationality. In other words, ideology is central to an organization's deep structure. Giddens (1979) contends that ideology functions politically in three ways to privilege the interests of one group over another. A concise summary of Giddens' claims is adapted from Mumby (1987):

1. *Representing sectional interests as universal.* Although the real organization may consist of competing constituencies and conflicting interests (e.g., management versus labor, staff versus line), ideology can tell us, "We're all in this together," (i.e., that the interests of one group really are the interests of all).

2. *Denying or transmuting contradictions.* From the vantage point of critical theory, capitalist society and organizations within capitalist society are fraught with fundamental contradictions. The ownership of the means for producing goods and services is private, yet, in organizations, the production is accomplished through a social process. Ideology can obscure the fundamental nature of these contradictions by making them appear to be nothing more than social conflict. Thus, ideology tells us that decision making is purely rational, when, in fact, it is political, or that we are "all equal here," when, in fact, we are not.

3. *Naturalizing the present through reification.* In effect, reification means that we make a socially constructed reality appear to be concrete (i.e., objective, fixed, and immutable). Ideology reifies meaning by telling us, "This is the way things are." As we pointed out in earlier chapters, the most obvious example of this probably is the concept of organizational hierarchy itself. It is taken to be concrete and is literally the natural order of things, but it has its existence only in shared meanings which shape our actions to fit the idea.

Mumby has added a fourth function, *control* to Giddens' list of three. Perhaps the control function already is implied in Giddens' list, but Mumby wants to make it clear that ideological control is not so much a matter of one group's domination over another as it is the ability of a group or class to make the interests of other groups appear to be consistent with its own. We think it is also important to specifically connect Mumby's idea of control with systematically distorted communication. *Members of dominated groups participate in their own oppression through self-deception by identifying with and actively consenting to the system of hegemony.* When this occurs, we have, as Gramsci (1971) suggested, the condition under which hegemony works best.

Critical Theory in Organizational Communication Research

Critical theory has produced some outstanding studies of power in work and organizational settings (e.g., Burawoy [1979], Clegg [1975], and Edwards [1979]), but it has begun only recently to exert influence in the study of organizational communication. One good example of this kind of research is a study by Mumby on the political use of **narratives,** literally, the use of storytelling in organizations. Mumby examined a story that purportedly was widely disseminated in IBM Corporation and that was told and retold by many members of this company. The story concerns an incident between IBM's chairman, Thomas Watson, Jr., and an IBM employee named Lucille Burger. While the exact form and content of the story might vary somewhat from one telling to another, the basic form published by Martin, Feldman, Hatch, and Sitkin (1983, pp. 439–440) goes this way:

Lucille Burger, a twenty-two-year-old bride weighing ninety pounds, whose husband had been sent overseas, had been given a job until his return. The young woman was obliged to make certain that people entering security areas wore the correct clear identification. Surrounded by his usual entourage of white-shirted men, Watson approached the doorway to an area where she was on guard, wearing an orange badge acceptable elsewhere in the plant, but not a green badge, which alone permitted entrance at her door. "I was trembling in my uniform, which was far too big," she recalled. "It hid my shakes, but not my voice. 'I'm sorry,' I said to him. I knew who he was alright. 'You cannot enter. Your admittance is not recognized.' That's what we were supposed to say." The men accompanying Watson were stricken; the moment held unpredictable possibilities. "Don't you know who he is?" someone hissed. Watson raised his hand for silence, while one of the party strode off and returned with the appropriate badge.

Martin, et al. have studied this story from an interpretive vantage point and have concluded that it conveys two important moral principles at IBM. For higher-level personnel, the moral is that they should certainly obey company policies and rules because even Watson himself does so. For lower-level personnel, the moral is "uphold the rules no matter who is disobeying" (p. 440). In effect, the overall moral is "At IBM, the rules apply to everyone." But Mumby demonstrates how this story can plausibly accomplish all of the political functions of ideology; how the story is, in effect, an instance of systematically distorted communication. Even though its ostensible purpose is to reinforce the morals described by Martin, et al., and every statement in the story may be factually correct, the story nonetheless obscures and mystifies the actual conditions of organizational life at IBM.

As interpreted by Mumby, the story implies that sectional interests are transcended by rules that are designed for the benefit of all, but it obscures the fact that the rules are "created *by* the corporate elite (of which Watson is head) to protect their own interests" (p. 121). The rules at issue in this story "are in place for the benefit of people like Watson, and not for people like Lucille Burger" (p. 121). Moreover, the story denies a fundamental contradiction and is, itself, a contradiction. It portrays Watson as an ordinary person who must obey Burger in her official capacity as an enforcer of the rules, yet also makes him "a larger-than-life figure about whom fables are told" (p. 122). More to the point, it is the fact that Watson really *is* an exception that makes the story compelling. Watson wisely used the occasion to make a dramatic statement about corporate rules by deferring to a relatively low-echelon employee. In fact, he could have walked right by Burger without any consequences at all.

Mumby argues that this story provides a very good instance of reification simply because it can be recounted over and over again as a statement not only about rules, but also about the rationale for enforcing them, not to mention latent statements about sex roles and status differences. In particular, Mumby says, "The story serves to reify ideologically the organizational rule system itself. . . . Lucille Burger's single-minded adherence to the rules reflects not so much a heightened sense of corporate loyalty, but rather an enforcing of the rules *because they exist*" (p. 123). Finally, the story serves the control function because it is not only recounted by high-level executives, but throughout the company as "an example of 'intellectual and moral leadership'" (p. 123). The story itself is actively recounted by employees, and its ideology is taken up and adopted by employees. Its illustration of Burger's commitment to the system is identified and equated with the legitimacy and appropriateness of that system.

Mumby's study of the Watson-Burger story suggests three goals for critical scholarship which are adapted from Deetz (1982):

1. *Richer understanding of naturally occurring events.* Deep structure elements of meaning are largely taken for granted. They shape our actions without much conscious reflection, examination, or questioning. Critical research attempts to produce insights not only for scholars, but also for organization members themselves by calling attention to the deep structure of meaning systems. This is similar to the idea of "consciousness-raising."
2. *Criticism of false consensus.* When we deceive ourselves through systematically distorted communication, the result is false consensus. As Deetz expresses it, false consensus "is reached by the power of definition rather than open discussion" (p. 140). If illusions and the conditions that make them necessary can be overcome, it is possible to have open dialogue among different organizational groups and constituencies. Returning to Habermas, the task of the critical theorist is to identify and criticize strategic action in order to move toward communicative action in society.

3. *Expansion of the conceptual base from which organizational members think and work.* Organization members need to learn how to engage in communicative action in order to have a better understanding of organizational life and to expand their concepts and languages in order to grapple creatively with the problems that confront them.

Critical Theory versus Interpretivism

Obviously, critical scholarship has some affinity with interpretive scholarship as we described it in chapter 5. For example, both perspectives are concerned with organization members' use of symbols and language and with the meanings that are created through discourse. In fact, Deetz even used the label, critical-interpretive, to describe his position in 1982. But there are some important distinctions between interpretive scholarship as we presently understand it and the activities of critical theorists. Most importantly, critical theory sees interpretivism as naive. Its emphasis on the organization as a negotiated order of pluralistic interests is politically naive because it ignores the fact of discrepancies in power and privilege. It is also naive about meaning and symbolism. As explained by Mumby, "While such research adequately describes organizational sense-making at a surface level, it does little to explicate the deep structure process through which certain organizational realities come to hold sway over competing world-views" (1987, p. 113).

One good way to see both the similarities and differences between interpretive and critical scholarship is to compare Mumby's study with the study by Martin, et al. (1983) in which the Watson-Burger story was described. The study by Martin, et al. was an interpretive study in which the story is treated as a moral lesson without any particular political implications. In Mumby's critical analysis, the same story became an exemplar of systematic distortion. It may also be helpful to compare Mumby's study to the study by Smith and Eisenberg (conflict at Disneyland) that we described in chapter 5. Both of these studies address matters of discourse and meaning. Smith and Eisenberg were concerned with shared understandings underlying metaphorical expressions in interview transcripts. Mumby was concerned with the meaning of a commonly recounted story. But Smith and Eisenberg deliberately sought to find some way of reconciling the conflict between management and labor at Disneyland by appealing to the metaphor of drama as common ground for both groups—a basis for a negotiated order. Mumby's objective in his study of narrative is to show how narratives symbolically "impose an order on 'reality' that . . . privileges certain interests over others" (p. 126) (e.g., those of management over those of workers).

Conflict

Most critical theorists are prepared to acknowledge that power is *not* simply imposed by dominant groups on subordinate groups or forced upon the oppressed by the elite. Subordinate groups must accept the legitimacy of the system of hegemony in order for it to work. More importantly, however, the legitimacy of institutional and organizational power can be challenged by these groups. In fact, Habermas's interest in the idea of legitimation was developed through his studies of student protest movements during the 1960s.

Mumby noted, "Even the ostensibly powerless can use organizational structure to their advantage" (1987, p. 114). When the less powerful assert their interests against those of the more powerful, or when persons or groups of roughly equal power find that their goals are incompatible, the result is **conflict.** Conflict is a common yet widely misunderstood phenomenon in group processes and intergroup relations. Classical theorists regarded conflict as an anomaly—an abnormal occurrence that was not supposed to happen under an organizational structure with exhaustive rules and a "fair day's pay for a fair day's work." Human relations theorists developed a better understanding of conflict in organizations, but even they regarded it as a negative and counterproductive force to be avoided (Dessler, 1980). As Redding (1985) noted, even the organizations of the 1980s are overwhelmingly characterized by a mentality of "go along in order to get along." Given the right situation and a good sense of timing, one can become an organizational hero or heroine by challenging the status quo, but more generally, anyone in conflict with prevailing organizational values or managerial prerogatives is quickly labeled a boat-rocker or troublemaker.

No one would deny that uncontrolled conflict can be harmful within groups and organizations. Richard Beckhard (1969) argued, "one of the major problems affecting organization effectiveness is the amount of dysfunctional energy expended in inappropriate competition and fighting between groups that should be collaborating" (p. 33). Conflict, however, also has a functional as well as dysfunctional side. Contemporary organizational theorists stress the point that conflict is an inevitable and even necessary aspect of group and organizational processes (Janis, 1972; Goldhaber, 1990; Robbins, 1977). It should not be suppressed and avoided but confronted, managed, and resolved.

Conflict can bring to the surface issues that require resolution, relieve tensions, and lead to the development of new channels of communication (Koehler, Anatol, & Applbaum, 1981). Avoidance or suppression of conflict leaves underlying issues unresolved. These issues, like Schein's (1969) personal emotional needs will continue to reemerge in forms that hamper the group's task efforts. Even when conflict is successfully suppressed, the effect may be poor decisions and solutions based on badly distorted conceptions of problems and situations.

Irving Janis (1972) identified a phenomenon known as "Groupthink," in which extreme efforts are made to suppress conflict and stop the input of any information that contradicts an established or dominant view. Individual group members surrender their own beliefs and begin to see things only from the group perspective. The group develops a dogmatic commitment to the "moral rightness" of its position and may even believe that it is being persecuted by enemies. Janis argued that the ill-fated Bay of Pigs invasion during John F. Kennedy's presidential administration was a product of "Groupthink." Virtually anyone outside Kennedy's cloistered group of advisors would have said that the concept of invasion to oust Cuba's Fidel Castro was misguided and unworkable, but suppression of competing views, avoidance of conflict, and a quest to gain consensus merely for its own sake resulted in a disastrous decision. Actions by members of the Nixon administration during the Watergate era and Jimmy Carter's decision to attempt a military rescue of American hostages in Iran may also have been products of "Groupthink."

Janis also illustrated how the phenomenon figures into corporate decisions to continue marketing inferior or hazardous products. In a film on the development of "Groupthink," Janis showed how a pharmaceutical company arrives at a decision to market a drug with some extremely dangerous side effects by downplaying the importance and validity of studies demonstrating the hazards. The management team justifies its decision by highlighting the benefits of the product and suggesting that those who have qualms about the drug are "not being team players." The group even develops a vision that it is a heroic paragon of moral virtue in standing behind the product.

Of course, all of these examples of "Groupthink" are easy targets for discussion because they resulted in failed policies or morally questionable decisions. In other cases, decisions that emerge under conditions similar to "Groupthink" are not subjected to such critical scrutiny because they achieve ends that, at least in the short term, appear to be very desirable. For example, when Soviet fighters destroyed Korean Airlines Flight 007, evidence that the Soviets had tragically mistaken the civilian airliner for a U.S. spy plane was supressed and ignored in order to allow for a more convenient interpretation that cast the Russians as perpetrators of terrorism, an interpretation that fit neatly with Ronald Reagan's "Evil Empire" vision of the U.S.S.R. Deviant opinions may also have been suppressed during the deliberations that led to the invasion of Grenada and, later, the incursion into Panama that resulted in the ouster and arrest of Manuel Noriega. If these military exercises had failed, there might have been discussion and "second-guessing" about the conditions under which the decisions were made.

Sources of Conflict

While it is possible to suppress conflict through "Groupthink," the suppression cannot go on indefinitely. Conflict arises from many sources within groups and organizations, including various forms of role conflict, value and goal differences, competition for limited resources, and ambiguity in authority, structure, and procedures.

Role Conflict

As we already have noted, conflict may arise from discrepancies between expected, perceived, and enacted roles. If your perception and enactment of a role differ substantially from the expectations of other members in your group, you may soon find yourself in the midst of controversy and struggle over this discrepancy.

Sometimes role discrepancies are reflected in *intrarole* conflict. Intrarole conflict occurs when a person in a given role is subjected to competing expectations for that role. Professors, for example, frequently struggle with the realization that some students in a course prefer the teacher to function as a discussion leader and facilitator, whereas others regard discussion as a waste of time, preferring a dynamic lecturer instead. Group leaders face a similar situation when some members prefer a democratic style, whereas others clearly are more comfortable with a highly structured autocrat.

Interrole conflict occurs when a person is placed in the position of making a choice between two or more competing roles that demand simultaneous performance. Members of organizations may have several different roles in various groups or may even be responsible for two or more roles in the same group (i.e., the member who wears several hats). Most organization members also have external role obligations (e.g., as a parent, spouse, community member). When mutually exclusive demands arise for enactment of different roles, the stage is set for conflict. If you are a member of two different committees that have scheduled meetings at the same time or the boss asks you to work late on a day when the baby-sitter wants you to pick up your children no later than 5:15 P.M., something has to give!

These first two forms of role conflict only involve conflict to the extent that an individual experiences the stress of mutually exclusive role requirements. Certainly, such conflicts are very important. Indeed, these forms of conflict probably will try your patience and your sanity on a daily basis throughout much of your organizational life. But the forms of conflict with which we are primarily concerned here are those that fit the definition of conflict advanced by Putnam and Poole as "the interaction of interdependent people who perceive opposition of goals, aims, and values, and who see the other party as potentially interfering with the realization of these goals" (1987, p. 552). The remaining sources of conflict all allow for conflict in this form.

Interpersonal role conflict involves competition between two or more individuals for the same role within a group. Such conflict may occur over the leadership position or for choice jobs within a work group. Even the presence of some system for designating role assignments (appointment, promotion, seniority) does not necessarily prevent interrole conflict. We once worked with a research group in which top management officially appointed the team leaders. Some other senior team members felt that they were better qualified for the job. They continually undermined the leader's authority by telling junior team members to ignore his instructions on the grounds that the instructions were erroneous or inappropriate. Even in speaking with us, some of the senior team members would implicitly cast aspersions about the leader's competence. For example, they might say, "Joe's a nice guy, but decision making isn't his strong suit" and "Joe's appointment is just an example of the company's failure to promote qualified women." We do not know whether Joe was incompetent. We do know that most of the complaining senior team members had, themselves, been passd over for promotion to the leadership job. Under the circumstances, even the official sanction of top management could not guarantee Joe's authority in the situation.

Value and Goal Differences.

Conflict is likely to occur when different groups or members within the same group have contradictory values and goals. This form of conflict sometimes arises between production and sales groups in manufacturing companies. The sales group, which is compensated on straight commission, wants rapid production for high-volume sales and quick delivery. The production group desires a slower pace that permits emphasis on quality. The two groups are most likely to clash when sales makes requests for special attention to "rush" orders or when production is slow in meeting schedules.

Conflicts arising from value and goal differences can be deep and very difficult to resolve. Problems and their solutions always seem to be value-laden. There is a problem only to the extent that it is an obstacle to some valued condition. A solution is good or acceptable only to the extent that it fulfills valued conditions. When human values and the goals that arise from these values come into conflict, the result can be anything from rivalry and feuding to all-out warfare. One need only consider the violent reaffirmation of government control at Tianamen Square in the People's Republic of China or, conversely, the literal crumbling of East European communism late in 1989 to realize just how powerful conflicts over values can be.

Competition for Resources.

Different groups and even members of the same group often must draw their resources from a common pool—money for raises or for new positions, supplies, staff support, and funding for projects. The economics of scarcity, which many organizations have been forced to face since the turbulence of the 1970s, has only compounded internal competition for resources. Simply stated, the organizational resource pie is only so large. If one group gets a larger piece, some other group must settle for a smaller one. When group A gets a new person, someone in group B is laid off in order to pay for it. When group B's paperwork receives special priority at the word-processing center, group A's work has to wait. Particularly when competing groups are interdependent, a denial of resources to one so that the other may have them heightens the potential for intergroup conflict and reduces cooperation.

Structural Ambiguity

Conflict often occurs in situations in which authority, responsibility, and procedures are unclear. This form of conflict may take on the appearance of a territorial dispute, with two or more groups claiming jurisdiction over the same organizational function or, conversely, denying responsibility for some problem or area of organizational operations. Consider the case of a federally funded program to assist the hard-core unemployed in obtaining work.

Participants in the program are assigned either to a counselor or a job developer. Those assigned to counselors usually have severe deficiencies in skills or other major problems that would prevent them from being employable. Those who are potentially employable in some occupation are assigned to job developers who are placement specialists. Agency policy makes it clear that counselees are the sole responsibility of the counselor until the counselor decides that they are ready for reassignment to a job developer. There is no policy, however, regarding program participants that job developers are unable to place in employment.

Lately, the counselor at one office has begun to "raid" the job developer's difficult cases by calling them in for special counseling programs and redesignating them as "counseling cases," without consulting the job developer. The job developer, whose performance appraisal is tied directly to the number of program participants placed in employment, is angry about the counselor's unilateral action. The job developer correctly points out that policy makes no provision for these reclassifications, but the counselor retorts, also correctly, "It doesn't prohibit them either!"

Managing Conflict

Dessler (1980) suggested that various strategies for managing conflict can be organized into three categories: establishment of superordinate goals, structural interventions, and conflict-resolution activities.

Superordinate Goals

Where conflict arises as a consequence of competing or contradictory values and goals, the establishment of goals and values that are superordinate to those of the competing parties may reduce conflict. According to Schein (1970), this mode of conflict management requires the identification of goals upon which competing parties can agree and of values that are mutually acceptable. Dessler also noted that the use of special incentive systems may reduce discrepancies between goals of competing parties. For example, some years ago, Sears had trouble understanding why its stores in a certain region would not cooperate with one another on sales and special promotions until someone pointed out that managers were rewarded solely on the basis of individual store performance. Sears started a new policy of rewarding managers not only for sales within their own stores, but also for their production across all stores in a certain area. Reportedly, improvement in cooperation was immediate.

Structural Intervention

Structural interventions involve changes in group structure and relationships. These include third-party mediation or arbitration of a conflict (often by levels of management higher than those represented by the competing parties), reduction of interdependency between groups, reduced sharing of resources, exchange of competing personnel (competing parties are required to assume one anothers' roles), creation of integrators or liaisons between groups, and increased communication between conflicting parties.

Conflict-Resolution Activities.

Conflict-resolution activities have been categorized in several ways. Lawrence and Lorsch (1967) suggested that three basic types of activities exist: confrontation, smoothing, and forcing. Confrontation involves a recognition of an attempt to work through and solve problems surrounding a conflict without suppressing or avoiding it. Smoothing is a form of avoidance or suppression—pretending that sources of conflict are not present in hopes that the conflict will dissipate on its own. Forcing involves an effort to bring the conflict to a resolution by soliciting third-party intervention. In this case, forcing is a type of structural intervention. According to Lawrence and Lorsch, effective organizations are more often characterized by confrontation than by smoothing and forcing.

Dessler's concise, but rather simple, conception of conflict management may imply that conflict management is straightforward and easily accomplished with the right techniques, but many complicated factors influence organization members' choice of strategies, including the level of the conflict itself and the ease with which conflicts can be resolved. Some of the more important factors are discussed in a recent analysis of research on interpersonal and intergroup conflict presented by Putnam and Poole (1987).

Interpersonal Conflict

Putnam and Poole note that most work on interpersonal conflict in organizations has centered on **conflict styles** in superior-subordinate relationships. Conflict style "refers to a characteristic mode or habitual way that a person handles a dispute" (p. 556). Models of conflict style vary somewhat, but most are consistent with an early model proposed by Blake and Mouton (1964) and revised by Hall (1969). The model, presented in figure 6.1, is based on two dimensions: concern for your personal goals in the conflict and the importance of your relationship with the other person in the conflict. Both are rated on a 1 to 9 scale (low to high). Your "style" of conflict presumably can be located by the coordinate of your ratings on these two dimensions. Although there are eighty-one possible coordinates, each coordinate falls into one of five basic style categories.

The 1/1 Avoiding Style. This style is based on low concern for personal goals and for the relationship. The avoider refrains from arguing, withdraws from the situation, or otherwise tries to remain disconnected from the conflict.

9/1 Forcing Style. The forcer has high concern for personal goals in the conflict, but low concern for the relationship. Consequently, the forcer is aggressive, competitive, and confrontational in an effort to get his/her way.

1/9 Accommodating Style. When high concern for the relationship is coupled with low concern for personal goals, the result is an accommodating style. The accommodator glosses over differences or downplays disagreements in an effort to maintain the relationship.

9/9 Collaborating Style. The collaborator has high concern for personal goals and for the relationship. The collaborator faces the conflict directly and works toward an integrative solution. An integrative, or "win-win" solution embraces the goals of both

Figure 6.1
Conflict Grid. From *Small Groups in Organizational Settings,* by R. Ross. Copyright 1989, Prentice-Hall, Inc. Reprinted with permission.

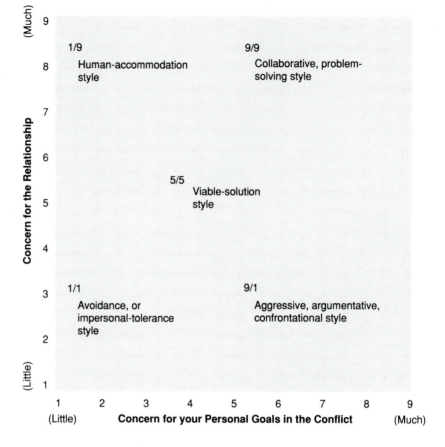

parties in the conflict. Hence, the collaborating style often is viewed as the ideal in conflict management. Since this approach addresses the conflict directly, it is sometimes referred to as the *confronting* style.

5/5 Compromising Style. Given a moderate concern for personal goals in the conflict and a moderate concern for the relationship, the compromiser is willing to "split the difference" with the other party in the conflict, where each party gets something, but the end result probably is less than ideal for either. This is sometimes called the *viable solution* approach to conflict.

Generally, research suggests that several factors in the *relationship* between conflicting parties influences choice of conflict strategy. Superiors most often rely on forcing as a method of handling conflicts with their subordinates, although first-line supervisors are more likely than either middle or upper level managers to exhibit a collaborative style (Putnam & Wilson, 1982). Perhaps not suprisingly, subordinates tend to adopt avoiding, compromising, or accommodating styles in conflicts with superiors. Burke (1970) found that subordinates preferred for superiors to use a collaborative or confronting style, but superiors regarded collaborating as effective only when the issues are negotiable and conflicts of interest are low. According to Robbins (1978), forcing was regarded as the most effective strategy under conditions of incompatible goals or organizational endorsement of a particular solution. In this case, "organizational endorsement" probably is a euphemism for top-management insistence. Lawrence and Lorsch (1967) found that accommodating and compromising were acceptable strategies to subordinates, but superiors regarded these strategies as counterproductive. Organizational members in general have reported that the avoiding style is neither desirable nor effective (Burke, 1970).

It is also important to note that some studies, in particular Putnam and Wilson (1982), suggest the organization members adapt the conflict styles across different types of relationships. Although the concept of conflict style assumes that a person typically engages in a particular mode of action, one's actions in handling a conflict clearly depend on the relationship within which the conflict occurs.

Conflict style also appears to be influenced by *conflict issues.* Where conflict involves incompatible values, forcing is likely to occur. Compromising and accommodating are more likely when the conflict involves competition for scarce resources or personality differences. Putnam and Poole concluded that personality traits and contextual variables, such as organizational climate, leadership style, and communication climate, do not influence the selection of conflict strategies, although high levels of member commitment to the organization are positively associated with collaborative styles of conflict management.

Recently, researchers have begun to extend the study of interpersonal conflict in organizations beyond the narrow boundaries of conflict style in superior-subordinate relationships. One good example of such work is a study by Papa and Pood (1988) on coorientational accuracy and differentiation in conflict management within coworker as well as superior-subordinate dyads in a large insurance company. Coorientational accuracy refers to "knowing where another person stands on an issue and what conflict tactics he or she prefers" (p. 401). Differentiation is "the process of clarifying differences in interactants positions and pursuing the reasons behind those positions" (p.401). Papa and Pood found that dyads entering a conflict with low coorientational accuracy spent much more time in differentiation than did high accuracy dyads. The finding is important because adequate differentiation is necessary in order to move conflict into an integration stage. According to Papa and Pood, "Dyads entering a conflict with low CA [coorientational accuracy] find it difficult to progress to the integration phase" (p. 418).

Coalitions and Intergroup Conflict

The large, complex organization provides a rich medium for the development of coalitions and the occurrence of intergroup conflict (i.e., conflict between different groups or units within the same organization). As Putnam and Poole point out, "When complexity increases, communication networks fragment and lead to different perspectives within units. If this condition is combined with high interdependence, conflict between units increases" (p. 575).

Intergroup conflict is affected by many contextual and structural factors in the organization. Factors as simple as physical separation of groups (e.g., different departments on different floors of a building or distances between field offices) may escalate conflict by making communication more difficult. Status distinctions between different groups also can lead to intergroup conflict (Dalton, 1959). As previously mentioned, competition for resources or ambiguous conditions in policy or authority may become sources of conflict. In the case of intergroup conflict, Zald (1981) found that groups increase their concern for equitable resource distribution in an effort to control their own destinies. Putnam and Poole also point out that " 'destabilizing' incidents, such as the departure of an executive or a financial crisis, often trigger struggles over the redistribution of power" (p. 576).

Not surprisingly, one of the major factors in intergroup conflict is the perception that groups have of their relationship. Those that see their relationship as competitive engage in misrepresentation, withholding of information, minimization of intergroup agreements accompanied by maximization of differences, discourse slanted favorably toward ingroup positions and unfavorably toward outgroup positions, and even charges of disloyalty against ingroup members who support positions taken by the outgroup (Walton, Dutton, & Cafferty, 1969; Blake et al. 1964).

Much of the research on intergroup conflict is concerned with formal intact groups, but many of the more interesting conflicts in organizations may involve **coalitions** that exist independently of the formal organizational structure. We touched briefly on the concept of organizational coalitions in chapter 4, saving the more detailed discussion for this chapter because coalitions are, by virtue of their very existence, agents of conflict. A coalition occurs when individuals band together in order to wield influence within the organization. Coalitional activity in large organizations seems to be as inevitable as the ebb and flow of the ocean tides, although the tides, unlike coalitions, are quite predictable. Stevenson, Pearce, and Porter say that a coalition has eight essential characteristics:

Interacting Group. Coalitions are considered to consist of members who communicate with one another about coalition issue(s) and potential coalition action.

Deliberately Constructed. Coalitions are explicitly constructed for a purpose. They can be distinguished from other informal groups by their self-conscious formation and design.

Independent of Formal Organization's Structure. A coalition is independent of formally designated groups such as departments, committees, or task forces. This does not mean that membership in coalitions and formally designated groups is necessarily mutually exclusive . . . the formally designated structure of the organization may—but usually will not—coincide with a mapping of the network of coalitions within the organization.

Lack of Formal Internal Structure. Not only are coalitions independent of the formal structure of the organizations within which they are embedded, but they also lack their own formal structure . . . coalitions lack a hierarchy of formal, legitimate authority and are much more dependent on attempts at informal influence among members.

Mutual Perception of Membership. Coalitions, as with other nonformal groups, are likely to have fuzzy boundaries. Nevertheless, some reasonable consensus about who is a member and whose commitment is questionable would be expected.

Issue Oriented. Coalitions are formed to advance the purposes of their members. When their members cease to interact around these issues, the group no longer exists as a coalition.

External Focus. The issue that the coalition addresses must be external to the coalition. . . . The coalition forms to influence some external agent. This means that a coalition does not form merely so that its members may debate or argue some issue among themselves. It is created in order to get *other* organization members or groups to yield to its purposes through persuasion, coercion, or other means of influence.

Concerted Member Action. An integral part of the definition of coalitions is that they must act as a group, either through a group action . . . or through orchestrated member action. (1985, pp. 261–262)

Stevenson et al. also point out that many of the factors associated with intergroup conflict in general also may be linked with the formation of coalitions. They argue that coalitions are more likely to form in an organization when there is a major change in the allocation of resources or when some organization members believe that comparable others are receiving more favorable treatment. They also argue that coalition formation is more likely when there are opportunities for frequent interaction among organization members and organization members have discretion in carrying out their job responsibilities. As the coalition itself becomes more visible, the issues pursued by the coalition also become more visible, and the likelihood increases that a "countercoalition" will form in order to block the aims of that coalition. Two examples of organizational coalitions that we have observed will illustrate, however, that the forms, motives, and methods of coalitions may be very diverse.

1. The accounting department of a large manufacturing firm has always had a male manager. Historically, all of the professional accountants in the department had also been men, although the clerks and bookkeepers had been women. During the past few years, however, more women had entered the department as accountants. Now, about one-third of the accountants are female, and over one-half of the department employees are women. Apparently, the manager had a long history of sexual harassment, but the female clerks and bookkeepers had always been reluctant to take any action because they were in vulnerable positions and harassment was "just something you put up with." But the new professional women in higher-status accounting positions were not so willing to "put up" with the situation, particularly given new laws that allow for action against sexual harassment in organizations that allow it to occur. Under these new conditions, the women soon coalesced in order to support each other and pursue sexual harassment charges against the manager.

Eventually, the department manager was fired, but he was replaced by another male who was promoted from within the department. While most of the women were relieved by the change, two of the more influential female accountants were incensed that yet another man was given the manager's position. The two began to engage in a series of covert actions designed to redirect the coalition toward the replacement of the new manager with a female. Among other things, they initiated a biweekly "Women's Night Out," when all of the female members of the department met for dinner to discuss their work-related problems, but the primary purpose was to encourage all of the women to create problems for the new manager (e.g., taking maximum sick leave, making difficult requests for resources or work schedules, asking the manager continually to repeat or clarify directives, etc.) and, during managerial performance reviews, to turn in negative subordinate evaluations of their superior. The strategy worked. Frustrated and angry, the new manager resigned after less then twelve months in the position. He was replaced by one of the two coalition leaders.

2. During the 1980s public health issues surrounding the hazards of cigarette smoking expanded because of the concern for the dangers to smokers, which included the health risks to nonsmokers exposed to secondary smoke. Many companies were required to handle the problem of developing policies on smoking in the workplace. In some cases, top level executives or personnel managers surveyed employees to determine their opinions toward various options (e.g., open smoking, smoking only in restricted areas, or a complete smoking ban), then implemented policies that seemed to have the broadest support in the surveys. In other cases, policies developed only as a response to coalitional action among nonsmoking employees. These coalitions were visible only through the efforts of a few core members who were very vocal on the issue, but who were given more force by the tacit support of the "silent majority" of nonsmokers who outnumbered smokers by two to one. A coalition of this type can be very loose in the sense that most of its "members" engage in little or no direct interaction about the issue and may not even know each other. Yet, efforts to ban or restrict smoking in public areas and in the workplace have been so effective that Philip Morris Corp., a major producer of tobacco products, has undertaken an active effort to promote "Smokers' Rights" groups throughout the country and to encourage countercoalitions to combat the actions of anti-smoking coalitions in organizations. *Philip Morris Magazine* even publishes what it calls a "Hall of Shame" list of companies that have imposed restrictions on workplace smoking.

In the first case, the coalition is small, localized in a specifc organizational unit, and works toward its objectives over a long period of time, sometimes overtly, sometimes covertly, with the concerted efforts of its members. In the second example, the coalition is large, with fuzzy boundaries. Status as a nonsmoker is the only specific defining characteristic of its members. Many of them may not really be "members" of the coalition, yet their presence in the organization and the policymakers' realization that they are nonsmokers tacitly lends force to the efforts of vocal core members. Curiously, neither of these examples involves the kinds of issues that organizational theorists typically see as the motivational forces in coalitional formation.

Bargaining and Negotiation

Bargaining and negotiation involve a special case of organizational conflict. As Putnam and Poole state:

Bargaining constitutes a unique form of conflict management in that participants negotiated mutually shared rules and then cooperate within these rules to gain a competitive advantage over their opponent. . . . Bargaining, then, differs from other forms of conflict in its emphasis on proposal exchanges as a basis for reaching a joint settlement in cooperative-competitive situations. (1987, p. 563)

In chapter 3, we mentioned Mary Parker Follett's work on redefining traditional ideas of power and authority in order to achieve integration of competing interests. Follett's ideas directly influenced the development of classic bargaining theory. In particular, Walton and McKersie (1965) extended on Follett's work to classify bargaining processes in four categories: distributive, integrative, attitudinal structuring, and intraorganizational bargaining. Putnam and Jones (1982) narrowed the focus to distributive and integrative bargaining for purposes of communication research. Putnam and Poole also suggest that much of the research on bargaining processes can be understood in terms of the distinction between distributive and integrative processes.

A **distributive** bargaining situation "is one characterized by the existence or the appearance of fixed-sum (zero-sum) alternatives; one party must win and the other party must lose" (p. 172). In contrast, an **integrative** bargaining "refers to situations where the potential outcomes can be expanded; inconsistent goals are combined to create a new alternative, one where neither side sacrifices his or her ultimate aims" (p. 172).

Distributive bargaining is characterized by deception, withholding of information, or the use of "disinformation" activities (i.e., directly disclosing information that obscures the negotiator's true objective). Bluffs, exaggerated demands, threats, and ambiguous cues are common in distributive bargaining. Negotiators conceal the strength of their positions, the outcomes that they really want, and the points that they are prepared to concede. Integrative bargaining is based on open communication, accurate disclosure of objectives, and sharing of information. Information is used for purposes of fact-finding, problem definition, and generation of alternative solutions (Putnam & Poole, 1987).

How does one know the difference between accurate disclosure in an integrative situation and the misinformation of the distributive situation? In some cases, the circumstances themselves—the bargaining issue, the parties involved, and the resources at stake—will define the situation as distributive or integrative. For example, a local school board faced with a severe decline in tax revenues due to plant closings in the community enters negotiations with a teachers' union. The board, having exhausted all other possible options to reduce costs, must eliminate some teaching positions in order to balance its budget, but the union is absolutely committed to a "no lay off" clause in the new contract. The resulting environment is tense and distributive. In another school district on the other side of the state, the community is enjoying a strong period of economic expansion. Here, the issues between the board and the union are entirely different and both parties are seeking the best ways in which to use the abundant resources available to them.

But bargaining situations often are "mixed" rather than purely distributive or integrative. Moreover, Putnam and Jones contend that many bargaining situations are defined inappropriately as distributive. The situation is treated as a win-lose dilemma when, in fact, it is possible to achieve an integrative, win-win settlement. Integrative strategies often do not appear until negotiators have gone through a lengthy period of distributive bargaining. In these situations, reciprocity is a critical factor in moving from distributive to integrative bargaining (e.g., when one party makes a concession and the other reciprocates). As we saw earlier in the study by Papa and Pood, differentiation also is critical for movement into integration stages of conflict, and differentiation appears to depend on coorientational accuracy. As Putnam and Poole point out, "integrative solutions emerge only after differences in perceptions of the problem are openly discussed" (p. 569).

Summary   The function of communication in constituting organizations depends upon the manner in which it is used to exercise two of the most pervasive phenomena in organizational life. These two phenomena are power and conflict. In hierarchically structured organizations, differences in members' status and power are a simple fact of life. Status refers essentially to the rank or importance of one's position in a group. Traditionally, power has been regarded as any means or resource that one person may employ to gain compliance and cooperation from others.

French and Raven provided an analysis of social power that has become a classic model for classifying the forms of power applied in organizational relationships. They described five basic types of power: reward, coercive, referent, expert, and legitimate. Social psychologists have claimed for many years that every exercise of power involves some form of exchange. One does not exact compliance from another without incurring some kind of cost—giving up something in return for compliance.

Traditional theories of power have tried to describe the forms of power that occur in social processes and have emphasized social exchange explanations for the operation of power. The result is an appealing, but somewhat sterile, account power that fails to account for the connection between power and communication and somehow seems to ignore the dark side of the organizational subservience. In view of modern critical theory, power is confounded with domination and oppression—conditions in the structure of society and in organizations that scholars should reveal and criticize. Critical theory also attempts to show how symbols are used to legitimate dominant forms of organizational reality, thereby restricting the interpretations and meanings that members can attach to organizational actions. In the process, critical theory relies heavily on showing how systematically distorted communication sustains hegemony.

Conflict is a common yet widely misunderstood phenomenon in group processes and intergroup relations. Classical theorists regarded conflict as an anomaly—an abnormal occurrence that was not supposed to happen. Contemporary organizational theorists stress the point that conflict is an inevitable and even necessary aspect of group and organizational processes. It should not be suppressed and avoided, instead, it should be confronted, managed, and resolved.

Conflict arises from many sources within groups and organizations, including various forms of role conflict, value and goal differences, competition for limited resources, and ambiguity in authority, structure, and procedures.

Various strategies for managing conflict can be organized into three categories: establishment of superordinate goals, structural interventions, and conflict-resolution activities. Many complicated factors influence organization members' choice of strategies, the level of the conflict itself, and the ease with which conflicts can be resolved. Some of the more important factors are examined in research on interpersonal and intergroup conflict. Most work on interpersonal conflict in organizations has centered on conflict styles in superior-subordinate relationships. Conflict style refers to a characteristic mode or habitual way that a person handles a dispute. Much of the research on intergroup conflict is concerned with formal, intact groups, but many of the more interesting conflicts in organizations may involve coalitions that exist independently of the formal organizational structure.

Bargaining and negotiation involve a special case of organizational conflict. Communication research on bargaining processes usually is based on a distinction between distributive and integrative processes. Distributive bargaining involves the existence or the appearance of fixed-sum, win-lose situation. Integrative bargaining involves situations where the potential outcomes can be expanded or inconsistent goals combined in win-win outcomes. Distributive bargaining is characterized by deception, withholding of information, or the use of disinformation activities. Integrative bargaining is based on open communication, accurate disclosure of objectives, and sharing of information. Information is used for purposes of fact-finding, problem definition, and generation of alternative solutions.

Discussion Questions/ Activities

1. In what ways does the critical perspective of power differ from the traditional treatment of power? Does the fact that our democratic society protects individual rights limit the application of critical theory to organizational communication? Why or why not?
2. In what ways are power and conflict intertwined in organizations?
3. Are there any problems with a stylistic approach to the study of interpersonal conflict? Is one conflict style more preferable than others? Why or why not?
4. Given the political nature of coalitions, under what conditions would it be ethically acceptable to form and work through coalitions in organizations? Are there circumstances under which coalitions might be unethical?
5. Assuming that integrative bargaining is superior to distributive bargaining, how does one move toward or encourage an integrative approach in the bargaining process? Can you think of any conditions under which distributive bargaining might be more effective than integrative bargaining?

Case Study

Eastern Air

On March 9, 1989, Eastern Air (EAL) filed for Chapter 11 Bankruptcy protection in a New York court. The union of Texas Air Corp. and EAL now seem to be losing the bitter war with Texas Air Chairman Frank Lorenzo. This bankruptcy strategy is only one small chapter in the stormy relationship Lorenzo has had with EAL's union since he acquired EAL in a low bid in 1986.

Many of these current problems stem from the dawn of the jet age, when former Chairman Eddie Rickenbacher, the World War I ace, cancelled an order of DC-8's, figuring he could still get by with prop-driven planes. Delta stepped in, picked up Eastern's order, and used the jets to surpass Eastern. EAL also has had a history of expensive executive power struggles, layers upon layers of management, and lavish executive perks. The company even found ways to lose money before the deregulation of 1978. EAL also failed to change a fundamental strategy of near-total dependency on north/south routes and the winter tourist trade. These fundamental problems set EAL's tragic course towards bankruptcy. Frank Borman took over in 1976 and tried to turn EAL around. Borman inherited a high cost/low yield airline with a poor service reputation and militant unions. Borman did lower overhead by persuading employees to make wage concessions. He also established a Kansas City hub to spread EAL routes from dependency on north/south corridors. His big blunder came when he decided to invest heavily ($1.4 billion) in fuel efficient planes. He did this just as deregulation started and oil prices crashed, thus removing what he thought would be a competitive advantage. The company also was faced with new competition by such competititors as People Express. To fight back, Borman cut fares and demanded more concessions from already cynical unions. As the losses and labor/management fighting escalated, Frank Lorenzo moved in 1986 to buy EAL for a mere $277 million in cash. At that time, EAL had a market value of $570 million.

Lorenzo's reputation preceded his arrival at EAL. In 1980, he created a nonunion New York Air and formed Texas Air (TA) as a holding company. He purchased Continental in 1982 for $154 million and successfully smashed the union via a "Chapter 11" bankruptcy strategy. He replaced his expensive union employees with much cheaper nonunion workers, successfully emerged from the bankruptcy courts, and made Continental profitable once again.

Lorenzo stepped into the EAL situation as the company's last hope. Since Lorenzo's take over, jobs have been cut by nearly 20 percent, and EAL has cut costs wherever possible. Just by eliminating meals on some flights, EAL has saved $20 million. Management is convinced that the company can't earn a profit unless the wage bill is reduced further. Thirty-seven percent of EAL's operating costs are due to wages, compared to the industry average of 35 percent and to the sister company Continental's meager 22 percent.

Pilots and flight attendants already have given big wage concessions. Lorenzo immediately demanded and got a 40 percent cut in pay and benefits. But the historically militant machinists' union has refused to accept Lorenzo's demands, even though it may mean the demise of EAL.

The machinists' union, which also represents cabin cleaners and baggage handlers, contends that management is overstating the company's problems to force unnecessarily large wage cuts. EAL already has laid off 4,100 workers (out of 40,000) and continues to sell off planes and spin-off airline assets to the parent company, Texas Air. To further reduce costs, it closed down its Kansas City hub, stopped service to eleven western cities, sold or grounded forty-four aircraft, and reduced systemwide flights from 1225 to 1085. Despite these cuts, the company was still losing $1 million daily.

By the summer of 1988, EAL was embroiled in tough negotiations with the Air Line Pilots Association (ALPA) and the International Association of Machinists (IAM). If Lorenzo gave in to the pilots, the machinists would have less pressure to settle. EAL would have to commit itself to maintain its size and only get $70 million of the more than $250 million in labor cost reductions that it wanted. Continental could also be in jeopardy of a reunionization. To avoid getting into such a mess, Lorenzo attempted to start a strike, sell assets, and move jobs to Continental. This action was stopped by the unions through the courts and the National Mediation Board (NMB).

By the fall of 1988, the IAM union offered Lorenzo three alternatives: (1) sell EAL to the unions in conjunction with another buyer; (2) spin off EAL and give unions a minority stake or (3) merge EAL with Texas Air's Continental. Several parties talked to Lorenzo and the unions, but Lorenzo tried to quiet rumors by stating that EAL was not for sale. Lorenzo wanted the unions to give in to his demands.

Two months later, some of TA's own directors were urging Lorenzo to cut his losses and sell EAL. The unions had still not budged on the concession issue, but Lorenzo vowed to keep on fighting. At this point, Lorenzo faced some tough choices: bankruptcy, merging EAL with Continental (thus facing unionization of Continental), or selling EAL to TWA's Carl Icahn at a humiliatingly low price. The National Mediation Board was giving Lorenzo fits during the negotiations. The NMB refused to grant an impasse in the negotiations. This action took away Lorenzo's right to force a 40 percent pay and benefit reduction in order to cause the strike he wanted so he could bring in nonunion workers. Angered by NMB's slowness to grant an impasse in negotiations, Lorenzo predicted publicly that the NMB would soon start the 30-day cooling off period necessary before Lorenzo could impose the cuts. The NMB didn't and its director was angered by Lorenzo's aggressiveness. Lorenzo, instead of continuing to persuade the NMB chairman, started a campaign to discredit him. Lorenzo said he would even sue the NMB.

By spring of 1989, Chairman Lorenzo was in danger of losing control of the company. EAL was grounded due to strikes by the pilots and machinists that started March 4th after the NMB finally agreed to an impasse. Texas Air, the parent company of EAL and Continental, had lost $555 million in three months. The pilots contended that Lorenzo had robbed EAL to benefit Continental. Only 10 percent of EAL's flights were running and the losses were mounting. The pilots asked the courts to remove Lorenzo as EAL's chairman because of his asset-stripping strategy. The unions also tried to convince the court that EAL must file a reorganization plan before Lorenzo sold more assets.

EAL's market position decayed quickly. The company frantically tried to replace striking pilots, machinists, baggage handlers, and flight attendants. Yet, by the summer of 1989, it appeared that Lorenzo's Chapter 11 strategy had beaten the unions. The laws of Chapter 11 give management the first chance to reorganize the company so it can pay off its debts. Lorenzo's plan for repaying EAL's debts convinced the court to let him retain control, thus avoiding a court-appointed trustee. Lorenzo claimed that he could rebuild operations without pilots crossing the picket lines. EAL put together a huge hiring and training program. By selling off more assets Lorenzo raised enough money to pay for operations, to pay $914 million to creditors, and to start a market effort to regain some of Eastern's lost market share.

The only certainty in EAL's future is that it will have fewer jobs. One striking machinist said, "We're stuck in the middle—pawns in a chess game." For Lorenzo, it now seems that beating the unions, for which he has little use, is the only thing that matters. "Three months ago, there was a lot of talk about using Eastern as a symbol of union power," Lorenzo says, "It was the last place they should have made Custer's last stand."

1. What forms of power are reflected in this case? Does the French and Raven model provide an adequate means of understanding the use of power by the various parties in the EAL dispute?
2. How would a critical theorist analyze what has occurred in the EAL case? Can critical theory, as described in this chapter, be applied appropriately to this case?
3. What does this case say about the relationship between power and conflict?
4. Use the concepts of integrative versus distributive bargaining to discuss the events that transpire in this case.

References

Bachrach, P., & Baratz, M. (1962). Two faces of power. *American Political Science Review, 56,* 947–952.

Beckhard, R. (1969). *Organization development: Strategies and models.* Reading, MA: Addison-Wesley.

Blake, R. R., & Mouton, J. S. (1964). *The managerial grid.* Houston: Gulf Publishing.

Blake, R. R., Shepard, H., & Mouton, J. S. (1964). *Managing intergroup conflict in industry.* Houston: Gulf Publishing.

Burawoy, M. (1979). *Manufacturing consent.* Chicago: University of Chicago Press.

Burke, R. J. (1970). Methods of resolving superior-subordinate conflict: The constructive use of subordinate differences and disagreements. *Organizational Behavior and Human Performance, 5,* 393–411.

Clegg, S. (1975). *Power, rule, and domination.* London: Routledge & Kegan Paul.

Dahl, R. (1957). The concept of power. *Behavioral Science, 2,* 201–215.

Dalton, M. (1959). Conflicts between staff and line managerial officers. *American Sociological Review, 15,* 342–351.

Deetz, S. A. (1982). Critical interpretive research in organizational communication. *Western Journal of Speech Communication, 46,* 131–149.

Dessler, G. (1980). *Organization theory: Integrating structure and behavior.* Englewood Cliffs, NJ: Prentice-Hall.

Edwards, R. (1979). *Contested terrain.* New York: Basic Books.

Emerson, R. M. (1962). Power-dependence relations. *American Sociological Review, 27,* 31–41.

Farrell, T. B., & Aune, J. A. (1979). Critical theory and communication: A selective literature review. *Quarterly Journal of Speech, 65,* 93–120.

French, J. R. P., Jr., and Raven, B. H. (1959). The bases of social power. In D. Cartwright (Ed.), *Studies in social power.* Ann Arbor: University of Michigan Press.

Frost, P. J. (1987). Power, politics, and influence. In F. M. Jablin, L. L. Putnam, K. H. Roberts, & L. W. Porter (Eds.), *Handbook of organizational communication: An interdisciplinary perspective* (pp. 503–548). Newbury Park, CA: Sage.

Giddens, A. (1979). *Central problems in social theory.* Berkeley: University of California Press.

Goldhaber, G. M. (1990). *Organizational communication* (5th ed.). Dubuque, IA: Wm. C. Brown.

Gramsci, A. (1971). *Selections from the prison notebooks* (Q. Hoeare & G. Nowell Smith, Trans.). New York: International Publishers.

Habermas, J. (1968). *Knowledge and human interests* (J. Shapiro, Trans.). Boston: Beacon Press.

Habermas, J. (1979). *Communication and the evolution of society* (T. McCarthy, Trans.). Boston: Beacon Press, 1979.

Hall, J. (1969). *Conflict management survey: A survey of one's characteristic reaction to and handling of conflicts between himself and others.* Monroe, TX: Telemetrics International.

Harsanyi, J. C. (1962). Measurement of social power, opportunity, costs, and the theory of two-person bargaining games. *Behavioral Science, 7,* 67–80.

Janis, I. L. (1972). *Victims of groupthink.* Boston: Houghton Mifflin.

Kelman, H. C. (1961). Processes of opinion change. *Public Opinion Quarterly, 25,* 57–78.

Koehler, J. W., Anatol, K. W. E., and Applbaum, R. L. (1981). *Organizational communication: Behavioral perspectives* (2nd ed.). New York: Holt, Rinehart & Winston.

Lawrence, P. R., and Lorsch, J. W. (1967). *Organization and environment.* Boston: Division of Research, Graduate School of Business Administration, Harvard University.

Lukes, S. (1974). *Power: A radical view.* London: Macmillan.

Martin, J., Feldman, M., Hatch, M. J., & Sitkin, S. B. (1983). The uniqueness paradox in organizational stories. *Administrative Science Quarterly, 28,* 438–453.

McGaan, L. (1983). *Critical theory and communicative action: An introduction to the work of Jurgen Habermas.* Paper presented to the Humanities Colloquium, Wabash College.

McPhee, R. (1985). *Four critical approaches to workplace power/control in organizational communication.* Paper presented at the annual meeting of the International Communication Association, Chicago.

Meyers, C. E. (1944). The effect of conflicting authority on the child. In K. Lewin et al. (Eds.), *Authority and frustration: Studies in topological and vector psychology* (Vol. 3). Ames: Iowa State University Press.

Mumby, D. K. (1987). The political function of narrative in organizations. *Communication Monographs, 54,* 113–127.

Papa, M. J., & Pood, E. A. (1988). Coorientational accuracy and differentiation in the management of conflict. *Communication Research, 15,* 400–425.

Putnam, L. L., & Jones, T. S. (1982). Reciprocity in negotiations: An analysis of bargaining interaction. *Communication Monographs, 49,* 171–191.

Putnam, L. L., and Poole, M. S. (1987). Conflict and negotiation. In F. M. Jablin, L. L. Putnam, K. H. Roberts, & L. W. Porter (Eds.), *Handbook of organizational communication: An interdisciplinary perspective* (pp. 549–599). Newbury Park, CA: Sage.

Putnam, L. L., & Wilson, S. R. (1982). Communicative strategies in organizational conflicts: Reliability and validity of a measurement scale. In M. Burgoon (Ed.), *Communication yearbook 6* (pp. 629–652). Newbury Park, CA: Sage.

Robbins, S. P. (1977). Managing organizational conflict. In J. Schnee, E. K. Warren, and H. Lazarus (Eds.), *The progress of management.* Englewood Cliffs, NJ: Prentice-Hall.

Robbins, S. P. (1978). "Conflict management" and "conflict resolution" are not synonymous terms. *California Management Review, 21,* 67–75.

Russell, B. (1983). *Power: A social analysis.* New York: Norton.

Schein, E. (1969). *Process consultation: Its role in organization development.* Reading, MA: Addison-Wesley.

Schein, E. (1970). *Organizational psychology.* Englewood Cliffs, NJ: Prentice-Hall.

Secord, P. F., and Backman, C. W. (1964). *Social psychology.* New York: McGraw-Hill.

Smith, R. C., & Eisenberg, E. M. (1987) Conflict at Disneyland: A root-metaphor analysis. *Communication Monographs, 54,* 367–380.

Stevenson, W. B., Pearce, J. L., & Porter, L. W. (1985). The concept of "coalition" in organization theory and research. *Academy of Management Review, 10,* 256–268.

Tannenbaum, A. S. (1962). An event-structured approach to social power and to the problem of power comparability. *Behavioral Science, 7,* 315–331.

Tjosvold, D. (1985). Power and social context in superior-subordinate interaction. *Organizational behavior and human decision processes, 35,* 281–293.

Walton, R. E., Dutton, J. M., & Cafferty, T. P. (1969) Organizational context and interdepartmental conflict. *Administrative Science Quarterly, 14,* 73–84.

Walton, R. E., & McKersie, R. B. (1965). *A behavioral theory of labor negotiations: An analysis of a social interaction system.* New York: McGraw-Hill.

Zald, M. (1981). Political economy: A framework for comparative analysis. In M. Zey-Ferrell & M. Aiken (Eds.), *Complex organizations: Critical perspectives* (pp. 237–262). Glenview, IL: Scott, Foresman.

Outline

Types of Information Systems
    Computerized Accounting
    Integrated Data Processing
    Integrated Management
        Information Systems
    Real-Time MIS
    Distributed Processing
Technological Consequences for
    Communication
    Changes in Organizational
        Structure
        Centralization School
        Decentralization School
        Neutrality School
        Research Findings

Effects on Staffing and Job
        Functions
    Research Findings
    Staffing Implications for
        Communication
Communication in the Information
        Network: LANs and WANs
    Limitations and Disadvantages
    Communication and
        Technological Skill
Summary
Discussion Questions/Activities
Case Study
References

Information Technology: The New Medium

Imagine for a moment that you are a corporate middle manager in the year 2000. You have just arrived at your office to begin another typical workday. Only a few years ago, you began your morning by exchanging greetings with your secretary, then reporting to a conference room for the daily management team briefing. But times have changed. Managers at your level no longer have secretaries, and the management group seldom has face-to-face meetings. Most secretarial functions have been taken over by an **automated office system.** This same system allows you to participate in meetings, to get information from other people, and to transmit reports, orders, and letters without ever leaving your office.

The automated office system has become your primary business tool. You know this system as an array of electronic gadgetry that occupies a worktable next to your desk. The centerpiece of the system is a **personal computer** (**PC**) with a keyboard, visual display, printer, and voice-to-machine translator. Your PC has time-sharing access to the company's large mainframe computer. It also has sophisticated data- and information-processing capabilities of its own. Moreover, it is tied into a companywide information network that permits direct communication with any other terminal in the system. Even your telephone is hooked into this system.

You switch on your PC, allowing it to warm up as you fumble with the lid on your coffee cup, and scan the front page of the *Wall Street Journal* (the only paper-medium information record in your office). You key in a request for the system to display your calendar for the day. The entire day's schedule flashes on the video display, indicating that you have an hour of open time before a morning teleconference.

Since you already have prepared your notes for the teleconference (the notes are stored on a computer disk), you decide to check your electronic mail. Another command to the PC yields a display of titles for various memos and letters awaiting your review. One internal memo is designated as a priority item. You call it up for display on your screen. The memo, which one of your subordinates sent to you, concerns a major problem in a work project. It refers to some records stored in the central computer data base. You identify yourself to the company's central computer with a number and a password in order to access the data base, but you receive a message on your monitor indicating that your password is no longer valid due to a policy change regarding data base security. You immediately call the data base manager in order to obtain an updated password, but you have to leave a computer-stored "voicegram" because the manager is not available. You do not want to waste time, so you also call your subordinate with a request to transmit the relevant information directly to your computer. While you await the transmission, you return to your own electronic mail.

These activities are only the beginning of your day. Before you leave the office tonight, you will dictate and send several memos with the aid of your voice-to-machine translator, speak with your boss by telephone about a report that both of you have displayed simultaneously on your terminals, leave computer-stored "voice-grams" for telephone transmission to people who were out of their offices when you tried to reach them, and access the central computer on various occasions for data to be used in preparing reports. Since you decided to "brown-bag it" for lunch today, you spend the entire day without seeing another human being.

Some of the technologies in this hypothetical scenario are not fully developed, but our description of the twenty-first century workday is hardly farfetched. Many of the capabilities described above are feasible with current **information-processing technology.** In fact, most are realities in today's work organizations.

Some observers believe that contemporary information-processing technology will have little effect on organizational life other than improved efficiency and productivity. Others claim that this technology, especially in its more sophisticated forms, will bring about profound changes within organizations and the society at large (Gratz & Salem, 1984; Olson, 1982). Creation of new jobs, elimination of some old jobs, changes in management functions, and higher levels of stress usually are included in the list of potential changes. However, Bjorn-Andersen (1981) pointed out that an even more compelling issue should draw the attention of social scientists to this technology:

One of the most important questions concerning this technology is whether there is a change in human relationships and in the way we handle complex interpersonal interaction. (p. 56)

In this chapter, we will describe some of the major developments in contemporary information-processing technology and the possible effects of its introduction on organizational structures and communication.

Types of Information Systems

Contemporary information-processing technology occurs in several forms. All of these forms have one thing in common. They are electronic and computer-based. Otherwise, they are quite different. Each form represents a technological advance over the forms that preceded it. Because the history of this technology is short but very active, the earliest as well as the most recent forms can be found in today's organizations. It is important to distinguish among the various types of information technology because the influence of technology on organizational communication depends, in part, on the form of the technology. Thierauf (1978) identified five major types of contemporary information-processing technology: (1) computerized accounting, (2) integrated data processing, (3) integrated management information systems, (4) real-time management information systems, and (5) distributed processing.

Computerized Accounting

The earliest large-scale electronic computers were invented in the late 1940s. The first-generation commercial versions of these machines were acquired by business in the 1950s (Sanders, 1974). In these early years, the business vision of the role of computers in organizations was limited. The computer was regarded only as a highly efficient calculator that expanded the mechanization of accounting functions. The computer was not used as a management decision-making tool, as its potential as a communications medium was unimagined. The computer was nothing more than another hunk of machinery in the accounting department. **Computerized accounting** did the arithmetic required for bookkeeping, inventory control, and payroll (Thierauf, 1978).

Integrated Data Processing

With the development of second- and third-generation computers in the 1960s and the growing recognition of the value of information as an organizational resource, designers developed systems that unified data from logically related organizational subsystems—human resources, finance, machinery, materials. These **integrated data-processing systems** introduced single-entry records for access by users in many areas of an organization. For example, several different departments might require access to some types of financial information. Under integrated data processing, this information is stored in one location for retrieval by authorized users. Integrated systems are designed to increase organizational flexibility by making it easier to coordinate functions, procedures, and work methods (Thierauf, 1978).

Integrated Management Information Systems

Integrated data-processing systems allow some use of computers in decision making, but the applications are confined primarily to areas such as production scheduling, ordering, and inventory control. During the 1960s, electronic data processing was not used extensively in managerial decision making although its *potential* for use in decision making was substantial. This potential was realized through creation of **management information systems** or **MIS.**

As described by Thierauf (1978), MIS is "a system designed to provide selected decision-oriented information needed by management to plan, control, and evaluate the activities of the organization" (p. 16). In order to bring

MIS into being, integrated data processing must be changed in two fundamental ways. First, the system must be able to produce reports with essential information in appropriate form for use in the performance of management functions. Second, performance of routine decision making must be computerized. The first change was accomplished through clearer definition of managers' information needs. The second was developed by stating criteria for routine decisions in operational terms that could be programmed for execution by a computer (e.g., automatic reordering of items when inventory is reduced to a certain level).

Joseph (1969) predicted that managers in the 1970s would have to employ MIS in order to carry out their daily activities. The prediction appears to have been correct because use of MIS became widespread in the late 1970s. MIS today is "a network of related subsystems, integrated to perform the functional activities of an organization" (Thierauf, p. 17).

Real-Time MIS

A conventional MIS is subject to one problem that also occurs with integrated data processing. Data for such systems are processed in "batch" form. This means that information is accumulated over a period of time, then entered into the computer all at once. As a result, users of conventional MIS sometimes work with the computerized equivalent of yesterday's news. Moreover, needs arise for information that cannot be retrieved because it is not yet in the system. This limitation can be overcome with **on-line, real-time systems.**

An on-line system has the capability for continuous entry of and access to data through remote terminals. The system serves users in real time when data are entered into the computer as soon as they exist and become immediately available to potential users (Greenless, 1971). On-line and real-time characteristics are important features of **time-sharing systems** in which two or more users at different remote terminals have virtually simultaneous access to a computer. As described by Thierauf, real-time MIS means that "the firm's data base (locally, regionally, or centrally located) is always updated as events occur and can be interrogated from many I/O [input/output] terminals" (p. 24).

Distributed Processing

Despite the differences between integrated data processing, integrated MIS, and real-time MIS, all of these systems generally operate with **centralized processing.** Centralized processing means that all operations are performed by one large computer complex. Even though input/output devices (terminals and printers) may exist at various locations in an organization, all rely on the central-processing unit (e.g., a mainframe computer). Centralized processing creates at least two conditions that some organizations find unacceptable. First, it depends on highly standardized systems of input, processing, and output that may fit the needs of some departments but are not appropriate for others.

Second, costs associated with downtime and communication between the central computer and remote stations (e.g., through phone lines) can be high. One response to these problems lies in **distributed processing.**

According to Thierauf, the basic concept of distributed processing is simple: "Small computers, located near the data, do much of the processing and send only summary information to headquarters" (p. 4). These small machines, known as minicomputers, can be deployed at logical locations such as departments, field offices, or profit centers that require some form of electronic data and information processing. Burnett (1975) describes three ways in which minicomputers can be used in a distributed system:

1. Minicomputers may be employed to control communication through a network by a large computer.
2. Minicomputers may be used to communicate with other machines in a network and to perform local computing functions.
3. Minicomputers can be linked together in a network in which any given computer performs a specialized function and can be called on by other minicomputers in the system for performance of that function.

The primary advantage of a distributed-processing system over a centralized system is the efficient placement of computer power where it is most needed. Distributed processing gives local users more control over their own information systems and reduces burdens placed on the central computer. Moreover, a distributed-processing system can be much less costly than a centralized real-time MIS (Thierauf, 1978). These features of distributed processing are enhanced even more by the large-scale adoption of microcomputer (PC) technologies in organizations during the 1980s. Figure 7.1 provides a comparative diagram of centralized- and distributed-processing systems.

Technological Consequences for Communication

The emergence of electronic information-processing technology has been greeted with dire predictions about its ultimate effects on organizations and society in general. Some experts have argued that the technology will eliminate many jobs, resulting in unemployment rates of 10 percent to 15 percent, the redefinition of the basic concept of management, the provocation of widespread worker resistance and the demands for more job security, and the creation of a more controlled social order (Barron & Curnow, 1979). Others point out that massive unemployment and other undesirable side effects of electronic information-processing technology are not occurring at present and are unlikely to occur in the future (West, 1981).

In the face of this debate, communication scholars are confronted with two critical questions. Do organizations use new technologies to alter structures, staffing, and job functions and what are the communicative implications of these changes? More to the point, do organization members alter the content and patterns of interaction with one another through use of this technology, especially when it is employed as a communications medium? Before

Figure 7.1
Examples of information-processing systems.

Centralized Processing

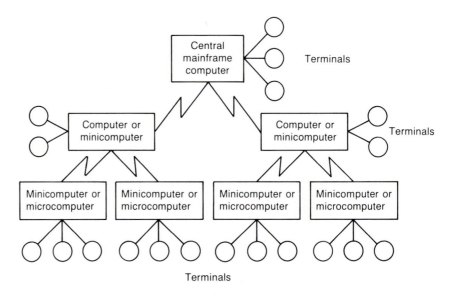

Distributed Processing

we try to answer these questions, we need to consider several factors that hamper any effort to assess the impact of information technology on organizations.

First, the technology is relatively new. Despite articles in popular magazines about the arrival of the "paperless office," electronic information technology is still a long way from becoming the dominant means for handling information in organizations. Davenport (1981) pointed out:

We live today in a paper information age. In every area of business and commerce, government, law, education, and health, our transactions are mainly paper documents. We have letters, memoranda, reports, specifications, executive orders, written policies, documentation, notes. . . . We are swamped with paper. (p. 1)

Even with the advent of PC's, Davenport's claim is still true. Until electronic information-processing technologies overtake paper as the medium of information storage and transmission, the effects of these technologies on communication will be difficult to assess.

Second, much of the impact (both positive and negative) of information technology depends on the extent to which it is automated rather than merely mechanized. West (1981) distinguished sharply between mechanization and automation. **Mechanization** involves the operation of a machine to accomplish a job that was formerly done manually (e.g., using a calculator rather than pencil and paper for computations). **Automation** means much more—the capability of the machine *to regulate itself* and to be put into operation with a set of instructions that it can execute without operator intervention. West claims that contemporary information technology has yielded neither the benefits nor the negative consequences that many have predicted because the systems implemented to date fall short of automation.

Third, as we pointed out earlier, the effect of the technology depends on the form in which it occurs. Where the computer is used for little more than accounting or for highly routine decision applications, the effects on organizational structure and communication may be negligible. In contrast, MIS and distributed-processing systems may result in extensive organizational change (House, 1971; Sanders, 1974). This problem is complicated by the variety of labels that writers use when discussing the technology. Terms such as *electronic data processing, computer-based systems,* and *automated information processing* are employed almost interchangeably and with no specific referent. When a writer offers predictions or reports the results of studies about the effects of technology on organizational life, those effects are difficult to evaluate unless one clearly understands the form of technology with which the writer is concerned. For example, Rice and Bair (1984) provide an excellent summary of thirty-one studies "on office automation impacts" (p. 210). Each of these studies is concerned with one or more forms of computer-based information processing (e.g., word-processing, electronic mail, and data base applications). An uninformed reader who assumes that "office automation" means only one thing might be quite confused by the various findings produced in these studies because the results of any given study only make sense when they are understood within the context of the form of technology considered in that study.

Finally, assessing the impact of technology on organizational structure and communication is difficult because there is some disagreement over the degree to which technology operates as a *causal* force in determining change. Some experts such as Rogers (1988) subscribe to a hypothesis of **technological determinism;** namely, "that certain social changes result from technological innovations" (p. 438). Others (e.g., Olson, 1982) reject the technological determinism hypothesis, pointing out instead that changes are a result of choices made by humans in their adoption and use of technology, not as a result of the technology itself. Even though we have spoken so far in this chapter with causal terminology (effects, impact, etc.), we are inclined to agree with Olson that social changes result from human choice rather than technological force.

Despite these limitations, we can draw some conclusions about the general consequences of innovations in information technology for organization structure, staffing, job functions, and communication. The remainder of this chapter includes a review of some early predictions as well as current research findings regarding these consequences.

Changes in Organizational Structure

To what extent will organizations alter their structural characteristics through the use of information technology? This has been a hotly debated question among management, information-processing, and communication experts since the late 1960s. The focal point of the argument centers on the extent to which new technologies foster centralization or decentralization of authority and decision making. If you recall the relationships described earlier in this book between communication and centralization (or decentralization), you will see immediately that this is an important question for communication scholars.

Centralization School

Before the arrival of more sophisticated forms of information technology, decentralization of authority and decision-making power clearly was a trend in American organizations (Sanders, 1974). While the trend developed in part from the influence of human resource and organization development theory, the primary force behind decentralization was much more utilitarian. Top managers, faced with greater complexity in organizations and with environments that demanded rapid response to new conditions, were virtually compelled to delegate authority to lower levels of management. Lower-level managers were closer to immediate problems and to the information required to solve these problems.

The basic argument of experts who predict a return to centralization (i.e., recentralization) rests on the fact that the new technology, especially in the form of MIS, creates the potential for top managers to recover delegated authority (Emery, 1964). Without a handy computer terminal, a top manager might have to wait for information to trickle up from lower levels or could be obliged to transpose large quantities of information from unusable to usable forms. Given a terminal, the top manager has information at a fingertip not only for strategic decisions concerning broad plans, goals, and objectives, but also for tactical decisions involving day-to-day organizational functions. Advocates of the centralization view claim that top managers not only will use technology to recover authority delegated to middle managers during the decentralization trend, but they also will actually extend their control over decisions into operational areas, bypassing middle managers who are now responsible for such functions.

Decentralization School

Some experts reject the claim that electronic information-processing technology leads to recentralization of authority. They argue instead that trends toward decentralization already in progress will be reinforced by information technology. Since top management's ability to monitor lower-level activity is greatly enhanced through technologies such as MIS, these managers will be more willing to delegate authority and to allow major decision making at lower levels (Sanders, 1974). Casbolt and Cherry (1983) argued that decentralization will be even more pronounced as distributed-processing systems take hold in organizations:

Traditionally, information in the organization has been controlled in an unintegrated fashion by service functions such as Data Processing, Personnel, Controller, and Office Services. Often these functional areas are politically antagonistic. As data-processing departments evolve to information resource management, the traditional walls of mystique and control are broken down. Managers become more responsible for their own information needs as DDP [distributed data processing] is implemented. Shared decision making and joint accountability create an interdependent cycle. (p. 3)

The arrival of contemporary **microcomputers**—the so-called personal computers so heavily marketed by IBM, Apple, ITT, and other major companies today—also has fueled the fires of the decentralization school (Danowski, 1983). Writers such as Hiltz and Turoff (1978) and Naisbitt (1982) argue that the capabilities of microcomputers will lead inevitably toward a "network" society with revolutionary implications for organizational life. According to Danowski, some authorities, in line with Rogers' technological determinism hypothesis, actually see the microcomputer as an *agent* of social change.

Neutrality School

A few observers have claimed that electronic information-processing technology, in and of itself, will not result in any particular form of structural change in organizations. Instead, the technology can be used to support moves in the direction of either centralization or decentralization. Management philosophy and the environment in which the organization operates will determine whether organizational structure becomes more or less centralized as a result of technological innovations. The technology "can be effective (or ineffective) in either a centralized or decentralized mode" (Kanter, 1972, p. 22). This position is similar to the view expressed by Olson.

Research Findings

Even though people have had a great deal of speculation about the effects of information technology on organizational structure, relatively little field research has been conducted in an effort to identify the kinds of changes that are occurring. Danowski (1983) concluded from his review of studies during the 1960s and early 1970s, "The dominant theme in this research was the effects of mainframe computing on centralization of organizational structure" (p. 13). Studies by Vergin (1967) and Brink (1969) are typical of those in this group. Brink interviewed leading business executives in a number of organizations. Vergin interviewed data-processing managers, system analysts, department managers, and senior executives in eleven Minnesota companies that ranged in size from 89 to 23,000 personnel.

Executives in Brink's study insisted that electronic information-processing technology had no impact on organizational structure in their companies. Even though they would not rule out the possibility of *future* impact resulting from MIS, they claimed that changes in organizational structure are driven by management philosophy and organizational circumstances. This finding supports the view of the neutrality group.

In contrast, Vergin concluded from his study, "Undoubtedly, the largest and most visible organizational change resulting from computer use in the eleven firms was a move toward recentralization of decision making" (p. 65). Although the technology may be used to support either centralization or decentralization, organizations in Vergin's study chose the path of greater centralization. In particular, managers elected to recover decision-making authority that had previously been delegated to lower levels.

Vergin did qualify his findings by pointing out that changes associated with recentralization were less dramatic than some forecasters had predicted. Moreover, structural changes seemed to be confined primarily to organizations with integrated data processing or some form of MIS. Virtually no changes occurred in organizations that employed computers as little more than accounting tools.

According to Danowski, the tendency toward centralization as a result of computer technology is best reflected in research by Whisler (1970), who produced a complete book from his studies. His major findings are summarized in table 7.1.

While the studies by Brink, Vergin, and Whisler are quite dated, more recent investigations by European researchers have produced similar results. Bjorn-Andersen (1981) concluded from studies of European organizations that

Table 7.1
Impact of Computers on Organizational Structure

1. Most study participants reported that the number of clerical personnel decreased, but some reported that the number remained unchanged or actually increased.
2. Most study participants reported that the number of supervisors and managers remained unchanged, but some reported either increases or decreases.
3. In most cases, span of control decreased. Some reported that span of control increased, while others reported no change.
4. Most companies reported no change in the number of organizational levels, but those that reported changes usually indicated a decrease.
5. Many changes in patterns of departmentalization were reported, including creation of new departments, elimination of old ones, transfer of activities from one department to another, and functional reorganization of departments.

Impact of Computers on Decision Making

1. All of the companies in the study reported consolidation of separate decision-making areas.
2. With a small number of exceptions, companies reported that decision making was pushed to a higher level of the organization.
3. All companies in the study reported shifts to quantification of decision areas that had been regarded previously as unquantifiable.
4. The primary effects of the computer on decision making occurred in middle management, with increased power and decision-making responsibility during transition to computer-based systems, followed by reduction of responsibilities after stablization of the systems.
5. A majority of the companies reported that computers made decision making more rigid and inflexible, although some claimed that flexibility increased as a function of improved access to information.

Impact of Computers on Authority and Control

1. All companies in the study reported increased centralization of control.
2. The overall response indicated that computer systems were used to control some aspects of human behavior such as initiation of action, specification of proper action to be taken, automatic performance of work, or monitoring of individual behavior.
3. Respondents were divided on whether computers affected clarity in lines of authority. Some reported increased clarity, some reported increased ambiguity, and others reported no change.

Impact of Computers on Job Content

1. Respondents were divided on whether computers affected routinization of clerical jobs. Some reported greater routinization and some reported job enlargement. Most reported no change with exception of accounting areas, where the net effect was greater routinization.
2. The content of the majority of supervisory jobs did not change. Those that did change generally involved increases in supervisory responsibilities.
3. Levels of interpersonal communication increased during transition to computer-based systems. Face-to-face communication declined after the systems were stabilized. Individuals spent more time working alone and communicated with others through the computer system.
4. Respondents overwhelmingly reported changes in skill requirements for clerical and supervisory jobs. Most reported that skill requirements increased, but 30 percent indicated downgrading of skill requirements in clerical positions.
5. Changes in skill requirements were less frequent for management positions, but in those cases where changes occurred, the effect almost always involved an increase in skill level.

Summary of findings in Whisler's study of nineteen insurance companies. From *The Impact of Computers on Organizations*, T. L. Whisler, 1970, Praeger Publishers.

technological innovations in information processing typically were followed by greater centralization. In particular, interdependence fostered among organizational units by integrated-processing systems—the same kind of interdependence that Casbolt and Cherry associate with distributed processing—actually had the effect of "limiting the discretion of individual managers" (p. 53). Bjorn-Andersen concluded from his studies that the introduction of sophisticated information-processing technology in an organization is followed by more rules, more policies, more methods, and more procedures. At the same time, day-to-day orders and advice from higher-level to lower-level managers *decrease*.

Bjorn-Andersen also noted marked separation between information system *planners* and system *users*. Even where information technology did not directly foster centralization, control of the system and knowledge about the system were centralized. In effect, "The system planner defines the need for information, designs the system, handles the programming, and implements the system. The user is often an astonished spectator" (p. 55). Although use of distributed-processing systems might correct this problem (Casbolt & Cherry, 1983), management has to make a conscious decision to adopt and support a distributed system.

Other studies by Roveda and Ciborra (1981) of five types of organizations in Italy produced results that differ somewhat from Bjorn-Andersen's findings. They observed evidence of centralization *and* decentralization occurring simultaneously, though in different levels or areas of the organization. Centralization of production control through integrated-processing systems was "often accompanied by delegation of decision power and autonomy to work groups" (p. 134). While control of the information-processing system itself was centralized and moved further up the organizational hierarchy, system failures and other unanticipated contingencies required an ability "to work in an 'informal' group, where hierarchical levels disappear and different personal expertise and know-how have to be integrated in ad hoc problem solving" (p. 134). But Roveda and Ciborra reported one major finding that fits some of the dire predictions of the centralization school. Supervisory and middle-management functions typically were "made redundant or emptied of control power" (p. 134).

The results of both American and European investigations are somewhat ambiguous. Although one must exercise caution in comparing American organizations to their European cousins, the study by Roveda and Ciborra is especially interesting because it suggests that centralization and decentralization may be interrelated. A move toward centralization in one application of information technology results in decentralization of some other application.

Effects on Staffing and Job Functions

An issue closely related to the centralization controversy is the extent to which electronic information-processing technology results in unemployment and redefinition of job functions. Barron and Curnow pointed out in 1979 that 65 percent of all occupations are concerned directly with acquisition, processing, and/or distribution of information. Even moderate increases in processing efficiency through electronic systems could result in high levels of unemployment for workers in such occupations.

While clerical and secretarial occupations would bear the brunt of personnel reductions, managerial positions are not immune from possible effects. Since much activity at middle-management levels is concerned with manipulating information rather than with decision making per se, integrated data processing and MIS could reduce the number of managers as well or, at least, redefine their jobs substantially. Especially in areas in which top managers use information technology to recentralize authority, middle managers would be eliminated. Those who survive would find that some of their functions are taken over either by a computer or by higher levels of management.

Other scholars argue that claims of massive unemployment are unwarranted. In particular, advocates of the decentralization view argue that information technology will create many new jobs and that middle-management roles actually will be enhanced, with less need to attend to routine matters and more opportunity for creative problem solving (e.g., see Emery, 1964; Sanders, 1974).

Research Findings

Studies to date lend some support to both of the positions described above. For example, large-scale personnel reductions have not resulted from innovations in information technology. West (1981) almost seems unhappy with the situation when he points out, "There are more clerical workers today than ever before. . . . We're not going to pick up a lot of savings in reduction of personnel [by adopting new information technology]" (p. 115). Vergin found in his study that no middle managers were terminated or downgraded in salary as a consequence of "the shift in duties to the computer" (p. 64).

On the other hand, job functions in many organizations clearly have been redefined by integrated data processing, MIS, and distributed processing. Clerical and secretarial personnel have become terminal operators and word processors rather than typists and paper shufflers. Middle-management functions also have changed. European researchers report loss of control, power, and discretion in management functions, although Bjorn-Andersen found that *staff* managers (those in support functions) gained influence as information gatekeepers. Vergin's study of U.S. companies indicated that computers had taken over some management functions in each organization that he examined. Moreover, some managers were moved to lower echelons of the organization, even though they retained their old salary levels. Changes in managerial job functions are not necessarily negative, at least as perceived by managers who are users of the new technologies. In a survey of 151 middle managers from 14 large organizations conducted by Millman and Hartwick (1987), most respondents indicated that office automation actually had enriched their jobs by making their work more important and interesting.

Staffing Implications for Communication

Technological effects on employment and job definitions, whether real or imagined, have several communication-related implications. If personnel believe that their jobs are jeopardized by electronic information processing, there could be extensive resistance to adoption of the technology accompanied by demands for more job security. Even job redefinition, especially at the management level, is likely to be resisted. Since middle managers highly value participation in decision making, Vergin argued that any serious use of information technology to recentralize decision making at top levels could result in "serious revolt [by middle managers]" (p. 68). The reaction of middle management might be like the militant unionism of the 1920s and 1930s, which resulted, in part, from scientific management and elimination of worker participation in planning.

Gouldner and Alvin (1955) pointed out that subordinates can use various upward communication strategies to exert pressure against downwardly imposed policies and changes. Top management's unilateral attempts to impose technological innovations could be met by some of these strategies if subordinates believe that the technology works against their interests. Consequently, organizations must consider communication planning in connection with decisions to implement information technology.

What kind of communication program should accompany the adoption of technological innovations? Brink (1969) concluded from his study that worker acceptance of information technology was greatest when management took two steps: (1) provided assurances that technology would not endanger job security; (2) kept the promise implied in these assurances.

As we already have seen, Brink's second step may be difficult to honor, and the first step should not be undertaken without the second. Wherever computer technology is used as more than a mere calculator, some change is almost inevitable. A simplistic internal public relations program designed to sell the technology to personnel may be woefully inadequate. Instead, the communication program should be based on active involvement of and consultation with those groups of organization members that will be affected by the change.

Organizational communication scholars traditionally argue that acceptance of change is more likely to occur when all parties affected by the change are able to participate in decisions and plans that lead to the change. Vergin's findings on adoption of information technology support this argument. He found that technological change occurred with less resistance in organizations that encouraged relevant departments to participate in both the design of the information system and in the planning for its implementation. Opposition and resistance were strongest in those organizations in which decisions about the system were made primarily in a centralized data-processing department without the participation of system users and others affected by the innovation.

Communication in the Information Network: LANs and WANs

Changes in organizational structure, staffing, and job definition as a result of technological innovation certainly raise issues with which communication scholars should be concerned. However, these issues are secondary to a more central question that we have not addressed fully—Bjorn-Andersen's question about the changes in complex human interaction that may occur in the wake of technological innovation. This question is important now because large organizations are just beginning to employ electronic information-processing technology in a more powerful form that we have not yet discussed. This "new" form of technology really involves a convergence of several information technologies in an electronic network that is sometimes called an **information bus** (Meisner, 1980). The information bus may involve a **wide-area network (WAN)** with hundreds of users or it may consist of **local-area networks (LANs)** that connect only users within a specific group (e.g., a department within a company). While the effects of technologies such as MIS are important, the use of LANs and WANs may have much more impact on human communication in organizations.

We already have described the concept of on-line, real-time systems that afford time-sharing access to a central computer through remote terminals. We also noted the capability of minicomputers to communicate with one another in distributed-processing systems. Given these basic capabilities, the next logical step is to allow system users to communicate with one another through terminals in a distributed system. In effect, the information bus implements this idea in LANs and WANs with a highly connected network of information-processing devices that have **multimode capability**—in Meisner's words, "the capability to transport audio, video, and digital information" within and between organizations (p. 151). The basic elements in an information bus are illustrated in figure 7.2.

LAN and WAN technology provides precisely the kind of system that is required for the turn-of-the-century scenario at the beginning of this chapter to become a reality. It is implemented through cable systems that can accommodate not only remote terminals and microcomputers, but also telephones, television, graphics devices, and other information-processing tools. In this form, electronic information processing literally becomes a communications medium that can complement or potentially replace other forms of communication. For example, consider Danowski's (1983) list of communication applications that are possible with current technology:

- computer messaging (private electronic mail)
- computer conferencing (group communication through terminals)

Figure 7.2
Elements in an information bus.

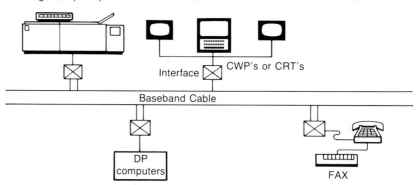

Intelligent copiers/printers

CWP's or CRT's

Interface

Baseband Cable

DP computers

FAX

- computer bulletin board
- computer newsletter (periodic on-line message distribution to a large group)
- data base access (both in-house and external)
- voicegrams (telephone messages computer-stored and transmitted)
- teleconferencing (audio, video, or both)

LANs also provide a medium for the use of "groupware," a form of software that, according to G. Berton Latamore, "holds the potential to vastly improve business communication and interaction" (1988, p. 72). Latamore noted that groupware packages combine electronic mail with individual and group scheduling, note taking, and a directory of group projects. With groupware, if you wish to schedule a group meeting, for example, you can call up each participant's electronic calendar, find an open time, schedule the meeting, and then send an announcement by electronic mail simultaneously to each person within a few minutes. Without groupware, the same task would require individual telephone calls and follow-up memos to each group member and might take hours to complete.

Meisner claims that computer conference and teleconferencing through LANs and WANs will substantially reduce the number of face-to-face meetings that now occur in organizations. On average, face-to-face meetings consume about 40 percent of the managerial workday. Voicegrams can reduce the problem of "telephone tag" that affects over 70 percent of business phone calls (Meisner, 1980). Telephone tag occurs when Person A calls B, B is not available, A leaves a message, then B later returns the call only to discover—as you probably have guessed—that A is not available! Other information bus capabilities such as word processing on microcomputers, computer messaging, and computer newsletters can increase efficiency and accuracy in the composition and transmission of letters, memos, and other documents.

Several studies of such applications of the technology appear to support these claims. For example, Rice and Case (1983) found that use of electronic messaging not only reduced paper and telephone traffic, but also increased work quantity and quality. Tapscott (1982) found changes in communication patterns and decreases in telephone usage and meetings. Steinfeld (1983) reported improvements in the timeliness and accuracy of information as well as in general coordination of tasks. Conrath and Bair (1974) found that reductions in telephone and face-to-face communication were accompanied by increased upward communication.

Some of the evidence regarding the influence of LANs and WANs on communication comes from popularized anecdotes and case studies. For example, Latamore (1988) reported excerpts of interviews with managers and secretaries from various companies about their experiences with LANs. A manager with Coca-Cola Foods claimed that her employees "want to live on the network" (p. 72). An assistant vice president with Banker's Trust of New York reported, "LANs make people look at what constitutes logical work groups so they can work together more effectively" (p. 77). An executive secretary at Prudential-Bache R & D Funding Corp. said that the company's LAN "has had a huge impact. It has opened a new channel of communication and made [me] more effective, able to do more in less time and with less effort and more fun."

Limitations and Disadvantages

Despite the glowing accounts about the benefits of LANs as reported by Latamore, information bus technologies do have limitations. First, some studies point to some undesirable results in the use of computer-mediated communication for group decision-making processes. Hiltz, Johnson, and Agle (1978) found that equality of member participation is greater in computer conferencing than in face-to-face meetings, but that computer-mediated groups engage in less communication, have more difficulty achieving consensus, and require more time to arrive at decisions. Kiesler, Siegel, and McGuire (1984) and Rice (1982) reported similar results. Such findings suggest that computer conferencing should not be substituted for face-to-face group meetings without first considering the relative advantages of each method.

Use of the information bus also poses a paradox that we described earlier in this book. On the one hand, organizations are faced with a growing need to acquire, process, and distribute large quantities of information in the most efficient way possible. On the other hand, Goldhaber (1990) contends that organization members typically express a desire for more face-to-face interaction in the workplace—a somewhat inefficient means of handling information. He suggests that the explosion of information technologies "may be producing a counter-revolutionary effect" (p. 143).

Other communication theorists express similar concerns. For example, Gratz and Salem (1984) are not so worried about interactive or conferencing capabilities but about long hours at terminals becoming a form of "human-machine" communication that steals time from human-to-human communication. Since human interaction is critical to the formation and stability of self and relationships with others, human-machine communication "has the potential for doing great harm to human relationships, even as our capability to handle information is expanded" (p. 100).

Karl Weick (1985) argued that contemporary information technology not only interferes with human interaction, but also interferes with our ability to make sense of events in organizations:

The growth of electronic information processing has changed organizations in profound ways. One unexpected change is that electronic processing has made it harder, not easier, to understand events that are represented on screens. As a result, job dissatisfaction in the 1990s may not center on issues of human relations. It may involve the even more fundamental issue of meaning: Employees can tolerate people problems longer than they can tolerate uncertainty about what's going on and what it means. (p. 51)

According to Weick, dependence on incomplete, abstract, or even cryptic displays of information at a computer terminal denies people access to the kinds of data and actions that they usually employ to validate their observations. Sandra O'Connell (1988) raised a similar concern when she said, "Meaning for the computer is established through precisely defined code. Humans . . . establish meaning through context and interpretation" (p. 474). For example, a good deal of ordinary "sense making" occurs by affiliating and deliberating with others. We decide "how things are" by comparing our thoughts and feelings with those of other people and negotiating with them to arrive at "some mutually acceptable version of what really happened" (Weick, p. 54). But technology isolates us from affiliation and moves too quickly for deliberation. While Weick is worried that "extensive nonsocial interaction with a terminal can atrophy social skills" and lead to "clumsy interactions" (p. 60), he is more concerned that it will lead to gross distortions in our interpretations of reality unless people learn to "simply push back from their terminals and walk around" (p. 61) in order to interact with one another and to use their ordinary sense-making capabilities.

Do contemporary information technologies threaten the quality of human organizational communication as well as organization members' sense-making capacities? No doubt, debate over this question will continue into the 1990s. Regardless of the final answer, reliance on these technologies certainly is increasing. Protests against their overuse are likely to fall on deaf ears in the management ranks of work organizations. If the trends identified thus far in research continue, we may see two related outcomes.

First, *job* satisfaction may actually increase with the introduction and use of electronic information-processing systems, especially if the technology permits more time for creative work, but organization members' sense of alienation and isolation from one another also will increase (Bjorn-Andersen, 1981). Second, organization members may have to develop new flexibility in their communicative behaviors. They must be able to work through a depersonalized electronic communications system, yet also function in a highly interpersonal environment when breakdowns and other problems force temporary abandonment of the system (Roveda & Cibbora, 1981).

O'Connell (1988) has gone even further in her assessment of the potential impact of new information technologies on organizational communication. She presented six hypotheses regarding the potential changes:

1. Opportunities for face-to-face contact will be diminished; information from nonverbal cues will be reduced. Consequently, opportunities for random, spontaneous information sharing will be reduced. Managers will need to structure work and relationships to provide more opportunities for face-to-face contact to occur. Meaning will be derived increasingly from text and symbols.

2. More informal message and "short-circuiting" of the hierarchy will occur as new formats are accepted due to the remote nature of an electronic network. Organization structure and formal information flow will be redefined.

3. Channel effects will mean that messages of affect and values will decrease. Digitized data, with less context and interpretation, will be the norm. Consequently, decision making may be impaired rather than enhanced. Ambiguity in interpreting information will increase, and the quality of decisions could decrease with the lack of organizational values and context. Organizations will need to work harder at communicating their values and corporate history. Managers will have to seek new ways of communicating the affective component of messages. New and improved decision-making skills will be needed.

4. Trust will play a changed role in communication. Trust develops with shared experience, values, give-and-take, which is the result of human communication. Satellites, electronic mail, and networks could reduce the dimensions of trust to which we are accustomed. New ones may spring up in their place.

5. The computer imposes a discipline of linear thinking. Data is processed at speeds that increase with each new version of the chip. Consequently, people may develop less patience and tolerance for individual styles of communicating. Organizations may find themselves less tolerant of people who do not think or perceive in a strict linear mode. They will need to find ways to encourage and protect nonlinear thinking and communicating.

6. Expectations of work performance may be machine driven. As we become accustomed to the speed and accuracy of the computer, we may expect employees to have the same qualities and produce in a similar manner. Employees in some organizations will perceive this as dehumanizing and cohersive [sic]. Unions will take up the human environment as an issues [sic]. New ways of defining and using performance standards will be needed. (pp. 480–481)

Communication and Technological Skill

We do not wish to close this chapter with the implication that "human communication" and "information technology" are antithetical. Indeed, some research suggests that communicative ability may be important in one's acquisition of new technology. Papa and Tracy (1987) studied the transition from one computer system to another in a large, multiline insurance company with specific attention to the relationship between each employee's communicative behaviors and their productivity with the new system. The transition involved a major change in the employee's tasks. According to their findings, "The more an employee was communicatively competent, a skillful listener, and talked frequently about the new task, the more productive that employee was likely to be using the new computer" (p. 17). Papa and Tracy also found that communicative competence and interaction frequency were negatively correlated with declines in productivity during the first week that the new computer was used and positively correlated with the speed with which employees returned to their past levels of performance. These findings may be particularly important, since those employees who were productive under the routine of the old system were not necessarily productive under the novel conditions of the new system.

Summary   Electronic information-processing technology occurs in several basic forms, including computerized accounting, integrated data processing, integrated MIS, real-time MIS, and distributed processing. Each form represents a technological advance over those that preceded it, but the history of the technology is so recent that all forms are found in contemporary organizations.

Changes in organizations as a consequence of information technology innovations depend to some extent on the form of the technology. Where computers are used only for accounting functions, few changes appear to occur. Other systems may foster various changes. In particular, use of the technology as a means for centralization or decentralization of decision making and authority has occupied the attention of management theorists. Some predictions and studies suggest that top managers use the technology to recentralize authority that they delegated in earlier decades. Others claim that MIS and distributed systems in particular foster decentralization. Some European research suggests that both conditions may follow as consequences of technological change. Advocates of the so-called neutrality position claim that information technology may be used for either centralization or decentralization.

While the impact of technology on centralization is not entirely clear, studies consistently suggest that jobs are redefined as a consequence of electronic information processing. Although the technology may not actually eliminate jobs, it may also be perceived as a threat to job security. Effects on staffing and job definitions mean that organizations must consider the kinds of communication strategies that they will employ in gaining acceptance of technology. Research on this problem seems to indicate that acceptance is greatest under conditions of active participation in decisions related to the technological change.

Most of the technological implications for organizational communication are linked to recent developments such as the information bus or fully integrated audio, video, and digital information networks in LANs and WANs. These systems have many capabilities that can complement or replace other forms of communication. Such capabilities include computer messaging, computer conferencing, teleconferencing, computer bulletin boards, computer newsletters, voicegrams, and data-base access. Research on the use of these technologies has produced both positive and negative results. In any case, some theorists believe that these contemporary technologies will change the character of complex human interaction in organizations.

Discussion Questions/ Activities

1. Given the different forms of electronic information-processing technology described in this chapter, which ones do you think are most likely to affect organizational communication? What kinds of changes, if any, are likely to occur as organizations adopt these technologies?
2. Some studies have found that adoption of electronic information technology is followed by organizational changes that have features of both centralization and decentralization. Can you think of some ways in which this might occur?
3. Have a discussion with someone who works in an organization that uses advanced systems of information technology. How does this person feel about the technology? Does this person feel that the technology has a particular effect on organizational communication?

The New System

Case Study

An American company has a large training facility where approximately 100,000 people are trained a year. Logistical requirements for the training of these personnel include the managing of classrooms and equipment, the coordinating of housing and meals, the scheduling of faculty, the booking of participants, and the arranging of inbound and outbound transportation. At any time, a potential exists for 45,000 people to make a request to hold a meeting or a training session. Each request involves all aspects of managing the facility. For example, if John Doe, vice-president of marketing, wants to hold a workshop for his marketing representatives, the following would have to be done:

1. Request made to facilities management specifying number of attendees and room preference.
2. If request is approved and space is available, detailed information needs to be provided to answer the following questions:
   A. Number of rooms? Layout of each?
   B. Number of attendees?
   C. Equipment needs (always a big production for marketing)? When? What?
   D. Special meals/events if appropriate (i.e., banquet last night or cocktails before dinner)?

    E. The names of attendees and faculty? When will they arrive? How long they will stay, and when will they need transportation to the airport?

    F. Charge number: How to bill? Who to bill?

3. Participants register with the registrar (one designated for each school). They communicate their arrival day/time and departure information by a registration form. This information is entered on a computer, which is accessed only by the registrar. A request for information about attendees is made by telephone.

4. Details about A, B, C, & D are communicated by the person requesting the program to facilities management. The information is keyed into a computer system that is accessed only by facilities management. That office prints copies of the completed request form and routes the form to the requestor for confirmation. Copies also are given to support staff, including Audio Visual Department, Room Set-up, Materials/Distribution, and Catering, when appropriate. Any requests for information or changes are made by telephone or by a revised form.

Two years ago, the company began designing a computer system that would enable all departments to access the same information through their computer network. The design phase required one year, and implementation was expected to take six months. This system would effect all the 500 people working at the Center. The goal of the system was to save time and, consequently, money. It would cut down on the number of telephone calls and the amount of paperwork. It would also increase the accuracy of information. Each person working directly in the Center would have access to the system at his/her desk. People outside the Center (e.g., those who requested programs or others who frequently needed information) would also have access. They would be able to input and review. Everyone would be able to use the computer at his/her desk to review information, to check for accuracy, or to check the status of the project. Departments no longer would be dependent on someone else to do their job. If a change was necessary, they could get on the system and make it themselves, rather than requesting that the change be made and then double-checking.

The potential benefits—and potential complications—of the system were substantial. Generally, the implementation of the new system was handled proactively and effectively.

- Users were involved in the design phase by being interviewed for suggestions.

- A steering committee was formed, which included one or two people from each area. These committee meetings kept people informed of progress and provided a forum to discuss major issues. Decisions were made in those meetings and then implemented.

- Once the system was operational, each area chose two or three people to get involved in a user acceptance test. This was an opportunity to both train end-users and to get feedback about the system.

- The people managing the design and implementation of the system were always accessible and continuously consulted users for information.

    Despite these safeguards, problems arose during and after the change.

- The conversion required substantial overtime.

- It took longer than expected for people to learn how to fully use the system. To date, the only form of training was a user's manual.

- Some employees experienced computer anxiety. They were afraid of making mistakes that impacted hundreds of other people.

- It was actually more difficult to expedite "special" or "rush" requests for programs that did not fit into the routine of the system design. When problems arose, some Center personnel used the limitations of the new system as an excuse not to solve the problem.

1. Are there any surprises in the case? That is, given what you read in the chapter, would you expect to see both the benefits and the problems that this company experienced with its new information system? Why or why not?
2. Evaluate the company's steps in designing and implementing the system. Was the process an effective way of meeting potential resistance to change?
3. What, if anything, could the company have done differently to make the implementation more successful?

References

Barron, I., & Curnow, R. (1979). *The future with microelectronics.* Milton Keynes, England: The Open University Press.

Bjorn-Andersen, N. (1981). The impact of electronic digital technology on traditional job profiles. In *Microelectronics, productivity, and employment.* Paris: Organisation for Economic Cooperation and Development.

Brink, V. Z. (1969, Jan.–Feb.). Top management looks at the computer. *Columbia Journal of World Business,* pp. 77–103.

Burnett, G. J. (1975). Computer options: Large centralized computers versus minicomputers. In F. W. McFarlan & R. Nolan (Eds.), *The information systems handbook.* Homewood, IL: Dow Jones-Irwin.

Casbolt, D. M., & Cherry, J. (1983). *The decentralization of an organization's information center: Organizational change issues and answers.* Paper presented at the annual meeting of the International Communication Association, Dallas.

Conrath, D. W., & Bair, J. (1974). The computer as an interpersonal communication device: A study of augmentation technology and its apparent impact on organizational communication. *Proceedings of the Second International Conference on Computer Communications.* Stockholm, Sweden, pp. 121–127.

Danowski, J. A. (1983). *Organizational communication: Theoretical implications of communication technology applications.* Paper presented at the annual meeting of the International Communication Dallas.

Davenport, L. L. (1981). Technology and the communication society: An informal overview. In M. Lehman & T. J. M. Burke (Eds.), *Communication technologies and information flow.* New York: Pergamon Press.

Emery, J. C. (1964). The impact of information technology on organization. *Proceedings of the 24th annual meeting, Academy of Management.*

Goldhaber, G. M. (1990). *Organizational communication* (5th ed.). Dubuque, IA: Wm. C. Brown Company Publishers.

Gouldner, A. W., & Alvin, W. (1955). *Patterns of industrial bureaucracy.* London: Routledge & Kegan Paul.

Gratz, R. D., & Salem, P. J. (1984).Technology and the crisis of self. *Communication Quarterly, 32,* 98–103.

Greenless, M. (1971). Time-sharing computers in business. In W. G. House (Ed.), *The impact of information technology on management operation.* Princeton, NJ: Auerbach.

Hiltz, S. R., Johnson, K., & Agle, G. (1978). *Replicating Bales problem-solving experiments on a computerized conferencing system. Report 8.* Newark, NJ: New Jersey Institute of Technology, Computerized Conferencing and Communications Center.

Hiltz, S. R., & Turoff, M. (1978). *Network nation.* Reading, MA: Addison-Wesley.

House, W. G. (Ed.). (1971). *The impact of information technology on management operation.* Princeton, NJ: Auerbach.

Joseph, E. C. (1969, August). The coming age of management information systems. *Financial Executive,* pp. 45–52.

Kanter, J. (1972, April). The impact of computers on the business operation. *Data Management,* pp. 20–23.

Kiesler, S., Siegel, J., & McGuire, T. (1984). Social psychological aspects of computer-mediated communication. *American Psychologist, 39,* 1123–1134.

Latamore, G. B. (1988). Why everyone works smarter when they're connected. *Working Woman,* October.

Meisner, N. B. (1980). The information bus in the automated office. In N. Naffah (Ed.), *Integrated office systems: Burotics.* Amsterdam: North-Holland.

Millman, Z., & Hartwick, J. (1987). The impact of automated office systems on middle managers and their work. *MIS Quarterly,* 478–489.

Naisbitt, J. (1982). *Megatrends: Ten new directions transforming our lives.* New York: John Wiley & Sons.

O'Connell, S. E. (1988). Human communication in the high tech office. In G. M. Goldhaber & G. A. Barnett (Eds.), *Handbook of organizational communication* (pp. 473–482). Norwood, NJ: Ablex.

Olson, M. H. (1982). New information technology and organizational culture. *MIS Quarterly,*

Papa, M. J., & Tracy, K. (1988). Communicative indices of employee performance with new technology. *Communication Research, 15,* 524–544.

Rice, R. E. (1982). Communication networking in computer conferencing systems: A longitudinal study of group roles and system structure. In M. Burgoon (Ed.), *Communication yearbook 6,* (pp. 925–944). Beverly Hills, CA: Sage.

Rice, R. E. (Ed.). (1984). *The new media: Communication, research, and technology.* Beverly Hills, CA: Sage.

Rice, R. E., & Bair, J. H. (1984). New organizational media and productivity. In R. E. Rice (Ed.), *The new media: Communication, research, and technology.* Beverly Hills, CA: Sage.

Rice, R. E., & Case, D. (1983). Computer-based messaging in the university: A description of use and utility. *Journal of Communication, 33,* 131–152.

Rogers, E. M. (1988). Information technologies: How organizations are changing. In G. M. Goldhaber & G. A. Barnett (Eds.), *Handbook of organizational communication* (pp. 437–452). Norwood, NJ: Ablex.

Roveda, C., & Cibbora, C. (1981). Impact of information technology on organisational structures. In *Microelectronics, productivity and employment.* Paris: Organisation for Economic Cooperation and Development.

Sanders, D. H. (1974). *Computers and management in a changing society* (2nd ed.). New York: McGraw-Hill.

Steinfield, C. (1983). *Communicating via electronic mail: Patterns and predictors of use in organizations.* Unpublished doctoral dissertation, University of Southern California.

Tapscott, D. (1982). *Office automation: A user-driven method.* New York: Plenum Press.

Thierauf, R. J. (1978). *Distributed processing systems.* Englewood Cliffs, NJ: Prentice-Hall.

Vergin, R. C. (1967, Summer). Computer-induced organizational changes. *MSU Business Topics,* pp. 61–68.

Weick, K. E. (1985). Cosmos vs. chaos: Sense and nonsense in electronic contexts. *Organizational Dynamics, 14,* 51–65.

West, J. M. (1981). Some questions about the new office technology. In M. Lehman & T. J. M. Burke (Eds.), *Communication technologies and information flow.* New York: Pergamon Press.

Whisler, T. (1970). *The impact of computers on organizations.* New York: Praeger.

part three

CONTEXTS

Outline

Theories of Dyadic Communication
    Motivational Theory
    Personality Theory
    Rules Theory
Superior-Subordinate
        Communication
    Subordinate Satisfaction
    Superior's Compliance Gaining
    Subordinate Behavior

Assimilation Theory
Conclusions from Superior-
    Subordinate Research
Unanswered Questions in Dyadic
    Communication
Summary
Discussion Questions/Activities
Case Study
References

Dyadic Communication

8

The **dyad,** or *two-person* relationship, represents the most basic level at which human interaction occurs in organizational settings. Many day-to-day episodes of organizational communication occur in a dyadic context (e.g., conversations with coworkers, communication between superiors and subordinates, and sending and receiving information to and from other organizational units).

Several scholars stress the importance of the dyad in organizational communication. For example, Karl Weick (1979) believes that **double interacts** provide the foundation of all human-organizing activity. A double interact occurs when "an action by actor A evokes a specific response in actor B . . . which is then responded to by actor A" (p. 89). According to Weick, most double interacts originate in dyads. Goldhaber, Dennis, Richetto, and Wiio also write about the significance of dyadic communication in organizations when they point out that "the relationship level [is] where most of the work of the organization is accomplished, where most of the communication difficulties are primarily encountered, and where the survival potential of the organization is qualitatively judged" (1979, p. 104).

Although dyadic organizational communication occurs in many different forms and types of relationships, organizational scholars have devoted almost all of their attention to only one type of dyad—the superior-subordinate relationship. With the exception of a few studies on the development of romantic relationships in organizations (Dillard & Witteman, 1985) and research on a special type of career relationship called the "mentor-protégé" relationship (Daniels & Logan, 1983), we generally have restricted systematic study of dyadic organizational communication to superior-subordinate relationships.

In part, this narrow focus developed from a belief that the most important episodes of organizational communication occur in superior-subordinate relationships (Eisenberg, Monge, & Farace, 1984). It also is based on a long-standing desire to identify the means of achieving organizational effectiveness through managerial control. In some cases, research is driven by the human relations assumptions that superiors gain compliance from subordinates by promoting interpersonal relationships and satisfaction of social needs. More recently, scholars have treated the superior's role as one of facilitation and creation of the proper climate for development of subordinates' capabilities (i.e., human resource development). In either case, *we have been preoccupied with revealing strategies for superiors to use in communicating with subordinates for accomplishment of organizational objectives.*

In this chapter, we review three different groups of theories and models that have been used to describe and explain dyadic organizational communication. We also summarize a number of important themes and conclusions from research on superior-subordinate communication. Finally, we describe some of the findings from the limited research conducted to date on other types of organizational dyads.

Theories of Dyadic Communication

Trying to explain just what occurs in the process of dyadic communication and why it occurs is no easy matter. Although scholars have developed many theories and models of interpersonal communication, three systems of explanation in particular have been applied to organizational dyadic relationships in order to make sense of the communication processes that occur there. These systems are **motivational theory, personality theory,** and **rules theory.**

Motivational Theory

Motivational theories are based on principles of drive reduction and need fulfillment. They view behavior as a response to drives that arise from unsatisfied needs. In other words, behavior occurs in order to satisfy needs. Motivational theories in this form have been applied to organizational relationships in two ways. First, motivational explanations are used to account for why individuals behave in particular ways. For example, certain styles of interpersonal communication might be attributed to a need to control others. Second, motivational models are used to provide prescriptions for influencing or gaining others' behavioral compliance. For example, what are the best communication strategies that supervisors can use to promote worker productivity?

One motivational theory that attempts to explain individual behavior in interpersonal relationships is William Schutz's (1958) fundamental interpersonal relations orientation (FIRO). According to Schutz, your fundamental orientation or typical behavior in interpersonal relationships depends on your particular "mix" of three interpersonal needs: inclusion, affection, and control.

Inclusion involves a need for interaction and participation with others in social relationships. **Affection** is a need for warmth and caring in one's relationships. **Control** refers to the need to exercise power and influence over others. We might expect, for example, that a person who is high in need for control and also prefers impersonal and distant relationships might be inclined to behave in an autocratic or manipulative manner. In contrast, an individual who has high needs for affection and inclusion but low need for control might be very submissive and compliant with others.

Many theories of motivation have been used to generate prescriptions for influencing or gaining others' compliance. One example of a theory that has been used in this way is Frederick Herzberg's (1966) motivator-hygiene theory.

Like other human resource development theories of the 1960s, motivator-hygiene theory is based on Maslow's need-hierarchy concepts, but Herzberg added two novel and unique features to his theory:

1. Satisfaction and dissatisfaction are *not* opposite conditions. The opposite of satisfaction is simply the absence of satisfaction.
2. The factors that lead to job satisfaction and motivation are *different* from those that lead to job dissatisfaction.

Herzberg observed in his studies of organizations that six factors seemed to contribute to job satisfaction and motivation for high levels of performance, while a different set of ten factors was related to job dissatisfaction. The satisfiers, called **motivators,** and the dissatisfiers, called **hygiene factors,** are as follows:

Motivators

Achievement
Recognition
Advancement
The work itself
Responsibility
Possibility of personal growth

Hygiene Factors

Company policy and administration
Technical supervision
Relationship with supervisor
Relationships with peers
Relationships with subordinates
Salary
Job security
Personal life
Work conditions
Status

Even a casual comparison of motivator-hygiene theory with Maslow's need hierarchy as described in chapter 3 will suggest that Herzberg's motivators correspond to Maslow's esteem and actualization needs, while hygiene factors correspond to the lower-level needs in Maslow's hierarchy. What is different is Herzberg's argument about the relationship of the two sets of factors to satisfaction and dissatisfaction. According to Herzberg, failure to provide for workers' hygiene needs will lead to dissatisfaction and poor performance, but meeting these needs does not produce motivation to improve performance. For example, if you do not feel that you are adequately paid, you may be dissatisfied and perform poorly. On the other hand, a pay raise is not likely to turn you into a better performer.

Herzberg's theory made the idea of job-enrichment programs very popular in business and industry during the 1970s. These programs look for ways to incorporate the six motivators into the work environment. In particular, such programs are concerned with enhancing the value of the work itself. But how does the motivator-hygiene theory apply to organizational *relationships?* Steinmetz and Todd (1975) claim that supervisory functions usually are organized around attention to Herzberg's hygiene factors. Hence, supervisory activity does not encourage subordinates to perform better. It merely discourages poor performance. Since interpersonal relations at all levels are presumed to be hygiene factors, Wayne Pace (1983) actually argues:

A supervisor who does a good job of creating positive relationships with employees will be disappointed if he or she thinks that those employees will be motivated to work harder as a result. . . . To motivate employees, the supervisor will need to find ways to give employees greater freedom and more responsibility in doing their work, or at least give them more recognition for work done well. (p. 89)

Personality Theory

While motivational theory explains behavior as a need-meeting or drive-reduction process, personality theory views behavior as the product of a central set of acquired traits and dispositions. This viewpoint is not necessarily inconsistent with motivational theory, but it does shift our focus in understanding human action to patterns of a person's behavior that are relatively enduring and stable over time and circumstance.

We should hasten to add that the concept of human personality as a set of individual traits and dispositions represents only one school of thought in personality theory. Other social scientists have argued for many years that our behavior is mostly a reflection of the situations in which we find ourselves rather than a result of so-called personality traits. Most probably subscribe to a more contemporary notion that personality is not so much an individual or personal phenomenon but an *interpersonal* phenomenon (Secord & Backman, 1964). Nevertheless, the individual disposition school is most often reflected in applications of personality theory to organizational life (e.g., see Spector, 1982).

One of the earliest attempts to explain behavior in organizational relationships in terms of personality traits was presented by Presthus in 1962. Presthus reported that three basic types of personalities are encountered in the typical bureaucratic organization: upward mobiles, indifferents, and ambivalents. The labels are to some extent self-explanatory, but some description of each "personality" is appropriate to understand how trait theories account for interpersonal behavior.

Upward mobiles identify strongly with the organization, seek power and prestige, are rule- and procedure-oriented (play by the book), and tend to have an internal locus of control (belief that they are captains of their own destinies, not victims of fate). Upward mobiles also are characterized as impersonal. They may, in fact, interact with others very frequently and very effectively, but they see human relationships primarily in utilitarian terms. They ask such questions as "What's in it for me?" or "What task or career function does this relationship serve?"

Indifferents might be best described as those organization members who are just trying to get by or working only as a means of earning a living. They do not see themselves engaged in the pursuit of a career or profession. They avoid or reject self-discipline, striving for success, and anxiety-provoking situations. In general, they separate private life and work life, closely protecting the latter from infringement by the former. According to Koehler, Anatol, and Applbaum (1981), indifferents may well constitute the great majority of workers in most organizations. They generally get along quite well with one another and reinforce their views of organizational life within their group.

Ambivalents are an organizational minority, but they may be more visible and troubling than indifferents because they are not complacent about their lot in life. Ambivalents face a conflict that seems to provoke a neurotic pattern of responses. Like the upward mobiles, ambivalents appear to desire status and power but they lack either the abilities, skills, or temperament to "play the game" and to compete for organizational success. Their frustrations are reflected in criticisms of the organizational status quo. They resist authority and rules, often seem to be out of step with others, and tend to be introverted, withdrawn, and inept at group processes. They may also be very bright, creative, and good at their jobs.

Presthus' description of personality types in organizations is somewhat outmoded and overshadowed today by other attempts to explain organizational behavior with reference to personality traits. Koehler, Anatol, and Applbaum (1981) devoted an entire chapter to personality in their text on organizational communication with discussions of many personality types in organizational settings, including authoritarians, Machiavellians, dogmatics, and others. In each case, they attempted to demonstrate how certain traits lead to stable patterns of behavior within organizational roles.

Rules Theory

Motivational and personality theories are concerned primarily with accounts of *individual* behaviors. Even though such theories may consider the behavior in the context of an interpersonal relationship, the question that they ask is still "Why does Person X act in a particular way?" In contrast to these theories, rules theory is *not* focused on individual behavior. Rules theory is explicitly a theory (or, more properly, a group of theories) about interpersonal communication. It attempts to account for the ways in which two or more individuals structure and coordinate their interaction. The foundation of this structure and coordination is the **communication rule.**

Generally speaking, a rule is an instance of "social knowledge" that a person uses to sequence and coordinate his or her actions with those of other people (Rose, 1985). These instances of social knowledge help us to distinguish different types of situations and relationships, to interpret others' behaviors, and to define our own actions in a situation. For example, the rules that define an "intimate relationship" and guide our actions in that relationship are different from those that apply to a "casual acquaintance."

One familiar type of rule is the social norm. A norm is an expectation shared within a group that provides a standard of appropriate behavior for individual members (Secord & Backman, 1964). Normative expectations are communicated to group members in various ways, and the group generates pressure on individual members to conform. If individual behavior deviates too much from the norm, the individual may be punished or sanctioned in some way.

"Rule" is a broader concept than "norm." All norms are based on rules, but all rules are not necessarily normative. A norm usually is regarded as a group standard that is imposed on the individual. Most of the rules that operate in day-to-day interaction seem to have little normative force. They are not so much fixed group standards for "correct" individual behavior, but flexible and sometimes highly personal guidelines for interpretations and actions that "make sense" or "fit" within a particular situation.

Since every interpersonal encounter involves many rules, describing how interaction is structured and coordinated through the use of rules can be very complicated. We will begin with a concrete example, then apply some of the key concepts in rules theory to show how they account for interaction.

Jamie Ryan was so pleased to get her first job with a small, local construction company after college graduation that she completely forgot to ask what time to report on her first day of work. She guessed that 7:45 A.M. would be about right, so she was pleased to see that the company president and the secretary/receptionist were just getting out of their cars as she pulled into the parking lot.

As Jamie approached the others, she called out, "Good morning. Are we the first ones here?" Mr. Harter, the president, smiled and replied, "You're a little early. The rest of the troops will be here at 8 o'clock. Valene and I get here about a quarter 'til to open up. By the way, Val, this is Jamie Ryan, our new purchasing agent. Jamie, this is Valene Smith, our gal Friday." "Hello," said Jamie. Valene, a fortyish woman with platinum blond hair, spiked heels, and heavy makeup, was unlocking the office door. In addition to her duties as secretary/receptionist, she used to help Mr. Harter with all of the purchase orders before he decided that the job had become big enough to warrant a full-time purchasing agent. She was hurt by his decision to hire a college kid, but she had kept this to herself. Without even looking at Jamie, she quipped, "Please to meetcha, honey." Val's tone seemed aloof to Jamie and Jamie resented the term, *honey*. She felt as if the older woman had just snubbed her.

Upon entering the office reception area, Valene immediately switched on an FM receiver behind her desk. The raucous sound of country and western music flooded the room. Jamie, who hated country and western music, questioned Val, "Do you play this stuff all the time?" She put the question in a light, humorous manner, but Valene clearly was not amused. She literally glowered at Jamie, then sharply snapped, "Listen, honey, this ain't no college sorority house. This is a construction company and we get a lot of rough, tough ole boys in and out of here all day. They like this music, I like this music, and you better get used to it." Jamie turned to see Mr. Harter's reaction, but he had already entered his own office. She sensed that she had violated the first commandment of office politics: Thou shalt not ruffle the secretary's feathers. She also sensed that Valene felt truly threatened by a newcomer in the office. "Sorry," said Jamie. "I didn't mean anything by it." Valene seemed to soften a bit. "Apology accepted, honey, just so long as you realize that this front office is *my* territory. I've done this job the same way every day for fifteen years and I don't plan any changes for at least fifteen more."

This example illustrates what rules theorists call **episodes,** "Communication routines that people view as distinct wholes . . . a patterned series of reciprocated speech acts" (Rose, p. 327). Episodes are defined by two types of rules called constitutive and regulative. **Constitutive rules** tell us what a particular behavior means, whereas **regulative rules** tell us what we should or might do in a situation; namely, what acts are supposed to precede or follow other acts (Pearce & Cronen, 1980).

The morning greeting ritual in our example is a fairly common episode in organizations. Participants in this episode probably have very clear constitutive rules for defining "greeting ritual" as well as regulative rules for how to conduct this ritual. But this morning's ritual is different because of Jamie's arrival. The normal exchange between Mr. Harter and Valene is restructured to accommodate a third party. Jamie not only applies a rule about initiating greetings when she says, "Good morning," but also uses the situation to resolve some uncertainty over when to report to work by asking whether she, Mr. Harter, and Val are the first arrivals. This reflects creative use of a regulative rule that makes sense in the context of this episode. Mr. Harter applies a constitutive rule to interpret Jamie's question as a request for information. He has a choice of regulative rules to follow. A simple "yes" would satisfy the obvious requirements of Jamie's question, but Harter uses the situation to explain a standard operating procedure. The rules allow this latitude, Harter uses it, and the outcome makes sense.

Introduction episodes also are very common and usually subject to social norms concerning politeness. However, in this example, Valene may be using the episode as an occasion to express disdain. In effect, Valene bends the rules of the situation to accomplish her own purposes. Jamie applies a constitutive rule about social rejection to interpret Val's quip in the context of an introduction as an arrogant snub and decides that silence is the best response (regulative rule).

The confrontation episode begins innocently enough. Jamie's question about the playing of country music might be interpreted in many ways, but her tone and phrasing may have suggested that she is hardly a fan. The constitutive rule that Val applies yields only one interpretation. The question is really a put-down and a challenge that asks Val to justify her preferences. Val's regulative rule in the situation calls for a counterattack. Here, we also see how rules are established through interaction. During the confrontation, the participants are testing rules of relationship control (i.e., dominance and submission). Valene quickly gains the upper hand and reinforces her position when Jamie yields with an apology. In effect, Val successfully defines a rule for the relationship: Everything will be fine so long as *you* know your place—honey!

Farace, Monge, and Russell (1977) pointed out that rules come into play for virtually every aspect of interaction. For example, rules are required to answer the following questions:

What topics will be discussed?
How will these topics be discussed?

How are topic shifts handled?
How are interruptions handled?
Who initiates conversations?
Who terminates conversations?
How are delays handled?
How often does interaction occur?
Are the communication rules satisfactory?

The authors also noted that the key to understanding how rules structure and coordinate interaction lies in the concept of **coorientation.** As we indicated earlier, a rule essentially is an instance of social knowledge that an individual possesses, but communication cannot be structured solely from one participant's knowledge of rules. For two or more individuals to communicate, they must, to some extent, achieve a common frame of reference on the rules that they apply in the situation. A and B must act toward each other in a reciprocal manner that has some degree of common meaning for both. This is coorientation.

Coorientation of rules in interpersonal communication includes two concepts: agreement and accuracy. Agreement occurs when two parties have the same viewpoint of the communication rules in a situation. Accuracy occurs when each person can reliably describe the other's viewpoint. Given these concepts, Scheff (1967) describes four conditions that can be regarded as coorientation states. These states are displayed in figure 8.1.

When agreement and accuracy are both high, the condition is called **monolithic consensus.** In this case, both parties agree and know that they agree. Suppose that we ask Jamie and Valene to describe the rules that define their relationship and to predict each other's descriptions. In monolithic consensus, we might see the following responses.

Jamie: The relationship is defensive, and I'm sure that's how she wants it.
Valene: It's stiff and uneasy, and that probably suits her just fine.

Where agreement is low but accuracy is high, the condition is **dissensus.** The parties disagree and can predict the disagreement. In this case, we might see these descriptions.

Jamie: The relationship is defensive, but I don't think she sees it that way.
Valene: The relationship is open, but I'm sure she doesn't see it that way.

Where agreement is high but accuracy is low, the condition is **pluralistic ignorance.** The parties agree but do not realize it. For example:

Jamie: The relationship is defensive, but she probably thinks it's open and friendly.
Valene: It's uneasy and tense, but I'm sure she thinks it's friendly.

The final condition, **false consensus,** occurs when both accuracy and agreement are low. The parties not only disagree in their viewpoints, but they also cannot predict the disagreement.

Jamie: The relationship is defensive, and I'm sure that's the way she likes it.
Valene: Well, we're pretty open and friendly, and I'm sure she'd tell you the same thing.

	Low	High
High	Pluralistic ignorance	Monolithic consensus
Low	False consensus	Dissensus

Agreement

Figure 8.1
Four conditions of agreement and accuracy on communication rules. From *Communicating and Organizing,* by R. V. Farace, P. R. Monge, and H. M. Russell, 1977. Reading, MA: Addison-Wesley. Reprinted by permission from Random House, Inc.

According to Farace, Monge, and Russell (1977), monolithic consensus is the ideal condition in communication, although too much consensus can result in stagnation of a relationship. Dissensus usually is regarded as healthy inasmuch as the differing points of view are at least expressed and acknowledged. Pluralistic ignorance and false consensus both pose problems. Either condition allows for substantial miscommunication as a result of the participants' differing perceptions of the rules and the relationship. Grunig (1975) reported evidence that managers and employees often may be cooriented in a state of false consensus. They not only disagree with one another in their perceptions of the kinds of problems and concerns that are important to the organization, but they cannot even predict the extent of the disagreement.

Motivational theories, personality theories, and rules theories have been applied in various ways to explain interpersonal relationships in organizations. The theories do not necessarily conflict with one another, but they do differ in the ways that they attempt to account for human action. Motivational theorists assume that all human behavior, including interpersonal behavior, serves need-meeting or drive-reduction functions. Personality theorists try to explain individuals' relatively stable and enduring patterns of behavior in social settings with reference to acquired traits and dispositions. Rules theorists argue that interpersonal communication is structured and coordinated through application and coorientation of rules—instances of social knowledge that help us to interpret situations and define our actions within them. Each of these approaches is reflected in research on the dyadic communication topic in which organizational communication scholars have been most interested—the superior-subordinate relationship.

Superior-Subordinate Communication

The very idea of organization not only implies coordinated action, including divisions of labor and role specialization, but also a hierarchy of authority in which those who occupy higher positions are accorded more status, privilege, and power than those who occupy lower positions. A person at any given level of an organization generally is **subordinate** to an immediate **superior** (the person to whom you report, from whom you take orders—the boss). Although the superior-subordinate relationship involves mutual dependence, the subordinate generally is in the more dependent position. In effect, a person in a superior position is able to exert more control over a person in a subordinate position.

Eisenberg, Monge, and Farace (1984) argued, "Of the communication processes that operate in organizations, the most important include those that regulate interaction between superiors and subordinates" (p. 261). Many scholars apparently share this belief because there are far more studies of superior-subordinate communication than of any other relational context in organizations. Fredric Jablin published a 1979 landmark review of these studies in which he observed, "Research examining superior-subordinate communication is diverse, strewn across a multitude of disciplines, lacks coherent organization and classification, and, in general, has not received sufficient review and interpretation" (p. 1201).

Jablin reviewed more than 150 studies, which he organized into nine categories: interaction patterns and related attitudes, openness in communication, upward distortion, upward influence, semantic-information distance, effective versus ineffective superiors, personal characteristics, feedback, and systemic variables. Although we have included a summary of Jablin's specific findings in table 8.1, we will not attempt a comprehensive discussion of research in all nine categories. Instead, we will concentrate on lines of research that have continued in the 1980s.

Table 8.1 Summary of Jablin's review on superior-subordinate communication. From Organizational Communication: Foundations for Human Resource Development, by R. W. Pace, Copyright 1982, pp. 98–100. Reprinted by permission of Prentice-Hall, Inc., Englewood Cliffs, NJ.

Interaction Patterns

1. Between one-third and two-thirds of a supervisor's time is spent communicating with subordinates.
2. The dominant mode of interaction is face-to-face discussion.
3. The majority of interactions is about task issues.
4. Superiors are more likely than subordinates to initiate interaction.
5. Superiors are less positive toward and less satisfied with interactions with subordinates than with their superiors.
6. A subordinate's job satisfaction is positively correlated with estimates of communication contact with superiors.
7. Superiors think they communicate more with subordinates than subordinates think they do.
8. Subordinates feel they send more messages to their supervisors than the supervisors think they do.
9. Superiors who lack self-confidence are less willing to hold face-to-face discussions with subordinates.
10. Role conflict and role ambiguity on the part of superiors are correlated with direct interactions with subordinates.
11. Subordinates seek informal help in their work setting more from their superiors than from peers or subordinates.
12. Superiors are more likely to serve as liaisons about production rather than maintenance or innovation issues.

Openness in Communication

13. Subordinates are more satisfied with their jobs when openness of communication exists between superiors and subordinates.
14. Openness of communication appears to be related to organizational performance.
15. The willingness of superiors and subordinates to talk as well as the actual talk on a topic is a function of the perception of the others' willingness to listen.
16. Superiors and subordinates prefer supervisor responses that are accepting and reciprocating rather than neutral-negative (unfeeling, cold, or nonaccepting).
17. Subordinates dislike disconfirming responses from a superior and prefer those that provide positive relational feedback.

Upward Distortion of Communication

18. In superior-subordinate relationships when one person does not trust the other, the nontrusting person will conceal his or her feelings and engage in evasive, complaint, or aggressive communicative behavior and under- or over-estimate agreement on issues.
19. Subordinates will tend to omit critical comments in their interaction with superiors who have power over them.
20. Mobility aspirations and low trust tend to have a negative influence on the accuracy of communication between subordinates and superiors; however, even if the subordinate trusts his or her superior, high-mobility aspirations reduce the likelihood of communicating potentially threatening information.
21. Subordinates seem to feel less free to communicate with superiors who have held the subordinate's position.
22. Subordinates tend to see greater appropriateness, expect fewer harmful consequences, and have a greater willingness to disclose important, yet personally threatening, information to superiors in organic as compared with mechanistic organizational climates.
23. Subordinate tendencies to distort upward communication can be reduced by increasing the superior's consideration or by increasing the accuracy with which the superior transmits downward information.
24. Intrinsically motivated subordinates tend to distort messages less than do extrinsically motivated subordinates.

Upward Influence of a Subordinate's Superior, or the Pelz Effect

25. Supervisors who exercise influence upward with their own superiors are more likely to have subordinates with high levels of satisfaction, although extremely high influence may separate subordinates from superiors.
26. Subordinates who see their superior as having high-upward influence also have a high desire for interaction with, high trust in, and a high estimation of accuracy of information received from the superior.
27. Subordinate confidence and trust in a superior are positively related to the superior's success in interactions with higher levels of management.

Semantic-Information Distance

28. The larger the semantic distance between superior and subordinate, the lower the subordinate's morale.

29. Superiors tend to overestimate the amount of knowledge subordinates possess on given topics.
30. Significant semantic distances exist between union and management personnel and between union leadership and their members.
31. Serious semantic distances are frequent between superiors and subordinates.

Effective versus Ineffective Superiors

32. More effective superiors tend to enjoy talking and speaking up in meetings, are able to explain instructions and policies, and enjoy conversing with subordinates.
33. More effective superiors tend to be empathic listeners, responding understandingly to silly questions; they are approachable and listen to suggestions and complaints.
34. More effective superiors tend to ask or persuade rather than tell or demand.
35. More effective superiors tend to be sensitive to the feelings and ego needs of subordinates.
36. More effective superiors tend to be more open in passing information along by giving advance notice of changes and explaining the reasons for policies and regulations.
37. Supervisory effectiveness tends to be contingent on such factors as task structure, superior-subordinate relations, and superior-position power.

Superior-Subordinate Personal Characteristics

38. Subordinates who have tendencies toward an internal locus of control see their superiors as more considerate than do external-control subordinates and are more satisfied with participative superiors.
39. Superiors who have tendencies toward internal locus of control tend to use persuasion to obtain subordinate cooperation, whereas externals tend to use coercive power more.
40. Superiors tend to rate subordinates as competent when they have values similar to those of the superior.
41. Superiors who are apprehensive communicators are not particularly well liked by subordinates.
42. Authoritarian subordinates seem most satisfied when they work for directive superiors.
43. Subordinate satisfaction with his or her immediate superior is related to the subordinate's perception of the superior's credibility.

Feedback from Superiors and Subordinates

44. Subordinate feedback responsiveness is greater when subordinates are told what needs to be done with completed assignments, when the superior makes the assignment to the subordinate, and when the subordinate feels that he or she can secure clarification about assignments from the immediate superior.
45. Positive feedback to a superior tends to make the superior more task-oriented.
46. The performance of superiors tends to improve after feedback from a subordinate.
47. Feedback from a superior that shows a lack of trust results in subordinate dissatisfaction and aggressive feelings.

48. The technology of an organization tends to affect superior-subordinate communication.
49. Upper-level superiors tend to involve their subordinates more in decision making than do lower-level superiors.
50. Organizations with flat structures tend to reward superiors who favor sharing information and objectives with more rapid advancement than do organizations with tall structures.

Our own review suggests that contemporary research in superior-subordinate communication is every bit as fragmented and diverse as Jablin claims, but three themes seem to be dominant:

1. Identification of factors in superior-subordinate communication that are related to subordinates' satisfaction with their jobs, their superiors, and the organization, and, in some studies, to superiors' satisfaction with and evaluation of subordinates.
2. Description and explanation of the processes by which superiors attempt to influence or gain compliance from subordinates.
3. Description and explanation of subordinates' behaviors in communicating with superiors.

A fourth theme also appears to be emerging. This theme concerns the assimilation of new members in organizations. Although the factors that influence the assimilation process involve much more than superior-subordinate communication, we will discuss the process here because Jablin, one of the leaders in assimilation studies, emphasizes in his own research that the "supervisor is a key person in the organizational assimilation process" (1984, p. 624).

Subordinate Satisfaction

Research in the first category is derived from traditional human relations values and beliefs in the linkage between communication and effective supervision. In organizational communication, one important source of these values and beliefs is a series of graduate research projects directed by W. Charles Redding at Purdue University. These studies classified supervisors as effective or ineffective on the basis of ratings by higher-level managers, then examined the supervisors' communicative dispositions. Redding (1972) drew five major conclusions from these studies.

1. The better supervisors tend to be more "communication-minded." For example, they enjoy talking and speaking in meetings; they are able to explain instructions and policies; and they enjoy conversing with subordinates.

2. The better supervisors tend to be willing, empathic listeners; they respond understandingly to so-called "silly" questions from employees; they are approachable; and they will listen to suggestions and complaints, with an attitude of fair consideration and willingness to take appropriate action.
3. The better supervisors tend (with some notable exceptions) to "ask" or "persuade," in preference to "telling" or "demanding."
4. The better supervisors tend to be sensitive to the feelings. For example, they are careful to reprimand in private rather than in public.
5. The better supervisors tend to be more open in their passing along of information; they are in favor of giving advance notice of impending changes and of explaining the "reasons why" behind policies and regulations. (p. 433)

Although the Purdue studies were not directly concerned with the effect of superiors' communicative behavior on subordinate satisfaction and morale, the tone of Redding's conclusions bears a strong resemblance to the prescription that earlier human relations theorists offered: Management promotes compliance by promoting morale and satisfaction. Morale and satisfaction depend on effective interpersonal relations; namely, empathy, sensitivity to social needs, receptivity, and two-way communication—essentially the same communicative behaviors that the Purdue studies link with "effective supervision."

In a classic investigation closely related to the ideal of the Purdue studies, Jack Gibb (1961) made a more direct connection between superiors' communication and subordinate satisfaction by distinguishing between climates of supportive and defensive interpersonal communication. According to Gibb, a supportive climate leads to subordinate satisfaction and accuracy in communication, while a defensive climate leads to dissatisfaction and distortion of communication. He identified the communicative behaviors of superiors that trigger the development of these climates. The resulting model is summarized in table 8.2.

Table 8.2 Descriptions of Gibb's defensive and supportive communication climates. From "Defensive communication," by J. Gibb, 1961, *Journal of Communication, 11,* pp. 141–148.

Defensive	Supportive
1. *Evaluation:* To pass judgment on another; to blame or praise; make moral assessments of another or question his [or her] motives; to question the other's standards.	1. *Description:* Nonjudgmental; to ask questions which are perceived as requests for information; to present feelings, emotions, events which do not ask the other to change his or her behavior.
2. *Control:* To try to do something to another; to attempt to change behavior or attitudes of others; implicit in attempts to change others is the assumption that they are inadequate.	2. *Problem Orientation:* To convey a desire to collaborate in solving a mutual problem or defining it; to allow the other to set his [or her] goals and solve his [or her] own problem; to imply that you do not desire to impose your solution.

3. *Strategy:* To manipulate another or make him or her think that he or she was making his or her own decisions; to engage in multiple and/or ambiguous motivations; to treat the other as a guinea pig.

3. *Spontaneity:* To express naturalness; free of deception; a "clean id;" straightforwardness; uncomplicated motives.

4. *Neutrality:* To express a lack of concern for the other; the clinical, person-as-an-object-of-study attitude.

4. *Empathy:* To respect the other person and show it; to take his [or her] role; to identify with his [or her] problems; to share his [or her] feelings.

5. *Superiority:* To communicate that you are superior in position, wealth intelligence etc.; to arouse feelings of inadequacy in others; to express that you are not willing to enter into joint problem solving.

5. *Equality:* To be willing to enter into participative planning with mutual trust and respect; to attach little importance to differences in ability, worth, status, etc.

6. *Certainty:* Dogmatic; to seem to know the answers; wanting to win an argument rather than solve a problem; seeing one's ideas as truths to be defended.

6. *Provisionalism:* To be willing to experiment with your own behavior; to investigate issues rather than taking sides; to solve problems, not debate.

The influence of the Purdue studies, Gibb's model, and other studies such as those on communication openness (see findings in table 8.1) have continued in the 1980s through many investigations of factors in superior-subordinate communication that are related to subordinates' satisfaction with their job, superiors, and organizations. Most of these studies concern the relationship between some aspect of the superior's communicative behavior and subordinate satisfaction. Some explore the impact of political factors that extend beyond the relationship itself (e.g., the subordinate's perception of the supervisor's ability to influence higher levels of management). A few scholars have even studied the relationship between satisfaction and rules coorientation in superior-subordinate interaction.

Some studies of superiors' communicative behaviors are direct extensions of research themes of the 1960s and 1970s. For example, Wheeless, Wheeless, and Howard (1984) studied subordinates' job satisfaction as a function of their satisfaction with superiors, their perceptions of superiors' receptivity to upward communication, and their level of participation in organizational decision making. While satisfaction with superiors and perceived receptivity to upward communication were strong predictors of job satisfaction, *the relationship between job satisfaction and participation in decision making for lower-level employees was weak.* This finding runs contrary to the assumptions of human resource development about the benefits of participative management.

O'Reilly and Anderson (1980) extended another traditional theme in superior-subordinate studies by investigating the effects of trust on subordinate perceptions of feedback from superiors. While it is generally understood that feedback is related to subordinates' satisfaction and performance, O'Reilly and Anderson argued that subordinates' trust of superiors would influence this relationship. They found that *quantity* of feedback is related to satisfaction when subordinates trust superiors (i.e., more feedback leads to greater satisfaction). When subordinates do not trust superiors, *relevance* and *accuracy* (rather than quantity) of feedback promote satisfaction.

The finding for accuracy seems paradoxical in a way, since earlier studies by O'Reilly and Roberts (1974) indicated that low trust leads subordinates to distort information in upward communication. This raises the curious possibility in low-trust conditions that subordinates want and expect accurate feedback from superiors even though the subordinates themselves may distort upward communication.

One new line of research in the 1980s concerns the impact of argumentativeness in the superior's communication style. Infante and Gorden (1985) contend that contemporary perspectives of organizations involve a "corporatist theory" of human performance that advocates sociopsychological and ideological integration of individual members with the organization as a whole. One of the consequences of a corporatist environment is dialectical and disputative communication (argument).

Drawing a distinction between argument as a constructive form of discourse and verbal aggressiveness as demeaning and alienating, Infante and Gorden hypothesized that the more subordinates perceive superiors to be high in argumentativeness and low in verbal aggressiveness, the more the subordinates also will be argumentative as well as satisfied with their jobs. Results provided strong support of this hypothesis, suggesting that "argumentativeness is a constructive communicative predisposition" (p. 123).

More recently, Infante and Gorden (1987) reported research indicating that "independent-mindedness" is highly valued in American organizations. According to Infante and Gorden, the communicative attitude associated with independent-mindedness is based on argumentativeness, but excludes verbal aggressiveness. In a study of superior-subordiante dyads in more than 100 U. S. organizations, they found that superiors who are argumentative but low in verbal aggressiveness are perceived by their subordinates to be friendly and attentive. Argumentative superiors also were seen to have more influence with high levels of management. Superiors also valued the trait of argumentativeness in their subordinates. Infante and Gorden have suggested that these findings are important because they indicate the value of independent-mindedness within our highly individualistic American culture. They claim:

American corporate productivity will be restored to preeminence not by emulating Japanese management which is founded firmly in their cultural values of collectivism, harmony, and deference to authority, but by organizations nurturing employee independent-mindedness. (p. 73)

Although the study of argument is a new theme in superior-subordinate communication research, the concept of argument as constructive discourse is hardly novel in human resource and organization development theories. Such theories traditionally regard conflict as a necessary and constructive aspect of organizational behavior, but they focus on conflict within a given organizational level or between different organizational groups. Examination of constructive conflict or argument in the superior-subordinate relationship considerably extends the traditional theories.

Scholars are just beginning to study political factors outside the immediate superior-subordinate relationship that nonetheless influence superior-subordinate communication. However one traditional line of research in this area has received prominent attention in organizational communication. This research concerns subordinates' perceptions of superiors' influence with higher levels of management or *upward influence*.

Interest in upward influence began with a study by D. P. Pelz in 1952. Pelz pointed out that the relationship between supportiveness in a superior's communicative behavior and subordinates' satisfaction seems so intuitively obvious that it requires no special demonstration. But Pelz thought that this relationship had been misunderstood because an important variable, the superior's upward influence, had not been considered. According to Pelz, the critical factor affecting satisfaction is the combination or interaction of supportiveness with upward influence. Unsupportive behavior has no effect on the level of satisfaction. Subordinates with unsupportive superiors are neither satisfied nor dissatisfied, regardless of the superiors' upward influence. When the superior is supportive and has high upward influence, satisfaction can be expected, but *supportiveness in combination with low upward influence will lead to subordinate dissatisfaction.* A model of this relationship is displayed in figure 8.2.

According to Pelz, supportiveness raises subordinates' expectations for individual and work group reward, but a superior without upward influence is unable to fulfill the expectations. Consequently, dissatisfaction results. Pelz's research findings provided strong support for this hypothesis. Later research by House, Filley, and Gujarati (1971) suggested that high upward influence also could result in dissatisfaction and that the Pelz model was inaccurate.

Jablin (1980) attempted to resolve the inconsistent findings by examining the effects of supportiveness and upward influence on subordinates' job satisfaction and the perceptions of communication openness in the superior-subordinate relationship. Jablin found that high upward influence was associated with high satisfaction and perceived openness, but the same result occurred for supportiveness regardless of the superior's upward influence. Dissatisfaction did *not* occur with supportive superiors who were low in upward influence. Consequently, Jablin's results support neither of the previous studies. One possible explanation is that organizational values and subordinates' expectations have changed over the years since Pelz's original study. Supportiveness in organizational relationships is now valued so highly that it compensates for lack of upward influence (Daniels & Logan, 1983).

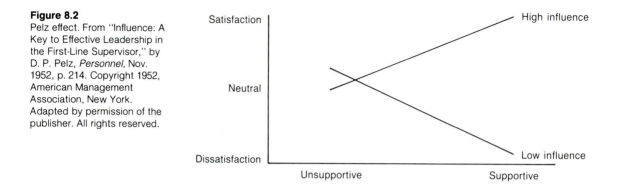

Figure 8.2
Pelz effect. From "Influence: A Key to Effective Leadership in the First-Line Supervisor," by D. P. Pelz, *Personnel,* Nov. 1952, p. 214. Copyright 1952, American Management Association, New York. Adapted by permission of the publisher. All rights reserved.

The studies described so far rely either explicitly or implicitly on motivational or personality theories. A few recent studies have attempted to explain subordinate satisfaction from a rules theory perspective. Eisenberg, Monge, and Farace (1984) applied the coorientation concept from rules theory as a predictor of subordinates' satisfaction with superiors and superiors' evaluations of subordinates. Specifically, they studied satisfaction as a function of agreement and accuracy on rules for initiating and terminating interaction. They found that *perceived* agreement was associated with the subordinate's satisfaction and the superior's evaluation. The superior's accuracy in perception of the subordinate's viewpoint on the rules also was associated with the superior's evaluation of the subordinate.

Ironically, *actual* agreement on communication rules was unrelated to either subordinate satisfaction or the superior's evaluation of the subordinate. In general, actual agreement and accuracy were both less important than perceived agreement. This may mean that false consensus as a coorientation state is not so bad after all. Put another way, sometimes ignorance is bliss.

Cline and Wilmoth (1987) extended this line of work by advancing a complex model of the relationship between coorientation and several other variables. They argued that greater frequency of communication leads to greater coorientation, which leads, in turn, to higher levels of communication satisfaction and job satisfaction. While they found that coorientation was, in their words, "causally related to communication satisfaction, which in turn, was causally related to job satisfaction" (p. 21), they found few connections between coorientation variables and frequency of communication.

Lamude, Daniels, and Graham (1988) attempted to explain factors that lead to the presence or absence of coorientation in superior-subordinate dyads. In particular, they focused on the sex composition of the dyad, hypothesizing that coorientation as well as communication satisfaction would be lower in female superior/male subordinate dyads than in dyads based on other sex combinations (male superior/male subordinate, male superior/female subordinate, female superior/female subordinate). The hypothesis was based on an assumption that female supervision of males is the least conventional arrangement, but the results of the study produced some surprises. Satisfaction was higher in same-sex dyads than in mixed-sex dyads, but coorientation was lower. Although male/male and female/female dyads reported greater levels of mutual communication satisfaction, they exhibited less accuracy and agreement on communication rules than did mixed-sex dyads. Perceived agreement also was much lower for male/male dyads than for other dyads, and perceived agreement among female/female dyads was greater than their actual agreement. These findings indicate that the relationship between coorientation and satisfaction is not as simple and straightforward as previous research has suggested.

Superior's Compliance Gaining

A second line of contemporary research in superior-subordinate communication involves description and explanation of communicative strategies that superiors use in order to gain compliance from subordinates. This line of research arises in part from earlier studies of feedback (see the feedback section in table 8.1). For example, Burke's (1970) finding that feedback expressing acceptance and encouragement is associated with subordinate satisfaction and Organ's (1974) conclusion that positive feedback leads to greater compliance from subordinates under conditions in which subordinates are subject to little surveillance from the superior.

Recent studies have been more concerned with the patterns of communication reflected in compliance gaining and more concerned with factors that may influence a superior's choice of compliance-gaining strategies. In particular, Fairhurst, Green, and Snavely (1984a; 1984b) have examined the strategies that managers use to correct or control poor performance by employees. They have emphasized the importance of studying control as a process that occurs over time, rather than as a single event. For example, one of their studies (1984b) described bank managers' use of face support in attempts to correct or control subordinates' poor performance. Face support includes two factors: (1) the degree of approval and (2) the degree of freedom given to poor performers to define a corrective course of action. The researchers found two different patterns in managers' behaviors over as many as four attempts to deal with a poor performer. The first pattern was punitive, consisting of direct disapproval (criticism and reprimand) and no freedom (threats and orders) throughout the entire sequence of correction attempts. The second pattern involved reliance on questions to discover the source of the problem and to identify possible solutions in early attempts (problem-solving approach), but this strategy was abandoned for the punitive approach in later attempts.

Fairhurst et al. offered this very insightful conclusion from their study:

Branch and personnel administrators in the banks we studied advocated the use of the punitive approach only after the problem-solving approach . . . repeatedly failed. Yet, in the field, we find that the punitive approach predominates from the start for many [while] the problem-solving approach is used by some but is quickly abandoned. (p. 289)

In other words, the managers professed commitment to problem solving as a strategy, but they showed little reliance on this strategy in actual attempts to control poor performance. In short, they simply did not practice what they preached.

Fairhurst et al. provide an interesting picture of the strategies that managers use for compliance gaining but little information that helps us to understand why they select these strategies. They do indicate that the choice of a control response probably depends upon whether the manager is closer to a "problem-solving" breakpoint or an "elimination breakpoint" in the control process. At the problem-solving breakpoint, the manager recognizes a performance problem and hopes that it can be corrected. At the elimination breakpoint, the manager has decided that the problem cannot be solved and that the employee is not worth retaining. But they also note, "There appears to be no 'formula' of necessary ingredients for determining whether a manager will issue a warning, choose only to 'counsel' the employee, request retraining, or whatever" (1984a, p. 587).

Other recent studies attempt to provide some insights on this issue. Conrad (1983) found that superiors' own perceptions of their supervisory skills are related to strategies that they choose to manage conflicts with their subordinates. In particular, superiors who perceived their skills to be low were more likely to rely on autocratic (threatening or coercive) strategies, while those who expressed low self-confidence avoided use of participative conflict resolution.

Riccillo and Trenholm (1983) found that superiors' levels of trust for subordinates affect their choice of strategies for influencing subordinates. Specifically, trusted subordinates are subjected to interpersonal persuasive strategies, while untrusted subordinates are subjected to coercion.

A final line of research on factors influencing the choice of compliance-gaining strategies is based on the concept of *locus of control*. Locus of control is said to be either *internal* or *external*. People who have external locus of control believe that they are victims of fate. Whether they attain desired goals or rewards depends on luck and circumstance rather than their own efforts. People who have internal locus of control believe that they control their own destinies (i.e., they are largely responsible for what happens to them). Spector (1982) summarized several studies that found relationships between locus of control and choice of compliance-gaining or influence strategies. Generally, these studies indicate that superiors who have internal locus of control tend to rely on interpersonal persuasive strategies, while those who have external locus of control rely on threat and coercion.

The factor of locus of control in compliance gaining is especially interesting because a good theoretical model can be developed to explain what happens. External locus of control appears to be related to authoritarian personality characteristics. Authoritarians are unduly submissive to authority, hostile toward anyone who defies or disregards authority, and preoccupied with use of power, conformity, and enforcing rules. Since people who have external locus of control believe they are victims of fate, it makes sense that they would rely on higher authority to mediate their fate, to "take care" of them by enforcing the rules. This style of thinking would lead easily to use of threat and coercion as a defensive strategy.

We should point out that the studies of subjects such as compliance-gaining and the effects of communication style on satisfaction are not the only lines of work on the communicative behavior of superiors. A great deal of research also has been conducted on the related subject of leadership style. We will consider some of this research when we discuss the theories of leadership in chapter 9.

Subordinate Behavior

The third line of contemporary research in superior-subordinate communication concerns the subordinate's communicative behaviors toward the superior. Historically, most of this research has addressed two themes, upward distortion and feedback. We know of no studies published in organizational communication literature after Jablin's 1979 review that specifically attempt description or explanation of subordinates' feedback to superiors. Consequently, we will assume that Jablin's conclusions on this topic (table 8.1) represent the current state of knowledge. Although most studies of upward distortion also occurred prior to Jablin's review, researchers in the 1980s have continued to show some interest in this topic.

Early studies of upward distortion indicated that subordinates' mobility aspirations (desire for promotion and advancement) are *negatively* related to accuracy in upward communication, while subordinates' trust in superiors is *positively* related (Read, 1962). As mobility aspirations go up, accuracy goes down. Increased trust is associated with increased accuracy. Other studies suggest that distortion is more likely to occur in rigid, machinelike organizational climates than in open, "organic" climates (Young, 1978).

Studies in the 1980s have extended past research by attempting to identify other variables that influence distortion of upward communication. For example, Krivonos (1982) reviewed studies suggesting that subordinates are more likely to distort information when that information reflects unfavorably upon them. He extended this research by distinguishing between task and non-task situations. Krivonos found that subordinates are more likely to distort unfavorable information in a task situation but actually seem to relay unfavorable information more accurately than favorable information in a nontask situation. He argued that distortion of unfavorable information occurs in task situations because superiors exercise more power over subordinates in such situations. The possible consequences of a "bad report" in a task situation are more ominous than they might be in a nontask situation. Since the nontask situation is less risky, subordinates might capitalize on "pratfall effect" by accurately reporting unfavorable information. Pratfall effect occurs when a person's admission of errors or mistakes actually increases his or her credibility with others.

More recently, scholars have turned their attention away from traditional topics such as feedback and upward influence in order to explore new themes on subordinates' behaviors in communicating with superiors. One new theme concerns subordinates' use of compliance-gaining strategies in upward communication. In a recent study of this topic, Lamude, Daniels, and White (1987) explored the influence of locus of control and situation on strategies that subordinates chose to gain compliance from superiors.

Given an assumption that external locus of control is closely tied to authoritarian personality characteristics, Lamude et al. argued that an external subordinate is more likely to attempt compliance gaining with a superior *only* in situations in which the superior's intervention is needed to enforce rules that protect the subordinate's interests (e.g., a conflict with coworkers). In contrast, an internal subordinate may be inclined to attempt compliance gaining with a superior in any situation in which some goal can be achieved by influencing the superior. Moreover, Lamude et al. argued that subordinates in general will be more likely to attempt compliance gaining with superiors who are perceived to be external in locus of control. Although such superiors are presumed to behave autocratically, their external orientation predisposes them toward compliance. Internals are presumed to be more resistant to compliance-gaining attempts (Spector, 1982).

Results of this study were only partially consistent with predictions, but they yielded some tentative conclusions. First, subordinates showed high inclination to use some compliance-gaining strategies regardless of situation and locus of control factors. These strategies included liking (being friendly in the compliance-gaining attempt) and altruism (asking a person to act unselfishly).

Second, external subordinates were more likely to use threats and aversive stimulation (e.g., harassing the superior until the superior complies) with internal superiors than with external superiors. This finding is consistent with arguments that external subordinates are likely to rely on coercive strategies, but it is inconsistent with the expectation that external superiors are more likely to be targets for compliance-gaining attempts. It is possible that the risk of threatening an external, autocratic superior is too great for the external subordinate and that the internal superior is perceived as an easier target.

Third, internal subordinates showed high inclination to use aversive stimulation under various circumstances. This is surprising because theory suggests that internals avoid the use of coercive strategies in relationships with others. Internal subordinates, however, showed little inclination to use threat. One explanation may be that internals like to exert direct control over their environments. Since a threat merely forecasts a future consequence, it is not as direct as aversive stimulation, in which one takes action against a target and continues the action until the target complies.

Finally, theory suggests that internals are more likely to respond to compliance-gaining attempts based on values and obligations than to attempts based on coercion (e.g., threat) or even relational identification (e.g., liking, esteem, or altruism). Value appeals include debt, moral obligation, and a strategy called altercasting (e.g., acting in a given way because this is what a "good" person would do). Subordinates may be aware of this predisposition in internals because they showed more inclination to use debt and altercasting with internal superiors. Curiously, subordinates showed virtually no inclination to use moral appeal in any set of circumstances.

Assimilation Theory

One final theme in scholarship on superior-subordinate communication that has received a great deal of recent attention concerns the assimilation of new members into organizations. Much of the attention given to the assimilation process is attributed to the efforts of Fredric Jablin. Jablin (1984, p. 594) began with the simple but powerful observation that "time may be a major independent variable affecting the development of organizational communication attitudes and behaviors" among individual organization members. The assimilation process provides a context in which to observe this development.

Borrowing from earlier work by Van Maanen on organizational socialization, Jablin (1982; 1984; 1987) argued that assimilation involves three distinct stages:

1. *Anticipatory socialization,* which occurs prior to one's entry into an organization. This stage may actually begin during one's childhood as one acquires attitudes and values about work, organizations, and communication through the influence of family, schools, peer, part-time jobs, and the media.
2. *Encounter,* which begins when one enters an organization and is confronted with the reality of its expectations, policies, and practices.
3. *Metamorphosis,* during which the new member acquires new attitudes and behaviors or changes old ones in order to meet organizational expectations and become an accepted, participating member.

It is important to note that Jablin goes a step further by distinguishing organizational assimilation from organizational socialization. Organizational socialization generally is defined as "the process by which a person learns the values, norms and required behaviors which permit him to participate as a member of the organization" (Van Maanen, 1975, p. 67). But Jablin argues that assimilation also includes the process of *individualization* as well as socialization. Just as the organization attempts to influence and mold the new member, the new member may attempt to put his or her own stamp on the organization, create an individual identity within the organization, stake out a territory, or in some other way oblige the organization to adapt to the new members goals, values, and needs.

In one six-month study of the assimilation process involving new employees in three nursing homes, Jablin (1984) compared "job survivors" with those who terminated their employment during the course of the study. He found that job survivors' expectations for the quality of the communication climate in their new organizations were consistently lower than the expectations of terminators; namely, those who quit, which suggests differences in anticipatory socialization between survivors and terminators. During the encounter phase of assimilation, new employees "were experiencing a form of 'communication deprivation' " (p. 622). They were receiving less information than they had expected to receive, but they did not compensate for this deficiency by seeking out information from others. At six weeks, the best predictor of employee performance was the degree of dependency on the supervisor for information. Better performers were more dependent on the supervisor.

The study also revealed changes in communication patterns and attitudes during the metamorphosis phase. At the end of nine weeks of employment, the new employees usually were initiating interaction with others rather than waiting for others to initiate interaction with them. They found communication with superiors to be more satisfying than communication with peers or patients. At eighteen weeks, the best predictors of employee performance included the degree of supportiveness in the supervisor's communication style and the supervisor's work-related upward influence with higher management. Jablin (1987) concluded from his own findings and from those of other studies that the quality of the relationship with the immediate supervisor is a key factor in determining the nature of a new employee's assimilation experience, particularly in the encounter phase.

Conclusions from Superior-Subordinate Research

If you have reviewed the summary of Jablin's (1979) findings in table 8.1 and the additional 1980s studies described here, you may be in a state of befuddlement. Trying to interpret so many studies of superior-subordinate communication is a bit like assembling a jigsaw with pieces that do not always fit together, but we can draw some general comments from this research.

First, we have substantial evidence, at least from organizational environments of the 1950s and 1960s, that effective supervision is correlated with positive, open, and receptive communication behaviors. We also know from three decades of research that factors such as openness, receptivity, supportiveness, feedback, upward influence, and trust are related to subordinates' satisfaction with jobs and superiors and, to some extent, with accuracy of communication. More recent research also suggests that factors such as constructive argumentativeness in a superior's style of communication and *perceived* agreement between superiors and subordinates on communication rules also may be related to satisfaction. With the exception of some aspects of feedback and openness, it is *not* clear whether any of these factors in superior-subordinate communication are connected with task performance.

Second, while a climate of open, supportive, and trust-based communication may be the ideal in superior-subordinate relationships, managers' claims that they have adopted these ideals may be based more on wishful thinking than fact. Recent studies of superiors' communicative behaviors in attempts of compliance gaining, influence, and conflict management with their subordinates suggest that coercive, threatening, autocratic, and punitive tactics are still quite common. Factors such as low self-esteem and confidence in one's supervisory abilities, external locus of control, and mistrust of subordinates continue to promote defensive styles of communication.

Third, subordinates' behaviors toward superiors also are far removed from a picture-perfect representation of openness and supportiveness. Studies continue to show that distortion is a common occurrence in upward communication and that various situational factors may contribute to this phenomenon. Moreover, although subordinates generally are in a less powerful position in the superior-subordinate relationship, they certainly are not powerless. They can and do attempt to influence their superiors and may well use some unsavory tactics such as threat and aversive stimulation in the process.

Finally, Fairhurst, Green, and Snavely's studies on managerial control of poor performance, as well as Jablin's recent work on assimilation, indicate that it is vitally important for research on superior-subordinate communication to examine the development of this relationship and the communication processes within it over time. As Jablin put it, we must reexamine "the implicit assumption of most research that superior-subordinate communication relationships, once formed, are somehow fixed" (1987, p. 709).

Unanswered Questions in Dyadic Communication

The overwhelming emphasis on studies of superior-subordinate communication in our field poses two problems. First, even in the context of superior-subordinate communication, relatively little research actually examines ongoing interaction in this relationship. For the most part, we have been concerned with characterizing the communication climate in the relationship or studying the communicative behaviors of one or the other party in the relationship. However, we have done little to examine the simultaneous participation of both parties in the relationship.

Second, as we already have noted, the study of communication in other types of organizational dyads has received scant attention. Although research seems to suggest overwhelmingly that the superior-subordinate dyad may be the single most important relationship within the organization, it seems counterintuitive to us to suggest that other forms of dyadic communication are unimportant in the daily affairs of organizational life. Recently, some scholars have begun to investigate the relationship between organization members' participation and involvement in communication networks to determine how this participation influences various outcomes. For example, the investigations include the commitment to the organization (Eisenberg, Monge, & Miller, 1983), the information diffusion (Albrecht & Ropp, 1984), and the ability to cope with occupational stress (Albrecht & Ropp, 1982). Since network participation or integration often is measured in terms of the number of contacts, frequency, and/or importance of interaction that one has with other individuals, it includes dyads as well as other communication contexts such as informal groups and formal groups. However, it does not focus specifically on particular dyadic relationships.

At least two lines of research have made some attempt to investigate dyadic communication within organizations in contexts other than the superior-subordinate relationship. These lines of research illustrate some of the possibilities for extending the frontier of dyadic communication research in organizational settings.

One line concerns romantic relationships. Citing evidence that changes in organizational life are making romantic involvements between members of the same organization more likely than ever before, Dillard and Witteman (1985) attempted to determine the prevalence of romance in the workplace, the characteristics of participants in these relationships, and the organizational factors that might be associated with the occurrence of these relationships.

Dillard and Witteman concluded from a telephone survey that organizational romance is very common (nearly one-third of the respondents claimed to have had one or more work-related romantic involvements). These work-related romantic involvements are most likely to occur between individuals with positions at the same level of the organizational hierarchy or between those at immediately adjacent levels, and most involvements are likely to occur in organizations with twenty to fifty members. Romantic involvements for women are negatively related to age, length of service in the organization, and rank in the hierarchy. Involvements for men have equal likelihood across various levels of age, tenure, and rank. Formalization in the organization appears to suppress romantic involvements, although other aspects of organizational climate appear to be unrelated to the occurrence of romantic relationships. Of course, as the authors themselves note, the conclusions from this study are strictly tentative because of limitations in the survey method and restriction of the sample to one region of the country. In short, the validity of these conclusions depends on the representativeness of the sample and whether the survey respondents were really telling the truth.

A second line of research concerns a special type of relationship called the mentor-protégé relationship. In many organizational and professional settings, integration and development of new members, especially in management, professional, and certain trade occupations, occurs in this type of relationship. The new member becomes a protégé to an older or more established member who functions as a mentor. The mentor role entails teaching, guidance, counseling, appraisal, and other developmental activities, including sponsorship and promotion of the protégé's career advancement (Bolton, 1980; Shelton, 1981).

Although a mentor may also be a protégé's immediate superior, the mentor frequently occupies another role (e.g., a higher-level manager or a more experienced peer at the same level of the organization). Moreover, the mentor role is inherently different from the definition of the conventional role of an immediate superior, in which the relationship is based on task rather than the objectives of career development.

To date, studies of mentor-protégé relationships have focused primarily on determining how common they are in the work world (e.g., Roche, 1979) and whether protégé participation in such relationships actually leads to career advancement (e.g., McLane, 1980; Shelton & Curry, 1981). One investigation by Daniels and Logan (1983) specifically analyzed the communicative features of mentor-protégé relationships. They restricted their study to female managers and professionals, comparing those who participated as protégés in career development (mentor-protégé) relationships with others who only had experience as subordinates in conventional superior-subordinate relationships. Daniels and Logan found that levels of supportiveness, influence, satisfaction, and overall communicative activity were perceived to be much higher in career development relationships than in conventional superior-subordinate relationships. They also found that the mentor's supportiveness and upward influence were both important to protégés' satisfaction with the relationship.

Summary

The dyad is regarded as the most basic level at which organizational communication processes occur. Some scholars believe that the most important organizational communication processes occur at this level.

Several groups of theories and models have been applied to describe and explain the features of dyadic communication in organizations. Three of the most prominent are motivational theory, personality theory, and rules theory.

Motivational theories attribute all forms of human behavior to need fulfillment and drive-reduction functions. Consequently, they are concerned primarily with explanations of individual behavior, although some theories are used to account for why an individual behaves in certain ways within social settings.

Personality theories are concerned with identifying and explaining relatively stable and enduring patterns of behavior. These patterns are attributed to underlying psychological traits and predispositions. Like motivational theories, personality theories account primarily for individual action.

Rules theories focus explicitly on interaction. These theories explain communication processes in terms of rule coorientation. Rules are regarded as instances of social knowledge that individuals use to sequence and coordinate their actions with others.

Most of the research on dyadic organizational communication focuses only on one type of dyadic relationship—the superior-subordinate relationship. This research bias has developed in part from a belief that the superior-subordinate dyad is the most important of all organizational relationships. The bias also occurs because of a traditional desire to achieve organizational effectiveness through managerial control. Since the principal means for such control are employed through hierarchical relationships, the relationship between effective supervision and effective communication has preoccupied scholars as well as practitioners.

The most comprehensive review of research on superior-subordinate communication was presented by Jablin (1979). He organized some 150 studies in nine categories: interaction patterns and related attitudes, openness in communication, upward distortion, upward influence, semantic-information distance, effective versus ineffective superiors, personal characteristics, feedback, and systemic variables.

Since Jablin's review, studies in the 1980s continue to reflect great diversity, but most are concerned with factors in superior-subordinate communication that influence subordinate satisfaction, superiors' communicative behaviors in influence and compliance-gaining attempts with subordinates, and subordinates' communicative behaviors toward superiors. Generally, the history of research on superior-subordinate communication suggests that a supportive, open, trusting climate is the ideal. Such a climate certainly is related to satisfaction, and some features may be related to performance. But belief in the value of a supportive climate is easier to advocate than it is to enact. The communicative behaviors of both superiors and subordinates continue to reflect theoretically undesirable characteristics, including threat, coercion, mistrust, and distortion of information.

Although relatively little research has been conducted on other types of organizational dyads, some recent investigations do point to new directions in the study of dyadic organizational communication. These lines of research include studies of network integration and participation, organizational romance, and mentor-protégé relationships.

Discussion Questions/ Activities

1. Some scholars believe that the dyad is the most important level at which organizational communication occurs. What is the basis for this belief? Do you agree or disagree? Why?
2. Compare and contrast motivational theories, personality theories, and rules theories as ways of understanding dyadic communication. Is any one of these perspectives better than the other two? Why or why not?
3. Identify some of the reasons for researchers' preoccupation with the study of superior-subordinate communication.
4. After studying the summary of Jablin's review in table 8.1 and the chapter discussion of the studies in the 1980s, write a summary of what we think we know about superior-subordinate communication. Are there any problems with some of the conclusions that we have drawn?
5. What are some of the other types of dyads in organizational settings that might merit attention from communication scholars? Why should we study them?

Case Study

Unrealistic Expectations

Marsha Hill is a successful small business owner at age 35. She began in the recruiting industry eleven years ago working for a midsized firm. After the first three years, she began to feel restricted by the rules and regulations. She had the dream of owning her own business and working for herself. During her time with that company, she learned a lot about the industry and felt certain that she could break out on her own. She had established strong relationships with many of the clients, and she believed that they would follow her if she started her own company. In fact, some of them were so pleased with her work that they had encouraged her to do just that.

Marsha had a real knack for this business. She was able to identify a person's strengths and weaknesses quickly, and she had "an eye" for matching them with employers. The average tenure for the people she placed was well above the industry average. She was often frustrated with her colleagues that they could not achieve the same results.

In 1981, Marsha struck out on her own, convinced that she would soon "rule the recruiting world." Thus, Hill Company was started in downtown Toronto. She was right. Some of her clients did follow her, and she quickly gained a solid reputation. Most all of her work came from referral. For eight years her firm did quite well with only three people—herself and two office assistants. Marsha wanted to expand her business by adding personnel, especially individuals with college degrees. Her vision was to expand her recruiting force and to create a marketing staff in order to sell the firm's services rather than to rely so heavily on referrals.

Throughout the years, Marsha had grown accustomed to working independently. She had grown accustomed to running the business her way and using techniques that had been successful throughout the years. She had always hired people with little, if any, formal education beyond high school. She had found these people to be very willing to take orders and to carry out requests without questioning her methods and without taking responsibility.

Her first step in expanding her business was to hire a marketing graduate, Ann Walters. Ann came from a well-to-do family in a high-class Toronto suburb. This was Ann's first job out of college, and she was excited about the responsibility of taking the firm into a new direction. She saw this as a possibility for using her education in a creative and innovative way. Ann was a social individual who also saw this as a way to meet and to interact every day with a variety of people. In fact this was a skill that served her well from a sales perspective. She was able to make acquaintances quickly and to establish rapport effectively. She was looking forward to learning about how to get things done from Marsha's experience and knowledge.

Ann was eager and willing to learn, but she needed guidance. Almost immediately, Marsha seemed to approach Ann as a mentor. Marsha was in love with the idea of taking her under her wing and watching her grow. The problem was that Marsha had unrealistic expectations about how long that process would take. After about two months, their relationship took a negative turn. In fact, Marsha began to act in a condescending way toward Ann, actually scolding her when she had done something wrong or trying to shame her into changing her ways.

Over time Marsha became increasingly dissatisfied with Ann's work. Rather than focusing on Ann's performance problems, Marsha picked on her at a personal level. She criticized Ann's interactions with others, her friends, and the way she spent her personal time. However, she never provided specific and objective information about what Ann could do better to improve her performance.

Marsha was inquisitive by nature, which served her well in her relationships with clients. However, her inquisitive nature took on negative characteristics when she began to feel frustrated about Ann's lack of progress. For example, Marsha began to ask suspicious questions. One day Ann returned to the office after an afternoon of cold calls. Marsha called her into her office. By the tone in her voice, Ann knew she was "in trouble."

"Where have you been all afternoon?" Marsha asked.

"I told you before I left, at the MCI plaza making calls," Ann replied.

"Who did you see?" Marsha suspiciously asked.

Ann replied, "I had an appointment scheduled with Mr. Brander of Teltronics, and I was able to get an appointment with John Reeds at Canadian Broadcasting. I also stopped by a dozen other businesses and dropped off my card. I plan to call them tomorrow for appointments."

"Is that all?" Marsha asked.

"Yes!" Ann responded.

Then Marsha said with a sarcastic tone, "Did you happen to get any shopping done?"

Ann, exasperated and aggravated, said, "No, Marsha. If that's what you think I do all day, why don't you just fire me instead of accusing and humiliating me!"

Marsha and Ann had many similar exchanges. Marsha's trust in Ann rapidly declined. Over time, Ann went from being a conscientious worker to fulfilling the prophesy Marsha had laid for her.

1. Which elements of Gibb's model of defensive communication are reflected in this case?
2. Given the major theories (personality, motivation, and rules) used to explain dyadic interaction, how would you account for what happened here?
3. What does this case say about the importance of the superior's behavior in setting the climate of relationships with subordinates?
4. Is there any way in which Ann might have defused this situation?

References

Albrecht, T. L., & Ropp, V. A. (1982). The study of network structuring in organizations through the use of method triangulation. *Western Journal of Speech Communication, 46,* 162–178.

Albrecht, T. L., & Ropp, V. A. (1984). Communicating about innovation in networks of three U.S. organizations. *Journal of Communication, 34,* 78–91.

Bolton, E. (1980). A conceptual analysis of the mentor relationship in the career development of women. *Adult Education, 30,* 195–207.

Burke, R. J. (1970). Methods of resolving superior-subordinate conflict: The constructive use of subordinate differences and disagreements. *Organizational Behavior and Human Performance, 5,* 393–411.

Cline, T. R., & Wilmoth, G. H. (1987). *Superior-subordinate communication, coorientation, and satisfaction.* Paper presented at the annual meeting of the International Communication Association, Montreal.

Conrad C. (1983). Supervisors' choice of modes of managing conflict. *Western Journal of Speech Communication, 47,* 218–228.

Daniels, T. D., & Logan, L. L. (1983). Communication in women's career development relationships. In R. N. Bostrom (Ed.), *Communication yearbook 7* (pp. 532–553). Beverly Hills, CA: Sage.

Dillard, J. P., & Witteman, H. (1985). Romantic relationships at work: Organizational and personal influences. *Human Communication Research, 12,* 99–116.

Eisenberg, E. M., Monge, P. R., & Farace, R. V. (1984). Coorientation of communication rules in managerial dyads. *Human Communication Research, 11,* 261–271.

Eisenberg, E. M., Monge, P. R., & Miller, K. I. (1983). Involvement in communication networks as a predictor of organizational commitment. *Human Communication Research, 10,* 179–202.

Fairhurst, G. T., Green, S. G., & Snavely, B. K. (1984a). Managerial control and discipline: Whips and chains. In R. N. Bostrom (Ed.), *Communication yearbook 8* (pp. 558–593). Beverly Hills, CA: Sage.

Fairhurst, G. T., Green, S. G., & Snavely, B. K. (1984b). Face support in controlling poor performance. *Human Communication Research, 11,* 272–295.

Farace, R. V., Monge, P. R., & Russell, H. M. (1977). *Communicating and organizing.* Reading, MA: Addison-Wesley.

Gibb, J. (1961). Defensive communication. *Journal of Communication, 11,* 141–148.

Goldhaber, G. M., Dennis, H. S., III, Richetto, G. M., & Wiio, O. (1979). *Information strategies: New pathways to corporate power.* Englewood Cliffs, NJ: Prentice-Hall.

Grunig, J. E. (1975). A multisystems theory of organizational communication. *Communication Research, 2,* 99–136.

Herzberg, F. (1966). *Work and the nature of man.* New York: Collins.

House, R. J., Filley, A. C., & Gujarati, D. N. (1971). Leadership style, hierarchical influence, and the satisfaction of subordinate role expectations: A test of Likert's influence proposition. *Journal of Applied Psychology, 55,* 422–432.

Infante, D. A., & Gorden, W. I. (1985). Superiors' argumentativeness and verbal aggressiveness as predictors of subordinates' satisfaction. *Human Communication Research, 12,* 117–125.

Infante, D. A., & Gorden, W. I. (1987). Superior and subordinate communicator profiles: Implications for independent-mindedness and upward effectiveness. *Central States Speech Journal, 38,* 73–80.

Jablin, F. M. (1979). Superior-subordinate communication: The state of the art. *Psychological Bulletin, 86,* 1201–1222.

Jablin, F. M. (1980). Superior's upward influence, satisfaction, and openness in superior-subordinate communication: A reexamination of the "Pelz Effect." *Human Communication Research, 6,* 210–220.

Jablin, F. M. (1982). Organizational communication: An assimilation approach. In M. E. Roloff and C. R. Berger (Eds.), *Social cognition and communication* (pp. 255–286). Beverly Hills, CA: Sage.

Jablin, F. M. (1984). Assimilating new members into organizations. In R. N. Bostrom (Ed.), *Communication yearbook 8* (pp. 594–626). Beverly Hills, CA: Sage.

Jablin, F. M. (1987). Organizational entry, assimilation, and exit. In F. M. Jablin, L. L. Putnam, K. H. Roberts, & L. W. Porter (Eds.), *Handbook of organizational communication: An interdisciplinary perspective* (pp. 679–740). Beverly Hills, CA: Sage.

Koehler, J. W., Anatol, K. W. E., & Applbaum, R. L. (1981). *Organizational communication: Behavioral perspectives* (2nd ed.). New York: Holt, Rinehart & Winston.

Krivonos, P. D. (1982). Distortion of subordinate to superior communication in organizational settings. *Central States Speech Journal, 33,* 345–352.

Lamude, K. G., Daniels, T. D., & White, K. (1987). Managing the boss: Locus of control and subordinates' selection of compliance-gaining strategies in upward communication. *Management Communication Quarterly, 1,* 232–259.

McLane, H. J. (1980). *Selecting, developing, and retaining women executives.* New York: Van Nostrand Reinhold.

O'Reilly, C. A., III, & Anderson, J. C. (1980). Trust and the communication of performance appraisal information: The effect of feedback on performance and job satisfaction. *Human Communication Research, 6,* 290–298.

O'Reilly, C. A., III, & Roberts, K. H. (1974). Information filtration in organizations: Three experiments. *Organizational Behavior and Human Performance, 11,* 253–265.

Organ, D. W. (1974). Social exchange and psychological reactance in a simulated superior-subordinate relationship. *Organizational Behavior and Human Performance, 12,* 132–142.

Pace, R. W. (1983). *Organizational communication: Foundations for human resource development.* Englewood Cliffs, NJ: Prentice-Hall.

Pearce, W. B., & Cronen, V. E. (1980). *Communication, action, and meaning: The creation of social realities.* New York: Praeger.

Pelz, D. P. (1952). Influence: A key to effective leadership in the first-line supervisor. *Personnel, 29,* 209–217.

Presthus, R. (1962). *The organizational society.* New York: Alfred A. Knopf.

Read, W. H. (1962). Upward communication in industrial hierarchies. *Human Relations, 15,* 3–15.

Redding, W. C. (1972). *Communication within the organization: An interpretive review of theory and research.* New York: Industrial Communication Council.

Riccillo, S. C., & Trenholm, S. (1983). Predicting managers' choice of influence mode: The effects of interpersonal trust and worker attributions on managerial tactics in a simulated organizational setting. *Western Journal of Speech Communication, 47,* 323–339.

Rose, R. A. (1985). Organizational adaptation from a rules theory perspective. *Western Journal of Speech Communication, 49,* 322–340.

Scheff, T. (1967). Toward a sociological model of consensus. *American Sociological Review, 32,* 32–46.

Schutz, W. (1958). *FIRO: A three-dimensional theory of interpersonal behavior.* New York: Holt, Rinehart & Winston.

Secord, P. F., & Backman, C. W. (1964). *Social psychology.* New York: McGraw-Hill.

Shelton, C. (1981, July). Mentoring programs: Do they make a difference? *National Association of Banking Women Journal,* p. 25.

Shelton, C., & Curry, J. (1981, July). Mentoring at Security Pacific. *National Association of Banking Women Journal,* p. 25.

Spector, P. E. (1982). Behavior in organizations as a function of employee's locus of control. *Psychological Bulletin, 91,* 482–497.

Steinmetz, L., & Todd, H. (1975). *First-line management: Approaching supervision effectively.* Dallas: Business Publications.

Van Maanen, J. (1975). Breaking in: Socialization to work. In R. Dubin (Ed.), *Handbook of work, organization and society* (pp. 67–120). Chicago: Rand McNally.

Weick, K. E. (1979). *The social psychology of organizing* (2nd ed.). Reading, MA: Addison-Wesley.

Wheeless, L. R., Wheeless, V. E., & Howard, R. D. (1984). The relationships of communication with supervisor and decision participation to employee job satisfaction. *Communication Quarterly, 32,* 222–232.

Young, J. W. (1978). The subordinate's exposure of organizational vulnerability to the superior: Sex and organizational effects. *Academy of Management Journal, 21,* 113–122.

Outline

Groups as Organizational
  Subsystems
Concepts in Group Communication
  Norms and Conformity
  Roles and Role Categories in
    Groups
  Leadership Behavior
    Leadership as Trait
    Leadership as Style
    Situational Theory
    Leadership vs. Management
Group Decision Making
  Decision Making and Culture
  Effective Group Decision Making

Group Decision Development
Prescriptive Models for Decision
  Making
Parliamentary Procedure
Reflective Thinking
Brainstorming
Delphi
Quality Circles
Groups, Values, and Sense Making
Summary
Discussion Questions/Activities
Case Study
References

Group Communication

9

Although interaction at the dyadic level may provide the most basic unit for organizing processes, communication within and between groups is so central to the character of organizations that some scholars such as Herbert Simon (1957) literally regard an organization as a group of groups. Richard Beckhard, a well-known organizational development theorist, argues, "Groups and teams are the basic units to be changed or modified as one moves toward organizational health and effectiveness" (1969, p. 16).

Organizations are comprised of many types of groups: special project teams, management teams, committees, functional work groups and departments, social groups, groups derived from occupational and professional communities, and coalitions of special interests that arise from organizational politics. Much of the problem solving, decision making, day-to-day work, and social activity of organizations occurs in groups. Consequently, communication processes within and between groups exert substantial influence on organizational performance and the quality of organization life.

Most of the research on group communication in organizations seems to focus on group decision-making and problem-solving processes, including models of effective decision making, the phases or steps that characterize group decision making, and factors that distinguish effective from ineffective decision-making groups (Littlejohn, 1989). But groups are more than mere decision-making mechanisms. Group membership often is a critical factor in the individual members' sense of identity and self-concept. Groups exercise power in order to gain and control resources. Groups provide values, justifications, and frames of reference from which individual members make sense of their organizational experiences. In this chapter, we will consider the importance of groups as organizational subsystems, the elements of group communication processes, basic research on group decision making, and other functions that organizational groups serve.

Groups as Organizational Subsystems

When Simon argued that an organization is a group of groups, he seemed to be saying that groups are the most obvious subsystems of an organization. Groups affect and are affected by the organizational system. Homans (1950) noted that certain types of activities, member interactions, and "sentiments" (members' feelings) are required for group survival. These required conditions, according to Homans, are imposed on the group by the larger organizational system. He referred to these imposed conditions as the **external system.** Other activities, interactions, and sentiments arise within the group that are different from and even at odds with the requirements of the external system. Homans called this emergent set of group behaviors the **internal system.** He argued that the emergent internal system is influenced by and, in turn, influences the external system. In particular, the internal system shapes the actions of individual group members and protects the group from outside interference.

Suppose that a special project team is assembled to reposition a company product that has leveled off in sales. The members are Ted, Sally, Juan, Bob, and Jessie, and they are from different departments. They all know one another, but they have never really worked together before. The group's objective is imposed by the larger system. In order to reposition the product, the group has to determine why its sales have declined, then figure out how to recover the old market or find a new market. In order to solve these problems, the group members are required to interact in certain ways. Moreover, the external system demands some feeling of commitment to the project.

The conditions of the external system seem clear, but as the group develops, "it elaborates itself, complicates itself, beyond the demands of the original situation" (Homans, 1950). Ted believes that the product has outlived its usefulness to the company and should simply be discontinued. He resents top management's insistence that it be repositioned in the market. Sally, a "radical feminist," and Bob, a "male chauvinist," quickly develop a severe interpersonal conflict. Juan, an accountant with no marketing background, can contribute little to the task. Jessie, the team leader, is a rigid authoritarian who wants unilateral control over all group decisions.

As the group members approach their task, they not only cope with demands of the external system, but they also adapt to individual idiosyncracies. The internal system that emerges from this coping and adaptation could have several features. For example, members do not ridicule Juan's inability to contribute to the task because it turns out that he is very adept at mediating conflicts and relieving tension in the group—a critical skill in light of Ted's opinion about the product, Sally and Bob's dislike for each other, and Jessie's aggressiveness. Jessie's need for control has to be reconciled with the other members' desire for a democratic approach to leadership. The group discards Ted's concerns about the product, establishing a shared expectation that some sort of solution will be developed. Yet, Ted's continued objections serve a purpose by stimulating the group to develop justifications for the project. The gender-related conflict between Bob and Sally creates many uneasy moments and occasional male versus female coalitions in the group, but Juan defuses these situations with humor. The group develops a pattern of conflict followed by humorous tension relief, although it never really resolves the conflict between Sally and Bob.

Any given organization may be composed of a number of identifiable groups. In open systems, these subsystems interact for a variety of purposes.

In some cases, the interaction and interdependence may be minimal. In other cases, interdependence of groups is essential to the organization's mission and functions.

The environment of contemporary organizations often is turbulent. Although the economic picture in the 1980s has been brighter than the one of the 1970s, in general, we can no longer count on the stability in markets, technology, government regulations, energy costs, tax revenues, societal needs, and a host of other factors that affect organizations. A turbulent environment seems to promote or even require high levels of intergroup dependence and cooperation (Lippitt, 1982). But which types of organizations are the most adaptive and flexible in the face of environmental change? Those characterized by high levels of coordination and interdependence among subsystems, or relatively awkward and uncoordinated loosely coupled systems? Weick (1976) argued that loosely coupled systems are more flexible and have a better chance of long-term survival. Lippitt also suggests that high levels of interdependence among organizational subsystems reduce adaptiveness. Yet, interdependence, coordination, and integration of subsystems is precisely what many scholars call for as a response to turbulent environments.

As we saw in the discussion of horizontal communication in chapter 4, many organizations, unaccustomed to the flexibility of communication required for cooperative effort, are finding it difficult to develop effective intergroup relationships. Even in organizations in which group subsystems are relatively independent and loosely coupled, these subsystems still may affect one another. As Beckhard pointed out, "By the very nature of organizations, there are bound to be conditions where, if one department achieves its goals, it frustrates the achievement of some other group's goals" (1969, p. 33). When subsystems are coupled (loosely or otherwise), cooperation and conflict within and between groups is a daily part of organizational life. Consequently, an understanding of intragroup and intergroup communication is essential to an understanding of organizations.

Concepts in Group Communication

Several concepts are important in developing an understanding of communication processes at the group level of organizations. Groups are characterized by **norms** that regulate the behavior of individual members. Members can generate pressure on one another to **conform** to these norms. Group members also enact **roles.** One of the more prominent roles is reflected in **leadership** behavior. Finally, even though group action is more or less a cooperative venture, group interaction often is characterized by **conflict** as well as cooperation. There are **status** differences between members and inequities in the distribution of **power.** Since the concepts of conflict and power were discussed in chapter 6, we will not address these issues here, but you should keep in mind that they are especially important in understanding group processes.

Each of these elements in group dynamics affects and is affected by communication processes, but the significance of communication in group dynamics runs a bit deeper than most treatments of group dynamics suggest. Social psychologists traditionally have regarded factors such as norms, roles, and power relationships as the causative or "driving" forces in group behavior. People behave as they do in groups because of normative expectations, role requirements, or compliance in the face of power. Now, there is no doubt that groups do develop normative expectations, role requirements, and differences in power. However, explaining group dynamics in these terms reduces communication to the status of just one more variable among many in group dynamics—a position that does not coincide with the beliefs of the communication theorists.

In the very beginning of this book, we argued that an organization really is constituted by its members' joint actions. The same thing may be said for groups. In fact, Blumer (1969) argued that a group cannot be understood without the concept of joint action among members. Joint action is constructed from interlinked individual actions. It can arise only when the interpretation of each participant in that action takes into account the interpretation of the other(s). As George Kelly once stated, "The person who is to play a constructive role in a social process with another person need not so much construe things as the other person does [but must] effectively construe the other person's outlook" (1955, p. 95). Joint action does not necessarily depend on mutual agreement in interpretation, but it does depend on some level of mutual understanding of one another's interpretations. This mutual understanding arises only through communication. Hence, all group dynamics, whether they take the form of cooperation, games, sense making, and even conflict, hinge on communication.

Norms and Conformity

In chapter 8, we discussed communication in dyads as a rule-bound process. Rules help to structure interaction in groups as well as in dyads by providing for certain regularities. In group communication, many of these regularities are derived from norms. As defined by Secord and Backman (1964), "A norm is a standard of behavioral expectations shared by group members against which the validity of perceptions is judged and the appropriateness of feelings and behavior is evaluated" (p. 323).

Norms—shared expectations for behavior, thought, and feeling—may be developed within the group or imported (brought in) from the larger system of which the group is a part (e.g., standards prevailing in the larger organization or mutual expectations acquired through prior experience in other groups). Importation is apparently what occurs in the orientation phase of Fisher's decision-development model. The internal development of norms occurs as the group negotiates and tests certain rules for interaction. Some of the characteristics in Homans' concept of internal systems are developed through such negotiation and testing.

Norms also may be explicitly stated or implicitly understood. Explicit normative standards could include policies, written rules, and verbally communicated procedures and standards. Implicit norms and other rules are not explicitly articulated, but the individual group member can observe and learn about their functions. Sometimes, new members of groups discover implicit norms only when they inadvertently violate such norms. This type of violation is illustrated in an example that one of the authors encountered at a luncheon meeting of an industrial project group.

The group often met over lunch in order to discuss problems associated with its project. However, on this particular day, the initial topic of conversation involved a recent string of losses by the local professional football team. Later, there was some specific discussion of work-related matters but nothing directly relevant to the project itself. Finally, during a lull in the conversation, a new member, who had been with the group for less than one week, made a remark about the unusually brutal November temperatures, then said, "I sure hope it clears up some. I hate for my kids to walk home in this kind of weather."

The comment seemed perfectly harmless, but there was no reply from the other members—only downcast eyes and sullen expressions. The new member was quite embarrassed by this response. When the author later asked some of the other members about their reaction to the comment, they testily replied that luncheons are "business meetings where personal topics like families and children are off-limits." Apparently, however, discussion of the football team's win/loss record was not regarded as inconsistent with the purpose of a "business meeting." In fact, the catalyst that triggered this uncomfortable situation may well have been gender. The new member was a woman. All the rest were men. As long as she talked about football like "one of the boys," everything was fine, but the mention of children provoked the men's stereotype of a "female" topic. The same remark made by a man might not even have been noticed.

This example illustrates one of the ways in which groups exert pressure for conformity to norms. Methods for producing this pressure include the following:

1. Delay action toward the deviant, allowing for self-correction.
2. Joke humorously with the deviant about the violation.
3. Ridicule and deride the violation.
4. Seriously try to persuade the deviant to conform.
5. Engage in heated argument with the deviant.
6. Reject or isolate the deviant.

Bormann (1969) indicated that these methods actually reflect several stages of pressure toward conformity. If conformity does not occur after delaying action, the group might engage in humor. Should deviance still continue, the group would move to ridicule. As pressure toward conformity progresses through these steps, the amount of communicative action directed at the deviant increases until, at stage six, attempts to communicate cease.

Rules and norms are essential to group action for at least two reasons. First, they help to reduce uncertainty. When we understand the norms and rules in a situation, we can have more confidence about the appropriateness of our own actions and in our expectations of others. Second, some predictability is required for joint action and cooperation. In order to collaborate at all, we must have some shared expectations for one another's behavior. But norms also have some unfortunate effects as well. As Baird and Weinberg (1981) noted, norms can hamper group creativity and protect inefficient and archaic practices. Such practices may take the form of certain traditions or so-called sacred cows. Norms also enforce inequities within and between groups. They can be used as instruments of repression that primarily serve the interests of a privileged few. Nevertheless, norms and rules are ever-present in group interaction. They help to define the basic *roles* that members enact.

Roles and Role Categories in Groups

The concept of roles has been defined in various ways. One traditional approach treats a role as a set of shared, normative expectations that people hold for the behavior of someone in a given social position (Levinson, 1959). Given this point of view, a role is regarded as something that exists apart from the person who assumes it. A person's behavior is determined by the role in the sense that he or she merely occupies it. Koehler, Anatol, and Applbaum (1981) referred to this position as the *deterministic* conception of role.

The deterministic perspective is quite limited. Even some social psychologists who adopt this position readily acknowledge that a role can be defined as any meaningful set of behaviors (Secord & Backman, 1964). George Kelly (1955) defined role as "an ongoing pattern of behavior that follows from a person's understanding [or misunderstanding] of how others who are associated with him in his task think" (p. 97). Simply stated, the enactment of a role depends on a person's interpretations of a given situation. It does not necessarily follow from others' expectations for what a person in the role is supposed to do.

Wofford, Gerloff, and Cummins (1979) attempted to clarify the idea of role by distinguishing between perceived, expected, and enacted roles:

The *perceived role* is the set of behaviors that the occupant of the position believes he or she should perform. The *expected role* is the set of behaviors that others believe he or she should perform. *Enacted role* is the actual set of performed behaviors. (p. 39)

There may be a high level of agreement between perceived, expected, and enacted roles, but the three frequently differ. Suppose that the members of a work group expect a supervisor to be a democratic leader, providing guidance and encouraging participation. The supervisor's perception of the leadership role, based on a belief in autocratic methods such as controlling decisions, dictating orders, and using punishment to gain compliance, is quite different from the members' expectations. Moreover, the supervisor's actual behavior— the enacted role—turns out to be a laissez-faire approach of "cool your heels on the desk and leave things alone," in which the supervisor actually relinquishes much of the leadership responsibility. As we shall see later, disparities between expected, perceived, and enacted roles can be significant sources of conflict in groups.

Any role is enacted. It is not only defined by others' expectations for appropriate behavior, but it is also defined by the perceptions, capabilities, and choices of the person who enacts it. Even so, there do seem to be some types of roles that frequently occur in task groups. A classic description of typical task group roles that Benne and Sheats developed in 1948 is still widely accepted today. Their description includes:

Task Roles
Initiator: defines problem, contributes ideas and suggestions, proposes solutions or decisions, offers new ideas.
Information seeker: asks for clarification, promotes participation by others, solicits facts and evidence.
Energizer: prods members into action.
Orienter: keeps group on track, guides discussion.
Secretary: keeps track of group progress, remembers past actions.
Maintenance Roles
Encourager: provides support, praise, acceptance for others.
Harmonizer: resolves conflict, reduces tension.
Comedian: provides humor, relaxes others.
Gatekeeper: controls communication channels, promotes evenness of participation.
Follower: accepts others' ideas, goes along with others.

Self-Centered Roles
Blocker: interferes with progress of group by consistently making negative responses to others.
Aggressor: attacks other members in an effort to promote his or her own status.
Dominator: monopolizes group time with long, drawn-out monologues.
Deserter: withdraws from group discussion by refusing to participate, engages in irrelevant conversations.
Special-interest pleader: brings irrelevant information into discussion, argues incessantly for his or her own point of view.

As you read the descriptions above, most may have seemed familiar to you from your own experience in group activities. It is very likely that you have seen some, if not all, of these roles enacted in task groups. Sometimes a particular individual consistently will enact one of these roles, but Benne and Sheats do not mean to imply that any given member has only one role. Generally, the actions of a given member will reflect some of these roles but show little or no evidence of others, and more than one member may enact any given role.

Leadership Behavior

Most organizational theorists believe that leadership is a central factor in the effectiveness of groups as well as organizations. We assume that leadership is required in order to initiate structure, to coordinate activities, and to direct others toward the accomplishment of group goals. Despite this belief, no one has been able to develop a uniformly accepted theory of leadership behavior (Koehler, Anatol, & Applbaum, 1981). Over the years, we have attempted to distinguish leaders from nonleaders on the basis of personality traits, to identify and describe ideal styles of leadership, and to determine the kinds of situations under which any given type of leadership behavior is likely to be effective or ineffective. Most recently, some scholars have even argued that "leadership" and "management" involve two different and sometimes inconsistent forms of behavior.

Leadership as Trait

The earliest theories of leadership attempted to distinguish leaders from nonleaders on the basis of certain personality traits. The list of distinguishing traits such as intelligence, responsibility, and others like them typically sounds as if it came from the pages of the Boy Scout or Girl Scout Handbook. Despite many efforts to identify a clear and consistent set of characteristics of leaders, results of the trait approach are mixed. Jennings (1961) argued that the trait school has "failed to produce one personality trait or set of traits that can be used to discriminate between leaders and nonleaders." On the other hand, Koehler, Anatol, and Applbaum believe that at least three specific traits are associated with effective leaders across a broad range of situations: intelligence, adjustment, and deviancy.

Leadership as Style

The stylistic approach to leadership behavior developed, in part, out of frustration with the earlier trait approach. As Koehler et al. pointed out, "Unlike the trait approach to leadership, the stylistic approach is concerned with what leaders do rather than the personal characteristics they possess" (p. 228). Two widely used models of leadership style were presented by White and Lippitt (1960) and by Blake and Mouton (1964).

White and Lippitt identified three basic styles of leadership that they labeled as **authoritarian, democratic,** and **laissez-faire.** Authoritarian leaders exercise strong control over decisions and tasks. They issue and enforce orders to ensure that their plans are executed in an acceptable manner. Democratic leaders are more oriented toward guidance than complete control of group activities. They share authority with subordinates and seek subordinate input in decision making. Laissez-faire leaders relinquish virtually all control of decisions and group processes to subordinates. Such leaders may remain available for consultation or problem solving but generally delegate all authority for tasks to subordinates.

A second and more widely used stylistic approach to leadership is presented in Blake and Mouton's Managerial Grid®. Blake and Mouton (1964, 1985) argued that eight basic managerial (i.e., leadership) styles can be identified according to their degree of concern for production and concern for people. Five of these styles can be located in a grid in which the two dimensions of managerial concern form axes. The remaining three are not displayed graphically in the grid. As the phrase, "concern for," implies, Blake and Mouton's concept of style is more *attitudinal* than behavioral. The Managerial Grid is presented in figure 9.1.

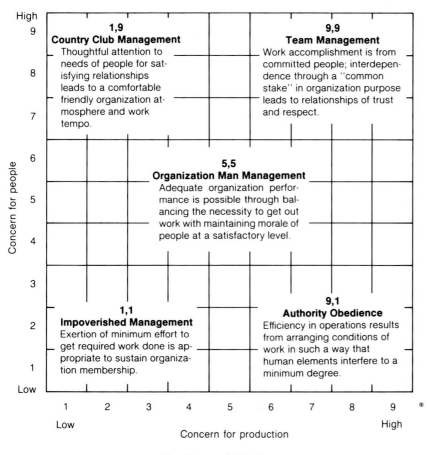

Figure 9.1

The Managerial Grid®

Source: The Managerial Grid Figure from The Managerial Grid III: The Key to Leadership Excellence, by Robert R. Blake and Jane Srygley Mouton. Houston: Gulf Publishing Company, Copyright © 1985, page 12. Reproduced by permission.

The 1,1, or **impoverished leader,** is theoretically the least effective. Given low concern for both production and people, the impoverished leader exercises no initiative and abdicates any responsibility for group outcomes. According to Blake and Mouton, the 9,1 **authority-obedience** and 1,9 **country club** leaders are not much more effective. The authority-obedience leader basically regards people concerns as obstacles to production accomplishment. This leader may use punitive and even abusive strategies to subordinate people concerns to the all-important goal of production accomplishment. In contrast, the country club leader thinks of nothing but people concerns. This leader strives primarily to maintain morale, satisfaction, and harmony among group members, even if production has to suffer in order to accomplish maintenance functions.

The 5,5, or **middle-of-the-road manager,** attempts to compromise and balance production and people concerns. The middle-of-the-road manager may believe that **production** and people concerns are competing and contradictory aspects of group behavior. In order to cope with the contradiction, the middle-of-the-road leader settles for moderately harmonious group relationships and adequate but not outstanding task performance.

The ideal style for leadership effectiveness presumably is the 9,9 or **team leader.** Whereas the 5,5 leader sees production and people concerns as competing, the team leader believes that group effectiveness depends on integration of people needs with production objectives. This leader personifies the ideals of human resource development theory as described in chapter 3. Specifically, group effectiveness is presumed to depend on the extent to which individual members are able to develop, assume responsibility, and function as a team. The team leader concentrates on bringing about this form of development.

Some writers (e.g., Goldhaber, 1990; Hersey & Blanchard, 1982) have claimed that the Managerial Grid is based on earlier studies of leadership behavior at the Institute for Social Research (ISR) in Michigan and at Ohio State University (OSU). The ISR studies identified two basic styles of leadership, job-centered and employee-centered. The OSU studies found two similar leadership variables—initiating structure and consideration. The OSU model regarded *both* variables as potential factors in a leader's behavior, whereas the ISR model viewed them as different styles. In either case, the job-centered and initiating structure factors represent a **task** dimension of leadership style, while employee-centered or consideration behavior represents a **maintenance** dimension. Despite the similarity of terms in all of these models, there are some important differences. The OSU and ISR models specifically are behavioral, while the Managerial Grid, as we noted earlier, is attitudinal. Moreover, Scientific Methods, Inc., the corporation holding the rights to the Managerial Grid, contends, "Blake and Mouton's research and writings are not based on either the ISR or the OSU studies" (Knause, 1990).

Situational Theory

Just as trait theories have been criticized for failing to produce clear distinctions between leaders and nonleaders, stylistic theory has been criticized for assuming that any one style of leadership can be effective in all situations. Situational or contingency theories of leadership argue that no one leadership style is ideal and that the circumstances of leadership will determine whether a particular style will be effective or ineffective.

Frederick Fiedler (1967) devised one popular contingency theory. Fiedler argued that the effectiveness of a leadership style will be influenced by three factors:

1. Leader-member relations, or the degree of confidence and trust that subordinates have in the leader.
2. Task structure, or the degree of certainty and routine as opposed to ambiguity and unpredictability in the task.
3. Position power, or the influence inherent in the leadership role (legitimate authority and ability to reward or punish).

Table 9.1 Fiedler's Situational Model. From *A Theory of Leadership Effectiveness,* by F. Fiedler, 1967. New York: McGraw-Hill

	Group Situation			
Condition	Leader-Member Relations	Task Structure	Position Power	Leadership Style Correlating with Productivity
1	Good	Structured	Strong	Directive
2	Good	Structured	Weak	Directive
3	Good	Unstructured	Strong	Directive
4	Good	Unstructured	Weak	Permissive
5	Moderately poor	Structured	Strong	Permissive
6	Moderately poor	Structured	Weak	No Data
7	Moderately poor	Unstructured	Strong	No relationship found
8	Moderately poor	Unstructured	Weak	Directive

Fiedler conducted a number of studies on directive and permissive styles of leadership under varying combinations of the three key situational factors. Results of these studies led him to propose a model of situational conditions under which each style would be most effective. Fiedler's model is presented in table 9.1.

The group and task characteristics identified by Fiedler probably are not the only factors that influence the effectiveness of a given leaderhip style. Eblen (1987) found that the relationship between leadership style and employee commitment varied across organizational contexts. Given the two basic leadership variables from the OSU studies, initiating structure and consideration, she found the consideration was positively related to employee commitment in hospitals, while initiating structure was positively related to commitment among employees in city government departments.

The sex of a leader also may mediate the effectiveness of a given style. Interestingly, studies have revealed no basic differences between male and female leaders on any behaviors related to initiating structure and consideration (Nieva & Gutek, 1981), but subordinates' evaluations of any given leadership behavior appear to depend on whether that behavior is exhibited by a male or a female. Studies by Wolman and Frank (1975), Hagen and Kahn (1975) and Bartol and Butterfield (1976) indicated that women who enact stereotypically "masculine" leadership behaviors are evaluated unfavorably by subordinates. On the other hand, women's stereotypically "feminine" enactments of leadership are associated with high levels of satisfaction among subordinates. This bias in subordinates' evaluations of leaders usually is attributed to sex role incongruence. As explained by Lamude and Daniels (in press):

When traditional sex role expectations for women are imported to the workplace, these expectations not only lead to the belief that women do not behave in the stereotypically masculine fashion associated with leadership, but also to the belief that they *should* not; that female enactments of "masculine" behavior are incongruent with sex role expectations.

Finally, there is some reason to believe that there are circumstances under which no style of leadership can be effective. For example, recall our brief discussion of Pettegrew's S.O.B. theory from chapter 3. Because resources in the hospital that Pettegrew studied were essentially "fixed," many administrative decisions resulted in "win-lose" reallocations of resources to different groups in the organization. Whether administrators were authoritative or participative in style had no effect on subordinates' perceptions of the administrators. Administrators inevitably were S.O.Bs.

Situational, as well as stylistic theories of leadership, also have one other very important limitation. They assume that leaders behave in a consistent manner toward all of the members within a group, exhibiting something like an "average leadership style" (ALS model). Graen (1976) challenged this assumption with a leader-member exchange (LMX) model, arguing that leaders discriminate significantly in their behavior toward subordinates.

Fairhurst and Chandler (1989) examined the LMX model in a qualitative study of interaction between the manager and three of his subordinates in the warehouse division of a large manufacturing company. One subordinate was an "in-group" member (worked under conditions of mutual trust, influence, and support with the manager), one was an "out-group" member (worked under conditions involving low trust and support along with exercise of the manager's formal authority). The third subordinate was a "middle group" member which fell between the conditions of the other two. Fairhurst and Chandler found both consistency and inconsistency in the manager's relationship with these three subordinates. The manager used indirect and ambiguous communication to exercise unobtrusive control with all three subordinates. As described by Fairhurst and Chandler, he was "a control-based manager who tries to appear noncontrolling and participative" (p. 230). At the same time, the manager's behavior and the patterns of interaction between the manager and subordinates clearly differed across in-group, middle-group, and out-group relationships. Both parties frequently challenged and disagreed with each other in the in-group relationship. The manager was somewhat more dominant in the middle-group relationship and exercised direct authority with the out-group subordinate. Interestingly, the out-group subordinate went to great lengths to maintain his outgroup status with communicative behaviors that created social distance between the manager and himself.

Of course, Fairhurst and Chandler themselves point out that one cannot draw general conclusions from a limited case study. Even so, their findings clearly show the simultaneous operation of the ALS and LMX models in this case, suggesting that more attention and research should be devoted to variations in leaders' exchanges with different group members.

Leadership vs. Management

One of the most intriguing themes in recent studies of leadership is the argument that leadership and management are qualitatively different organizational roles. This theme is reflected in several works from the middle and late 1970s (e.g., Maccoby, 1976; Zaleznik, 1977), but it probably is most pronounced in the work of Warren Bennis. Basically, Bennis (1976a; 1976b) contended that management functions are defined in terms of accomplishing specific organizational tasks, whereas leadership functions are (or should be) more concerned with providing direction for a group or organization. Fulfilling a true leadership role has become much more difficult in contemporary organizations because leaders must respond to many competing demands and voices, both within and without the organization. Leaders' choices are severely limited by threats of legal and regulatory interference from the outside and political dissension from within. In order to function effectively, leaders must meet the following seven basic challenges:

1. Develop vision and assertiveness to make effective decisions.
2. Concentrate on the organizational "big picture" rather than becoming preoccupied with day-to-day details.
3. Be able to interpret events and situations in light of the organization's unique history and goals.
4. Have the courage to make difficult decisions and to take calculated risks.
5. Be able to gather relevant information for planning and decision making and to interpret messages from many different sources.
6. Shape the culture of the organization to promote cooperation and loyalty.
7. Have the self-confidence and assurance required to handle the stress of leadership.

Group Decision Making

Many organizational groups exist primarily for decision-making and problem-solving purposes. Project teams, task forces, and committees typically serve such functions. Sometimes groups are created temporarily to deal with one special contingency. The members of such ad hoc groups work through to the solution of a particular problem, then disband and move on to other projects. The importance of group decision making to organizations has led researchers in small group communication to study these processes almost to the exclusion of any attention to other aspects of communication in group action (Littlejohn, 1983).

Group decision making is a rule-bound process, but members often seem to be aware only tacitly of the norms, roles, and regularities that they enact in the process. Status and power factors are accepted implicitly without reflection or examination. Members often note the presence of conflict, but they do not seem to understand its nature. Certain patterns of interaction and ways of doing things are simply taken for granted. Thus, as Schein argued, groups are not always aware of their own processes for problem solving and decision making, even when these processes are inefficient and ineffective.

Schein (1969) pointed out that groups typically make decisions in one of six ways, even though members may not recognize that their groups are operating in these ways.

1. *Lack of response.* This method is evident in a group when ideas are introduced, then immediately dropped without discussion. In effect, the ideas are vetoed by silence.
2. *Authority rule.* In this case, the power structure in the group places final authority for decision making with one person, usually the leader. The group may discuss an issue, share information, and suggest ideas, but the authority figure has the last word.
3. *Minority coalition.* Schein describes this method as a process of "railroading" decisions through a group by a vocal minority, especially a minority with a powerful member. When other members remain silent in the face of strong minority support for an idea, it can create the impression that the group has reached a consensus. In fact, most members may be opposed to the idea, but no one voices an objection for fear of disrupting what appears to be a consensus.
4. *Majority rule.* This is a familiar system of decision making through voting. Majority rule is typical of highly formal decision-making procedures. An issue or problem is discussed, then a policy or proposal is adopted or rejected on the basis of the percentage of members who favor it.
5. *Consensus.* When the members of a group are prepared to accept an idea, even though they may have some reservations about it, a group has a consensus. Schein is careful to point out that consensus does not necessarily mean that the group unanimously and enthusiastically endorses an idea. Consensus only implies that discussion of the problem has been open and all points of view have been considered. Although group members may not be in complete agreement, the solution or proposal falls within their range of acceptability.
6. *Unanimity.* This rare but ideal mode of decision making occurs when all of the members in a group are in full agreement on a point of view, proposal, policy, or problem solution.

Schein regards consensus and unanimity as preferred modes of arriving at decisions. Although the processes required to achieve consensus can be inefficient and time-consuming, the result is more effective implementation of the decision. Decisions that are made by authority, minority coalition, and majority rule may be arrived at quickly, but those members with other viewpoints may feel frustrated and have little incentive to support the decision.

Why are some groups able to achieve consensus-based decision making, while others are not? The answer to this question probably involves many complex factors, but Beatty (1989) argued that one very important factor is the similarity of individual group members' *decision rule orientations*. For example, some people might apply a *maximin* [sic] rule orientation by making decisions that are designed to minimize the risk of losses, while others might apply a *maximax* principle designed to maximize gains regardless of risk. Still others might apply a *maximum expected utility* (MEU) orientation that attempts to obtain the highest average payoff across all future conditions. Beatty hypothesized that groups composed of members who are identically matched in their decision rule orientations will achieve consensus more often than groups composed of members who have different orientations.

Beatty tested this hypothesis by comparing fourteen groups in which members were identically matched on decision-rule orientation (two groups of maximax members, eight of MEU members, and four of maximin members) to fourteen mixed groups (i.e., groups whose members had varying decision rule orientations). Members in one-half of the groups (seven matched and seven mixed) were allowed to interact in face-to-face meetings, while those in the other groups were required to work as individuals isolated from each other. All seven of the matched, interacting groups achieved unanimous consensus, a condition "unequalled by any other group" (p. 289).

Decision Making and Culture

The contrast between different methods of arriving at decisions is easy to see when one compares the methods of traditional Western organizations to those of Japanese organizations. As Ryutard Nomura, chairman of Japan's Triyo Industries, pointed out, the "bottom-up" consensus-based decision methods of Japanese organizations are painfully slow and cumbersome, but most decisions are implemented effectively because support has been developed among all essential participants during the decision-making process. In contrast, decisions are made quickly with traditional Western methods such as reliance on centralized authority, but implementation is slow and uncertain. According to Nomura, "Opposition and misunderstanding which inevitably arise emerge *after* the decision has been announced" (1981). One only has to examine the American political system to see that losing factions often are more interested in regaining power, winning the next decision, and stalling unwanted decisions than in cooperating with the winner.

Differences between cultures in their methods of group decision making can be explained in part by the degree to which a given culture is *individualistic* or *collectivistic*. As explained by Hofstede and Bond (1984, p. 419), people in individualistic cultures "are supposed to look after themselves and their immediate family only," while those in collectivistic cultures "belong to ingroups or collectivities which are supposed to look after them in exchange for loyalty." The term, "ingroup," does not mean the same thing in this context that it means in the study conducted by Fairhurst and Chandler. When Hofstede and Bond talk about ingroups, they are referring to people such as coworkers, colleagues, and classmates. Outgroups include strangers, or anyone who is not specifically a member of an ingroup.

Gudykunst, Yoon, and Nishida (1987) argued that ingroup relationships are more intimate in collectivistic cultures than in individualistic cultures. Consequently, ingroup communication should be more personalized, better coordinated, and less difficult in collectivistic cultures than in individualistic cultures. Results from their study of ingroup communication among students from Korea (highly collectivistic), Japan (moderately collectivistic) and the United States (highly individualistic) supported this hypothesis. Ingroup communication was more personalized, better coordinated, and less difficult for the Koreans than for the Japanese, and more personalized, better coordinated, and less difficult for the Japanese than for the Americans.

These results do not necessarily mean that we should all initiate a cultural revolution in an effort to make American society more collectivistic. Individualistic values may offer some communicative advantages. Gudykunst, Yoon, and Nishida also found that U.S. students had somewhat better experiences than the Japanese and Koreans with *outgroup* communication. Interaction with strangers was easier and better coordinated (though less personal) for U.S. students. You may also recall from chapter 8 the studies on argumentativeness and the value placed on independent-mindedness in U.S. organizations, along with Infante and Gorden's claim that these conditions are necessary for productivity and therefore are nurtured in an individualistic culture.

Effective Group Decision Making

What distinguishes effective decision-making groups from ineffective groups? Social scientists have been interested in this question for several decades, but much of the research has been more concerned with comparing group performance to individual performance. These studies indicate that groups generally produce more and better ideas than individuals working alone, but the evaluative judgments of groups are not as good as those of the very best individuals.

Research on the characteristics of interaction in decision-making groups has not yet provided a comprehensive picture of the differences between effective and ineffective groups. A series of studies by Randy Hirokawa provides several clues about the difficulties that small group communication scholars face in the study of decision-making processes.

Hirokawa has devoted most of his career to the study of group decision making. In one of his early investigations (1980), he noted that the question of differences between effective and ineffective groups had received almost no systematic scrutiny in communication research. He assembled laboratory groups to study a problem for which experts already had devised a correct solution. Effective and ineffective groups were distinguished on the basis of agreement between their solutions and the expert solution. Once the two types of groups were separated, Hirokawa was able to classify all of the statements made during these groups' decision-making processes according to various task and socioemotional functions, then compared the patterns of interaction in effective and ineffective groups.

Surprisingly, Hirokawa found many more similarities than differences between effective and ineffective groups. Only one major difference occurred in the communicative behaviors and interaction patterns: *effective groups were much more attentive to the procedures used to solve the problem.* Specifically, one member would make a statement of procedural direction (e.g., "Why don't we set up some evaluation criteria?"), and the others would adopt this direction.

Later, Hirokawa (1982a) extended his research into the effects of consensus-based decision making. In this study, he found evidence of a relationship between consensus and the quality of group decisions, but only when the group approached its task in a systematic manner. Moreover, there was no clear relationship between consensus and group members' satisfaction with decisions. This may mean that assumptions about the superiority of consensus for effective implementation of decisions are questionable, since effective implementation is associated with satisfaction and commitment to the decision.

Gradually, Hirokawa became concerned that studies of group decision making, including his own, were contributing "very little to our already limited understanding of how group interaction affects (i.e., improves or impairs) group performance" (1982b, p. 135). He reviewed a number of recent studies and concluded that they had two general problems:

1. failure to distinguish between group behaviors that are relevant to a task and those that are not relevant;
2. failure to focus on communication behaviors that are related theoretically to effective decision making.

In a later investigation, Hirokawa (1983) tried to correct both of these problems by examining only group communication acts that served one of five functions: (a) *establishing operating procedures,* (b) *analyzing the problem,* (c) *establishing evaluation criteria,* (d) *generating alternative solutions,* and (e) *evaluating solutions.* Results of the study indicated a positive relationship between effectiveness of a group's decision and the group's efforts to analyze the problem, but the relationship between effectiveness and attempts to establish operating procedures was *negative.* Moreover, there was no association between effectiveness and attempts to establish evaluation criteria, to generate alternative solutions, or to evaluate solutions.

The results of Hirokawa's studies are disturbing because they lack consistency and because they contradict some cherished assumptions about the essential communicative elements in effective group decision making. Hirokawa concluded once again that we still know very little about the role of communication in group effectiveness.

Since his early studies relied on predetermined categories for classifying communication behaviors, Hirokawa decided that the classification schemes themselves might be masking some of the critical differences between effective and ineffective groups. In other words, real differences might exist, but Hirokawa was not finding them in the systems that he used to analyze group behavior. In his most recent research, Hirokawa and Roger Pace (1983) abandoned the use of predetermined behavioral categories in hopes of deriving classifications unique to group interaction itself. This strategy led them to conclude that the quality of group decisions seems to depend on four factors:

1. *The manner in which group members attempt to evaluate the validity of opinions and assumptions advanced by fellow members.* Evaluation was more rigorous in high-quality decision groups.
2. *The manner in which group members attempt to evaluate alternative choices in light of established criteria.* Again, high-quality groups were more careful and rigorous.
3. *The nature of the decisional premises employed by the group.* High-quality groups based decisions on facts and inferences grounded on information about the problem, whereas low-quality groups used questionable facts and inferences that were not based on relevant information.
4. *The nature of influence exerted by influential member(s) of the groups.* In high-quality groups, influential members tended to act in a positive, facilitative way. In low-quality groups, influential members were negative and inhibiting.

These conclusions are not, by any means, the last word on the group effectiveness issue. While Hirokawa and Pace seem to have developed some new insights about the distinctions between effective and ineffective groups, they point out that the major value of their study is its potential to generate a new line of research in small group communication. They believe that their findings will gain more credibility if further studies yield similar results. Hirokawa's personal exodus and soul-searching over the group effectiveness issue reveals much of the frustration that arises from inconsistent and ambiguous research findings on the role of communication in group decision making. However, it also promises some fresh viewpoints on the problem for the first time in many years.

Group Decision Development

In addition to Hirokawa's work on the differences between effective and ineffective group decision making, another important line of research has addressed the *stages* or *phases* of decision development within groups. One of the most complete treatments of this topic was developed by B. Aubrey Fisher (1970), who identified four stages in group decision-making processes: **orientation, conflict, emergence,** and **reinforcement.**

The orientation phase begins as the members of a group meet for the first time. The members experience uncertainty; they are not sure what to expect. Behavior is based on members' understanding of social norms regarding politeness and initiation of relationships. These norms are brought into the situation, since the group has evolved no rules of its own.

Politeness norms become less important as members acquire some familiarity with one another, and the group moves into a conflict phase characterized by disputes, disagreements, and hostility. The group gradually works through conflict, entering an emergence stage in which increased tolerance for ambiguity in opinions is reflected. Ambiguity at this point allows for face-saving and reconciliation of conflicts. Finally, the group moves to a reinforcement stage in which the members develop and endorse a decision. The idea of reinforcement implies that group members engage in a mutual process of justifying and committing themselves to the decision. For example, they might say, "This is the right decision because . . ." or "This solution is better than the other possibilities."

Many studies of group development, including Fisher's own studies, have examined the processes of groups during a relatively limited time frame (e.g., over several meetings or even in only one meeting). The results of these studies suggest that group development occurs in an orderly, linear fashion, proceeding from one step to the next. Fisher points out, however, that a phase model may not apply to all task-oriented groups. The limitations of phase models like Fisher's are reinforced in a recent series of studies by Marshall Scott Poole (1981, 1983a, 1983b). Poole found that the stages of decision development in small groups may follow any one of several possible sequences. He concluded that a "logical" or unitary sequence of problem-solving steps may provide normative expectancies that influence the group, but the group's actual course of action emerges from many complicated factors. In other words, groups in different situations act in different ways. Even when group decision making fits a phase model, the specific types and cycles of interaction within any given phase differ substantially from group to group.

Since Poole's studies were based on groups that had a prior history of working together and expectations of working together in the future, it is tempting to argue that phase models such as Fisher's are best applied to groups with limited life spans and specific objectives. For example, a special ad hoc project team is similar in some ways to groups that are assembled only to participate in an experimental study. Such groups exist for only one purpose and disband when the purpose is accomplished. But two recent studies by Poole and Roth (1989a; 1989b), which employed "experimental" as well as "real" groups, provide no evidence to support this argument.

In their first study (1989a), Poole and Roth found that groups in general exhibited "complex decision paths with traces of the normative unitary model, intermittent disorganized periods, the existence of breakpoints" (p. 347)—results all consistent with Poole's basic contingency model. But the second study attempted to predict group decision paths from characteristics of the task and group structure. The results indicated that "group structure variables [power, size, cohesiveness, and conflict history] were by far the best predictors of the overall properties of the decision path" (1989b, p. 585). Large groups with low cohesiveness, shared power, and a history of conflict were more likely to exhibit unitary decision making sequences (i.e., logical phases) and to engage in more problem analysis, while smaller, more cohesive groups with high power concentration were more likely to exhibit complex, solution-oriented decision paths. A unitary sequence also was more likely when the group's goals were unclear and the task required a detailed analysis.

Although there may be conditions under which group decision making is likely to follow a unitary model, much of Poole's research does suggest that groups go through *cycles* in their decision development. Instead of moving through phases in a linear fashion, such groups repeat certain stages. This tendency to recycle activities might be even more pronounced in long-lived groups as a consequence of changes in group membership, groups' goals, and environmental demands. Frequently, groups seem to languish at a particular stage, suffering something like a case of arrested development. You may have had the experience of working in student groups that become mired in conflict and never seem to move beyond this phase.

The idea that group development is characterized by cycles is reflected in a model developed by Edgar Schein (1969). Schein, who based his model on earlier work by Benne and Sheats (1948), argued that newly formed task groups and decision-making groups typically go through a period of **self-oriented behavior** before entering a phase of **task and maintenance behavior.** This argument is not based on systematic studies such as Fisher's or Poole's but on Schein's experience over the years as a consultant to private industry.

Schein's concept of the self-oriented phase is very similar to Fisher's conflict phase. According to Schein, individual members face several problems upon entering a new group. These problems include identity or role in the group (Who am I in the group?), influence and power in the group (Can I exert control over other members?), acceptance by other group members (Will they like me?), and congruence between personal needs and group goals (Do the group goals and values fit my own?). During the early development of a group, members are concerned primarily with meeting their individual needs and coping with obstacles to fulfill their needs.

The coping behaviors that members use during self-orientation may reflect hostility, dependency, or withdrawal. For example, a member who desires leadership and power may cope by resisting authority. One who is more concerned about being liked and accepted by other members may be very supportive of their ideas. The coping behaviors may, on the surface, be connected with *substantive* issues concerning the group's task (ideas, procedures, etc.), but under the surface, according to Schein, such behaviors really reflect *emotional* issues.

The main point about Schein's analysis is that many groups never seem to progress successfully beyond the self-oriented phase. In an effort to get to the heart of the task itself, the group may attempt to suppress or avoid personal, emotional issues rather than to confront and resolve them. As long as such issues remain unresolved, they will continue to hamper the group's task efforts.

Groups that meet infrequently may be particularly susceptible to developmental problems. For example, boards of directors, organizational committees, university department faculties, student senates, city councils, and others that meet formally for a few hours a month or even less never have a chance to progress through self-orientation or they continually repeat various phases of decision development for each new problem that comes along.

Prescriptive Models for Decision Making

The history of scholarship in small group communication suggests that we should be cautious in offering any particular set of procedures or methods as a tried and true path to effective group decision making. Nevertheless, many prescriptive models for group problem solving and decision making have been developed and used by organizational groups over the years. Examples of such models include parliamentary procedure, reflective thinking, brainstorming, the Delphi method, and quality circles.

Parliamentary Procedure

Parliamentary procedure is a common system of decision making in Western societies. Rooted in English parliamentary law, this system is over 700 years old. Basically, parliamentary procedure involves the presentation of proposals in the form of motions, followed by debate, amendment, and votes on these motions. Although many organizational and communication theorists bemoan the cumbersome inefficiency of this method, the system does enforce the right of the majority to act while protecting the right of the minority to debate, vote, and, perhaps, become the majority. The procedure is best applied in large assemblies and formal business meetings. Some types of groups are *legally* obligated to use some form of parliamentary procedure for any official meeting. A working familiarity with a handbook of parliamentary procedure (e.g., Robert, 1970; Sturgis, 1966) is useful for anyone who must work in such a group.

Reflective Thinking

McBurney and Hance (1950) developed a standard agenda for group problem solving that is based on John Dewey's model of reflective thinking. Dewey tried to describe the logical sequence of steps that a person normally would use in order to think through a problem. The McBurney-Hance agenda is based on Dewey's sequence:

1. Define the limits of the problem.
2. Analyze the problem (data and information on the problem).
3. Suggest possible solutions.
4. Consider the advantages and disadvantages of each solution.
5. Implement the best solution.

The McBurney-Hance agenda and similar reflective thinking models have been the stock-in-trade for training in group problem solving, but the value of such models is questionable. When Hirokawa used such models in order to compare effective and ineffective groups, he found few reliable differences on the kinds of activities that these models prescribe.

Brainstorming

Brainstorming is one of the most popular techniques for generating ideas in small groups. The concept was introduced by A. F. Osborn in 1957. Strictly speaking, brainstorming is not a complete problem-solving model because its application usually assumes that the problem already has been defined clearly. The purpose of brainstorming is to generate possible solutions. The rules for the process are very simple, but they demand strict adherence.

1. Adverse criticism is taboo.
2. Freewheeling is encouraged.
3. Quantity of ideas is desired.
4. Combination and improvement of ideas is sought.

According to Coon (1957), brainstorming relies on suspension of a critical attitude that might sabotage a potentially good idea before it can be developed. Anyone and everyone is to participate in offering ideas, no matter how strange or ridiculous they may sound. Criticism of ideas at this stage is not permitted. The goal is to generate as many ideas as possible, then refine them through combinations, "hitchhiking," and other techniques. The process is moderated by a facilitator who enforces the rules.

Delphi

Delphi was developed in the 1950s by Rand Corporation, a private think tank that does work for the federal government. The technique was designed for purposes of developing expert consensus on solutions to unstructured and ambiguous problems, but the basic design has been modified in order to accomplish other purposes (e.g., to generate several perspectives on a problem). Whatever its purpose, Delphi is based on interaction between a monitor team and a group of respondents. It usually includes the following steps.

1. The monitor team develops a questionnaire on the problem and submits this questionnaire to the respondent group. Depending on the purpose, the respondents might be experts from a single field or from various fields or even nonexpert laypeople.
2. Members of the respondent group complete the questionnaire under *nominal group* conditions. This means that they work in isolation from one another, never meeting or interacting directly during the Delphi.
3. The monitor team summarizes data from the questionnaire responses and returns the summary to the respondent group along with a second questionnaire to explore areas of agreement and disagreement within the group. This step may be repeated several times with modifications in the questionnaire.
4. The monitor team develops a final summary of questionnaire results, relaying it as information for use by decision makers.

Although Delphi can be a very powerful technique in the problem analysis phase of decision making, its use has sparked a surprising amount of controversy. Linstone and Turoff (1975) published an extensive collection of readings on the methods, uses, and effectiveness of Delphi. Some critics feel that Delphi places too much faith in the monitor team. Others argue that it fails in its attempt to remove problem analysis from the social pressures of group process by having respondents work in nominal conditions because group feedback still occurs through the monitor team. Generally, however, Linstone and Turoff give Delphi high marks and suggest many ways in which to use the technique.

Quality Circles

A quality circle (QC) is an informal problem-solving group composed of workers and their supervisors in an organization. It really is more properly a *context* for group problem solving than a prescriptive model for decision making, but we will discuss it here because of its recent popularity in American organizations. The group's activity focuses on improving job-related quality and productivity (Rehder, 1981). The QC concept originated in America during the so-called zero-defect movement, but its emphasis on employee participation did not fit well with traditional American organizations. When the concept was exported to Japan after World War II, Japanese organizations quickly realized the role for QC's in their decentralized decision-making processes.

The QC's include a number of basic features. The ones listed below are adapted from Kaoru (1968) and Rehder (1981).

1. The basic assumption underlying QC's is the belief that neither managers nor workers independently know the causes of quality and productivity problems, but given proper tools, training, and time, QC's can solve these problems.
2. A QC operates as an ongoing study group in the organization.
3. All participants, including workers, supervisors, and managers, are volunteers.
4. A QC emphasizes practical applications developed from studies of actual problems.
5. Organizations must support QC's with technical assistance and training in participative management, problem-solving, and statistical analysis techniques.

The impact of QC's in Japanese industry has been dramatic. During the 1950s, the label, "Made in Japan," evoked images of cheap imitations of Western products. Today, Japanese quality is envied throughout the industrialized world. Although many factors have accounted for the Japanese success story, some American industries stung by Japanese imports began to revive the QC concept here. The trend has spread to the point that hundreds of major U.S. companies and even governmental agencies are employing QC's today (Coonfield, 1984).

The fact that quality circles have been adopted with such uncritical enthusiasm has begun to worry some experts on the technique. For example, Meyer and Stott (1985) claimed "We are aware of no discussion of failures and only limited exploration of potential problems in implementing quality circles" (p. 34). They reviewed two case studies of large-scale QC implementation that point to several problems. First, the concept of QC may be incompatible with existing reward systems, decision-making processes, work-flow arrangements, and staffing policies. These inconsistencies promote tension and opposition to QC's. Second, a QC program begun when production demands are slack may be sidetracked when market pressures increase. Third, any existing labor-management conflicts may spill over into QC activity. Finally, QC meetings themselves exhibited the following problems:

1. Supervisors tended to dominate the meetings, pushing their own ideas until they were adopted by the group.
2. Leaders and members sometimes had no clear sense of the meeting agenda or their specific responsibilities.
3. Many groups began to stray from recommended problem-solving procedures and got bogged down in an "analysis paralysis" that set in and months would pass without a solution.
4. Members of some groups complained that their supervisor or circle leader was open in the group meeting but on the shop floor rarely asked for ideas and ignored any that were offered.
5. It was not uncommon for the facilitators to take over as group leaders and become increasingly involved in doing the group's work.

Despite the problems with quality circles in the two cases observed by Meyer and Stott, at least one comprehensive study conducted by Cynthia Stohl (1986) indicates that quality circles can, in fact, fulfill many of the positive expectations that have led to their popularity.

Groups, Values, and Sense Making

Small group communication scholars have focused so much attention on groups as decision-making systems that it sometimes seems as if organizational groups have no other purpose. But the importance of group communication in organizations may extend far beyond the impact on decision-making processes. Evidence from the Hawthorne studies suggested that work group relationships provide the primary context from which individual values and attitudes toward the organization are derived. We also know from recent studies of occupational communities (a concept discussed in chapter 4) that shadowy group structures cutting across various areas of the formal organization give rise to and reinforces powerful values as well. Given the implications of "Groupthink," as described by Janis and the antiboat-rocking sentiments of contemporary organizatons (Redding, 1985), one of the most important functions of group communication may be to provide the basic frames of reference from which individual members understand, enact, and justify the organization and its mission.

Unfortunately, contemporary scholarship in small group communication has devoted little energy to the study of value-setting and sense-making functions in organizational groups. There has been so much devotion to the idea that the relationship with one's immediate superior is the central force in one's experience of organizational life (e.g., see Jablin, 1984) that the potential influence of group communication on the individual has essentially been ignored.

Summary

Groups constitute the most obvious and, perhaps, most important organizational subsystems. Communication within and between groups can be channeled toward cooperation or conflict. In either case, group action must be understood as joint action. A group not only serves the functions of a larger system, but it also strives to survive within that system. Hence, the goals of different organizational groups are not always consistent with one another or with the goals of the larger system.

Groups, like living organisms, appear to move through stages of development. In some cases, the stages seem orderly and sequenced, but activities of many groups take on cyclical characteristics. Interaction in groups is a rule-bound process based on normative expectations and role enactment. Group members are accorded varying levels of power and status within the group. One of the more prominent and powerful positions is that of group leader. The importance of leadership to group effectiveness is emphasized in our culture, yet no one has developed a uniformly accepted theory of leadership. Over the years, we have attempted to understand leadership by identifying leader traits, behavioral styles, and situations in which particular styles are likely to be more or less effective.

Most communication research on small group processes has been concerned with decision making. Hirokawa's studies are fairly typical of research in this area. Few consistently reliable differences have been found between effective and ineffective groups, although recent studies suggest that communicative behaviors involving evaluation of opinions, evaluation of alternatives, decisional premises, and the styles of influential group members may explain some of the differences. Although the usefulness of specific problem-solving procedures is in question, several prescriptive models for problem solving continue to be used widely. Examples of such models include parliamentary procedure, reflective thinking, cycle models, brainstorming, Delphi, and quality circles. Other potential functions of organizational groups (e.g., the role of group processes in organizational sense making) have received much less attention in communication scholarship.

Discussion Questions/ Activities

1. Observe a group in a decision-making process. What kinds of communicative behaviors seem to influence the group's effectiveness? Can the group's decision-making process be characterized by any of the models or procedures described in this chapter?
2. Do you think that group memberships within an organization play an important role in shaping individual members' values? Can you provide some examples to support your conclusion?

3. Some organizational scholars have argued prescriptive models of group decision making are undesirable and should be avoided. Do you agree with this position? Why or why not?
4. How important is leadership to effective group performance? What style of leadership do you think is most likely to be effective in a wide variety of situations?

Case Study

Developing Human Resources at Anderson Medical Center

Tom Benson was delighted to learn that he had just been named director of the new department of human resource development (HRD) at Anderson Medical Center. The new department consolidated all training and development in the 750–bed, 2,200–employee hospital. Before HRD was created, training was split among three departments: personnel, which handled job-related and safety training for support (nonhealth care) staff; in-service education, which was responsible for nurses, orderlies, and other health care personnel; and management services, which identified training needs and conducted training programs for line administrators and managers.

The new department was created because top administration felt that training activities at Anderson had become too fragmented. Although the training objectives and functions in each of the three departments seemed well-defined, the right hand did not know what the left hand was doing. Part of the problem was that some training programs were redundant. For example, in-service education did a program on performance appraisal interviewing for nursing supervisors, while management services did a similar program for administrative department heads. Moreover, much of the training had become routine. Administration wondered if the real training needs in the hospital were being served.

The new department pooled the old in-service education and management services departments and removed all training functions from personnel. Tom knew that the people in the personnel department were glad to be rid of the training function, since they believed that their real responsibilities were hiring, negotiating labor contracts, and administering the benefits and safety programs. He was not so sure about the feelings of former in-service education director, Clara Carson, and former management services chief, Bob Roth. Carson was a registered nurse with more than fifteen years of nursing experience and ten years as an in-service education director. Roth was a retired military officer who believed firmly in the human relations principles espoused by Dale Carnegie during the 1930s.

Carson and Roth both had received hefty salary increases along with their "promotions" as Benson's new associate directors, but Benson suspected that they might be displeased by the new arrangement. After all, Benson was 33-years-old, had a Ph.D. in Organizational Behavior, and was much younger than either Carson or Roth. Also, he had been brought in "from the outside" to start up and manage the new HRD department, although he had worked as a consultant to Anderson Medical Center for more than a year. In fact, the decision to create HRD developed out of needs assessment research that Benson had done for the hospital. Tom had never directly suggested that this be done, but when the chief administrator decided to make HRD a reality, he was happy to be offered the position of director.

The other members of the new HRD department included two registered nurses who had worked for Carson at in-service education, a program developer and a human relations trainer from the old management services group, and two technical trainers, formerly with the personnel department. Benson knew that the new members of HRD would experience some disorientation while the department was being organized. Prior to the change, their roles and jobs had been defined clearly. Now, everything was unclear.

On the first day of HRD's operations, Benson called Roth and Carson in for a meeting. He asked them whether they had any reservations about the new department and their roles in it. Carson asserted that she was "happy as a clam." Roth said that he was looking forward to learning about the idea of basing training programs on formal needs assessments, though he still thought that tapes of Norman Vincent Peale speaking on the "Power of Positive Thinking" were the best training programs that money could buy. Benson was not entirely pleased with these answers, but he let the matter drop.

Benson then discussed his ideas for the first few months of HRD's existence. Since they, rather than the hospital administrators, were the experts on training and development, HRD would have to develop its own statement of mission, objectives, and functions within broad guidelines laid down by top administration. Benson suggested that the department should continue with "business as usual" during the first few weeks. Members would continue with the training projects that already were underway in the in-service education, management services, and personnel departments before HRD was created. During this same time frame, HRD would work on a mission statement. After all current projects were completed, HRD would set up a list of new project priorities and develop some general plans for their execution. Carson and Roth praised the plan.

The three broke up their own meeting and reconvened with the entire group. Benson explained the general plan. Outside of some casual jokes about the uncertainty over job functions, no one expressed any concerns. The two training specialists from the personnel department did seem somewhat remote and withdrawn. Even so, the group hammered out a schedule for completion of projects already underway, then set up a series of six meetings over the next three weeks in order to develop a mission statement. Benson asked everyone to consider two questions before the first planning meeting: "Who are we and what do we do?" Members spent the rest of the day organizing their new office.

Planning Meeting 1

Benson was surprised to discover at the first planning meeting a few days later that no one had given much thought to his questions. In general, members simply said, "I know what *I* do, but I have no idea what anyone else here does."

Benson was uncertain about how to proceed. He had planned on a lively discussion. Carson finally said, "Look, I'm really confused by this whole question." The remark was followed by nods of agreement all around the table. Roth, agitated over the lack of progress, suggested that Benson prepare his own version of a functional organizational plan for HRD to use as a "springboard for discussion" at the next meeting.

Planning Meeting 2

Benson began by laying out a functional organization chart. The idea was simple. Carson and the two registered nurses would still have responsibility for all health care delivery training. Roth, along with his two former staffers and the technical trainers from personnel, would cover all nonhealth care areas from top administration to cafeteria workers. All projects would be reviewed by the entire group as it worked toward developing a model for collecting data on training needs, translating that data into training objectives, and designing training and development programs. At this point, one of Carson's nurses became angry at the idea of collaborating with non-nurses on training programs designed for nurses. Roth, perceiving the remark to be directed at him, said that he was not very pleased about trying to work with "a gaggle of geese like hard-headed nurses." Carson attacked Roth for his lack of professionalism, announced that she was late for a training seminar, and then left the meeting, remarking that she hoped the next meeting would yield some productive ideas. With the meeting in shambles, Benson asked all members to think through their concerns and ideas about the plan, then write them down for discussion at the next meeting.

A few days after the meeting, Benson discovered that the director of personnel had asked the hospital administrator, "What in the world is going on at HRD? If they can't get their act together, maybe we ought to recover our trainers and just pick up where we left off." The administrator replied, "Well, let's give it two or three weeks. If things aren't under control by then, we'll have to make some changes."

1. How would you characterize Benson's style of leadership in this situation? In light of situational theories of leadership, could Benson get more effective results by changing his approach?
2. Given what you read in the chapter about basic concepts in group dynamics, explain why this group is not really developing as a group.
3. Does research on small group decision-making processes provide any insights that might help to explain why HRD is having problems and how these problems might be corrected? Explain your answer.

References

Baird, J. E., Jr., and Weinberg, S. B. (1981). *Group communication: The essence of synergy* (2nd ed.). Dubuque, IA: Wm. C. Brown.

Bartol, K. M., & Butterfield, D. A. (1976). Sex effects in evaluating leaders. *Journal of Applied Psychology, 61,* 446–545.

Beatty, M. J. (1989). Group members' decision rule orientations and consensus. *Human Communication Research, 16,* 279–296.

Benne, K. D., and Sheats, P. (1948). Functional roles of group members. *Journal of Social Issues, 4,* 41–49.

Bennis, W. (1976a). Leadership—A beleaguered species. *Organizational Dynamics, 5,* 3–16.

Bennis, W. (1976b). *The unconscious conspiracy: Why leaders can't lead.* New York: American Management Association.

Blake, R. R., & Mouton, J. S. (1964). *The managerial grid.* Houston: Gulf.

Blake, R. R., & Mouton, J. S. (1985). *The managerial grid III: The key to leadership excellence.* Houston: Gulf.

Blumer, H. (1969). *Symbolic interactionism: Perspective and method.* Englewood Cliffs, NJ: Prentice-Hall.

Bormann, E. (1969). *Discussion and group methods.* New York: Harper & Row.

Coon, A. M. (1957). Brainstorming: A creative problem-solving technique. *Journal of Communication, 7,* 111–118.

Coonfield, T. (1984). *Evaluating quality circle effectiveness.* Panel presentation at the annual meeting of the International Communication Association, San Francisco.

Eblen, A. L. (1987). Communication, leadership, and organizational commitment. *Central States Speech Journal, 38,* 181–195.

Emerson, R. M. (1962). Power-dependence relations. *American Sociological Review, 27,* 31–41.

Fairhurst, G. T., & Chandler, T. A. (1989). Social structure in leader-member interaction. *Communication Monographs, 56,* 215–239.

Fiedler, F. (1967). *A theory of leadership effectiveness.* New York: McGraw-Hill.

Fisher, B. A. (1970). Decision emergence: Phases in group decision making. *Speech Monographs, 37,* 53–66.

Graen, G. (1976). Role-making processes within complex organizations. In M. D. Dunnette (Ed.), *Handbook of industrial and organizational psychology* (pp. 1201–1245). Chicago: Rand McNally.

Gudykunst, W. B., Yoon, Y., & Nishida, T. (1987). The influence of individualism-collectivism on perceptions of communication in ingroup and outgroup relationships. *Communication Monographs, 54,* 295–306.

Hagen, R. L., & Kahn, A. (1975). Discrimination against competent women. *Journal of Applied and Social Psychology, 5,* 362–376.

Hirokawa, R. Y. (1980). A comparative analysis of communication patterns within effective and ineffective decision-making groups. *Communication Monographs, 47,* 312–321.

Hirokawa, R. Y. (1982a). Consensus group decision making, quality of decision, and group satisfaction: An attempt to sort "fact" from "fiction." *Central States Speech Journal, 33,* 407–415.

Hirokawa, R. Y. (1982b). Group communication and problem-solving effectiveness I: A critical review of inconsistent findings. *Communication Quarterly, 30,* 134–141.

Hirokawa, R. Y. (1983). Group communication and problem-solving effectiveness II: An exploratory investigation of procedural functions. *Western Journal of Speech Communication, 47,* 59–74.

Hirokawa, R. Y., and Pace, R. (1983). A descriptive investigation of the possible communication-based reasons for effective and ineffective group decision making. *Communication Monographs, 50,* 363–379.

Hofstede, G., & Bond, M. (1984). Hofstede's culture dimensions: An independent validation suing Rokeach's value survey. *Journal of Cross-Cultural Psychology, 15,* 417–433.

Homans, G. C. (1950). *The human group.* New York: Harcourt Brace Jovanovich.

Jablin, F. M. (1984). The assimilation of new members into organizational communication systems: A longitudinal approach. In R. N. Bostrom (Ed.), *Communication yearbook 8*. Beverly Hills, CA: Sage.

Jennings, E. (1961). The anatomy of leadership. *Management of Personnel Quarterly, 2*.

Kaoru, I. (1968). *QC activities*. Tokyo: Union of Japanese Scientists and Engineers.

Kelly, G. A. (1955). *The psychology of personal constructs* (Vol. 1). New York: Norton.

Knave, C. (1990, March). Letter stating the position of Scientific Methods, Inc., on the origin of the managerial grid.

Koehler, J. W., Anatol, K. W. E., and Applbaum, R. L. (1981). *Organizational communication: Behavioral perspectives* (2nd ed.). New York: Holt, Rinehart & Winston.

Lamude, K. G. & Daniels, T. D. (in press). Mutual evaluations of communication competence in superior-subordinate relationships: Sex role incongruency and pro-male bias. *Women's Studies in Communication*.

Levinson, D. (1959). Role, personality, and social structure in the organizational setting. *Journal of Abnormal and Social Psychology, 172*.

Linstone, H. A., and Turoff, M. (1975). *The Delphi method*. London: Addison-Wesley.

Lippitt, G. L. (1982). *Organization renewal: A holistic approach to organization development* (2nd ed.). Englewood Cliffs, NJ: Prentice-Hall.

Littlejohn, S. W. (1989). *Theories of human communication* (3rd ed.). Belmont, CA: Wadsworth.

Maccoby, M. (1976). *The gamesman: The new corporate leaders*. New York: Simon & Schuster.

McBurney, J., and Hance, K. (1950). *Discussion in human affairs*. New York: Harper & Row.

Meyer, G. W., and Stott, R. G. (1985). Quality circles: Panacea or Pandora's box? *Organizational Dynamics, 13*, 34–50.

Nieva, V. F., & Gutek, B. A. (1981). *Women and work: A psychological perspective*. New York: Praeger.

Nomura, R. (1981). West learns Japanese ways, executives wear workclothes. *Neihon Keizai Shimbum*. Translation Service Center, the Asia Foundation.

Osborn, A. F. (1957). *Applied imagination*. New York: Scribners.

Pettegrew, L. S. (1982). Organizational communication and the S.O.B. theory of management. *Western Journal of Speech Communication, 46*, 179–191.

Poole, M. S. (1981). Decision development in small groups I: A comparison of two models. *Communication Monographs, 48*, 1–24.

Poole, M. S. (1983a). Decision development in small groups II: A study of multiple sequences in decision making. *Communication Monographs, 50*, 206–232.

Poole, M. S. (1983b). Decision development in small groups III: A multiple sequence model of group decision development. *Communication Monographs, 50*, 321–341.

Poole, M. S., & Roth, J. (1989a). Decision development in small groups IV: A typology of group decision paths. *Human Communication Research, 15*, 323–356.

Poole, M. S., & Roth, J. (1989b). Decision development in small groups V: Test of a contingency model. *Human Communication Research, 15*, 549–589.

Rehder, R. (1981, April). Newly emerging nontraditional organizations: What American and Japanese managers are learning from one another in the productivity race. *Business Horizons*, pp. 63–70.

Robert, H. M. (1970). *Robert's rules of order, newly revised.* Glenview, IL: Scott, Foresman.

Schein, E. (1969). *Process consultation: Its role in organization development.* Reading, MA: Addison-Wesley.

Secord, P. F., and Backman, C. W. (1964). *Social psychology.* New York: McGraw-Hill.

Simon, H. A. (1957). *Administrative behavior.* New York: Free Press.

Stohl, C. (1986). Quality circles and changing patterns of communication. In M. McLaughlin (Ed.), *Communication yearbook 9* (pp. 511–531). Newbury Park, CA: Sage.

Sturgis, A. (1966). *Sturgis standard code of parliamentary procedure.* New York: McGraw-Hill.

Weick, K. W. (1976). Educational organizations as loosely coupled systems. *Administrative Science Quarterly, 21,* 1–19.

White, R., and Lippitt, R. (1960). *Autocracy and democracy,* New York: Harper & Row.

Wofford, J. C., Gerloff, E. A., and Cummins, R. C. (1979). Group behavior and the communication process. In R. S. Cathcart and L. A. Samovar (Eds.), *Small group communication: A reader* (3rd ed.). Dubuque, IA: Wm. C. Brown.

Wolman, C., & Frank, H. (1975). The solo woman in a professional peer group. *American Journal of Orthopsychiatry, 45,* 164–171.

Zaleznik, A. (1977). Managers and leaders: Are they different? *Harvard Business Review, 55,* 67–78.

Outline

Characteristics of Public
    Communication
  The Source in Organizational
    Public Communication
  Public Communication as
    Transaction
Grunig's Multisystems Theory
Internal Public Communication
  Orientation and Indoctrination
  Safety and Loss Prevention
  Compensation and Benefits
  Organizational Change and
    Development
  Morale and Satisfaction

External Public Communication
  Public Relations and Image
    Building
  Public Affairs and Issues
    Management
  Issues Management and
    Organizational Change
  Issues Management and Issues
    Advocacy
Summary
Discussion Questions/Activities
Case Study
References

Public Communication

Amy Stone, a new college graduate, recently was hired as an assistant dietitian at a large, urban hospital. On her first day at work, she reported to the personnel office, where she was told that she, along with several other newly hired employees, would participate in a daylong orientation program. During the program, Amy and her companions saw a 30–minute videotape about the history, services, and "caring tradition" of the hospital. They received copies of the employee handbook, along with a detailed review of hospital organization and policies. They also received a portfolio of information about employee benefits such as health insurance, pension plans, and credit union membership. They even got a personal welcome from the hospital administrator.

Later in the week, Amy received her first copy of the hospital's monthly newsletter. The newsletter was a slick, professional production with stories about activities in several hospital departments, employee-of-the-month awards, an article by the administrator on the importance of delivering high-quality health care, and an "action line," in which designated managers answered questions and complaints from employees.

A few days after this, Amy noticed an advertisement in the city newspaper that the hospital had sponsored as a "public service." The ad described the growing need to control health-care costs and some of the factors that cause these costs to go up. One of these factors was competition among hospitals when too many serve the same community. According to the ad, competition in health care does not have the expected effect of reducing costs but actually causes the cost of health care to increase. Amy mentioned the ad to her supervisor and said that she was glad to be working for an organization that believes in sponsoring public service messages. The supervisor explained to Amy that the hospital's top administrators decided to sponsor this advertisement as a part of their strategy to prevent a national medical corporation from obtaining approval to build a new hospital in the city.

Each of these three episodes (the orientation, the newsletter, and the advertisement) is an obvious instance of **public communication**—the effort of a particular source or agent to communicate with a given audience or public. Each episode also includes features of *organizational* public communication that are less obvious. First, public communication in the organizational context can require a substantial commitment of resources: production facilities for newsletters, company magazines, and video programs; advertising space in print and electronic media; salaries for the professionals who write, edit, and produce public communication programs. Second, top-level executives ultimately control these resources. Although the content of public communication programs is influenced by employee groups, communities, special-interest groups, and in some cases, even legal requirements, those who control organizational resources also control the agenda for public communication.

When executives decide to commit resources to organizational communication, they often have some form of public communication in mind. Generally, these forms may be classified as **internal** or **external.** Internal public communication has become synonymous with the term *employee communications* (Williams, 1978). **Employee communications** is management's effort to provide information to and exert influence with organizational membership in general. External public communication traditionally has included advertising and public relations efforts designed to influence consumers, communities, special-interest groups, voters, regulators, and legislators.

In this chapter, we will describe various forms and examples of internal and external public communication. Although an organization's advertising and promotion of its products or services are a form of public communication, we will not be concerned with this activity. Instead, our treatment of external public communication will focus on the traditional public relations image-building activity and a recent transition in some major U.S. organizations away from traditional public relations to a concept known as **public affairs** and **issues management.** First, we will review some of the basic characteristics of public communication. We also will consider a theory that has been used to explain how organizations and individuals use systems of public communication. This theory is Grunig's (1975) multisystems theory of organizational communication.

Characteristics of Public Communication

Public communication has been described as a process of *one communicating with many* (Wiseman & Barker, 1967). One person, who functions as a message source, creates and transmits a message to many others, who function as receivers. Unfortunately, this intuitively obvious definition of public communication oversimplifies the idea of a "source" in organizational public communication activities and also fails to recognize the transactional character of communication.

The Source in Organizational Public Communication

Conventional definitions of public communication treat the source of messages as a specific individual. While this may apply in some situations, messages intended for public communication in organizations often are originated and produced by organizational subsystems composed of many individuals. This point is illustrated in the following example.

Unitech Industries has never had a formal system for appraisal of employee performance. The personnel department has just developed a system for companywide appraisal of performance and then has persuaded management to adopt it. Since the new system will be used for decisions involving pay raises, promotions, and terminations, top management wants to ease potential employee concerns over the change in policy. At this point, top management decides to tell the communication department to develop an informational program that will explain to employees the appraisal system and the reasons for its adoption. Executives from top management, communication, and personnel groups will collaborate on deciding the content of the informational programs. After they decide what employees will be told, staff members in the communication department will write a series of articles based on these informational decisions and run the articles in the company newsletter.

In the Unitech example, top management makes the initial decision to provide employees with information on a policy change. Although the communication and personnel departments collaborate with top management on decisions about information provided to employees, in a real sense, it is management's message that is transmitted to the internal employee public. The communication department acts as a staff arm of management in producing and executing the informational programs. As the example indicates, organizational public communication can be a complex process in which a number of units and individuals contribute to the dissemination of messages.

Public Communication as Transaction

Public communication usually is regarded as a linear process. Most of us seem to understand public communication in terms that are similar to Berlo's model—a source-oriented view of presenting messages in ways designed to secure a desired response. Since the purpose of public communication often involves persuasion and gaining compliance, the image of the successful public communicator is one of a person who has discovered some formula for using words to mold an audience like putty. This idea is quite misguided. Sources do gain compliance from receivers, but acceptance of an idea is an act that arises from the receivers' choices. No universal formula in public communication exists for guaranteeing that receivers' choices will be consistent with the intentions of the source.

Public communication, like other communication contexts, may be more appropriately characterized as a transactional process that merely takes on a deceptively linear appearance. Even though the "source" and "receiver" roles in any given episode of public communication may be relatively fixed, the people in these roles are participants in a process of creating shared meaning. They interpret the situation at hand, act within the situation, and influence one another simultaneously. Grunig emphasizes this point in his "multisystem theory of organizational communication."

Grunig's Multisystems Theory

Grunig (1975) defined communication as motivated behavior that occurs in two forms: **synchronic** and **diachronic.** The synchronic form of behavior occurs when an organization or individual first *gives* information and then seeks feedback (i.e., a response to the information). Diachronic behavior occurs when the organization or individual attempts to solicit or *acquire* information prior to giving any information. According to Grunig, communication behavior is most likely to occur in "decision situations" in which one must recognize and choose among alternatives. In other words, Grunig believes that people communicate "in a situation that is problematic to them, and that they have no need to communicate in nonproblematic situations" (1976, p. 4).

Grunig contends that two basic factors in a person's perception of a situation—**problem recognition** and **constraint recognition**—can be used to predict the kind of communication behavior in which the person (or even an organization or a public) will engage. An individual who can recognize a problem in a situation is said to be an open individual. One who cannot or will not recognize a problem is said to be a closed individual. If a person recognizes that the structure of the situation allows some alternatives in solving the problem, the situation is said to be open or unconstrained. A structure that is perceived to allow no alternatives is closed or constrained. The combinations of these conditions lead to four basic types of behavior: **problem facing, routine habit, fatalism,** and **constrained decision.** The conditions and behavior types are displayed in figure 10.1.

Theoretically, the problem-facing condition in which one recognizes a problem and perceives alternatives should lead to diachronic communication in which the person or organization actively seeks out information. People in a constrained condition also will seek information, but only up to the point at which they perceive that some constraint will prevent them from using the information. Communication in the routine habit condition takes the form of defending and reinforcing the habitual behavior. Although a person perceives alternatives to the habitual behavior, he or she cannot or will not recognize problems in the behavior. Communication functions to justify such behavior. In the routine habit situation, there is no need to seek information—only to send it. Under the fatalistic condition, people demonstrate little recognition of problems in their situation and see many constraints that would prevent them from adopting any alternative to the situation. Consequently, they seldom communicate about their situation.

Since Grunig is concerned only with communication in decision situations and defines communication as only one form of motivated organizational behavior (1975, pp. 101–104), his theory really is too restrictive to be a general theory of organizational communication. It is, however, a good theory of *public* communication because it is concerned primarily with the kind of information that is most often the subject of public communication programs; namely, topics about the organization or its products and services rather than matters pertaining directly to one's job or relationships with others in the organization.

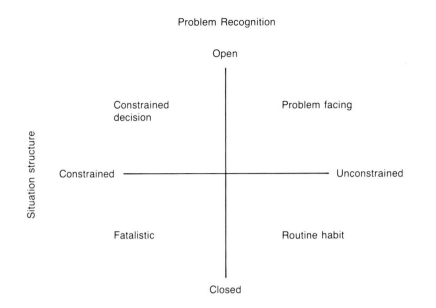

Problem Recognition

Open

Constrained
decision

Problem facing

Situation structure

Constrained ——————————————— Unconstrained

Fatalistic

Routine habit

Closed

Figure 10.1
Grunig's model of decision situations. From "A multisystems theory of organizational communication," by J. E. Grunig, 1975, *Communication Research, 2* pp. 99–136. Adapted by permission.

Grunig calls his theory "multisystems" because he has applied it to answer questions about public communication behavior in several types of systems (internal employee publics, management groups, and external publics such as consumers or even other organizations). His studies have produced a number of interesting results. For example, Grunig found in one investigation that organization members could be classified under three of the four conditions specified in his model. Constrained older workers adopted a fatalistic orientation. Dissatisfied younger workers were problem-facing types. Managers' behavior reflected routine habit. As predicted, communication behavior differed across the three groups. Problem-facing younger workers were more likely than fatalistic older workers to acquire information about the organization and to do so from a wider variety of media. Routine habit managers possessed information about the organization, but this seems to have occurred mainly because the kinds of information in Grunig's study originated at the management level. Managers also were the only ones to positively evaluate the company's formal media (newsletter, magazine, bulletin board).

In studies of consumers' use of advertising messages, Grunig again found three basic groups: fatalistic working-class consumers, problem-facing middle-class consumers, and slightly fatalistic professionals. Grunig wanted to know whether the consumers had acquired information about four consumer programs that a company in Washington, D.C., sponsored. As expected, middle-class problem facers were more likely than working-class fatalists to have heard about the programs, but professionals had acquired more information than either of the other groups. The result for professionals was surprising, since this group was slightly fatalistic. Actual use of advertising messages, however, was consistent with Grunig's theory. Use of advertisements among middle-class consumers was greater than use among professionals. Use among professionals was greater than use among working-class consumers.

Grunig also has applied his theory to explain organizations' strategies in relating to external publics and ways in which communication *from* external publics can influence organization members. He has been able to identify only two categories of organizations: problem-facing and fatalistic. Fatalistic organizations neither seek nor provide information and employ public relations professionals "primarily to react to the mass media in a time of crisis and to keep up interpersonal contacts with linkages needed for the organization's survival" (1975, p. 128). Problem-facing organizations use public relations as a tool for giving information but not for purposes of acquiring information. These organizations probably have other means of acquiring information about their external environments.

The influence of communication from external publics on the organization itself is an issue that is almost entirely ignored in traditional linear views of public communication. Grunig (1978) has attempted to identify "the conditions under which accurate information from an external public flows into an organization" (p. 40). He predicted that employees' levels of involvement within the organization (internal), their involvement with publics outside the organization (external), and their perceptions of situations will influence their ability to accurately perceive public attitudes toward the organization. Specifically, Grunig asked employees to predict the publics' responses to the following questions about the company in which the employees worked:

1. What comes to mind when you hear the name [*company*]?
2. What are the most frequent problems that you have experienced with the company?
3. How would you rate the service you get from the company (0 to 100)?
4. How would you rate the company's concern for customers?

Grunig assumed that those employees who could accurately predict public response somehow were obtaining accurate information. Generally, he found that problem-facing employees with high external involvement and low internal involvement both "actively seek information from the public and achieve accuracy" (1978, p. 51). Fatalistic employees did not achieve accuracy. According to Grunig, these employees passively processed and then simply agreed with information coming in from outsiders, but such information usually had a negative bias and did not accurately reflect the entire publics' attitudes.

Grunig has interpreted the results of studies based on his theory to mean that organizations' public communication efforts must not only be concerned with transmitting information in order to influence various publics but it must also be concerned with *acquiring* information from these publics and with understanding how various publics seek and use information. All of these functions are reflected in our review of internal and external public communication.

Internal Public Communication

Management often engages in efforts to disseminate messages and information through the entire structure of an organization to employees as a public or to specific groups within the organization. This is *internal public communication* or, as it is often called, *employee communications*. A 1978 survey of chief executive officers in major U.S. and Canadian corporations found that the majority regard employee communications as an important feature of their management plan and a contributor to organizational effectiveness and productivity (Williams, 1978).

The means for internal public communication may include any of the following media and methods:

employee meetings
newsletters
internal magazines
manuals and handbooks
general memos
pay-voucher inserts
posters and bulletin boards
public-address systems
videotape, film, and slides
closed-circuit television

Some large organizations with ample resources for communication programs employ all of these systems.

Organizational efforts at internal public communication occur for many reasons. These reasons often are managerially biased in the sense that they represent management views and objectives. Whether this bias is appropriate or not, it is important that you understand that managerial bias influences the choice of topics and the content of messages involved in internal public communication. Many of the conventional internal public communication topics can be grouped under five functional areas: **orientation and indoctrination, safety and loss prevention, compensation and benefits, organizational change and development,** and **morale and satisfaction.**

Orientation and Indoctrination

Imagine that you are a new employee in a large organization. You have just been hired for a job in which you are well-trained, but is your immediate task to gain knowledge about all that you want or need to know about the position and the organization? More than likely, it is not. You may arrive with a number of unanswered questions that range from "What is the company philosophy?" and "How does my job relate to the total organization?" to "When do I receive my first paycheck?" and "Where is the cafeteria?"

Many organizations provide answers to such questions through some type of formal orientation program. An orientation program may include topics that pertain to the organization as a whole (policies, procedures, operating philosophy, and structure), your specific position (scope of authority, job duties, work procedures), and other personal concerns.

Completion of orientation does not mean that you will never again be exposed to messages on organizational matters or your role within the organization. The maintenance and integration functions of communication that we described in chapter 4 often are carried out in part through a continuous program of public communication aimed at indoctrination and socialization of organization members. Such programs often are intended to build an organizational image with the internal employee public and to present and reinforce specific values, beliefs, and practices.

An example of an intensive orientation and indoctrination effort is reflected in programs conducted by Junior Achievement, Inc., a national nonprofit educational corporation. Junior Achievement franchises local program operations throughout the United States. Typically, the only full-time paid staff members in these local programs are the executive directors, who work in relative isolation from the national office as well as from one another. This kind of isolation in combination with the franchise relationship means that the national office cannot directly control the executive directors of the local programs. Isolation also can have adverse effects on the directors' motivation and commitment to the goals of the national program. Consequently, the national office conducts an intensive two-week orientation program for all new field executives. Most of the content involves national policies and procedures along with methods and standards for local program operation, but the orientation also is an open attempt to cast the new executives in the national mold. The orientation is conducted with a group of new executives who are not only exposed to formal training, but who are also placed in informal situations where they can interact, form friendships and alliances, and reinforce organizational values with one another. After they return to their own local offices, the national office continues indoctrination and reinforcement through frequent newsletters, bulletins, regional meetings, and occasional visits from internal consultants.

Safety and Loss Prevention

Organizations have two reasons for the promotion of safety and loss prevention. One is the conservation of organizational resources. The other is the welfare of organization members. Inventory shrinkages, theft of company property, and job-related accidents jeopardize both of these objectives, though it is probably fair to say that many organizations are more concerned with resource conservation than with member welfare because the former has a direct connection with costs and profits. Thus, many organizations make a conscientious effort to control losses and promote safe working practices through internal public communication.

For example, in the late 1960s, the Santa Fe Railway was plagued by a poor safety record. Accidents resulted in lost time and increased insurance risks. In an effort to improve, the Santa Fe management began a "Zero in on Safety" program that was promoted through internal publications, meetings between supervisors and top management, a safety film, employee-designed posters, and even a safety-incentive reward program. Within two years, Santa Fe's safety record advanced from nineteenth to first among the nation's large railroads (Industrial Communications Council, 1975). Even though it would not be appropriate to say that the public communication effort "caused" this improvement, the presence of the program clearly was a major factor in focusing attention on safety at Santa Fe.

In a limited sense, internal public communication regarding safety is required by the Occupational Safety and Health Administration (OSHA). For example, OSHA requires the posting of warning and regulatory signs in hazardous work areas. But OSHA's authority under the 1970 Occupational Safety and Health Act focuses primarily on *compliance* with safety standards rather than on *promotion* of safety through public communication programs. According to some safety and loss-prevention experts, any organization that really wants to promote safety and loss prevention "must go beyond OSHA compliance activities" (Petersen, 1975, p. 117). Public communication programs may form a major portion of these additional activities.

Compensation and Benefits

Whether or not work organizations wish to implement and maintain employee benefits, public communication programs concerning employee benefits are virtually mandatory. The Employee Retirement Income Security Act, which became federal law in 1974, requires organizations to make full and understandable disclosure of employee benefit programs.

Benefit programs in large organizations can be very elaborate. In addition to basic health protection, life insurance, and pension plans, these programs may also include credit union participation, use of company recreation facilities, child-care services, family and personal counseling services, and profit-sharing plans. Development of a public communication program that can effectively and efficiently provide information on benefit packages can also be complicated. Many organizations manage to incorporate information about benefits in orientation programs as a simple means of meeting legal requirements with new personnel. However, changes in benefit packages also require systematic dissemination of information to all personnel.

Organizational Change and Development

Change is a stressful process even when it is desirable. This is especially true for organization members who do not participate in the basic decisions on such matters. When organizations undergo substantial change, many of the members may be very uncertain about the impact that the change will have on the organization and their positions within it. Members may need a great deal of new information in order to understand the purposes and effects of major change.

A classic instance of a massive, yet rapidly executed internal public communication effort to cope with uncertainty over a major organizational change arose out of AT&T's divestiture agreement with the federal government. In return for dismissal of a government antitrust suit, AT&T agreed to sell more than twenty of its operating companies, including Mountain Bell Telephone. Mountain Bell executives, who had some forewarning of the decision, were advised by AT&T one morning in January 1982 that the agreement with the government would be made public later *on the same day.*

Mountain Bell executives were concerned that company employees (more than 50,000 in number) would get their first information about the decision on evening news programs. These executives understood that organization members can be very displeased and disconcerted when they don't receive important information within the organization before it appears in the media. Moreover, the situation was ripe with the possibility for morale-devastating rumors about the consequences of the change; in particular, the situation was ripe for rumors about massive layoffs, forced retirements, job changes, and transfers.

Mountain Bell attempted to mount an internal public communication effort that would reach as many of its members as possible within the few hours remaining before the evening news programs. Obviously, tactics such as a special newsletter, a company magazine article, or an attempt to relay the message from level to level in the organization were useless in this situation. Instead, the company president appeared on Mountain Bell's internal closed-circuit television system to announce and explain the AT&T decision. All of the personnel who worked in offices with access to the television system were convened to hear the president's announcement. The presentation was reinforced later in employee meetings at all Mountain Bell locations. The one-day effort reached about 60 percent of the organization members.

Public communication concerned with organization change usually does not occur in the crisis atmosphere reflected in the Mountain Bell example. Frequently, it is an ongoing process intended to familiarize members with long-term goals, objectives, plans, and progress. Yet, if you recall our discussion of information adequacy in chapter 4, these are precisely the kinds of topics on which many organization members think they are inadequately informed. Apparently, either many organizations do a poor job of public communication regarding organizational change and development or most members simply ignore the information.

Morale and Satisfaction

The final functional area in internal public communication includes the promotion of morale and satisfaction among organization members. Messages concerned with any of the other four areas may serve this purpose too, but promotion of morale and satisfaction includes many types of messages that are unrelated to these other areas. Messages that serve maintenance and human functions often fall into this group. For example, an employee-of-the-month column in a company magazine or notes about departmental accomplishments in the newsletter are instances of messages that have as their primary objectives the improvement of members' self-concepts, interpersonal relationships, and attitudes toward the organization.

External Public Communication

J. W. Hill (1977) argued that every private-sector corporation in contemporary America is faced with two tests: maintaining profitability and meeting the expectations and demands of society. A similar admonition can be offered to public-sector and nonprofit organizations by changing "maintaining profitability" to "providing services within budget" (although one wonders whether this will ever apply to the federal government!). In either case, contemporary organizations are faced with the problem of meeting societal demands.

Much has been written in recent years about growing public disenchantment with large corporations and institutions (Gallup, 1979). Hill believed that this problem developed, in part, because of public dependence on large organizations—dependence that brings about public frustration when such organizations fail to meet legitimate public needs and expectations. External public communication is a means through which organizations can understand and respond to public expectations in ways that allow an organization to meet its other tests.

External public communication occurs in at least three major forms: (1) *advertising and promoting products and services,* (2) *creating a desirable public image for the organization,* (3) *shaping public opinion on issues that are important to the organization.* In this text, we are concerned with the second and third functions. Traditionally, public communication concerned with **image building** has been the responsibility of public relations practitioners. During the past 20 years, however, many organizations have expanded the concept of public communication to include a new function—the management of **public issues** and **public affairs.** In fact, some types of organizations exist solely for the purpose of advocating and gaining acceptance of positions on public issues. For example, virtually everyone has at least some familiarity with organizations such as the National Consumers Union, Public Interest Research Group, Sierra Club, National Organization for Women, and the Urban League. Frequently, public-interest organizations and special-interest groups challenge business and government policies when these policies adversely affect the environment, consumers, minorities, and communities. Some corporations have attempted to cope with these challenges by shifting away from image building to identifying and tracking public issues that concern the organization. An organization may try to change in order to respond to public criticism or it may try to influence public opinion on important issues by advocating its own position in the public arena (Sethi, 1982).

Public Relations and Image Building

Gerald Goldhaber (1990) described **image building** as a process of creating the "identity an organization wants perceived by its relevant publics" (p. 336). Image building involves an organization's attempt to cultivate a public impression that a set of positively valued features defines the essential character of the organization.

Corporate and business concerns over image building date back to at least the mid-1950s, when the *Harvard Business Review* published a landmark article on business image (Gardner & Rainwater, 1955) and many major companies made definite efforts to change their corporate images (Finn, 1962). Typically, such changes are accomplished by developing and publicizing specific organizational characteristics and behaviors that are consistent with the image being cultivated. The art of image building usually is associated with the field of public relations. Clearly, it is inappropriate to equate the whole field of public relations with nothing more than image-building activity. In fact, Heath and Nelson (1986) indicate that the primary distinction between public affairs and public relations occurs in their relative focus on commercial or noncommercial concerns and in their power to direct corporate planning:

If public affairs is concerned primarily with the noncommercial aspects of corporate communication, public relations could be designated as being responsible for commercial communication, excluding paid product and service advertising . . . generally, public relations has no power to direct corporate planning departments. . . . (p. 27)

While Heath and Nelson point out that public relations functions may include activities such as media relations, marketing publicity, and internal communication, the process of image building has become, nonetheless, a major feature of public relations practice. For example, public relations has been defined as "the management function which evaluates public attitudes, identifies the policies and procedures of an individual or an organization with the public interest, and executes a program of action to earn public understanding and acceptance" (Cutlip & Center, 1964, p. 4). The second part of this definition, identifying an individual or organization with the public interest, lies at the heart of the image-building process. Hence, Scott Cutlip and Allen Center, whose text on public relations is a classic in the field, argued in 1964 that farsighted, contemporary public relations practice is concerned with developing public appreciation of good organizational performance. Presumably, this appreciation is a public image of what the organization is or does.

Image building continues to be a major concern in many types of organizations. In the 1970s, Ford automobiles were humorously called cars that one must *Fix Or Repair Daily*, and Henry Ford II openly admitted in a segment of "Sixty Minutes" that the company had manufactured some bad products. Today, Ford works hard (at least in its corporate advertising) to be known as the company where "Quality Is Job One." Labor unions, struggling with dramatic losses of membership during the 1970s, attempt to redefine their relevance to workers, while the National Democratic Party, demolished in the last three presidential elections, realigns its positions to achieve identification with voters. Even the notorious motorcycle club Hell's Angels is trying to shake its image as a loose assemblage of thugs and sociopaths and to replace it with a public view of the Angels as community-minded, upstanding citizens.

Despite the prevalence of image building in public relations practice, serious questions exist about the real purposes served by such activity. When public relations is equated with public appreciation of good organizational performance, the equation presumes that the performance is, in fact, good. But what happens when performance is not good? Chandler (1988) provided an interesting answer to this question in his examination of annual reports issued by Fortune 500 companies. The annual report is a "colorful, expensive document [that] allows the organization almost total rhetorical flexibility in choosing how to describe performance and communicate that description to the organization's audience" (p. 5). Chandler studied the reports of twenty profitable companies as well as those of twenty unprofitable companies. He found, perhaps not surprisingly, that corporations attributed poor performance to external factors beyond management control (e.g., legal contraints, government regulation, poor economic conditions, unfair competition, or labor problems). In contrast, good performance was attributed to management decisions such as product innovations or new marketing strategies.

Public relations tools and strategies can provide valuable information to audiences, but they also can be instruments of concealment and deceit for covering up poor performance or downplaying harmful actions. More importantly, much of the emphasis on developing public image may have more to do with fulfilling the psychoemotional needs of managers and executives than with influencing public opinion. David Finn (1962) described the problem this way.

The recent interest of organizations and public figures in images—besides compensating for self-doubt and rationalizing overweening ambition—is also a search for meaning in a confused period of history. The fact that corporate images have turned out to be just another fictitious wardrobe for the Emperor who still walks naked in the streets is not important. The image is so tenacious, not because it dresses up the organization, but because it answers a basic need for finding a convincing purpose for the corporate enterprise.

Public Affairs and Issues Management

In recent years, several types of organizations, especially some large corporations, have moved beyond traditional image-building functions of public communication in order to deal more effectively with social and political issues that affect organizations and their relationships with various publics. This new and emerging concern often is identified by the label **public affairs** and **issues management.** Richard Armstrong (1981) noted that public relations and public affairs overlap to some extent, but corporate executives draw a line between the two functions. Unlike public relations, public affairs developed primarily out of concerns over issues that lead to laws and government regulations affecting organizations. Issues management is a principle vehicle through which public affairs can accomplish its objectives. As described by Arrington and Sawaya (1984), issues management involves foresight, policy development and advocacy. Buchholz (1982) reported that 91 percent of the Fortune 500 companies have implemented issues management programs.

Organizations become involved in public affairs and issues management for various reasons. In the case of a public-interest or special-interest group, the principal purpose of the organization is to create public awareness of issues and to influence local, state, or federal government policies on these issues. These influence efforts frequently challenge business and industrial organizations, which respond with their own attempts to influence public policy. Such attempts at influence not only arise from conflicts between business and public-interest groups, but they also arise among entire industries. Industry versus industry confrontations have occurred several times during the 1980s. For example, in 1985, the federal government proposed to ease its standards for automobile fuel economy. Ford and General Motors, whose products did not on average meet 1984 standards, favored the reduction. Chrysler, a company that invested heavily in the technology required to meet the standards, opposed the change. Other recent examples include the furor created in the boxing industry when the American Medical Association called for a ban on the sport and the furor raised within the American Medical Association over the insurance industry's ideas for controlling physicians' fees!

Virtually every working organization in America is subject to some form of legal regulation that has an effect on operations and effectiveness. Heavily regulated industries and trade groups traditionally have relied on legislative lobbying to influence the regulatory process. The basic idea in lobbying is to obtain passage of laws that favor your industry or group and to ensure the failure of unfavorable legislation. But influencing legislative and regulatory processes pose two problems for industries and trade groups. First, many public issues do not become the objects of legislative action until they have grown, developed, and become politicized. In this case, lobbying is a *reactive* approach to a matter on which public opinion may already be frozen (i.e., not easily changed). Second, many organizations have used political and legislative influence strategies in ways that are almost exclusively self-serving, without regard for the real public interest in a situation. Hence, as the late J. W. Hill (1977) pointed out, failure to address public issues adequately is a major weakness in many organizations.

Public issues often represent adversity to executives and managers precisely because they raise challenges to the organization's established traditions and modes of operation. It is not surprising that managers avoid such issues until an effect on the organization seems inevitable. As Jones and Chase argued, "The most significant explanation of the failure of business to gain respect for its positions on public issues is that corporate leadership either does not recognize or ignores, the discernible trends which always precede issues" (1977, p. 3). James E. Post (1978) has developed a model of corporate responses to public issues that helps to explain how such failures occur.

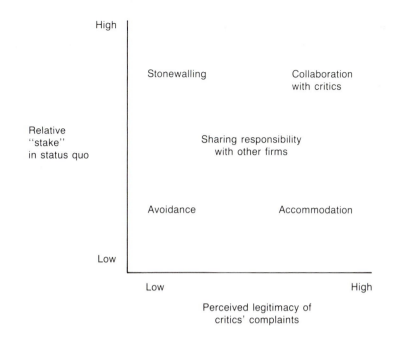

Figure 10.2
Modes of corporate response. From *Corporate Behavior and Social Change,* by J. E. Post, 1978, Reston, VA: Reston Publishing. Adapted by permission of John Wiley & Sons from "Conflict and conflict management," by K. Thomas, 1976, in M. Dunnette (Ed.), *Handbook of Industrial and Organizational Psychology,* Chicago: Rand-McNally.

Post characterizes organizational responses in light of two factors: (1) the organization's stake in maintaining the status quo (i.e., in continuing its current practices) and (2) the perceived legitimacy of public complaints against the status quo. According to Post's model in figure 10.2, organizations will avoid a public issue if both the stakes and perceived legitimacy are low. If the stakes are high and perceived legitimacy is low, organizations tend to "stonewall" with cover-ups, distortions, and other methods. Where stakes are low and perceived legitimacy is high, the organization attempts to accommodate critics through some form of change. If both the stakes and perceived legitimacy are high, the organization attempts to collaborate with critics.

Avoidance and stonewalling are based on a perception that the legitimacy of complaints arising from a public issue is low, but executives' *perceptions* of legitimacy may have little to do with the actual impact that a public issue may have on an organization. The only way to assess the importance of a public issue and to develop an appropriate response to the issue is through some means of tracking and monitoring the issue as it develops. This process is the central feature of issues management (Jones & Chase, 1977).

Raymond P. Ewing (1979) pointed out that issues management is concerned with "emerging issues whose definition and contending positions are evolving in the public arena and legislation or regulation is likely in a moving time frame of 18 to 36 months" (p. 15). He described several techniques that organizations can use to track and predict the development of such issues. Some of the more common techniques include the following:

1. *Trend extrapolation.* A factor or variable is measured over time and statistical forecasting techniques are used to project a trend from these measurements.

2. *Trend impact analysis.* This technique is a variation on trend extrapolation. After a trend is extrapolated, experts identify future events that would affect the extrapolation and the trend is modified in light of these events.
3. *Scanning.* A relatively simple technique in which issues that might affect an organization are identified and monitored by use of volunteers who regularly scan print and electronic media for useful information.
4. *Monitoring.* This method may be used in conjunction with scanning. Scanning identifies potential issues, while monitoring tracks these issues through systematic analysis of data. Monitoring may include public opinion polling and other forms of social science research.
5. *Scenario writing.* This technique begins by asking the question, "What would happen if X came to pass?" Given an assumption that X occurs, a chronological projection into the future is written. According to Ewing, some large organizations hire novelists and playwrights to develop and write such scenarios.

The kinds of tools that Ewing described help organizations to gather and interpret information on emerging public issues. However, development of a meaningful information base on a public issue is only one component of an issues management project. The other important component involves the use of this information in decision-making processes that lead to organizational action on the issue. This action typically takes one of two forms: organizational change or issue advocacy.

Issues Management and Organizational Change

Sometimes issues management may mean changing the organization and communicating with relevant publics about this change. A classic case of corporate change in response to public issues is reflected in the experience of Giant Food Corporation, which we discussed briefly in an earlier chapter. Giant operated many of its stores in urban inner-city areas. These urban communities were inhabited largely by minority groups who suffered the devastating effects of institutionalized racism—high unemployment, low education, poor housing, and, worst of all, little hope of real improvement in these conditions. Under the guidance of Paul Forbes, a private community relations consultant, Giant executives began to recognize that their customers also were members of a disenfranchised and increasingly frustrated segment of American society.

Many corporations that operated in inner-city areas during this period either didn't recognize or simply ignored the oppressive economic and social forces that mired these communities in a cycle of poverty. In the eyes of these communities, such companies were viewed as the agents of oppression—profiteers who took a great deal away, while returning nothing. Giant executives decided that they did not want this role for their company, but their actions went far beyond the simple mechanics of image building. The corporation undertook a careful study of inner-city problems, then responded with an equal employment opportunity program long before the federal government required such programs. Giant recruited minority job applicants and devised on-the-job training programs in order to merge corporate and community interests.

Sometime later, violence erupted throughout urban Washington, D.C., just after the assassination of Martin Luther King, Jr. The stores of many of Giant's competitors (who, according to Forbes, openly poked fun at Giant's community action programs) were demolished by riots and looting. The total damage to Giant Food facilities consisted of one broken store window. The company's stores had been defended and saved by community residents. It is obvious that the commitment to social change through corporate change resulted in a "payoff" for Giant Food not only because company property was protected, but also because Giant had become a publicly valued member of the communities that it served.

Issues Management and Issues Advocacy

While organizational change is sometimes an appropriate response to public issues, another legitimate form of action is advocacy of the organization's positions on these issues. Public communication programs based on issues advocacy are quite different from the traditional image-building activities of public relations. As described by Prakesh Sethi, traditional image building is "usually rather general in scope and bland in character," whereas issues advocacy "addresses itself to specific controversial issues, presenting facts and arguments that project the sponsor's viewpoint . . . to try to influence political decisions by molding public opinion" (1982, p. 162). Sethi probably should have added that advocacy campaigns often are intended to preserve the organizational status quo.

One of the most obvious public issues that has generated considerable advocacy is the problem of environmental protection. Any organization that has a significant impact upon ecology because of its operations will have to answer to government and to the public at large. Some large industries have actively resisted environmental protection regulations. Others have taken a more realistic approach to the issue. For example, Public Service Company of New Mexico, an electric company operating in a region with a rapidly growing demand for power, decided to meet the increasing demand with coal-fired generating stations that require very expensive "scrubbers" to minimize air pollution. The costs of pollution control are passed on to the company's customers. Obviously, this means higher electric bills.

Rather than opposing the environmental protection laws that require control of air pollution, Public Service Company of New Mexico has taken a middle-of-the-road position on the issue. A major theme in the company's public communication campaigns is the need for balance between rates that customers pay for electricity and the cost of environmental protection. In advertising messages prepared primarily for its customers, the company affirms its own commitment to a clean environment, but it also argues that clean air cannot be attained without paying a price. The company suggests to customers that they, as voters, are really the ones who set environmental protection standards. In turn, as consumers of electricity, they will pay for their standards. The implication in this message is fairly obvious. If you want clean air, you had better be prepared to pay for it. If you want to control the rates you pay for electricity, then you have to control the clean air standards that the company is required to meet (see figure 10.3).

Of course, the outcome of an advocacy campaign may not be exactly what the advocate expects. A good example of an unanticipated outcome is reflected in the case of another environmental campaign waged by American Electric Power (AEP) in the mid-1970s. AEP, like PNM, wanted to present a case for coal-fired generating stations, but got caught on the controversial issue of sulphur dioxide emissions from coal. According to Heath and Nelson (1986), AEP admitted that scrubber technology could control most of the emissions, but argued that disposal of sludge from scrubbers would destroy the land. While Sethi (1977) and Hush (1983) contend that the AEP campaign was very successful, AEP's use of fear appeals in the campaign drew the editorial wrath of the *Washington Post* and *New York Times,* and the Environmental Protection Agency (EPA) received more than 200 letters of protest about the campaign. The campaign failed to defeat interest in scrubber technology. EPA officials believed that their efforts to promote tougher clean-air standards "were strengthened by the AEP campaign, since the public learned more about scrubbers than it would have otherwise" (Heath & Nelson, p. 98).

Although some issues advocacy campaigns focus on a single issue that is salient to an organization, others are quite complex and involve several different types of public issues. Sethi (1982) provides an example of this kind of complexity in an extensive case study of advocacy campaigns conducted by Bethlehem Steel during the 1970s. Bethlehem executives identified six public issues that concerned their company and the steel industry in general.

1. Capital formation and federal tax reform.
2. Energy conservation
3. Pollution and the environment
4. Government overregulation
5. Business concentration
6. Steel imports and foreign trade policy.

You probably would not have to engage in much guesswork to figure out the company's positions on most of these issues. Obviously, the steel industry is not pleased with foreign competition because American steel companies have been decimated by cheaper foreign products. Furthermore, the use of the term *over*regulation in issue 4 is a sure-fire giveaway of the company's position. According to Sethi, Bethlehem budgeted $1.5 million in 1978 for advertising messages on these issues, but the company's problem was not as simple as just spending a lot of money to argue positions on these issues. For example, issues 4 and 6 put the company in a paradoxical situation. How can you argue against government regulation in one message, then ask for government intervention

ENERGY AND THE ENVIRONMENT:
HOW MUCH IS ENOUGH?

Figure 10.3
Example of issues advocacy advertising. Reprinted by permission of Public Service Company of New Mexico.

Balancing the need to develop adequate energy supplies with the need to maintain a clean environment in New Mexico is the constant challenge facing each of us. As the number of our customers increases and their demand for electricity grows, PNM must build generating plants and transmission lines to serve that demand. But at what cost to the environment? If steps are taken to reduce the effect on the environment, how much will you, the rate-payer, pay? And who will make the rules defining acceptable environmental standards? These are the questions facing all of us, you and PNM.

There is a strong link between environmental concerns and the economics of scarcity. Consider San Juan Generating Station. When increased demand necessitated additional electrical generation in New Mexico, coal was the obvious choice as a fuel source. Why? Because New Mexico is rich in coal resources. A power plant using natural gas would have been easier to operate, quicker to build and cheaper in the short run. The problem is that availability and price of future supplies of natural gas are in doubt. Besides, rather than being used as a boiler fuel, natural gas is better used for other societal needs, such as chemical and pharmaceutical purposes. Also, using the fuels we have reduces our nation's dependence on foreign imports.

Therefore coal, which we have in abundance, was chosen to be the boiler fuel at San Juan. But when burned, coal produces considerable pollutants—among these, fly ash and sulfur dioxide. These pollutants can have a major effect on air quality. To solve this problem, PNM constructed San Juan with "state of the art" pollution control equipment. Today the plant is a model for the electricity industry. But at a price. The sulfur dioxide scrubbers for the first two San Juan units, for instance, cost more than $120 million.

But environmental concerns at PNM extend beyond clear air. Energy development can also have a major impact on land, water and cultural resources. To make sure that PNM's activities have a minimum impact on the environment at the most reasonable cost, the company has a large environmental affairs department. Employing biologists, archaeologists, chemical engineers, land use planners, forestry and range specialists, atmospheric scientists, chemists and others, the department is charged with putting into action PNM's commitment to a clean and healthy environment.

Some of their work is nationally recognized as superior, such as the Chaco Canyon study recently featured on the PBS **Odyssey** program; or the department's long-term study of birds of prey; and, of course, San Juan Generating Station itself. But what is important is that PNM has demonstrated that energy development can go forward in harmony with the concern we all have of protecting our environment. Again, at a price. **Today, about 10 percent of your monthly electric bill goes to pay for environmental activities.** Should you pay more? Should you pay less? As a society, we need to agree on what environmental standards we want and how much we are willing to pay to meet them.

You, PNM'S customers, make the rules through your vote and through participating in the regulatory process. You pay to meet the environmental standards. And you benefit from those standards.

Please remember, all of mankind's activities affect the environment. That is unavoidable. Even the garden you planted drastically changed the ecology of your backyard. **The basic question then remains: how much is enough?** What standards do we as a society want for clean air? For land use? For cultural resources? And how much are we willing to pay to meet these standards? Energy is produced for your use; therefore, consider the resources at your command and command them wisely.

This is the fifth of a series of six statements designed to confront the issues and concerns about energy: its availability, cost and impact. The entire series is being paid for by the stockholders of PNM, 5,300 of whom reside in New Mexico.

PNM
Public Service Company of New Mexico

to control imports in another? Formulating argumentative strategies that resolved such problems required time and resources that went well beyond mere advertising costs.

If one takes the Bethlehem Steel, Public Service Company of New Mexico, and American Electric Power cases as typical examples of issues advocacy (and we believe that they are typical), then the social justification for issues advocacy seems questionable because the programs are one-sided and apparently self-serving. Indeed, the most controversial campaigns in this respect have been those run by Mobil Oil Corporation, one of the leading companies in issues advertising. Mobil's efforts to point out media bias against business, to protect the free enterprise system, and to chide the government for ill-conceived regulations and ineffective management have been described even by corporate executives of major American companies as "too strident" (Heath & Nelson, p. 81).

It is important to remember, however, that advocacy campaigns frequently are initiated in response to some specific challenge that is creating a public issue. In a pluralistic, free society, organizations, like individuals, have a right to speak out on issues. Hence, Mobil Oil contends that its campaigns are designed to promote the exercise of First Amendment rights, "to present our views and our ideas along with established facts to assist the public in making decisions" (quoted in Heath & Nelson, p. 81). Moreover, as we noted earlier, the growing sophistication of the advocacy concept often brings large organizations and entire industries into public conflict. Issues advocacy is no longer simply a case of a public-interest group versus a large corporation, but it is sometimes one corporation versus another or even one interest group versus another.

Recently, some issues advocacy campaigns have either eliminated or toned down their self-serving characteristics. In these cases, organizations are advocating positions that not only involve their interests, but also involve the welfare of society as a whole. In the early 1980s, the W. R. Grace Corporation began a series of advocacy messages intended to encourage more efficient U.S. industrial production in the face of foreign competition. At one point, however, the Grace campaign became something of a public issue itself when the company was accused of anti-Japanese rhetoric in its messages. By 1985, Grace had moved its campaigns into an attack on the federal budget deficit and another call to efficiency, this time directed at the federal government. Yet, W. R. Grace Corporation is not threatened directly by either foreign competition or the federal budget deficit. The selection of such issues for advocacy campaigns seems more dependent on the Grace executives' perception of public interest than immediately tangible corporate interests.

The Grace Corporation experience also points out some of the obstacles to successfully mounting an issues advocacy campaign. In 1986, the company wanted to sponsor a highly controversial television message on the federal budget deficit. The advertisement portrayed a futuristic setting in which young people were conducting criminal court proceedings against former government officials. These officials in this America of the future had been charged with destroying the economy through their failure to halt deficit spending. Grace officials wanted to air the advertisement immediately after President

Reagan's State of the Union Address, but all three of the major television networks refused to accept it. Some weeks later, Grace obtained limited access to air the message on network television.

Summary

Public communication in organizations is a complex process. Despite its linear appearance, it has the transactional characteristics of other communication contexts. Public communication emerges from the efforts of various individuals and organizational units, although much of the public communication agenda is regulated by management through control over the resources that are required for public communication programs.

Public communication programs should be concerned not only with transmission of messages in order to influence various publics, but also concerned with ways in which publics seek out and use information. Grunig has been concerned extensively with this problem in his multisystem theory of organizational communication. Grunig believes that communication (information giving and seeking) is motivated behavior that can be predicted on the basis of a system's (i.e., person, group, or organization) problem recognition and constraint recognition in a decision situation. Various combinations of problem and constraint recognition result in problem-facing, routine habit, fatalistic, and constrained conditions. Each condition leads to a particular form of communication behavior.

An organization's public communication efforts can be classified generally as internal or external. Internal public communication, sometimes referred to as employee communication, usually involves management efforts to exert influence with organization members in general. Some of the most common uses of internal public communication include orientation and indoctrination, safety and loss prevention, provision of information on compensation and benefits, explanation and facilitation of organizational change, and promotion of member morale.

External public communication is a means through which organizations adapt to and influence relevant publics, including customers, voters, communities, regulators, and legislators. Traditionally, external public communication has been dominated by public relations image-building strategists. Image building is a process of developing and publicizing specific organizational characteristics and behaviors that are consistent with the image being cultivated.

More recently, many organizations have turned their resources toward public affairs and issues management activities that differ from traditional image building. Issues management involves a process of identifying and tracking public issues that may affect an organization. In some cases, organizations respond to issues by changing and communicating with relevant publics about the change. In other cases, organizations couple issues management with issues advocacy—a strategic attempt to shape public opinion on issues before political action on these issues results in legislation or regulation that affects the organization.

1. Find some examples of internal public communication. What kinds of topics and problems are addressed in these examples? What do you think the main purpose of internal public communication seems to be?
2. Find some examples of external public communication concerned with *organizational* (not product or service) image building. What are the organizations behind these messages trying to accomplish? How?
3. Watch some segments of television programs such as "Face the Nation" and "Meet the Press." Can you identify some examples of issues advocacy in the advertisements on these programs?
4. Who controls the agenda for organizational public communication? What are the ethical and philosophical issues involved in such control?

Case Study

Crafting an Image

For years the chemical industry has been battling a poor public image. In the last decade, a growing concern for environmental protection has created a new wave of legislation that has placed greater restrictions on the chemical industry and added to its decreasing credibility with the American public.

In 1979, the North American Chemical Association (NACA) created a special task force to investigate the industry's image problems. The task force was comprised of communications managers from various chemical companies throughout the United States and Canada. They began by compiling information on the public's concerns with the industry. When their research was complete, they had reached two conclusions: (1) the public was convinced that chemicals contributed to a high standard of living and (2) they were also apprehensive about the potential dangers to human beings and to the environment. Specifically, data indicated that the public appreciated the benefits of chemicals and approved of them, but the public also felt that the chemical industry was jeopardizing the health of America through faulty operating practices. Overall, the public image believed that the chemical industry was doing a poor job of managing waste disposal and of protecting against air and water pollution.

Based on this information, NACA decided to launch a public communication campaign to address the concern for health and safety and highlight the industry's commitment and continuing efforts to protect the environment. The purpose of the campaign was to change the image of the industry, to make the public more aware of its current safety practices, and ultimately, to influence the government and financial community in order to reduce restrictive legislation.

Due to limited resources, NACA did not direct the campaign toward the entire public; rather, it targeted key groups within the country that would impact public opinion and public policy the most. These groups included politically active individuals, government representatives, educators, communicators, and "plant neighbors"—those individuals living in areas with a high concentration of chemical plants.

The advertising campaign was designed for the print media and included leading magazines and newspapers, such as *Time, Newsweek, The New York Times,* and the *Washington Post.*

NACA conducted a two-phase advertising campaign with an advertising expenditure of $8 million to be spread over a three-year period. The first phase presented a chemical industry comprised of high technology and scientific innovation. One ad was titled "Improving Chemical Product Safety" and listed five steps the industry was taking to minimize risks to people and to the environment, such as improving detection methods and finding safer new chemicals and products.

Although persuasive, these ads contained little human interest, so they were replaced by a new wave of ads. The second advertising phase focused on the human side of the industry; namely, its employees. By featuring employees, who were simultaneously chemical engineers and concerned parents, as spokespersons for the industry, the chemical industry attempted to show that their employees were citizens first and engineers second. Essentially, the ad tried to convey the message that these employees would not be working for the chemical industry if they did not believe that the industry was concerned about the public's health and safety. For example, one ad quoted an employee who said, "I'm a chemical industry engineer but a concerned father first. I'm working to improve water quality for my kids and yours."

The NACA concluded its public advertising campaign in 1982 with mixed results. Although those exposed to the ads were viewing the chemical industry in more positive terms, the public as a whole still perceived the industry as making little effort toward controling waste disposal and air/water pollution by comparison to other industries.

1. Does this case involve an "public relations" campaign, an "issues management" campaign, or elements of both? Explain why?
2. Evaluate NACA's strategy in planning and implementing the campaign. What steps were effective? What could have been improved?
3. Why do you think the results of the campaign were mixed?

References

Armstrong, R. A. (1981, Fall). Public affairs vs. public relations. *Public Relations Quarterly,* p. 26.

Arrington, C., Jr., & Sawaya, R. N. (1984). Managing public affairs: issues management in an uncertain environment. *California Management Review, 26,* 148–160.

Buchholz, R. (1982). Education for public issues management: Key insights from a survey of top practitioners. *Public Affairs Review, 3,* 65–76.

Chandler, R. C. (1988). *Causal attributions in organizational communication about positive and negative performance: An empirical investigation of corporate annual reports.* Paper presented at the annual meeting of the International Communication Association, New Orleans.

Cutlip, S. M., and Center, A. H. (1964). *Effective public relations* (3rd ed.). Englewood Cliffs, NJ: Prentice-Hall.

Ewing, R. P. (1979, Winter). The uses of futurist techniques in issues management. *Public Relations Quarterly,* pp. 15–18.

Finn, D. (1962). Stop worrying about your image. *Harper's Magazine,* p. 225.

Gallup Public Opinion Index, June 1979.

Gardner, B. B., and Rainwater, L. (1955). The mass image of big business. *Harvard Business Review, 33,*

Goldhaber, G. M. (1990). *Organizational communication* (5th ed.). Dubuque, IA: Wm. C. Brown.

Grunig, J. E. (1975). A multisystems theory of organizational communication. *Communication Research, 2,* 99–136.

Grunig, J. E. (1976). Organizations and public relations: Testing a communication theory. *Journalism Monographs,* No. 46, 1–59.

Grunig, J. E. (1978). Accuracy of communication from an external public to employees in a formal organization. *Human Communication Research, 5,* 40–53.

Heath, R. L., & Nelson, R. A. (1986). *Issues management: Corporate public policymaking in an information society.* Beverly Hills, CA: Sage.

Hill, J. W. (1977). Corporations: The sitting ducks. *Public Relations Quarterly, 22,* 8–10.

Hush, M. (1983). Corporate advertising: Stacking the odds. *Grey Matter: Tough Ideas on Advertising and Marketing, 54,* 1–12.

Industrial Communication Council (1975). *Case studies in organizational communication.* New York, NY.

Jones, B. L., & Chase, W. H. (1979). Managing public policy issues. *Public Relations Review, 5,* 3–23.

Peterson, D. (1975). *The OSHA compliance manual.* New York: McGraw-Hill.

Post, James E. (1979). Corporate response models and public affairs management. *Public Relations Quarterly, 24,* 27–32.

Sethi, S. P. (1977). *Advocacy advertising and large corporations: Social conflict, big business image, the news media, and public policy.* Lexington, MA: D. C. Heath.

Sethi, S. P. (1982). *Up against the corporate wall: Modern corporations and social issues of the eighties* (4th ed.). Englewood Cliffs, NJ: Prentice-Hall.

Williams, L. C., Jr. (1978). What 50 presidents and CEO's think about employee communications. *Public Relations Quarterly, 23,* 6–11.

Wiseman, G., and Barker, L. (1967). *Speech—Interpersonal communication.* Chicago: Chandler.

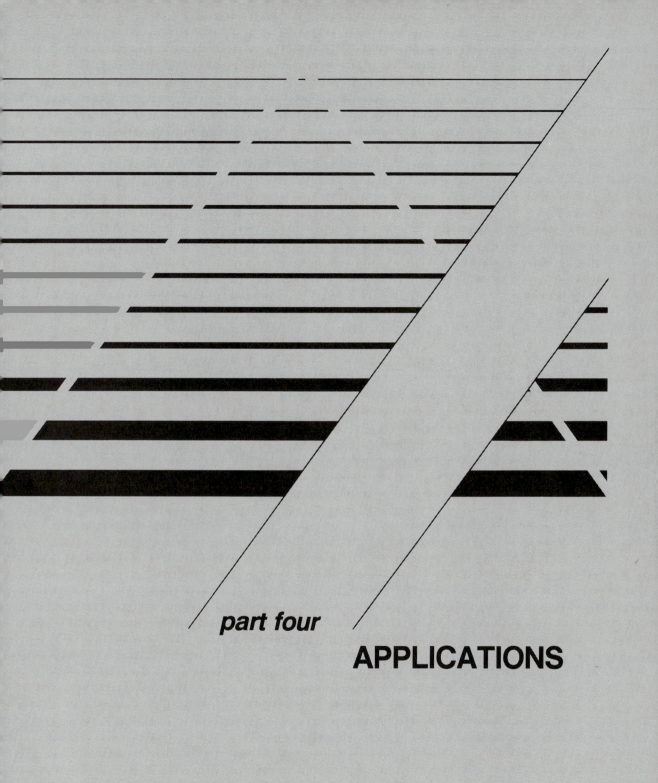

part four

APPLICATIONS

Outline

Basic Occupational Roles
Consultation Models
    Provision Model
    Prescription Model
    Collaboration Model
    Organization Development
        Planned Change
        System

        Managed from the Top
        Effectiveness and Health
Professional Politics
Professional Ethics
Summary
Discussion Questions/Activities
Case Study
References

Communication Professionals
in Organizations

11

Peter Drucker commented on the importance of communication in organizations when he observed, "As soon as you move one step from the bottom, your effectiveness depends on your ability to reach others through the spoken and written word." In today's era of quality circles, labor-management cooperation, participative decision making, and an economic shift to service and information-based industries, Drucker's argument sometimes can be applied to the lowest echelon of the organization as well.

Ideally, one should acquire both communication skills and an understanding of organizational communication during the course of one's education. In practice, elementary and secondary schools are concerned mainly with reading and writing skills rather than with speaking, listening, and other interpersonal skills. These programs typically offer no formal preparation in concepts and principles of organizational communication. Although appropriate theoretical and practical courses are available at most colleges and universities, many students obtain little exposure to communication skill offerings and virtually no conceptual background in the communication process of organizations.

The arrival of the communication and information age, the realization that communication study is a demanding field in its own right, and the rather lean preparation that many organization members have acquired in organizational communication skills and concepts have led to the emergence of several organizational roles for the communication professional. In this chapter, we will review the occupations available to communication professionals, will describe the basic models from which these professionals work, and will consider some of the political and ethical issues that confront them in their organizational roles.

Before we begin our review, we do want to reiterate a caution that we mentioned in chapter 1 regarding career preparation in organizational communication. The study of organizational communication is, in an important sense, more properly related to liberal arts education than to professional school training. If you major in a field such as accounting, education, engineering, nursing, pharmacy, or other professional school programs, you can expect to find occupational titles in the job market that correspond *directly* with your major. Even though preparation in the field of organizational communication fits well with several different occupations, you may never see a job advertisement that says, "Wanted: New college graduate with degree in organizational communication." Moreover, some of the appropriate occupations for a person who has preparation in organizational communication now virtually require graduate-level education (Redding, 1979).

Basic Occupational Roles

Communication professionals in organizations work in many different occupational specialities. Goldhaber (1990) reviewed some surveys of such professionals in order to develop a list of occupational areas that included internal communication, external corporate communication, media, publications, research, and training. Each of these six areas included several more specific occupations and job titles. Most of the specific occupations that Goldhaber described seem to fall in two basic groups: (1) **public relations and public affairs;** and (2) **training and development.**

The public relations and public affairs group is comprised of people who perform the functions of internal and external public communication, including employee communications, traditional public relations, and issues management and advocacy functions described in chapter 10. Their jobs usually involve creating and disseminating messages to internal and external publics through various forms of print and electronic media. Professionals in this area are most likely to be trained in journalism, mass communication, advertising, and related fields. There is some evidence, however, that this trend is changing. Neff (1987) and Wakefield (1988) have reported that public relations courses are taught by departments *other than* journalism or mass communication in nearly one-half of the U.S. undergraduate programs that offer public relations. Frequently, these courses are found in departments of speech communication or business, but there is one problem associated with this shift. Although the 1987 Commission on Undergraduate Public Relations Education, sponsored by several professional associations concerned with public relations education, recommended a highly interdisciplinary model for undergraduate public relations programs, the Accrediting Council on Education in Journalism and Mass Communication—the only officially recognized agency for accrediting public relations programs—refuses to accredit any public relations program that is not housed in journalism or mass communication (Wakefield, 1988).

When an organization's public communication efforts require extensive use of oral communication, specialists in speech communication, even though they may not have strong backgrounds in public relations, often are employed to coordinate these efforts and train others in the necessary skills. For example, many large businesses and institutions traditionally maintain speaker bureaus composed of organization members who make speech presentations to civic clubs, schools, or other interested groups (Grala, 1964). The topics in these presentations usually concern the organization's products, services, mission, or relationship with the community. Robert Heath (1980) also has pointed out that the kind of training provided in speech communication programs is ideal for occupations in issues management and advocacy.

Communication professionals in the training and development group are concerned with maintenance and change in organizational communication functions, structures, and the communication processes that occur at various systems levels, including dyads, groups, intergroup relations, and organization-wide network processes. Although professionals in the training and development group often become involved in maintenance of certain patterns in communication processes, *improvement* of organizational communication is, in theory, the primary function of such roles.

Communication professionals help organizations to improve communication by (1) identifying differences between actual and desired conditions of communication and (2) devising ways to close the gap between actual and desired states. The first function involves **organizational communication evaluation** (gathering, analyzing, and interpreting data about an organization's communication processes). The second function is referred to as **intervention** (actions taken to improve organizational communication). These skills often are provided in advanced organizational communication courses offered in the departments of communication or speech communication.

People who perform organizational communication evaluation and intervention activities may be members of the organization or outside agents brought in to perform specific projects. The inside member usually is in a staff position or staff department that supports the line organization and is responsible to upper levels of management. The outside agent usually is a representative from a private company that provides such services to other organizations or a college professor who has expertise in the area. In any of these cases, the communication professional in training/development is a **consultant** whose functions are best regarded as *helping* activities (Lippitt, 1982; Redding, 1979). The consultant's expertise may be in organizational communication evaluation, intervention, or both.

The internal and external public communication functions associated with the public relations/public affairs group are well established and widely recognized in the organizational world. Terms such as *employee communications, public relations,* and even *issues management* are a part of the daily vocabulary in many large corporations and institutions. In contrast, the professional who specializes in organizational communication evaluation and intervention is a relatively new species in organizational life (Eich, 1977). Moreover, training and development professionals come from several other fields as well as from organizational communication (e.g., education, psychology, and management) and their occupational titles usually do not include the term *communication.* Since communication professionals in training and development are not as well recognized as their counterparts in public relations and public affairs, the rest of this chapter is concerned with the training and development role. We will consider the models that professionals in this role use to provide evaluation and intervention services as well as the political and ethical issues that they confront in the process. Specific tools for organizational communication evaluation and intervention are presented in chapters 12 and 13.

Consultation Models

Consultancy roles in organizations are enacted through a number of different models. Since communication professionals in training and development are in such consultancy roles, models of the consultation process can help us to understand how these professionals do their work. At least three models of consulting, as described by Kurpius and Brubaker (1976), are relevant to the work of communication professionals. These models are (1) provision, (2) prescription, and (3) collaboration. The collaboration model usually is associated with a more general theory of organizational change known as organization development or, simply, OD. Consequently, we have included a separate section of OD and its influence on communication professionals.

Provision Model

In the **provision model,** a client usually approaches the consultant with a request for a specific service. The client asks the consultant to provide an intervention that responds to a problem that the client has identified and defined. Communication training programs frequently are offered under the provision model.

In order to see how the provision model works, consider the case of a midwestern corporation that had made a major expansion in its engineering division. As a result of the expansion, a number of line engineers were promoted to supervisory positions over engineering groups. Top management promoted these people because they had outstanding records as engineers. However, good engineering is based on technical competence. It does not necessarily require the social and communication competence associated with effective supervision.

Management recognized that its new supervisors might not be well prepared for their new roles. The supervisors themselves soon confirmed this suspicion by reporting that they were uncomfortable with their new jobs. Engineering machinery was not the same task as supervising people. In order to help the new supervisors, management hired outside consultants to design and implement a series of training programs on communication skills for supervisors. Specifically, management requested training on day-to-day interaction with subordinates, interviewing skills, and horizontal communication across departments.

This example illustrates several important points about the provision model. The consultant assumes complete responsibility for the intervention based on the client's definition of the problem. Typically, there is no formal evaluation of needs or, if a formal evaluation has been made, the consultant is not involved in this phase of the project. Consequently, success of the provision model depends on the client's accuracy in diagnosing the problem and describing it to the consultant (Schein, 1969). For example, are skills in day-to-day interaction, interviewing, and horizontal communication the only ones required for new supervisors? To what extent do they already possess such skills? Are they really receptive and enthusiastic about assuming their new positions? All of these factors, along with the competence of the consultant's intervention, may affect the success of the project.

In this particular case, the effectiveness of the training program was limited. For one thing, the necessary communication skills may have been too narrowly defined. The training also occurred in an artificial, laboratory situation that differed in several important ways from actual conditions that the supervisors faced on the job. Although the managers and supervisors reported that they generally were pleased with the training program, they probably encountered new problems later on for which the program had not prepared them. We can write with some authority on this particular case, since we were the consultants who designed and ran the training programs.

One variation on the provision model involves the use of prepackaged or so-called canned intervention programs. Outside consultants use such programs as do internal staff professionals. Training and development departments in some large organizations buy canned programs for management, technical, and communication training, then offer these programs on a regular basis to organization members. Sometimes, training departments literally market these services to other units of the organization through slick promotional campaigns. Such programs can be very effective, but they are highly generic—not really adapted to the specific needs of a given organization. Organizations are wise to exercise some caution in purchasing and using prepackaged interventions.

Prescription Model

The **prescription model** places responsibility on the consultant for evaluation of needs as well as intervention. The client has a problem that can be stated only vaguely or only in terms of symptoms. The consultant performs a systematic evaluation of the problem, then recommends and possibly executes an appropriate intervention. This model sometimes is called the doctor-patient model because the "doctor" consultant "diagnoses" the "patient" client's problem, then offers a "prescription" to cure it.

In some cases, the client has no specific complaint but merely wants a checkup to see whether there are any problems in the organization. A top management group might request a general evaluation of organizational communication. The managers believe that the organization basically is healthy, but they want a better understanding of strengths and weaknesses in communication processes. If they also insist on specific recommendations for interventions to respond to any problems identified in the evaluation (e.g., ineffectiveness in important communication functions, bottlenecks in the information network, inadequate channels for upward communication, lack of openness and trust in superior-subordinate relationships), the stage is set for use of the prescription model.

Typically, a prescription model consultancy includes a formal evaluation project, a written report of evaluation results, and recommendations for specific interventions to respond to problems. The consultant assumes ownership of the client's problem by taking primary or even sole responsibility for gathering, analyzing, and interpreting data, then recommending and even carrying out the interventions.

The prescription model has at least two important risks. First, it creates the impression that evaluation and intervention are two separate processes. This is not really the case. The evaluation itself may be a form of intervention in organizational processes. Organizational communication evaluations often include survey questionnaires, formal interviews, and direct observation. These methods are rather obtrusive. You cannot always be sure that people's reports in questionnaires and interviews are honest and accurate appraisals of conditions. People who are aware that they are being observed may not act in the same ways that they would in unobserved situations. More importantly, evaluation usually takes some time, and organization members may well be discussing it among themselves as the process occurs. The evaluation itself is a source of information that members interpret and act on in various ways without the consultant's ever being aware of what is happening (Webb, Campbell, Schwartz, Sechrest, & Grove, 1981).

Second, the client sometimes is unwilling to take the prescription. The bookshelf of an executive office is hardly complete if it does not contain at least one or two evaluation research projects with recommendations that were never implemented! In some cases, this problem occurs because the client has not been actively involved in either the evaluation process or the decisions about the most appropriate means for intervening in problems (Schein, 1969). In some cases, evaluation itself may be little more than a ploy or cover to create the impression that something is being done to respond to problems when, in fact, the client never had any intent to implement changes.

Collaboration Model

The **collaboration model** focuses on *joint* participation between the client and consultant in both diagnosis and intervention. Rather than directly providing or prescribing solutions to problems, the collaborative consultant guides the client through a process in which the *client* identifies and acts on problems. The collaborative consultant does not need to be an expert in production, control systems, accounting, marketing, and so forth, but must be well versed in human processes such as interpersonal and group communication and in the skills required for evaluation and intervention through helping relationships.

Edgar Schein (1969) referred to the collaboration model as "process" consultation specifically because it is concerned with human rather than technical processes. He identified several principles that are important in this model.

1. Most managers want to improve conditions in their organizations but need help in determining what to improve and how to do it.
2. Organizations can become more effective by learning how to identify their own strengths and weaknesses. *The consultant's task is to transfer these skills to the client.*
3. Consultants (at least those who are outside agents) presume too much if they believe that they can ever know enough about the organization's culture to suggest unilaterally appropriate interventions. The consultant should work jointly with those who do know the culture (i.e., with the members of the client system).
4. It is essential that the consultant know how to diagnose and how to develop helping relationships.

Organization Development

Collaboration or process consultation usually is associated with **organization development** (Schein, 1969). Organization development (OD) is a theory for applying social and behavioral science concepts and methods to bring about organizational change. Although OD is not primarily a theory of organizations or organizational effectiveness, the goals of the OD change process are based on principles of organizational structure and function, managerial strategy, and organizational effectiveness drawn from a synthesis of the human resource development and system theories that we reviewed in chapter 3.

Richard Beckhard (1969) pointed out that the activity of OD includes four basic features:

1. It is a *planned change* effort.
2. It involves the total "*system.*"
3. *It is managed from the top.*
4. It is designed to *increase organizational effectiveness and health.* (p. 9)

Planned Change

Organization development efforts are directed toward long-range organizational improvement according to a strategic plan. The basic tool for developing this plan is a method called *action research*. **Action research** helps the organization to diagnose and develop interventions for problems in planning, decision making, leadership, conflict, role definitions, and communication (French & Bell, 1978). The techniques for diagnosis and intervention are based on socio-behavioral science concepts and methods. The organization is introduced to this method through the assistance of an outside consultant or internal OD specialists on the staff of the organization itself. In either case, the ultimate goal of OD practitioners is to transfer their skills to members of the client organization.

System

Organization development change efforts involve "systemwide" activities. This does not necessarily mean that the change strategy is directed at the entire organization. It does mean that the target of OD must be a system that is "relatively free to determine its own plans and future" (Beckhard, 1969, p. 9). Organization development assumes that elements and subsystems within an autonomous (freely acting) system are interdependent and that change in one area will affect other areas of the system.

Managed from the Top

Organization development theorists argue that strategic, planned change must be managed from the top of the organization, but the concept of top-down management presents an image of control over decision making that is quite different from the idea that these theorists actually have in mind. The point is that OD will not succeed unless top-level managers understand the concept, are committed to OD goals, and support the methods used to attain these goals (Miles, 1979).

Effectiveness and Health

Organization development theory is similar to human resource development theory in its concept of organizational effectiveness, but there is one important difference. Human resource development is concerned with *individual* motivation. Organization development applies principles from system theory to shift the focus on organizational effectiveness from the motivation of individuals to systemwide improvement of human processes. The general goal of OD is to make organizations more adaptive—capable of solving their own problems and responding flexibly to new demands and environmental changes.

According to Beckhard, organizational adaptiveness requires ten characteristics. Although he points out that these characteristics are his personal standards for organizational effectiveness, many other OD theorists subscribe to similar characteristics (French & Bell, 1978). These characteristics include the following:

1. The total organization manages work against goals and plans.
2. Form follows function. The task determines organizational structure rather than the structure's determining the task.
3. Decisions are made by those closest to information about the problem or situation "regardless of where they are located on the organization chart."
4. Managers are rewarded not only for short-term profit, but also for developing subordinates and "creating a viable working group."
5. Communication is multidirectional and relatively undistorted.
6. Inappropriate win/lose competition is minimized.
7. Conflict occurs over substantive rather than emotional issues because most "interpersonal difficulties. . .have been generally worked through."

8. Organization members understand their organization as an open system of interdependent relationships.
9. Organization members value (and management supports) maintaining the integrity and uniqueness of each person and subsystem in an interdependent environment.
10. The organization creates, uses, and learns from feedback mechanisms and action research. (pp. 10–11)

Organization development implications for organizational communication are obvious since several of Beckhard's organizational effectiveness standards refer directly to communication, interpersonal, and group processes. The task of the communication professional is to help create the kind of communication climate that fosters OD goals. The parallel between organizational communication and OD is so close that Redding predicted, "By the early 1980s, as many as two-thirds or three-fourths of all communication consultants will be functioning in roles almost indistinguishable from those of OD practitioners" (1979, pp. 350–351).

Although OD is the most prominent theory of organizational change, OD objectives are not as straightforward as they might seem. The practice of OD often occurs in the face of a difficult paradox. On the one hand, it requires top management support. On the other, it is intended to serve the interests of the system as a whole, and these interests do not always coincide with the motives of managers (Beer, 1980). Moreover, the collaboration or process model of consultation on which OD depends also has several risks. Many organizations simply are not prepared for the intensive demands of OD and collaborative consultation.

Despite Redding's claim about the influence of OD on communication consultants, many who work under the banner of "organization development" may not actually be performing OD activity. Data from a survey by Rudolph and Johnson (1983) suggest that communication consultants probably are delivering conventional training programs under a provision model more often than performing OD under a collaboration or process model. This is not especially surprising. The provision model merely requires that the consultant be a competent interventionist. The prescription model not only requires competence in intervention, but it also requires technical skills in evaluation research and diagnosis. The collaboration model requires all of these competencies, plus the ability to transfer them to clients through a helping relationship.

The roles of communication professionals in organizations can be characterized generally by provision, prescription, and collaborative models of the consultant-client relationship. Each model has particular strengths and weaknesses. Although the collaboration model usually is regarded as ideal, especially where OD objectives are involved (Schein, 1969), use of any one of these models requires the professional to cope with some complex political dynamics when providing consultancy service.

Professional Politics

We pointed out early in this text that organizations are not merely decision-making and information-processing systems or structures for task performance. They also are political systems. Organizational communication professionals work daily within a complex political milieu.

The services of any provision model consultancy are not only paid for by management, but they are also typically defined by management. The consultant who contracts to provide these services is politically obligated to management. A prescription model may allow the consultant more autonomy from the client in the sense that the consultant both diagnoses and prescribes, but acceptance of the prescription may depend on how well it fits within the organization's prevailing political scheme. It may also be tempting for the prescription consultant to bend, shape, or outright distort both diagnosis and recommendations to provide what the client may *want* to hear instead of what the client *should* hear.

Cobb and Margulies (1981) claimed that collaborative organization development practitioners present a special political irony in organizations. Generally, they are politically unsophisticated, yet much of their activity has clear political implications. Since the concepts of collaboration, participation, and realization of human potential are central ideas in organization development, Cobb and Margulies argued that organization development requires supportive political conditions:

If the consultant is to achieve collaboration and participation in the social subsystem, supportive changes must occur in the political subsystem to allow it. Some of these changes include the general reduction of power differentials between organizational members, the transfer of power to those who are to participate in decision making, and the removal of structural obstacles to the flow of power in the organization generally and between levels of authority in particular. (p. 51)

The changes described by Cobb and Margulies are reflected in the political position of the individual organization member, in the quality of superior-subordinate relationships, and in overall organizational structure. While it is obvious that the goals of organization development are consistent with organizational communication scholars' prescription for organizational communication climate as described in chapter 3, Cobb and Margulies remind us that such prescriptions inherently are political because they affect the distribution of power and resources.

The practitioner can adopt political stances of pacifism, activism, or moderation. Pacifism is a naive position in light of organization development values, but activism often has a Machiavellian character. Cobb and Margulies worry that the activist practitioner too often "maintains that 'the ends justify the means' and advocates such strategies as limiting and channeling communication for political purposes, the use of covert or hidden agendas, and the political use of intervention research" (p. 54). They recommend a moderate position in which the practitioner is a political mediator and facilitator who guides organization members toward adoption of organization development values.

The concept of organization development as political facilitation seems ideal, but others point out that the practitioner's problem is not quite so simple. According to Michael Beer, the practitioner faces a daily dilemma. On the one hand, change requires the use of power. Since power is centered primarily at higher levels of the organization, the practitioner must cultivate the confidence of top management. Yet, organization development requires the support of other organizational constituencies and is intended to serve the interest of the organization as a whole. In Beer's words, "The problem then is how to achieve neutrality and independence even with respect to top management, while developing enough power to be effective and survive" (1980, p. 258).

Organization development practitioners do not have to become political activists in the sense that Cobb and Margulies described activism, but Beer said that they must participate in organizational politics. This participation includes demonstrations of competence that promote trust, cultivate a reputation for success, secure multiple sponsorship for organization development activities, gain control of resources, and create cohesion within the organization development group itself.

Even so, the power of management to distribute rewards, invoke sanctions, and restructure activities may mean that organization development fails to effect equitable change and actually may *maintain* inequities under the status quo. R. L. Forbes claimed, "I have found that many OD consultants, employed by members of management . . . seem actually to function as *restabilizing agents* rather than change agents. Their real purpose . . . is not to foster growth and improvement, but to restore a lost homeostatic balance" (1977, p. 12). If Forbes is correct, then the end result of organization development may be no different from results produced by human relations models of the 1930s and 1940s. Once again, participation leads to satisfaction, and satisfaction leads to greater compliance with organizational authority.

Professional Ethics

Redding characterized the organizational communication consultant as a person engaged in "playing God for a fee" (1979, p. 346). The power of a consultant to seriously harm as well as to help clients requires the true professional to pay scrupulous attention to ethics. As Lippitt pointed out:

The work of all professional helpers requires the constant exercise of discretion and judgment. Their clients may not be qualified to appraise the quality of service being offered or the risks involved and therefore may have to rely for support and protection on the helper's standards of conduct. (1982, p. 364)

The client's need to rely on the consultant creates many ethical issues in professional practice, yet some prominent practitioners openly admit that the profession lacks a well-developed philosophy of ethics (Miles, 1979).

Discussion of ethics in any human endeavor often seems simple and straightforward. Given commonly held standards for behavior in a professional community, a practitioner acts in certain ways and does not act in others. In the words of Mike Farrell's character, B. J., from the well-loved "M.A.S.H."

series, "Some things are wrong and they're always wrong." But the situation in which B. J. voiced this value was not so clear for Alan Alda's Hawkeye. Hawkeye decided to remove a healthy appendix from a gung ho infantry colonel in order to keep the officer's casualty-ridden brigade out of a major battle. B. J. objected, but Hawkeye went ahead with the operation. The ethical dilemma was created to remind us all that it is not always easy to distinguish right from wrong.

Ethical relativism—the idea that a given behavior can be wrong in one situation but right in another—seems to have become the order of the era in American society. Whether or not you like the idea of ethical relativism, you almost certainly will have to confront it. When a society believes in general that ethical evaluations of behavior must account for time, place, and circumstance, there is sure to be disagreement over the ethical codes that should drive our professional practice.

Disagreements aside, there are some commonly accepted principles for ethical consultant behavior that most practitioners would endorse. These principles are contained in ethical codes drawn up by professional associations such as the American Society for Training and Development, the Academy of Management, and others.

First, ethical consultants should never undertake evaluations or interventions for which they are not qualified. They should not misrepresent their qualifications to perform these activities. Second, the consultant should not violate conditions of confidentiality in the disclosure of information by organization members. However, at least one ethical code suggests that this standard can be discarded if the consultant becomes aware of illegal activity in the organization or is called to testify in legal proceedings. Third, the consultant should not exploit the client by recommending or performing services that are known to be unnecessary or inappropriate and should not continue to perform services that clearly are not helping the client. In our opinion, this third standard is especially important when the consultant's actions actually help some organizational groups, but in ways that disadvantage or harm other groups. Finally, the consultant should not misrepresent the realistic outcomes of interventions (e.g., the potential for training programs to produce long-term improvements when the task environment differs greatly from the training environment).

Even though most organizational communication professionals subscribe to the standards that we have described, we know that some certainly do not. We know of a West Coast management consultant who earns a great deal of money by teaching seminars in which he promises that "you, too, can earn $1,000 per day and more in your own consulting business." He will gladly teach you how to become a consultant—for a large fee, of course. The primary requirement for admission to these seminars is ability to pay, not qualifications to act as a consultant.

In recent years, we have seen literally dozens of advertisements in trade journals and television markets in which consultants offer everything from training sessions and seminars to books and cassette tapes with an unequivocal promise that "following these simple methods will make your organization more effective." Curiously, we have yet to see any money-back guarantees!

Unethical actions and outright malpractice are not unique to organizational communication consulting. Every helping profession has its share of quackery and hucksterism. However, many helping professions are regulated through standards for licensure or certification to practice in the field (e.g., medicine, nursing, pharmacy, accounting, law, or engineering). In contrast, the activities of training and development consultants are essentially unlicensed and unregulated.

In the 1970s, the International Communication Association implemented a program to certify its members in the use of communication audits, but the program was discontinued after problems developed in administering it. Both the International Communication Association and the Speech Communication Association sponsor programs on professional ethics, but neither association has a certification program for organizational communication consultants, and states do not require licensure for such consultants. Consequently, there are few actions that can be taken against incompetent or unethical practitioners besides waiting for their own poor reputations to catch up with them.

Summary

Growing recognition of the importance of communication to organizations has led to many occupational specialties for communication professionals. Most of the occupations seem to fall in two basic groups: (1) public relations and public affairs and (2) training and development. The first group is comprised of practitioners involved in internal and external public communication. Those in the second group are concerned with organizational communication evaluation and intervention.

Training and development practitioners work from at least three different models: provision, prescription, and collaboration. The provision model typically includes only intervention service. The prescription model includes both evaluation and intervention. The collaboration model differs from both of the others in the sense that the consultant does not assume primary responsibility for the client's problems and solutions to these problems. Rather, the objective is to improve the client's own diagnostic and problem-solving ability by transferring the consultant's skills to the organization. The collaboration or process model is the ideal model for organization development, but provision and prescription models may be used more heavily in actual practice.

Consultants confront a variety of political and ethical issues that are important to organizational communication professionals. By nature, organizational communication evaluation and intervention have political implications because the processes influence the distribution of power and resources. In organization development activities, the practitioner is supposed to work for the interests of the organization as a whole. However, the practitioner also has to achieve a complicated balance among commitments to various organizational constituencies in order to accomplish this objective. Sometimes the consultant may reinforce the very conditions that should be changed.

Clear ethical standards for professional practice are difficult to develop because the concept of ethical relativism is pervasive in our society. Nevertheless, it is clear that any form of misrepresentation or deception involving the consultant's capabilities or the effectiveness of services is regarded as unethical.

Discussion Questions/ Activities

1. Try to find a local organization that employs communication professionals in some capacity. Conduct an interview with one of these professionals in order to find out what this person's job is like on a day-to-day basis.
2. What is implied in the claim that the communication professional essentially is a consultant who performs helping activities?
3. Consider the three models of consulting described in the chapter (provision, prescription, and collaboration). What are their comparative advantages and disadvantages?
4. We discussed several political and ethical issues that face communication professionals in organizations. Can you think of some others that we may have missed? What are they and why are they important?

Case Study

Making It On Your Own

When Sam Vincent decided two years ago to leave his job as a speech professor at a state university in order to start his own business as a communication consultant, he knew the transition wouldn't be easy. Packaging and delivering good training programs on topics such as public speaking, team-building, supervisory communication, and interviewing was no problem. Afterall, he had ten years of experience teaching these skills in speech and organizational communication courses. But marketing these services in a highly competitive environment was another matter.

Sam barely managed to generate enough business to maintain a small suburban office, pay for a part-time secretary, and still make a living. He spent only one or two days a week actually doing training. Most of his time and energy—four or five days a week, ten to twelve hours a day—went into developing new clients and repeat business from old clients, so he was jubilant when he received a phone call from Martina Brittan, the senior customer service representative with Communication Dynamics, Inc., one of the largest consulting companies in the country. Marty (as she preferred to be called) was offering Sam a chance to do five one-day workshops on public speaking with AXOCO Energy, a large company that Communication Dynamics had just acquired as a client.

Sam was anxious to get this contract, but he also was a street-wise trainer. Why wasn't Communication Dynamics using one of its own trainers for this project? Why did AXOCO go "outside" instead of relying on its own internal training department? Marty had quick answers. She explained that the AXOCO program would involve the company's top 100 managers and executives. AXOCO's own training department delivered programs primarily for lower-level managers, supervisors, and employees. Although it delivered excellent programs, it had no credibility with the executive group at AXOCO. In other words, AXOCO executives felt that they could learn nothing useful from a department that serviced lower-echelon personnel. As for Communication Dynamics, Marty explained that the company no longer employed its own trainers. Competitive pressures had forced the company to concentrate 100 percent of its energy on marketing. "All of the actual training work is subcontracted to people like you, Sam. We just sell the service." Sam agreed to take the subcontract for $3,000 ($600 per workshop), plus travel and preparation expenses. He knew that Communication Dynamics probably would charge AXOCO at least two or three times this amount for the service.

One week later, Sam and Marty had a conference call with Jack Barnes, the vice president of operations for AXOCO. Barnes indicated that the decision to put AXOCO's top 100 managers through this program had been made by the company's executive committee and discussed in subsequent meetings with all participating managers. There was a real need for the training, and the company was looking forward to the program. Barnes indicated that the program should concentrate mainly on formal presentation skills. Sam described the program that he would present for each workshop. A morning session would consist of an orientation and a review of basic concepts in message preparation and delivery. This would be followed by two videotaping sessions in the afternoon. In the videotape sessions, each participant would make a short presentation to the entire group, would immediately see the tape of the presentation, and then would receive feedback from Sam and from other managers in the group. Marty told Barnes that she would accompany Sam as an observer.

Two weeks later, Sam and Marty arrived at AXOCO headquarters on the evening before the first day's workshop. During a meeting with Barnes that night, Sam discovered to his horror that the first day's program participants had been told that they would be videotaped, but they had *not* been told to come with prepared presentations. Sam was sure that he had told Barnes during the conference call that all participants should have prepared presentations. Could he have been unclear about this? He immediately asked for access to a PC so that he could revise the program agenda to allow for some preparation time before the afternoon taping sessions.

The next morning began awkwardly. During the standard "ice-breaking" exercise with the first group of twenty managers, several of the participants indicated that they weren't sure why they were called to corporate headquarters for this program. What was this all about? Sam spent the first hour just talking about the importance of good presentation skills for executives, but the group seemed aloof and unreceptive. Sam ended the program one hour before lunch in order to give them time to prepare for the afternoon taping sessions. Just before lunch, Sam pulled Marty aside to discuss the situation with her. She thought the attitude of the managers was a clear indication that AXOCO needed to implement a formal team-building program, and she spent the lunch hour explaining to Barnes just how Communication Dynamics could effectively provide this service. Barnes listened intently.

As the afternoon session was about to begin, one of the division managers in the group openly challenged Sam. "I want you to explain in detail why we're doing this workshop. Since I'm about to stand up here in a few minutes and make an ass of myself on videotape, I think you at least owe me an explanation." A few others mumbled support for the challenger. One member even applauded. Sam managed to recover some control and persuaded the group to go through the videotaping. But the tone of the entire program had soured. Nobody was enjoying this exercise, least of all Sam. As it turned out, most of the members in the group were pretty good speakers—organized, articulate, and comfortable in front of a group, despite the fact that they were being taped. Sam offered a lot of comments designed to help the participants recognize and play to their strengths. Peer feedback was limited and restricted mostly to comments about how well everyone had done.

1. What model of consulting describes this project? What, if anything, should have been done differently before the workshops started?
2. Given the present situation, what can Sam do to improve the situation for the second workshop—the one he has to do tomorrow morning?
3. Keeping in mind that consultancy is a helping relationship, are there any ethical problems with the behavior of the participants in this case? With Sam? With Marty? With Barnes?

References

Beckhard, R. (1969). *Organization development: strategies & models.* Reading, MA: Addison-Wesley.

Beer, M. (1980). *Organization changes and development: A systems view.* Santa Monica, CA: Goodyear Publishing.

Cobb, A. T., and Margulies, N. (1981, January). Organization development: A political perspective. *Academy of Management Review,* pp. 49–59.

Eich, R. (1977). *Organizational communication consulting: A descriptive case study of consultant practices and prescriptions.* Unpublished doctoral dissertation, University of Michigan, Ann Arbor.

Forbes, R. L., Jr. (1977). Organization development: Form or substance? *OD Practitioner, 9,* 12–13.

French, W. L., and Bell, C. H., Jr. (1978). *Organization development: Behavioral science interventions for organizational improvement* (2nd ed). Englewood Cliffs, NJ: Prentice-Hall.

Goldhaber, G. M. (1990). *Organizational communication* (5th ed.). Dubuque, IA: Wm. C. Brown.

Grala, W. (1964). Industry's best defense: The speakers bureau. *Public Relations Journal, 20,* 12–13.

Heath, R. L. (1980). Corporate advocacy: An application of speech communication perspectives and skills—and more. *Communication Education, 29,* 370–377.

Kurpius, D., and Brubaker, J. C. (1976). *Psychoeducational consulting: Definition, functions, preparation.* Bloomington: University of Indiana Press.

Lippitt, G. L. (1982). *Organizational renewal: A holistic approach to organization development* (2nd ed.). Englewood Cliffs, NJ: Prentice-Hall.

Miles, M. B. (1979, October). Ethical issues in OD intervention. *OD Practitioner,* pp. 1–10.

Neff, B. D. (1987). *Accreditation issues in undergraduate public relations programs.* Paper presented at the annual meeting of the International Communication Association, Montreal.

Redding, W. C. (1979). Graduate education and the communication consultant: Playing God for a fee. *Communication Education, 28,* 346–352.

Rudolph, E., and Johnson, B. (1983). A survey of consulting activities of members of the American Business Communication Association. Paper presented at the American Business Communication Association Convention, New York, NY.

Schein, E. (1969). *Process consultation: Its role in organization development.* Reading, MA: Addison-Wesley.

Wakefield, G. (1988). Caution: PR education ahead. *Central States Speech Journal, 39,* 88–98.

Webb, E. J., Campbell, D. T., Schwartz, R. D., Sechrest, L., and Grove, J. B. (1981). *Nonreactive measures in the social sciences* (2nd ed.). Boston: Houghton Mifflin.

Outline

Purposes of Organizational
Communication Evaluation
OCE Perspectives: Inner and Outer
General OCE Methods
  Direct Observation
  Interviews
  Survey Questionnaire
  Documents
  Specific OCE Tools

Communication Audits and Their
  Limitations
Content Analysis
Interaction Analysis
Episodic Communication
  Channels in Organizations
Summary
Discussion Questions/Activities
Case Study
References

Organizational Communication Evaluation

12

Any effort to change or improve organizational communication presumes that the communication behaviors and related values, motives, and habits of organization members differ somehow from desired conditions. Sometimes, this judgment is based on vague, intuitively felt needs. In others, it arises from formal and systematic evaluation.

Organizational communication evaluation, or **OCE** for short, involves two separate but related features: (1) gathering and analyzing data about an organization's communication system and practices and (2) defining the desired conditions and values that frame interpretation of these data. Communication professionals frequently are responsible for gathering and analyzing data. Defining desired conditions is a more complicated political matter that may be controlled largely by top-level managers. However, other organizational groups and constituencies, including communication professionals, can influence this process.

Formal, systematic OCE implies that you must know what to look for and how to look for it. In order to know *what* to look for, you need a set of concepts to direct your inquiry. Knowing *how* to look requires a set of methods and procedures for gathering data. The idea of formal OCE in this sense dates back to the early 1950s in work by Keith Davis (1953), George Odiorne (1954), and others. Since that time, the field of organizational communication has amassed a virtual armory of tools and techniques for OCE. When Howard Greenbaum, Susan Hellweg, and Raymond Falcione (1988) reviewed work in OCE, they compiled an extensive manuscript that included dozens of studies and methods designed to assess organizational communication climate, information flow, message content, and communication training at interpersonal, group, and organization-wide levels.

Our review of OCE in this chapter obviously will not be as comprehensive as the survey that Greenbaum et al. developed. We will consider the principal purposes of OCE, the basic perspectives from which OCE can be performed, general methods for gathering evaluation data, and some of the specific tools used in the OCE process.

Purposes of Organizational Communication Evaluation

Organizational communication evaluation can be regarded as a research process that is designed to answer questions, but it differs from the kind of scholarly research that you have been reading about throughout much of this text. Scholars answer research questions and test hypotheses in ways that are intended to develop *general* knowledge and, hopefully, sound theories about organizational communication. The communication professional involved in OCE faces a different task. Instead of building theory and general knowledge, the professional *applies* this knowledge in order to draw conclusions about organizational communication in *specific* instances. The two types of research do overlap, but their purposes certainly are not identical. Greenbaum et al. argued that OCE can serve specific organizational interests in five ways.

1. OCE develops benchmarks (i.e., it gathers information so that management is aware of the status of communication systems).
2. OCE improves the internal communcation system (i.e., the kinds of information furnished by the evaluation process improve the factors influencing the communication systems, as well as variables affected by the system).
3. OCE aids the management process of planning and control (i.e., the improvement of the communication system enables management to do a better job of planning and controlling operations, resulting in better outcomes in the form of employee satisfaction, adaptiveness, and performance).
4. OCE improves the external communication system (i.e., it provides an awareness to organizations of the environmental conditions affecting the organization . . . activities of government, minority groups, consumer activists, and other special publics).
5. OCE bridges many existing organizational communication gaps, namely, (a) the lag in communication system adaptation to the needs of the organization, (b) inadequate attention to interpersonal and group communication processes within and between organizations, (c) the failure to recognize the interrelationship of internal and external communication, and (d) the inability of the individual organization to compare the status of its own communication system to that of comparable organizations. (p. 277)

Of course, these five purposes are not quite as straightforward as they might seem. Some of the political and ethical issues that we described in chapter 11 are deeply embedded in these claims. For example, who should have the right to define what constitutes "improvement" of organizational communication? Should OCE work to improve management control if the welfare of other organizational groups is jeopardized by that control? Does improved organizational communication really result in improved organizational performance? There are no easy answers to these questions. The debate that they provoke is one of the reasons why it is important to understand the various perspectives on organizational communication. The perspectives that we reviewed in chapter 1 are not merely abstractions designed for the amusement of academic intellectuals. The practice of OCE itself is very much dependent on such perspectives.

OCE Perspectives: Inner and Outer

Joseph Chilberg (1980) argued that organizational communication researchers use tools and methods that depend on either an outer or inner perspective of organizations. In Chilberg's words, those who work from the **outer perspective** seek to draw conclusions *about* the organization's "life-world," whereas those who work from the **inner perspective** seek to draw conclusions *from* the life-world. Broadly speaking, we might think of a life-world as everything that is going on in the organization as experienced and shared by its members. The outer perspective of this life-world usually is associated with functionalism, whereas the inner perspective is consistent with interpretivism.

When OCE is performed from the outer perspective, the researcher gathers and analyzes data through established concepts such as those described in chapters 4, 8, 9, and 10 (communication functions, networks, formal and informal systems, and communication processes in dyads, groups, and public contexts). The researcher uses these concepts as a way of asking questions and understanding organizational communication. For example, what kinds of messages support the maintenance function? How much grapevine communication occurs? Are subordinates satisfied with their superiors' communication styles? Outer observers have their own language for talking about what they have observed.

Chilberg also pointed out that OCE data obtained from the outer perspective are *measurement-centered*. We measure everything from organizational communication climate to the amount of information that flows through the network. Such data often are provided through rating scales in survey questionnaires, coded from interviews, or obtained in other forms that permit quantification and statistical analysis. The results are cast in the form of percentages, ratios, averages, measures of variability, correlations, and other numerical information from which the researcher draws conclusions about communication systems and processes.

The outer perspective of functionalism contrasts sharply with the inner perspective of interpretivism. According to Chilberg, the researcher who takes the inner perspective is concerned with the meanings of actions and symbols and the ways in which social actions are constructed. The inner researcher tries to discover the experience of organization members *as they understand it* without reference to a set of preestablished concepts. From the inner perspective, knowledge of organizational communication is revealed in the language of organization members rather than in the language of the researcher. Chilberg actually goes a step further by insisting that the inner researcher must study organizational communication from a *naive* standpoint (i.e., without any preconceptions about communication).

We are not sure just how naive a trained professional can actually be. Any OCE *method,* by definition, makes assumptions about what is to be examined and contains a conceptual language for communicating the results to others. As we saw in chapters 5 and 6, some forms of interpretive and critical scholarship have very clear notions about what is to be studied and how it is to be studied. Even so, some methods impose themselves more forcefully than others on the organization that is being studied. For example, when organization members respond to a typical rating-scale survey, they do so in terms of concepts that are built-in to the questionnaire (e.g., adequacy of information, openness of communication channels, or supportiveness and trust in superior-subordinate relationships). In contrast, simply asking members to describe communication in their own terms allows for much more freedom and potential to discover members' own frames of reference on their experiences. *The more a method imposes its concepts on the organization, the more important it is for the researcher to be sure that those concepts are relevant in that organizational setting.*

General OCE Methods

At the most general level, OCE data can be obtained in four ways: direct observation of behavior, interviews, survey questionnaires, and review of documents. The OCE usually depends on one or more of these methods.

Direct Observation

Even though it might be possible to conduct OCE without setting foot inside the organization, OCE usually requires the researcher to be present physically—on-site in the organization. Physical presence brings with it the opportunity for direct observation of day-to-day communication among organization members. The information that you can gather through your own eyes and ears in this process can be very important, especially when you combine it with other methods and if you have some system of recording and classifying what you see and hear. Webb, Campbell, Schwartz, Sechrest, and Grove (1981) identified five kinds of data that can be obtained through direct observation.

1. Exterior physical signs, including the appearance and dress of people, slogans on signs and posters, the general condition of facilities and equipment.
2. Expressive movement or kinesic behavior, including facial expression, posture, gestures, gait in walking.
3. Physical location or proxemics, including the arrangement of objects in space, seating positions, distance between people in various situations, space violations.
4. Language behavior, including topics of conversation, vocabulary, modes of verbal expression, rules for initiating, conducting, and terminating conversations, and vocal characteristics such as pitch, tone, and inflection.

5. Time duration or chronemics, including the speed with which tasks are completed, the importance that people attach to time, how time is used, and the regularity in cycles of behavior.

Direct observation can lead to errors in interpretation if the observer's viewpoint is biased or if subjects change their behavior as a consequence of being observed. Moreover, isolated bits of data from any of the five categories described by Webb et al. may mean nothing until they are placed in a broader context. Even so, if we observed an organization in which members spoke frequently about "maintaining peak operating efficiency," all wore dress suits, carried on meetings and conversations in a highly formal style, never touched one another except in ritual greetings such as handshakes, moved with an air of precision, and looked at their watches a lot, we could probably draw some fairly interesting conclusions about the life-world of that organization!

Interviews

The interview is one of the most widely used methods for data gathering in OCE. Interviews may be conducted in one-to-one encounters with organization members or in small groups in which the interview strategy is mixed with discussion. In either case, the interview is an organized effort on the researcher's part to solicit answers to questions. Generally speaking, interviews are not conducted in a random hit-and-miss fashion. Rather, they are strategically designed out of decisions about the information objectives that are to be attained and the kinds of questions that will be asked (Stewart & Cash, 1988).

Interviews can range from directive to nondirective and can involve questions that range from open to closed. In a **directive interview,** the interviewer has specific, clearly defined informational objectives. The interviewer controls the content and course of the interview in order to attain these objectives. The course of the interview is directed by soliciting specific information about a topic, probing for clarification or extension when necessary, and then moving to a new topic once the necessary information has been obtained. Informational objectives in **nondirective interviews** are more general and less clearly defined. The interviewee is allowed considerable latitude in defining the content and course of the interview. In a sense, the nondirective interviewer initiates the process, then relinquishes control and follows the interviewee's lead. The outcome depends less on what the interviewer wants to know and more on what the interviewee wants to say.

Questions in an interview can range from highly closed to highly open. **Closed questions** are designed to restrict the interviewee's answer options in some way. Questions that solicit a yes-no response or provide a set of alternatives from which the interviewee must choose are obvious examples of highly closed questions. In contrast, **open questions** allow the interviewee freedom in defining answers and providing information. For example, "How would you describe your relationship with your boss?" is more open than "Would you describe your relationship with your boss as good, fair, or poor?"

The interview can be used alone or it can be used as a tool that complements other approaches to data collection. For example, if the OCE project includes a highly structured survey questionnaire, it may be a good idea to support it with a more open-ended set of interviews in order to tap perceptions, values, and issues that are not revealed in the survey data.

Survey Questionnaire

A survey questionnaire usually takes the form of some pencil-and-paper medium through which organization members provide information to the researcher. The survey questionnaire is similar to the interview in the sense that it may range from unstructured and open to highly structured and closed.

A highly structured, closed questionnaire consists of items for which the answer options are specified. These options may be presented as points on a rating scale, multiple-choice alternatives, or rank orderings of objects. The respondent *selects* an answer from options that the researcher provides in the questionnaire.

An unstructured, open questionnaire consists of items for which the respondent *supplies* rather than selects answers. The topic in the request for information may be fairly specific, but there are no constraints on the respondent's alternatives for answering. This is something like a short-answer or essay item in a classroom exam, except that in OCE the answers are not right or wrong. They simply reflect the respondent's point of view on a topic.

The survey questionnaire may be an attitude scale or a measure of some concept such as communication climate, supportiveness, or satisfaction. Such scales usually consist of several items that are related to the attitude or concept being measured. The researcher may want to add up the numerical values for a respondent's answers to these items in order to get a score that represents this person's attitude or perception of the concept. In this case, the researcher must be sure that the scale is valid and reliable (i.e., it measures what it claims to measure and does so consistently).

Survey questionnaires do not always have to be multi-item measures of some attitude or concept. In many OCE projects, a questionnaire explores members' perceptions about a number of factors in organizational communication, but each factor is addressed with only one item or a few items. The answers to the items may be numerically coded, but there is no assumption that the researcher can add up a respondent's answers in order to get anything like an attitude score. The only scores are the answers to individual items. Conclusions about a given item may be drawn by looking at the percentages of respondents in each answer category, from the average for all respondents' answers to the items, or by some other means.

Questionnaires may also take the form of diaries in which members record their communicative activities or even open-ended narrative reports of members' experiences in the organization. While data from such forms can be categorized and coded for descriptive statistical analysis, they also can be analyzed through qualitative methods.

Documents

The last general source of data lies in the organization's written, audiotaped, and videotaped records. The information in questionnaires, diaries, and narrative reports exists through the researcher's solicitation. The information in organizational records and archives exists as a result of day-to-day organizational functions. Such records may include statements of mission and philosophy, policy manuals, employee handbooks, newsletters, magazines, tapes of meetings and presentations, letters, memorandums, and internal reports. Some of these materials may be easier to obtain than others. An organization might willingly include policy manuals and newsletters in data for an OCE project, but it might hesitate to reveal the contents of internal memorandums and reports. Some records may be off-limits as a matter of law or organizational policy (e.g., confidential personnel records).

Functionalist approaches to OCE often use documents and records as background information (Goldhaber & Rogers, 1979). Some documents such as newsletters may be employed directly to draw conclusions about organizational communication, but most of the available records are used simply to understand more about the specific organizational context in which OCE is occurring. In contrast, some interpretive methods depend heavily on documents and records as a source of data because they provide direct examples of organizational discourse.

Specific OCE Tools

Many specific tools and techniques are available for use in OCE. We will consider four tools that can be applied in OCE: communication audits, content analysis, interaction analysis, and analysis of episodic communication channels in organizations (ECCO analysis).

Communication Audits and Their Limitations

The term **communication audit** first appeared in the work of George Odiorne (1954). The usage implies that communication processes can somehow be audited and evaluated in much the same way that financial records are reviewed. During the 1970s, the term was adopted as a label for one of the most visible and controversial OCE systems developed to date. This system is the International Communication Association Communication Audit. Despite some of the controversy that surrounds this system, it is important to review because it is a widely used package that actually consists of several OCE tools (Greenbaum et al., 1988). Potential users should be aware that the International Communication Association allows copying and general public use of the instruments in this package, but the association does not endorse or sponsor audits and has denied authority for any group to use the association's name in connection with a communication audit (Falcione, Goldhaber, Porter, & Rogers, 1979).

When Odiorne came up with the idea of auditing communication, he was thinking in terms of systematic evaluation. However, the state of work in OCE from that point until the 1970s could hardly be called systematic. Typically, OCE would be conducted with a single tool such as a questionnaire. It would be performed at a fixed point in time as a "single shot." Reliability and validity of results generally were open to serious questions (Richetto, 1977). In order to correct this situation, the International Communication Association, with the contributed efforts of more than 150 of its members, began in 1971 to develop its own OCE system as "the only broad-based coordinated attempt. . .to develop standardized instrumentation specifically associated with the investigation and classification of communication variables in complex organizations" (Sincoff & Goyer, 1977).

Today, at least two other communication audit systems exist, the LTT audit and the OCD audit, both developed in Finland by Osmo Wiio and his colleagues. The LTT is a relatively simple questionnaire that is easy and inexpensive to administer. The OCD is an improved version of the LTT with some ingenious procedures for involving organization members in the evaluation process (Wiio, 1978). The International Communication Association system is the most comprehensive of the three. It is described in detail by Goldhaber and Rogers (1979), but we will review its basic components.

The Communication Audit is a multipurpose OCE system that is designed to accomplish a number of specific objectives. According to Goldhaber and Rogers, these objectives include:

1. Determining the amount of information underload and overload associated with the major *topics, sources, and channels* of communication.
2. Evaluating the *quality of information* communicated from and/or to these sources.
3. Assessing the *quality of communication relationships,* specifically measuring the extent of interpersonal trust, supportiveness, sociability, and overall job satisfaction.
4. Identifying the *operational communication networks* (for rumors, social, and job-related messages) and comparing them with planned or formal networks (prescribed by organizational charts).
5. Determining potential *bottlenecks and gatekeepers of information* by comparing actual communication roles of key personnel (isolates, liaisons, group members, etc.) with expected roles (provided by job descriptions).
6. Identifying categories and examples of commonly occurring positive and negative *communication experiences and incidents.*
7. Describing individual, group, and organizational patterns of *actual communication behaviors* related to sources, channels, topics, length, and quality of interaction.
8. Providing general recommendations, derived from the audit, which call for changes or improvements in attitudes, behaviors, practices, and skills.

The audit system itself consists of five separate but related tools: interviews, survey questionnaire, communication experience forms, network analysis, and a communication diary. Each instrument can be used alone or in combination with others in the package.

Audit *interviews* generally occur in two phases: preliminary interviews that provide exploratory information and follow-up interviews that help to explain or corroborate results from other instruments. The preliminary interviews—the first step in the audit process—are conducted with a small random sample of organization members or with key people who are targeted specifically for participation. The preliminary interview guide is highly structured, with questions based on most of the communication concepts that are underlined above in Goldhaber and Roger's first seven audit objectives. The content and structure of follow-up interviews depend on the results obtained in other audit instruments.

The *survey questionnaire* contains over 130 items. Some of these items provide background information on the organization members who answer the survey. More than 120 of the items are designed to measure organization members' perceptions of organizational communication conditions in eight general areas:

1. The amount of *information on important job-related and organizational matters that you receive* from others versus the amount that you would like to receive.
2. The amount of *information on selected job-related matters that you send* to others versus the amount that you would like to send.
3. The amount of *follow-up taken on information that you send* to subordinates, coworkers, supervisors, and managers versus the amount that you would like for them to take.
4. The amount of *information that you receive from key sources* (subordinates, coworkers, supervisor, managers, etc.) versus the amount that you would like to receive.
5. The *timeliness of information that you receive from key sources.*
6. The amount of *information that you receive through various channels* (face-to-face, telephone, memorandums, newsletters, etc.) versus the amount that you would like to receive.
7. The levels of *trust, supportiveness, and satisfaction in organizational relationships* (with coworkers, supervisors, and managers).
8. The levels of *satisfaction with various job and organizational conditions and outcomes.*

Each item in the eight categories is associated with a one (very little) to five (very great) rating scale to assess the extent of the condition as organization members perceive it. Members complete and return the survey under conditions of anonymity and confidentiality.

The *communication experience form* asks organization members to write narrative reports of incidents or examples that reflect effective or ineffective communication in the organization. Copies of this form may be inserted after each of the eight major categories in the survey questionnaire in order to connect the quantitative data from the survey scales to qualitative information in the experiential reports. The respondent is asked whether the items in a survey category evoke memories of some recent experience. If so, the respondent is asked to describe the experience, indicate the organizational level involved, and label the experience as an example of effective or ineffective organizational communication.

The *network analysis* is based on organization members' perceptions of their frequency of communication with one another and the importance that they attach to these interactions. You may remember that we included a simple network analysis procedure in chapter 4. The audit procedure is much more complicated, but the basic idea is the same. Members estimate the number of times that they interact with others during a designated time period. The number of interactions is weighted by the importance of the interactions. This information is analyzed with sophisticated computer software that produces diagrams of network structure based on the organization members' reports. The analysis identifies group members, liaisons, bridge links, and isolates as well as interaction patterns within and between groups.

The *communication diary* essentially is a logbook of each interaction that a member has with others during a designated time period. The diary may include identification of participants in an episode of interaction, the type of channel, the importance, and various other factors. The network analysis is memory-based (it asks members to recall past interactions), but the diary is a current record (members are supposed to record episodes of communication as they occur). Consequently, the diary can help to corroborate the network analysis as well as provide other information about organizational communication that may not be obtained with the other tools.

The exact steps and procedures involved in a communication audit vary from one OCE project to another. Generally, an audit is preceded by meetings between the auditor and client in which expectations for the project are clearly defined (e.g., what is to be done, how it is to be done, when the project will be completed, how much it will cost). If the auditor is an outside consultant, a formal contract probably will be negotiated for the service. In large organizations, a liaison committee may be established to work directly with the auditor. The committee can help the auditor to become familiar with the organization. It also provides some assurance of the organization's involvement in and commitment to the OCE project.

The audit itself begins with preliminary interviews. The results of the interviews may lead to some modification in the survey questionnaire (addition or deletion of items, changes in terminology, etc.) or in the audit procedures. Other instruments are then administered, the data are analyzed, and conclusions are developed. The conclusions may lead to a series of follow-up interviews in which the auditor attempts to clarify or corroborate interpretations of results.

After all audit data are analyzed and interpreted, the audit culminates with a final report. Goldhaber and Rogers (1979) recommend that such reports should begin with highlights of important conclusions and recommendations, followed by supporting information on methods, procedures, and results. The full report is presented to those who will use the information in decision-making and policy-making processes. A brief version of the report is distributed organization-wide for review by all members. The report phase of the audit also includes meetings in which conclusions are discussed and attempts are made to develop action plans. This phase of informational feedback is discussed in chapter 13 as an intervention activity.

The Communication Audit has been a controversial technique for several reasons. Most of the concerns revolve around limitations of the technique. Anyone who decides to conduct a Communication Audit should be aware of these limitations.

First, much of the data in the audit is based on member *perceptions* of organizational communication that may not necessarily correspond to actual communicative behavior (Downs, Clampitt, & Laird, 1981; Smilowitz, 1983). Although Goldhaber and Rogers claim that the system identifies actual behavior, this occurs only in the communication diary. The diary usually is not employed in audits, and its accuracy depends on organization members' reliability in recording information.

Second, the scales in the survey questionnaire yield results that are too general and difficult to interpret (DeWine, James, & Walence, 1985; Downs et al., 1981). For example, if organization members indicate that they need more information about management decision-making processes, what does this really mean? Do members need more information about who makes the decisions, how decisions are made, the issues involved, or all of these things?

Third, the audit can be a time-consuming and an expensive project. It requires the organization's active commitment to the project (DeWine et al.). In 1981, we conducted an OCE project with International Communication Association instruments in a 2,500–person organization that required six months to complete and cost more than $25,000, even with unpaid assistants and donated computer time. Many organizations are unprepared to make this kind of investment in an OCE project.

Fourth, the audit defines organizational communication too narrowly, although critics who point out this weakness have very different ideas about what is wrong here. Downs et al. argue that the audit should be expanded to relate communication effectiveness to productivity, profit, and cost-effectiveness concerns. Their view reflects traditional functionalist ideas about the connection between organizational communication and managerially defined criteria for organizational effectiveness. In contrast, Smilowitz also feels that the audit is too narrow, but his concerns have little to do with profit and productivity. He is worried that the audit simply ignores many important features of day-to-day organizational communication. We can support his criticism through our own experience in using the audit as a tool for scholarly research.

It is so heavily focused on the role of communication in meeting the information needs of organization members as *individuals* that it provides practically no information about the *social* dynamics of communication in organizations.

Finally, auditors require a number of special skills in the design of measurement tools, statistics, and use of computer software for data analysis. They also must be sensitive to the political dynamics of the organization because these dynamics can exert a tremendous influence on the conduct and outcomes of an audit.

In our opinion, OCE objectives are best served when researchers avoid canned or prepackaged methods such as the International Communication Association Communication Audit. Instead, researchers should devise a good conceptual framework for OCE that is relevant to the situation and to the organization involved in the project. At best, any canned package will require at least some modification in light of this framework. At worst, you will have to design your own instruments from scratch. You may also find that a number of other specific tools may be useful in OCE. Some examples include content analysis, interaction analysis, and ECCO analysis.

Content Analysis

According to Berelson (1952), **content analysis** involves "the objective, systematic, and quantitative description of the manifest content of communication" (p. 18). In its simplest form, content analysis requires that you select a sample of messages and then categorize the content characteristics of these messages according to some classification system. Characteristics are recorded in categories according to frequency of occurrence.

Greenbaum et al. (1988) pointed out that content analysis in OCE usually has specific purposes such as determining the readability of messages (e.g., the content of newsletters), identifying common themes (e.g., values expressed in policies, mission statements, memos), and describing the characteristics of language (e.g., do executives use subjunctive rather than indicative mood so that interoffice memos consist mainly of simple sentences or complex sentences, or how often do certain words or phrases occur in messages?).

Content analysis usually is associated with analysis of written messages and documents, but it can also be applied to transcripts from audiotapes, videotapes, or to interviews and discussions, provided that the transcripts are complete and accurate. Moreover, despite Berelson's claims, content analysis can be used in qualitative or interpretive research orientations. For example, it might be useful to know how extensively organization members use certain metaphors to describe their experience (e.g., we're all just one big happy family here!).

Interaction Analysis

Interaction analysis may be one of the purest forms of communication research because it examines the content and structure in patterns of interaction. It is similar to content analysis in the sense that it categorizes interaction according to some classification system. However, it works with statements that occur in ongoing, here-and-now interaction rather than with after-the-fact analysis of narrative discourse like those found in written statements.

Interaction analysis is used frequently in academic communication research. For example, Randy Hirokawa's studies in group interaction that we described in chapter 9 provide good examples of interaction analysis through categorical classification of behaviors. We suspect that the technique is seldom used in OCE, but Greenbaum et al. feel that it can be applied for OCE purposes.

One of the oldest systems of interaction analysis is Robert Bales' (1950) interaction process analysis system. Bales identified twelve classes of statements in group interaction. These classes can be organized under four general types of statements: positive reactions, attempted answers, questions, and negative reactions. Bales also argued that each of the twelve statement classes is associated with one of six problems that occur in group interaction: orientation, evaluation, control, decisions, tension reduction, and reintegration. The complete system is displayed in table 12.1.

Table 12.1   Bales's interaction process analysis. From *Interaction Process Analysis,* by R. Bales, 1950, Reading, MA: Addison-Wesley. Used by permission of University of Chicago Press.

Social-Emotional Area: Positive	Problem Type	Statement Type
1. *Shows solidarity:* raises others' status, provides assistance and rewards.	f	A
2. *Shows tension release:* jokes, laughs, shows satisfaction.	e	A
3. *Shows agreement:* gives passive acceptance, understands, complies, concurs.	d	A
Task Area: Neutral		
4. *Gives suggestion:* offers direction while implying autonomy for other.	c	B
5. *Gives opinion:* provides elevation, analysis, expression of feeling or wish	b	B
6. *Gives information:* provides orientation, repetition, clarification, confirmation.	a	B
7. *Asks for information:* requests orientation, repetition, clarification, confirmation.	a	C
8. *Asks for opinion:* requests evaluation, analysis, expression of feeling or wish.	b	C
9. *Asks for suggestion:* requests direction while maintaining autonomy.	c	C

Social-Emotional Area: Negative

10. *Disagrees:* gives passive rejection, formality; withholds help.	d	D
11. *Shows tension:* asks for assistance; withdraws.	e	D
12. *Shows antagonism:* reduces others' status; defends or asserts self.	f	D

Problem Types	Statement Types
a. Problems of orientation	A. Positive reactions
b. Problems of evaluation	B. Attempted answers
c. Problems of control	C. Questions
d. Problems of decision	D. Negative reactions
e. Problems of tension reduction	
f. Problems of reintegration	

The lowercased letter next to each of the twelve statement classes indicates the problem type. The uppercased letter indicates the general statement type. In order to use the system, you assign each statement that occurs during interaction to one of the twelve statement classes. One approach is to keep a tally of the number of statements in each class over intervals of time (i.e., to use a matrix table in which row headings are identified by the twelve statement classes and column headings are time intervals). During each time interval, you simply tally the number of occurrences for each statement class. Then you interpret the results in light of the statement type and problem type that are associated with each class in order to characterize the interaction patterns.

For example, suppose that the statements in one time interval fall primarily into classes four through nine. In the next time interval, most of the statements fall into classes one through three. This would suggest that the group moved from a period of questions and attempted answers revolving around problems of orientation, evaluation, and control to a period of positive reactions involving problems of decision, tension reduction, and reintegration.

Bales' system is only one example of interaction analysis. The specific method can take on various forms. You might even want to develop your own system for doing an interaction analysis. Decide what you are going to observe and how it is to be categorized and then design and apply your system. For example, you might study supportive and defensive communication in superior-subordinate interaction by using Gibb's characteristics of supportive and defensive climates (chapter 8) as a classification system. Of course, you might also want to recall Hirokawa's experience as a small group scholar with predetermined classification schemes for analyzing interaction. He abandoned these systems in his most recent research in favor of devising classification schemes out of the interaction itself.

Episodic Communication Channels in Organizations

Episodic communication channels in organizations (ECCO) analysis is a system that Keith Davis (1953) developed for describing the flow of information through these channels. The ECCO analysis is initiated by placing a message into an organizational communication system at known points of origin. The organization's message-diffusion process takes over, and the message is relayed from the point of origin to other areas of the organization. At the end of some specified time period, each organization member is asked to indicate whether he or she received the message, how it was received, when it was received, and from whom it was received? The researcher uses this information to reconstruct the pattern of message diffusion in reverse—from the end to the beginning. You determine which members received the information last, find out where they obtained it, and then go to those sources in order to discover how they received the information until you finally return to the point of origin.

ECCO analysis sounds like network analysis, but it is not quite the same thing. ECCO analysis is "episodic" because it is based on a specific episode of message diffusion. It identifies the channels used in that diffusion episode. The technique can answer questions about information flow between line and staff areas and across functional divisions of the organization. It indexes the speed of the diffusion process and the media of communication. It also is relatively easy and inexpensive to use.

Like other techniques, ECCO analysis has limitations. Analysis of a single instance of message diffusion does not necessarily provide a picture of the overall communication network. The patterns identified in ECCO analysis can be highly dependent on the type of information included in the messages, as Davis himself demonstrated. ECCO analysis also is restricted to a picture of serial message transmission or linear communication from one person to another, while linkages in network analysis are based on reciprocal interaction. To some extent, these limitations can be controlled by using several different types of messages and by including questions about reciprocal exchanges of informtion, but the results could be very unwieldy and difficult to analyze.

Summary

Organizational communication evaluation is designed to answer questions about the relationship between actual and desired conditions of organizational communication. It is conducted in order to provide benchmarks, improve internal and external communication, aid in management control, and bridge communication gaps, although the value and desirability of these purposes are points on which organizational communication scholars disagree.

OCE can be conducted from outer or inner perspectives, but it usually is associated with the outer perspective of functionalism. Generally, data gathering in OCE depends on interviews, survey qestionnaires, direct observation, and documents. Use of these general methods is reflected in more specific OCE tools such as the International Communication Association Communication Audit, content analysis, interaction analysis, and ECCO analysis.

OCE is a complex but necessary step in the process of improving organizational communication. The communication professional who conducts OCE research must be skilled in the use of its tools and techniques and be able to work effectively with a client organization. If these conditions can be met, OCE can lead to effective intervention activities designed to improve organizational communication. The types of interventions used by communication professionals are described in chapter 13.

Discussion Questions/ Activities

1. Consider the purposes of OCE as described by Greenbaum, Hellweg, and Falcione 1988. Are there any important political or ethical implications embedded in these purposes? Why or why not?
2. Why is it important to draw a distinction between inner and outer perspectives for OCE as described by Chilberg? Can you think of any circumstances under which a researcher would want to use the inner perspective? Is it possible to approach OCE from a naive standpoint?
3. Compare the use of interviews, questionnaires, direct observation, and documents as sources of data in OCE. What are the relative advantages and disadvantages of each?
4. Suppose that an organization approaches you with a request for a communication audit, but the organization really knows very little about this OCE technique. How would you describe and explain the purposes, procedures, and limitations?

Case Study

Communication Audit Gone Bad

A large midwestern financial services company was contacted by XYZ consultants to investigate the possibility of a consulting relationship. The president of XYZ, Pam Zurich, knew the vice president for the financial services company, Steve Hamilton, because they were both members of a prominent civic club. During a discussion at one of their civic club meetings, Steve expressed interest in a communication audit. A meeting was set for the following week.

During the initial proposal meeting, Pam and two of her assistants presented the benefits of a communication audit, an overview of the communication audit methods, and the objectives of the communication audit. Steve had questions about what the communication audit measured. Pam explained that the communication audit measured communication underload and overload, the quality of information and communication relationships, the operational communication networks, the potential bottlenecks and gatekeepers, the positive and negative communication experiences, and patterns of communication reacted to sources, channels, topics, length, and quality of interactions. Steve noted each of the items measured and seemed interested in pursuing the communication audit. However, he felt that he should pass the idea along to the other vice presidents and the president before making a final decision. The meeting closed with an agreement that Steve would call Pam during the next week.

The following week, Pam received a call from Steve. Steve wanted to conduct a communication audit for his company. Another meeting was scheduled to discuss the logistics for implementing the audit. At that meeting, Steve brought in a manager and a secretary. Their role was to assist the communication audit team with their implementation plans. Time lines and resources were discussed during the meeting. Steve informed the audit team that he would be out of the office during the first week of the audit but that he would inform the office of the audit and express his support of it before he left.

During the following week, Pam gathered her team of consultants to discuss the audit implementation plans. During that meeting, one of the consultants suggested that they add some new questions to the communication relationships section of the survey. These questions would solicit information about organizational politics and the effect of organizational politics on employees' relationships with each other and with their superiors. After a brief discussion, the group agreed to add the questions to the survey.

During the following week, the survey was distributed to a random sample of employees in the organization. Interviews with some organization members also were conducted that first week. Steve's manager and secretary were very cooperative with providing needed resources and assisted with the scheduling of interviews.

During the second week of the audit, Steve returned. His name happened to be included in the random sample for the survey. While reading the survey, Steve noticed the questions related to organizational politics. He was upset and immediately called one of the audit consultants to his office. He demanded to know what the questions about organizational politics had to do with a communication audit. He walked through the measurement items that he had reviewed in an earlier meeting and questioned the applicability of political questions to any one of the items. The consultant tried to explain why items on organizational politics could be very important, but Steve was still very upset and demanded to speak with Pam as soon as possible. The consultant called Pam and explained the situation. Pam agreed to meet Steve for lunch that day.

At the lunch meeting, Steve reiterated his anger about the additional questions. Pam listened to Steve's concerns, but she was very surprised by the intensity of Steve's reactions. Steve made it clear that any revelations about organizational politics in the company would be embarrassing to management and that any employee involved in any form of "political intrigue" could risk being terminated. As the discussion continued, Pam was able to infer from Steve's comments that Steve himself apparently was a member of a covert coalition trying to oust the company president and that the purpose for requesting the audit was to get information that could make the president look bad. He was afraid that the items on organizational politics might somehow reveal the existence of the coalition. Steve decided to discontinue the audit.

1. What went wrong here is fairly obvious, but how did it happen?
2. What should Pam have done differently?
3. Would your assessment of this situation be the same if Steve had not been angered by the items on organizational politics?

References

Bales, R. (1950). *Interaction process analysis: A method study of small groups.* Reading, MA: Addison-Wesley.

Berelson, B. (1952). *Content analysis in communication research.* Glencoe, IL: Free Press.

Chilberg, J. C. (1980). *An ontological approach to interpersonal communication education.* Paper presented at the annual meeting of the International Communication Association, Acapulco.

David, K. (1953). A method of studying communication patterns in organizations. *Personnel Psychology, 6,* 301–312.

DeWine, S., James, A. C., & Wallence, W. (1985). *Validation of organizatinal communication audit instruments.* Paper presented at the annual meeting of the International Communication Association, Honolulu.

Downs, C. W., Clampitt, P. G., & Laird, A. (1981). *Critique of the ICA communication audit.* Paper presented at the annual meeting of the International Communication Association, Minneapolis.

Falcione, R. L., Goldhaber, G. M., Porter, D. T., & Rogers, D. P. (1979). *The future of the ICA communication audit.* Paper presented at the annual meeting of the International Communication Association, Philadelphia.

Goldhaber, G. M., & Rogers, D. P. (1979). *Auditing organizational communication systems: The ICA communication audit.* Dubuque, IA: Kendall-Hunt.

Greenbaum, H. H., Hellweg, S. A., & Falcione, R. L. (1988). Organizational communication evaluation: An overview 1950–1981. In G. M. Goldhaber & G. A. Barnett (Eds.), *Handbook of organizational communication* (pp. 275–317). Norwood, NJ: Ablex.

Ordione, G. (1954). An application of the communication audit. *Personnel Psychology, 1,* 235–243.

Richetto, G. M. (1977). Organizational communication theory and research: An overview. In B. D. Ruben (Ed.), *Communication yearbook 1.* New Brunswick, NJ: Transaction Books.

Sincoff, M. Z., & Goyer, R. S. (1977). Communication audit critque: The researcher's perspective. *Journal of Business Communication, 15,* 57–63.

Smilowitz, M. (1983). *An examination of the philosophy and application of the ICA audit.* Paper presented at the annual meeting of the Western Speech Communication Association, Denver.

Stewart, C. J., & Cash, W. B., Jr. (1988). *Interviewing: Principles and practices* (5th ed.). Dubuque, IA: Wm. C. Brown.

Webb, E. J., Campbell, D. T., Schwartz, R. D., Sechrest, L., & Grove, J. B. (1981). *Nonreactive measures in the social sciences* (2nd ed.). Boston: Houghton Mifflin.

Wiio, O. A. (1978). *Organizational communication studies: The LTT and OCD procedures.* Paper presented at the annual meeting of the International Communication Association, Chicago.

Outline

The Concept of Intervention
Models of Intervention
Organizational Communication
    Interventions
  Agenda Setting
    Process Analysis
    Standard Testing
    Conceptual Inputs

Feedback of Observations
Coaching and Training
Structural Suggestions
Summary
Discussion Questions/Activities
Case Study
References

Changing Organizational Communication

13

Frequently, the outcomes of organizational communication evaluation (OCE) lead to efforts to change organizational communication systems and practices through the use of *interventions*—"sets of structured activities . . . related directly or indirectly to organizational improvement" (French & Bell, 1978). Even though such activities are undertaken increasingly by organization members themselves, interventions usually are carried out under the guidance of a trained consultant. As we indicated in chapter 11, the consultant may be an outside agent or a staff professional within the organization.

We also noted in chapter 12 that consultants who engage in OCE must have special skills. This point applies with even more force to those who engage in interventions. Incompetence or carelessness in the performance of interventions can be extremely costly to the organization. Redding (1979) illustrated this point by drawing an analogy between the consultant and the physician. We go to great lengths to protect the public from inept physicians. Yet, Redding argued quite literally that an inept consultant is in a position to harm many more people in a much shorter period of time. We stress this point because the material in this chapter is designed only to acquaint you with some of the common interventions that communication consultants use. It provides neither the theory nor the skills that are required for competent performance of intervention activities. Given this caution, we will describe the concept of intervention, two basic models of intervention, and several specific types of organizational communication interventions.

The Concept of Intervention

Although some scholars argue that a consultant is not necessarily a "change agent," the concept of intervention usually is associated with the idea of bringing about change in the organization. The very presence of a consultant may lead to "change" if organization members begin to alter their interpretations and actions as a consequence of this presence. The "common sense" assumption that **evaluation** and **intervention** are different activities or separate phases in the consultation process can be very misleading (Schein, 1969).

We learned this principle in a most painful way as graduate students during the conduct of a communication audit. A few weeks after the audit began, we discovered that turnover in the organization had begun to increase. Elimination of various hypotheses to explain this change left us with the conclusion that *we* were the culprits. Our needs assessment had become something of a consciousness-raising experience for organization members. Problems began to take on a new significance as members shared them with us through interviews and surveys. The audit served as a catalyst for discussion and conflict over these issues with the organization. Even though the organization (including top management) viewed the end result of the project as highly useful, we still did some soul-searching over the impact of our presence. The increase in turnover was not, by itself, a serious problem. The real difficulty was our failure to realize at the outset that the *entire* consultancy process is an "intervention." We simply neglected to anticipate the kinds of changes, planned and unplanned, that might result from such an intervention.

While most consultants probably would agree with the point of our story, the term *intervention* usually is reserved for planned, structured activities that have the objective of organizational improvement—actions that are intended to bring about a change for the better. These intentional acts arise from a diagnosis of needs. All too often, interventions are based on very limited diagnosis (e.g., as in the purchase model of consultation). Ideally, interventions should be developed through a process known as **action research** (Corey, 1953; Shepard, 1960; Whyte & Hamilton, 1964). The action research model includes the following steps: (1) diagnosis and data gathering, (2) feedback of results to client organization, (3) discussion of results within the client organization, (4) action planning, and (5) action (French, 1969).

If we accept the idea that an organization is a living, open system of interdependent elements, then virtually any intervention in one area is likely to have some ripple effect on other areas. Communication interventions are especially subject to this principle, since virtually all organizing functions are accomplished through communication. Interventions in an organizational communication system and behaviors, as well as in the values and perspectives on which they are based, "will influence, and will be influenced by, innumerable organizational variables" (Redding, 1979, p. 349). Consequently, it is critical that such interventions be based on valid and reliable data and that they be planned with a thorough understanding of their purpose and role in organizational change.

Models of Intervention

Various models have been developed to describe interventions in organizational processes. Blake and Mouton (1983) presented one of the more sophisticated models. Since their model is concerned with interventions in an organization's *human* processes, it is employed in various social and behavioral science disciplines, including communication. The model (displayed in

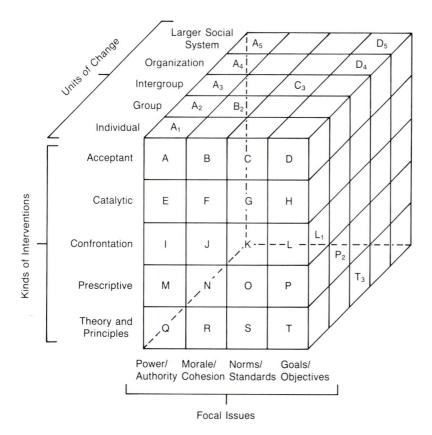

Figure 13.1
Blake and Mouton's Consulcube™. From CONSULTATION, by R. Blake and J. Mouton, pg. 11, figure 1.1. Copyright 1983, Addison-Wesley Publishing Company, Inc., Reading, Massachusetts. Reprinted with permission.

figure 13.1) is based on three dimensions of intervention: the *kind* of intervention, the *issue* that is addressed by the intervention, and the system level or *unit* that is the object of change.

Blake and Mouton's analysis includes five kinds of interventions:

1. *Acceptant* interventions intended to create openness in the consultant-client relationship (e.g., supportive behavior that encourages the client to discuss problems).
2. *Catalytic* interventions that assist the client with data collection, diagnosis, and interpretation of organizational conditions.
3. *Confrontation* interventions that challenge the client to examine values, assumptions, and ways of looking at the organization.
4. *Prescriptive* interventions based on the consultant's recommendations for specific solutions to problems.
5. *Theory and principle* interventions in which the consultant introduces the client to tested conceptual frameworks for understanding organizational situations (e.g., new ways of looking at old problems).

The issues addressed in any given intervention are, in essence, areas in which difficulties and problems arise. Blake and Mouton organize many issues into four broad categories: *morale* and *cohesion; power* and *authority; standards* and *norms;* and *goals* and *objectives.* They also suggest that interventions that focus on these issues may be directed at one or more system levels or units of change. These include *individual, group, intergroup, organization,* and *larger social system* (e.g., the community in which an organization is located).

The model in figure 13.1 represents Blake and Mouton's combination of these elements in a schema called the Consulcube®. It reflects all possible combinations of the five kinds of intervention, the four issues, and the five change units (a total of 100 different combinations). We have no intention of subjecting you to examples of organizational communication interventions for every combination in the Consulcube, but it does provide a convenient illustration of the extensive range of interventions that might be conducted in organizational communication.

A somewhat simpler model of consulting interventions—one more useful for our purposes—was offered by Schein (1969). He organizes interventions into four types: *agenda setting, feedback of observations and data, coaching and counseling,* and *structural suggestions.* Like Blake and Mouton, Schein is concerned specifically with interventions in human processes. According to Schein, "The important elements to study in an organization are the human processes which occur. A good diagnosis of an organizational problem may go beyond an analysis of such processes but it cannot afford to ignore them" (p. 9).

What are these **human processes?** Schein includes communication, member roles, group processes (including decision making and problem solving), group norms and group growth, leadership and authority, and intergroup relations as those that are most esssential to organizational effectiveness. Although communication is identified as a distinct process, even the casual reader of this text should be aware by now that communication is the very foundation of all processes in Schein's list. Hence, his conception of intervention is especially relevant to the field of organizational communication.

Organizational Communication Interventions

Agenda Setting

Agenda-setting interventions are directed primarily at the group level of the organization—management teams, committees, project teams, and other work groups in which members must interact to accomplish some organizational function. Agenda-setting interventions are intended to lead such groups into a conscious awareness and analysis of their own processes. For example, what are the taken-for-granted communication rules in the group? What stages typify group problem solving? How are member roles and role relationships defined in the group? How do members feel about these roles and relationships? How does the group deal with conflict? How do all of these factors affect the group's ability to accomplish its functions?

Since Schein is an advocate of the process or collaborative model of consultation, he endorses agenda-setting activities over other types of interventions. Even though a process consultant may use other types of interventions, agenda-setting activities are employed more often because they are most consistent with the basic values of process consultation. The consultant certainly must realize the answers to questions about the characteristics of a group's processes, but the goals of process consultation would be undermined if the consultant simply conveyed these answers to the group. The essential role of agenda setting is to *facilitate* the group's *own* discovery of these answers as well as its process of acting upon such discovery.

We should point out that the consultant does not simply leap into an agenda-setting intervention because there appears to be a problem in group processes. Before intervening, the consultant must assess the group's readiness to accept the intervention and to act on the problem at which it is directed.

Agenda-setting interventions may occur in several forms. Three common forms are process analysis, standard testing, and conceptual inputs.

Process Analysis

Process analysis often is employed in connection with group meetings. Typically, a period of time near the end of the meeting is reserved for a review of the group's outcomes and the processes and events that led to these outcomes. In its simplest sense, process analysis requires group members to reflect on and discuss *what* they did and *how* they did it. This intervention attends to members' feelings and attitudes about the dynamics of the group and may involve critical evaluation of these dynamics.

An example of process analysis can be drawn from an experience in the city planning department of a southern municipality. The department chief was concerned with the impact of the city's rapid growth on the ability of the department to do its job. In particular, the chief feared that work group supervisors had become so preoccupied with day-to-day operations in their own units that they had lost touch with overall department goals and the relationships among various projects. The chief decided to begin a series of weekly "update" meetings for supervisors. An internal staff consultant for the city was asked to sit in on the meetings.

The meetings were held on Friday afternoons. Basically, each supervisor presented a report on activities within his or her work group. After presentation of reports, the chief asked for questions or comments. These were usually few in number, so meetings often were adjourned within a few minutes after the reports were read.

After a few update meetings, the consultant simply suggested that the group take some time near the end of one meeting to "process" the session. Initially, the analysis was superficial. Members said that the meetings were "a good idea," but they took up "too much time." When the chief expressed doubt over whether the meetings really served to "give everyone the big picture," other members began to communicate more openly about the reasons for this difficulty. Each individual supervisor's report still focused on that supervisor's work group operations. Moreover, members were more concerned about presenting their own reports than listening to others. The reports themselves generally were unconnected with one another, involving little more than after-the-fact summaries of each group's work since the last update meeting. Friday afternoon scheduling reinforced these problems. Finally, some supervisors noted that they did not participate in the decision to begin the meetings. The chief's unilateral action created the impression that the objective of the meetings really was to provide information to the chief.

The process analysis led to a discussion in which the group as a whole decided that the department chief's "big picture" objective would be attained by making some changes in the meetings. Group members agreed that the meetings should focus on the discussion of specific projects and their relationships rather than on the presentation of unintegrated unit reports. Several actions were taken to bring about this change in orientation. In the process, the supervisors gradually began to function as a coordinated team. The consultant facilitated this process without actually becoming a "change agent" and solving the problem for the group.

Standard Testing

Standard testing interventions are related to and may even arise from process analysis. They involve an examination of rules and norms. Groups tend to reflect certain regularities in their processes. Even though these regularities may be unique to a given group, that group tends to function "as a rule" in certain ways. These rules may be based on formally articulated norms or on taken-for-granted expectations that are shared tacitly. Standard testing involves attempts to examine these rules and to decide whether they will be maintained or changed. This form of intervention sometimes involves confrontation in the sense that Blake and Mouton (1983) defined it.

A second example of group meetings illustrates the use of standard testing. Boards of directors for nonprofit organizations typically run monthly business meetings under parliamentary procedure, since state government regulations require such organizations to maintain legal minutes of these meetings. Sometimes, various committees in these organizations will employ the same parliamentary standards. Committees simply assume that this is the way to conduct business, so the use of parliamentary procedure is taken for granted. This was true of the seven-member finance committee in a large, nonprofit educational corporation that depends on public donations for its survival.

The organization had been very stable for many years. Funding always was available for its operations, so the functions of the finance committee had become quite routine. Motions were placed on the floor, received limited discussion, and usually were passed or rejected on unanimous votes. When the tough economy of the early 1980s forced the organization into a more competitive position with other nonprofit organizations, the finance committee began to deal with some very complex issues surrounding the ways in which funds were raised and allocated. Discussions over motions for action on these issues became more heated. Conflict was frequent and intense. The divisions among committee members were reflected in increasing numbers of 4-to-3 votes. Even when issues were decided, the execution of action was hampered by lack of support from those who opposed it.

The committee members were all aware of the conflict and its sources, but they did not know how to resolve it until a new board member, who happened to have a strong background in group processes, was assigned to the finance committee. During the next committee meeting after this assignment, the new member questioned the use of parlimentary procedure as a decision-making tool for the group. Although the new member's timing probably was poor (others might have perceived the action as a power play or some other type of threatening challenge from the "new kid on the block"), the basic idea was correct.

Since parliamentary procedure decides matters on win/lose votes, it is not a consensus-building method of decision making. It is very useful in large groups and assemblies in which majority rule may be the only means of arriving at decisions, but it may only factionalize and disrupt small groups. Unless losers are prepared to accept majority rule, parliamentary procedure does not resolve conflicts. It merely makes them a matter of public record.

Fortunately, the new committee member was a well-respected business-person in the community. The other members were unoffended by the challenge, chose to discuss it, and ultimately decided to abandon parliamentary procedure in favor of other methods. This change did not prevent conflicts from occurring, but it made it possible to resolve conflicts through development of consensus positions based on input from all committee members without the win/lose stigma of voting.

Conceptual Inputs

A third agenda-setting intervention, the **conceptual input,** is very similar to Blake and Mouton's theory and principle intervention. A group may face a problem that is consistently viewed from a restricted perspective that hampers the development of a solution. To use a well-worn metaphor, you cannot see the forest for the trees. When this situation occurs, the difficulty sometimes can be overcome by devising an alternative way of looking at the problem. In this case, the consultant does not prescribe solutions or actions but offers information that puts the problem in a new light. Once the group understands the problem in a different way, it may begin to see possible solutions and actions.

In chapter 11, we described the case of a midwestern company that had experienced major expansion and restructuring in its engineering division. Engineers who had been promoted to supervisory positions over project teams were having difficulty with their new positions. During our initial meetings with the top management team, these executives spoke consistently about the engineers' lack of supervisory skills and the need for "retraining technical engineers to be people engineers." It was clear that management saw the problem in terms of individual skill deficiencies among the new supervisors, so we offered the provision model training program in communication and supervisory skills that management wanted. However, we knew that other explanations might account for the supervisors' complaints of uncertainty in their new positions.

Given the extent of organizational change that had occurred in a short period of time, one alternative explanation for the supervisors' difficulties involved lack of role clarity and ambiguity in top management's expectations. During the period when we were running the training program for supervisors, we also intervened with top management through a conceptual input about the concept of role clarity and a specific tool for defining roles known as job expectation technique (JET). We simply sent the information along with a memo to the executive vice president with a suggestion that the information might be useful. The management team advised us that it was familiar with JET but had ruled it out because it is too time-consuming. Nevertheless, in our next meeting with the management team, discussion of supervisory effectiveness problems shifted from skill deficiencies to the possibilities of an "information gap" resulting from management's failure to define the functions of project group supervisors.

At this point, the management team seized the initiative and, in a manner of speaking, left us in the dust. While we were busy with the training program, the top executives went on a three-day retreat. They returned with the rough draft of their new company handbook for project team supervisors! We never found out whether the supervisors favorably received management's initiative because our involvement ended with the completion of the training contract.

Feedback of Observations

The concept of **feedback** as an intervention is relatively simple, although its use requires considerable skill and tact. Essentially, the consultant gathers data, makes observations, and reports this information to the client. Feedback interventions may be directed at individual, group, or organization-wide levels. The use of feedback is a true intervention in the sense that it may lead to change by making the client aware of information that is relevant to an understanding of problems and to action planning (French & Bell, 1978). Feedback may provide support for beliefs that the client already holds. Sometimes, it disconfirms these beliefs. In other cases, it introduces issues that the client has never considered.

Since the concept of feedback is easy to grasp, our examples of its use as an intervention are undetailed and simple. Feedback at the individual level might, for instance, involve discussion with a top-level manager regarding consultant or subordinates' perceptions of this executive's communication style. At the group level, a consultant might gather data from individual members on their perceptions of decision-making processes, then feed back a summary of these perceptions in a group meeting. At the organization-wide level, feedback of needs assessments is common. For example, reports of communication audits are made not only to top management, but they are also traditionally disseminated in some form to all organization members. This may involve full reports of methods, results, and conclusions, abstracts of full reports, meetings with departments and work groups, or some combination of these methods.

The basic simplicity of the feedback concept does not mean that it is easy to use as an intervention. Whether the consultant is providing feedback to a group on direct observation of its processes or reporting the results of a large-scale diagnostic study to an entire organization, the feedback inherently reflects the consultant's perceptions and interpretations. The information included in feedback depends on the consultant's selective perception of phenomena in the organization. Values and background influence what the consultant "sees" or regards as significant.

Survey data, which may be regarded as objective in the sense that they are separate from the consultant, must still be acquired through instruments that the consultant selects or designs. Since the selection or design of a survey instrument clearly is not separate from the consultant, the data derived from such an instrument depend on choices that the consultant makes. For example, if organization members are to report their perceptions of communication in a survey, their reports are limited by the survey designer's judgments regarding those aspects of communication that are relevant for inclusion and the ways in which they will be measured.

Observation is not separate from interpretation, but feedback of observations can reflect *degrees* of interpretation. We would suggest that feedback be made as *descriptive* as possible, free of any judgmental or *evaluative* character. This is essentially the same distinction that Gibb (1961) made between descriptive and evaluative actions in communicative behavior. Scholars in intervention techniques seem to agree with Gibb that judgmental behavior contributes to defensiveness. Bowers and Taylor (1973) noted that executives frequently are unreceptive to "bad news—any information interpreted as unfavorable to the organization. Research by organizational communication scholars supports this assertion (e.g., Koehler & Huber, 1974). Evaluative interpretations of data in unfavorable terms may be greeted only with rejection.

Does this mean that the consultant's feedback intervention ends with a descriptive presentation of data? Probably not. For instance, Schein (1969) noted that feedback should be descriptive, but he also said that the consultant's objective must be to "ensure understanding of the data and to stimulate acceptance of it, so that remedial action of some sort can be effectively undertaken" (p. 113). Blake and Mouton go so far as to suggest that feedback alone will be ineffective as an intervention. The consultant must be able to present not only data, but also explanations of data and suggestions regarding their interpretation and use.

A review and synthesis of information provided by Blake and Mouton (1983), French and Bell (1978), and Nadler (1977) suggest that feedback intervention is effective under the following conditions:

1. The content of the feedback is adapted to the receiver's ability to comprehend and to use it.
2. Feedback is sought by the client rather than imposed by the consultant.
3. The consultant facilitates the group's movement from reception of data to interpretation of data and formulation of action plans.
4. The rights of interviewees, survey respondents, and other information sources to anonymity and confidentiality are protected.
5. Feedback to *specific* organizational units includes data about that unit as well as overall or aggregate results from the entire assessment, but it does not include data that permit the unit to compare itself to other specific units.

Coaching and Training

Schein noted that the provision of feedback usually leads to **coaching or counseling interventions.** When clients recognize difficulties in organizational communication, they want to know how to change the communication system and practices. Schein regards coaching and counseling as means of addressing this question by helping the client to see alternatives to the status quo and to analyze the costs and benefits of these alternatives.

We should point out that Schein does not actually discuss "training" as an intervention. While **training** is similar to other interventions in the sense that it is designed to improve the knowledge and skills of individuals or groups, it differs in the sense that the consultant assumes an overt *instructional* role. A trainer is engaged in teaching others how to do something by structuring their learning activities, directing these activities toward specific objectives, and providing feedback and evaluation on the extent to which the objectives are being attained. Consequently, training interventions frequently are employed in purchase or prescription models of consultation. Although training interventions seem to be somewhat inconsistent with the basic assumptions of process consultation, they constitute a significant means of intervention for organization development practitioners (French & Bell, 1978; Schmuck & Miles, 1971).

As Goldhaber (1990) observed, consultant recommendations in organizational communication evaluations and diagnoses frequently call for some form of training. Typically, these training programs have the objective of developing organization members' skills in and knowledge of interpersonal, group, or public communication processes. Training models in organizational communication are quite sophisticated (communication scholars have been devising and modifying them since the time of Aristotle), but this does not mean that training is always an appropriate solution for problems in organizational communication. Unfortunately, training is sometimes used as a "quick fix" panacea, especially when the organization operates under pressure to produce quick and visible results. Under such conditions, the results of training may be temporary at best and unresponsive to the real problems at worst. The engineering company discussed earlier provides a good example. The consultant might have suggested supervisory skills training to correct individual deficiencies, but behavioral skills training for supervisors would not have addressed the underlying problem with role clarity.

When training is executed through purchase or prescription models, clients often are dissatisfied with the end result (Schein, 1969). One of the greatest problems arises when organization members receive training under circumstances that differ substantially from the situations in which they must function within the organization. Frequently, skills and knowledge acquired in a training context are not (or cannot be) transferred to the work setting. For example, we know of a government human services agency that spent a large sum of money to train caseworkers in empathic listening skills, then returned them to work settings in which they were interviewing dozens of clients per day, as well as processing paperwork on each case. The structure and demands of the work setting were fundamentally incompatible with the objectives of the training program. In general, training interventions should be undertaken only when they are clearly responsive to the problem and when there is a reasonable expectation that skills and knowledge can be successfully acquired and applied.

Goldhaber (1990) has proposed a general model for communication training in organizations that may help the consultant to avoid some of the problems with this form of intervention. This model, based on work by Kibler, Barker, and Miles (1970) and Brooks and Friedrich (1973), includes four basic steps: (1) a pretraining analysis to identify training needs; (2) development of informational and behavioral objectives for the training program; (3) selection, design, and execution of training techniques to accomplish the objectives; and (4) posttraining evaluation and feedback on program effectiveness. Goldhaber's model is displayed in figure 13.2.

Pretraining analysis essentially is equivalent to needs assessment or some other form of diagnosis. Goldhaber is quite specific in his recommendation that this phase be as thorough as possible in order to avoid inappropriate training efforts and ineffective results. The development of training objectives—specific statements of desired outcomes against which trainee performance can be assessed—depends critically upon this analysis phase.

In turn, training techniques depend on the objectives that are to be attained. In communication training, these techniques frequently include behavioral modeling, skill exercises, structured experiences (e.g., games and simulations), role playing; and case studies, supported by lectures, discussions, and media materials.

The effectiveness of the training program itself is subjected to some form of evaluation in the last phase. In many instances, evaluation is limited to postsession feedback forms on which trainees report their satisfaction with the program and their perceptions of its value. This form of feedback has many similarities to course evaluation systems with which most university students

Figure 13.2
Goldhaber's Communication Training Model. From *Organizational Communication,* by G. M. Goldhaber, Copyright 1986 by Wm. C. Brown Publishers, Dubuque, Iowa. All rights reserved. Reprinted by permission.

are quite familiar. Evaluation through postsession feedback from trainees has some utility, but it does not address the issue of transfer of learning. A complete evaluation requires some assessment of the extent to which skills and knowledge are carried over into the work setting.

Structural Suggestions

The final type of intervention involves the use of structural suggestions. **Structural suggestions** are consultant-initiated recommendations for specific changes in the organization. As applied in organizational communication, such recommendations often are concerned with both the structural and functional aspects of an organization's communication system. Examples of such suggestions include:

1. creation of mechanisms for upward communication (e.g., suggestion systems, complaint systems, employee meetings);
2. modification of elements in a communication network (e.g., designating liaisons to facilitate horizontal communication);
3. development of feedback mechanisms with which to respond or report follow-up on upwardly communicated messages (e.g., an "action line" column in a company newsletter);
4. adoption of new models of group decision making and problem solving;
5. development or modification of policies on the kinds and amounts of information available to various units of the organization;
6. conduct of interpersonal skills training programs;
7. development and dissemination of policies, goals, and objectives for organizational communication;
8. creation of a communication department with responsibility for organization-wide media and internal consulting on matters involving all aspects of organizational communication.

Recommendations for structural or functional change in organizational communication systems frequently are included in reports of large-scale diagnostic projects such as communication audits. Although some scholars have argued that such needs assessments are consistent with process consultation and organization development assumptions, this consistency is easier to claim that it is to create.

A formal needs assessment may require weeks or even months for execution. Since it is assumed that diagnosis will occur prior to any discussion of interventions, a long-term assessment reinforces the perception of a separation between diagnosis and intervention. The client comes to expect that the consultant will assume the role of "expert" and will tell the organization specifically what should be done in light of assessment results. This can generate a great deal of pressure for the consultant to move into a prescription model by recommending and perhaps actually even implementing solutions to problems. Generally, formal needs assessment results are effective in process consultation only if they avoid specific structural suggestions and only if they are used instead as feedback to facilitate the *client's* interpretations of and actions on organizational communication problems.

Does their inconsistency with process consultation assumptions mean that structural suggestions should not be offered? Our answer to that question lies in the fact that we have employed them in their own work and that we probably will continue to do so. For example, a communication audit that we conducted in one company yielded data suggesting communication problems in performance appraisal procedures.

The organization had a companywide performance appraisal policy. Appraisal was to be conducted every six months with a standard evaluation form. Results were to be discussed with the appraisee in a face-to-face interview. Data indicated four problems in this system: (1) some managers and supervisors either failed to conduct appraisals or simply completed the form without the interview; (2) the standard evaluation form included criteria that simply were not applicable to many jobs; (3) many appraisers experienced discomfort with and a desire to avoid interviews; and (4) appraiser discomfort was reflected in organization members' perceptions that the interviews were defensive—characterized by judgmental statements, domination of the interaction, and a strict "tell and sell" approach on the appraisers' part. Our report included the following conclusion and recommendations for possible action:

Conclusion
Organization members perceive that communication of performance appraisal information is generally ineffective and reflects little consistency across organizational units.

Recommendations

1. Reinforce policy by alerting appraisers when personnel evaluations are due.
2. Establish appraisal criteria and procedures *within* functional job areas.
3. Train appraisers in the use of the performance appraisal system and the conduct of appraisal interviews.
4. Establish a feedback mechanism to check for adherence to performance appraisal standards and procedures throughout the organization.

Recommendations 1, 3, and 4 have obvious communication implications, but recommendation 2 seems to be a "management" intervention rather than a "communication" intervention. This points out one of the key problems in the use of structural interventions. Evaluation data often yield information on other organizational issues such as the content of management decisions, personnel policies, or organizational philosophy. A consultant might be in a position to draw clear conclusions about such issues without really possessing the proper qualifications to make recommendations in light of these conclusions.

When you consider the pervasive nature of communication in organizations and its potential relationship to many other organizational processes, it is obvious that situations will arise in which consultants are tempted to offer structural recommendations on matters outside their immediate area of expertise. Such recommendations must be approached with great caution. In our example, we were comfortable with the second recommendation only because some of the audit team members had training and experience in the design and use of performance appraisal systems.

We have no hard-and-fast rules for deciding when it is appropriate to use structural suggestions instead of other forms of intervention. We do believe that structural suggestions are warranted when an organization is not sufficiently prepared to undertake self-evaluation and change, even under the guidance of a consultant. Consultants may also be pressured into such recommendations when the client has an unalterable expectation for "expert" advice. In some cases, the use of structural intervention may be a necessary first step in the organization's process of learning to deal with itself.

Even so, we have encountered precisely the kinds of problems with structural interventions that lead advocates of collaborative or process consultation to view structural suggestions with disfavor. Clients often are either surprised or confused by the recommendations. When the consultant takes over ownership of the client's problem by prescribing such interventions, it is easy for the client to become defensive and hostile about the recommendations and to blame the consultant if such recommendations fail.

Research from various disciplines of organizational studies, beginning with a classic study by Coch and French (1948), consistently indicates that people generally are more receptive to decisions when they are actively involved in formulating these decisions. This applies to clients as well. Even if the consultant does have more expertise in the problem (and this is not necessarily the case), intervention works best when it represents the client's solution to the problem. Structural changes in particular should emerge from the client's problem-solving process, not from the consultant's insistence.

Summary Intervention in organizational communication involves structured activities related to organizational improvement. However, remember that virtually any consultant activity in an organization potentially is an intervention that can initiate change, unanticipated as well as expected. Consultants who engage in organizational communication interventions must be very well versed in the activities that they perform.

Various models of the intervention process exist. Blake and Mouton described five kinds of interventions: acceptant, catalytic, confrontation, prescriptive, and theory/principle. Schein classified interventions as agenda setting, feedback, coaching/counseling, and structural suggestions. With some modification, Schein's model provides an excellent characterization of organizational communication interventions.

Agenda-setting interventions in organizational communication include process analysis, standard testing, and conceptual inputs. Feedback involves results of formal organizational communication evaluation as well as informal assessments. Coaching and training is one of the major forms in which organizational communication intervention occurs. Structural suggestions may include recommendations about changes in channels and media of information flow, network roles, and group memberships, although they also may lead the consultant into interventions that are vaguely related to communication and outside the consultant's area of expertise.

Discussion Questions/ Activities

1. Try to find a faculty member at your college or a private consultant who performs intervention activities for organizational clients. Interview this person to find out what kinds of problems he or she has encountered in this type of work.
2. Is it really the consultant's responsibility to be a change agent for the organization? Why or why not?
3. What are the comparative advantages and disadvantages of agenda setting, feedback, training, and structural interventions in organizational communication? When would you choose one type of intervention over another?
4. What kinds of skills should a consultant have in order to be competent in organizational communication intervention?

Team Building PDQ

Case Study

Linda Johnson is a manager at Smith & Co., a medium-sized management consulting firm. One afternoon, Linda received a call from her director, Pat Williams. Pat told Linda that she had just received a call from Steve Johnson, the human resource manager at ATI/BC Corporation. Steve was interested in talking to someone at Smith & Co. about a two-day team-building workshop for his management team. Pat asked Linda to call Steve to get the details. Pat said that Smith & Co. had been trying to get in the door at ATI/BC Corp. and this looked like an excellent opportunity.

Linda called Steve and received the following details:

- ATI is a major manufacturer of farm equipment.

- ATI has ten plants located throughout the Midwest.

- One year ago, ATI purchased BC Corporation, a small manufacturer of farm equipment with seventy-six employees.

- All of AT's plants have switched to just-in-time (JIT) Manufacturing.

- Each member of the management team at ATI/BC has twenty-five and thirty years of experience at BC Corporation—except for Steve Johnson and Russ Jones. Russ, the plant manager, was transferred from the Detroit plant to oversee the purchase of BC Corp. and run the new operation.

- Russ' goal was to switch the ATI/BC Corp. plant over to JIT within the next twelve months.

Once Linda had the basic information about the company, she asked Steve to give her a description of each member of the management team. The descriptions Steve provided follow:

John	**Vice President Production**
	25 years with BC Corp. Hostile about the purchase because his boss and good friend was forced into early retirement. No college education. Highly resistant to any discussion of JIT manufacturing.
Lisa	**Controller**
	30 years with BC Corp. Three years until she retires. Thinks the plant operates just fine the way it is. Does not want to have to learn a whole new system when she is so close to retirement.
Vince	**Vice President of Sales**
	20 years with BC Corp. Joined right out of college. Prides himself on knowledge about industry and products. Is intimidated by JIT because he has no experience with it. Had a falling out with John five years ago. Since then, he avoids contact whenever possible.
Jerry	**Manager, Quality Control**
	25 years with BC Corp. Has always worked independently. He, too, is angry about the purchase of his company. He refuses to discuss JIT and subtly sabotages every attempt that Russ has made to obtain employee buy-in. Jerry is afraid that any change may result in losing his job. He has a high school education.
Russ	**Plant Manager**
	10 years with ATI. Russ has an MBA from Stanford and has moved through the ATI ranks very quickly. His perception is that the employees at BC Corp. resent him because of his education and because he replaced a plant manager that was very popular and well respected.

Steve summarized the discussion by restating Russ' goals—to bring the management team together. Russ feels that unless they are committed to working together and accepting JIT, it will be a failure. Russ also feels that they must work together as a team before they can help their employees do the same. Russ' experience tells him that teamwork is the heart of JIT.

Linda thanked Steve and told him that she would call him back the next day to discuss alternatives. Linda then met with Pat to discuss what she had learned. Pat told Linda that she felt confident that a two-day team-building workshop, similar to the one Linda had done with another large company, would be a great idea. Pat was also excited that ATI/BC Corp. wanted to switch to JIT. Maybe Smith & Co. could help them with the transition because they had five experts on JIT manufacturing.

Linda called Steve the next day and proposed the following:

Phase 1: In order to work well together, people need to understand their own communication style and habits. We have an instrument that measures both communication styles and team interaction preference. I can send the instruments to teach team members. They will complete them and mail back to me for processing. I will bring each individual's results to the workshop.

Phase 2: Two-day workshop, off-site. The goal of the workshop will be two-fold. First, allow each person to learn more about JIT manufacturing and discuss all of their concerns. Second, provide each person with information about successful teams. We will do this by giving them information about their own team interaction preferences and then show them how to work together so that they achieve their own outcomes and produce work that is superior to what they could have produced alone.

Linda explained that she would like to bring in an outside expert on JIT. She felt that the group might accept the information from an outside expert more readily than from Russ. She also stressed that it was important to achieve buy-in on JIT before any team building could begin. She felt that allowing for open discussion without any fear of retribution would be the best way to obtain buy-in.

Steve liked Linda's ideas and asked her to put them in writing. They ended the conversation by agreeing that Steve would have the proposal by the end of the week.

Russ hired Smith & Co. to do a two-day team-building workshop. Day one was an open forum on JIT manufacturing. The result of day one was a list of concerns the management team had about JIT to be submitted to Russ. If Russ could satisfy the group that their concerns would be dealt with individually, they agreed to accept the possibility that JIT would be a good decision. Day two consisted of lecture, discussion, and role playing on forming successful teams. At the end of day two, the team left with:

a. An anchor plan to ensure that they interacted with their coworkers.
b. Suggestions to foster team interaction with their subordinates.
c. Information about the role successful team interaction plans in JIT Manufacturing.

1. In your opinion, did Linda propose the best solution? What would you have done differently?
2. Will ATI/BC Corporation successfully switch to just-in-time manufacturing in the next twelve months?
3. Should the consultant's role end here?

References

Blake, R. R., and Mouton, J. S. (1983). *Consultation.* (2nd ed.) Reading, MA: Addison-Wesley.

Bowers, D. G., and Taylor, J. (1973). Survey of organizations. University of Michigan Institute for Social Research *Newsletter 3,* no. 6.

Brooks, W., and Friedrich, G. (1973). *Teaching speech communication in the secondary school.* Boston: Houghton Mifflin.

Coch, L., and French, J. (1948). Overcoming resistance to change. *Human Relations, 1,* 512–532.

Corey, S. M. (1953). *Action research to improve school practices.* New York: Bureau of Publications, Teachers College, Columbia University.

French, W. (1969). Organization development objectives, assumptions, and strategies. *California Management Review, 12,* 23–24.

French, W. L., and Bell, C. H., Jr. (1978). *Organization development: Behavioral science interventions for organization improvement* (2nd ed.). Englewood Cliffs, NJ: Prentice-Hall.

Gibb, J. (1961). Defensive communication. *Journal of Communication, 11,* 141–148.

Goldhaber, G. M. (1990). *Organizational communication* (5th ed.). Dubuque, IA: Wm. C. Brown.

Kibler, R. L., Barker, L., and Miles, D. (1970). *Behavioral objectives and instruction.* Boston: Allyn and Bacon.

Koehler, J. W., and Huber, G. (1974). *Effects of upward communication on managerial decision making.* Paper presented at the annual meeting of the International Communication Association, New Orleans.

Lippitt, G. L. (1982). *Organizational renewal: A holistic approach to organization development* (2nd ed.). Englewood Cliffs, NJ: Prentice-Hall.

Nadler, D. A. (1977). *Feedback and organization development: Using data-based methods.* Reading, MA: Addison-Wesley.

Redding, W. C. (1979). Graduate education and the communication consultant: Playing God for a fee. *Communication Education, 28,* 346–352.

Schein, E. (1969). *Process consultation: Its role in organization development.* Reading, MA: Addison-Wesley.

Schmuck, R. A., and Miles, M. B. (Eds.). (1971). *Organizational development in schools.* Palo Alto, CA: National Press Books.

Shepard, H. A. (1960). An action research model. In *An action research program for organization improvement.* Ann Arbor: The Foundation for Research on Human Behavior, University of Michigan.

Whyte, W. F., and Hamilton, E. L. (1964). *Action research for management.* Homewood, IL: Irwin-Dorsey.

Agle, G., 187, 194
Albaum, G., 98, 114
Albrecht, T. L., 104, 105, 108, 114, 223, 228
Alexander, E. R., III, 89, 114
Alvin, W., 184, 194
Anatol, K. W. E., 42, 51, 54, 80, 83, 91, 96, 115, 140, 150, 167, 203, 229, 238, 240, 262
Anderson, J. C., 214, 230
Applbaum, R. L., 42, 51, 54, 80, 83, 91, 96, 115, 140, 150, 167, 203, 229, 238, 240, 262
Armstrong, R. A., 277, 287
Arrington, C., Jr., 278, 287
Aune, J. A., 144, 166

Bachrach, P., 140, 166
Backman, C. W., 139, 140, 142, 168, 202, 204, 230, 236, 263
Bair, J. H., 177, 193, 194
Baird, J. E., Jr., 32, 34, 50, 238, 260
Bales, R., 321, 326
Baratz, M., 140, 166
Barawoy, M., 147, 166
Barker, L., 266, 288, 339, 346
Barley, S. R., 109, 116
Barnard, C., 61, 71, 79, 99, 114
Barron, I., 175, 183, 193
Bartol, K. M., 243, 260
Bateson, G., 41, 51
Beatty, M. J., 247, 260
Beavin, J., 35, 42, 51
Beckhard, R., 17, 24, 150, 166, 298, 306
Beer, M., 17, 18, 24, 301, 306
Bell, C. H., Jr., 18, 25, 97, 114, 132, 137, 297, 298, 306, 329, 336, 338, 346
Benne, K. D., 239, 252, 261
Bennis, W., 245, 261
Berelson, B., 41, 50, 320, 326
Berlo, D. K., 43, 50
Bertalanffy, L. V., 70, 79
Birdwhistell, R., 38, 50
Bittner, J. R., 42, 51
Bjorn-Andersen, N., 172, 180, 182, 188, 193

Blake, R. R., 155, 158, 166, 240, 261, 331, 332, 334, 338, 346
Blanchard, K., 8, 25, 242
Blumer, H., 236, 261
Boase, P. H., 7, 24
Bolton, E., 224, 228
Bond, M., 247, 261
Boren, R., 94, 115
Bormann, E. G., 120, 121, 122, 123, 124, 136, 237, 261
Bosmajian, H. A., 13, 24
Bowditch, J. L., 5, 24, 70, 79
Bowers, D. G., 337, 346
Brammer, C., 131, 137
Brink, V. Z., 179, 184, 193
Brooks, W., 339, 346
Brubaker, J. C., 294, 306
Buchholz, R., 278, 287
Burgoon, J. K., 36, 50
Burgoon, M., 44, 50
Burke, R. J., 156, 157, 166, 217, 228
Burnett, G. J., 175, 193
Burrell, G., 8, 24
Butterfield, D. A., 243, 260

Cafferty, T. P., 158, 168
Campbell, D. T., 296, 307, 312, 326
Carey, A., 64, 79
Carlson, C. V., 7, 24
Carnegie, D., 62, 79
Casbolt, D. M., 179, 182, 193
Case, D., 186, 194
Cash, W. B., Jr., 313, 326
Center, A. H., 276, 287
Chandler, R. C., 277, 287
Chandler, T. A., 127, 129, 137, 244, 247, 261
Chase, A. B., 93, 114
Chase, W. H., 278, 279, 288
Cheney, G., 127, 128, 137
Cherry, J., 179, 182, 193
Chilberg, J. C., 311, 326
Cibbora, C., 182, 188, 194
Clampitt, P. G., 319, 326
Clegg, S., 145, 147, 166
Cline, T. R., 216, 228
Cobb, A. T., 300, 301, 306

Coch, L., 342, 346
Cohen, G., 125, 137
Compton, C., 131, 137
Conrad, C., 32, 51, 132, 137, 218, 228
Conrath, D. W., 193
Coon, A. M., 254, 261
Coonfield, T., 255, 261
Corey, S. M., 330, 346
Crawford, J. S., 13, 24
Cronen, V. E., 205, 230
Culbert, S. A., 95, 114
Cummins, R. C., 238, 263
Cunningham, M. A., 34, 50
Curnow, R., 175, 183, 193
Curran, K. E., 89, 114
Curry, J., 225, 230
Cutlip, S. M., 276, 287
Cyert, R. M., 84, 109, 114

Dahl, R., 139, 166
Dalton, M., 158, 166
Daly, J. A., 87, 114
Damhorst, M. L., 87, 114
Dance, F. E. X., 36, 50
Daniels, T. D., 70, 79, 87, 88, 89, 93, 114, 115, 199, 215, 216, 220, 225, 228, 229, 243, 262
Danowski, J. A., 179, 185, 193
D'Aprix, R., 74, 79
Davenport, L. L., 176, 193
Davis, K., 93, 95, 99, 114, 309, 323, 326
Davitz, J. R., 37, 50
Deal, T. E., 119, 121, 130, 137
Deetz, S. A., 15, 18, 24, 32, 51, 125, 137, 148, 166
De La Zerda, N., 38, 50
Dennis, H. S., III, 8, 25, 199, 229
Dessler, G., 8, 25, 53, 61, 71, 79, 150, 154, 166
DeWine, S., 88, 116, 131, 137, 319, 326
Dickson, W., 63, 80
Dillard, J. P., 199, 224, 229
Di Salvo, V., 5, 25
Downs, C. W., 319, 326
Dutton, J. M., 158, 168

Eblen, A. L., 243, 261
Eden, J. M., 95, 114
Edwards, R., 147, 166
Eich, R. K., 6, 25, 293, 306
Eisenberg, E. M., 16, 25, 33, 50, 74, 75, 79, 80, 86, 114, 126, 127, 137, 149, 168, 199, 208, 216, 223, 229
Ekman, P., 35, 38, 50
Emerson, R. M., 140, 166, 261
Emery, J. C., 178, 183, 193
Ewing, R. P., 279, 287

Fairhurst, G. T., 217, 218, 223, 229, 244, 247, 261
Falcione, R. L., 16, 25, 87, 114, 309, 315, 326
Farace, R. V., 19, 25, 70, 75, 79, 80, 83, 84, 85, 86, 87, 94, 107, 114, 199, 205, 207, 208, 216, 229
Farrell, T. B., 144, 166
Fast, J., 36, 50
Faules, D. F., 68, 80, 122, 137
Fayol, H., 54, 55, 56, 57, 79, 97, 114
Feldman, M., 147, 149, 167
Fiedler, F., 242, 243, 261
Filley, A. C., 215, 229
Finn, D., 276, 277, 288
Fisher, B. A., 14, 25, 250, 251, 261
Follett, M. P., 60, 61, 79
Forbes, R. L., Jr., 301, 306
Foss, S. K., 33, 50
Frank, H., 243, 263
Franke, R. H., 64, 79
French, W. L., 18, 25, 97, 114, 132, 137, 140, 166, 292, 298, 306, 329, 336, 338, 342, 346
Friedrich, G., 339, 346
Friesen, W. V., 35, 38, 50
Frost, P. J., 143, 167

Gardner, B. B., 276, 288
Geist, P., 127, 129, 137
Gerloff, E. A., 238, 263
Gibb, J., 212, 229, 337, 346

Giddens, A., 146, 167
Glassman, R. B., 103, 114
Goldhaber, G. M., 8, 19, 24, 25,
32, 39, 50, 68, 79, 83, 86, 87,
91, 93, 94, 96, 109, 114, 115,
150, 167, 187, 193, 199, 229,
243, 276, 288, 292, 306, 315,
316, 319, 326, 338, 339, 346
Goodall, H. L., Jr., 19, 25
Gorden, W. I., 214, 229
Gouldner, A. W., 184, 194
Goyer, R. S., 30, 50, 316, 326
Graen, G., 261
Graham, E., 216, 229
Grala, W., 292, 306
Gramsci, A., 145, 147, 167
Gratz, R. D., 172, 187, 194
Green, S. G., 217, 223, 229
Greenbaum, H. H., 309, 310, 315,
326
Greenless, M., 174, 194
Grove, J. B., 296, 307, 312, 326
Grunig, J. E., 207, 229, 266, 268,
269, 270, 288
Gudykunst, W. B., 248, 261
Gujarati, D. N., 215, 229
Gutek, B. A., 243, 262

Habermas, J., 144, 145, 146, 167
Hagen, R. L., 243, 261
Hall, E., 39, 50
Hall, J., 155, 167
Hamilton, E. L., 330, 346
Hance, K., 253, 262
Harre, R., 127, 137
Harris, S. G., 90, 115
Harrison, R., 35, 50
Harsanyi, J. C., 142, 167
Hartwick, J., 184, 194
Hatch, M. J., 147, 149, 167
Heath, R. L., 276, 282, 284, 288,
293, 306
Hellweg, S., 99, 100, 115, 309,
326
Helms, M. M., 89, 114
Hersey, P., 8, 25, 242
Herzberg, F., 200, 201, 229
Hill, J. W., 275, 278, 288
Hiltz, S. R., 179, 187, 194
Hirokawa, R. Y., 248, 249, 261,
321
Hoffman, L., 96, 115
Hofstede, G., 247, 261
Homans, G. C., 233, 234, 261
Hopper, R., 38, 50
House, R. J., 215, 229
House, W. G., 177, 194
Howard, R. D., 213, 230
Howell, W. S., 120, 121, 124, 136
Huber, G., 96, 115, 337, 346
Huse, E. F., 5, 25, 70, 79
Hush, M., 282, 288

Infante, D. A., 214, 229

Jablin, F. M., 14, 25, 208, 211,
215, 219, 221, 222, 223, 225,
229, 257, 263
Jackson, D., 35, 42, 51
Jacoby, J., 103, 115
Jaeger, A., 98, 115
James, A. C., 319, 326
Janis, I. L., 150, 167
Jennings, E., 240, 263
Johnson, B., 299, 307
Johnson, B. M., 32, 50
Johnson, K., 187, 194
Jones, B. L., 278, 279, 288
Jones, T. S., 167
Joseph, E. C., 174, 194

Kahn, A., 243, 261
Kahn, R. L., 3, 25, 70, 79, 95,
115
Kanter, J., 179, 194
Kanter, R. M., 86, 115, 119, 131,
137
Kaoru, I., 255, 262
Katz, D., 3, 25, 70, 79, 95, 115
Kaul, J. D., 64, 79
Kelly, G. A., 236, 238, 262
Kelman, H. C., 141, 167
Kennedy, A. A., 119, 121, 130,
137
Kibler, R. L., 339, 346
Kiesler, S., 187, 194
Knapp, M., 39, 50, 51
Knause, C., 242, 262
Koch, S., 32, 51, 125, 137
Koehler, J. W., 42, 51, 54, 80, 83,
91, 96, 115, 140, 150, 167,
203, 229, 238, 240, 262, 337,
346
Koontz, H., 103, 115
Kreps, G. L., 70, 80
Krivonos, P. D., 96, 115, 219, 229
Krone, K. J., 14, 25
Kurpius, D., 294, 306

Laird, A., 319, 326
Lakoff, R., 37, 51
Lamude, K. G., 216, 220, 229,
243, 262
Landsberger, H., 64, 80
Langer, S., 31, 51
Larson, C., 39, 51
Larson, C. E., 36, 50
Latamore, G. B., 186, 194
Lawrence, P., 70, 80
Lawrence, P. R., 155, 157, 167
Lesniak, R., 87, 94, 115
Level, D. A., 87, 115
Levinson, D., 238, 262
Likert, R., 67, 80
Linstone, H. A., 254, 262
Lippitt, G. L., 235, 262, 293, 301,
306
Lippitt, R., 240, 263
Littlejohn, S. W., 38, 41, 51, 71,
75, 80, 233, 245, 262

Logan, L. L. 199, 215, 225, 228
Lorsch, J., 70, 80, 155, 157, 167
Lukes, S., 145, 167

Maccoby, M., 119, 137, 245, 262
Machaver, W., 95, 115
Maier, N., 96, 115
March, J. G., 70, 80, 84, 109,
114, 115
Margulies, N., 300, 301, 306
Martin, J., 147, 149, 167
Maslow, A. H., 65, 66, 69, 80
Mayo, E., 62, 64, 80
McBurney, J., 253, 262
McCroskey, J. C., 39, 51
McGaan, L., 144, 167
McGregor, D., 66, 69, 80
McGuire, T., 187, 194
McKersie, R. B., 161, 168
McLane, H. J., 225, 230
McPhee, R., 144, 167
Mee, J., 72, 80
Meisner, N. B., 185, 194
Mellinger, G. D., 95, 115
Meyer, G. W., 255, 256, 262
Meyers, C. E., 142, 167
Miles, D., 339, 346
Miles, M. B., 17, 18, 25, 298,
301, 307, 338, 346
Miles, R., 65, 67, 80, 92, 115
Miller, G. R., 41, 51
Miller, K. I., 18, 25, 75, 80, 223,
229
Millman, Z., 184, 194
Monge, P. R., 18, 19, 25, 70, 71,
75, 79, 80, 83, 84, 85, 86, 87,
94, 107, 114, 199, 205, 207,
208, 216, 223, 229
Moss, S., 30, 42, 51
Mouton, J. S., 155, 158, 166, 240,
261, 331, 332, 334, 338, 346
Mumby, D. K., 15, 25, 143, 145,
146, 147, 148, 149, 150, 167

Nadler, D. A., 338, 346
Naisbitt, J., 179, 194
Neff, B. D., 292, 307
Nelson, R. A., 276, 282, 284, 288
Nichols, R. G., 120, 121, 124, 136
Nieva, V. F., 243, 262
Nishida, T., 248, 261
Nomura, R., 97, 115, 247, 262
Norton, R., 39, 51

O'Connell, S. E., 188, 189, 194
O'Donnel, C., 103, 115
O'Donnell-Trujillo, N., 12, 20, 25,
119, 122, 137
Olson, M. H., 172, 177, 194
Ordione, G., 309, 315, 326
O'Reilly, C. A., III, 96, 116, 214,
230
Organ, D. W., 217, 230
Osborn, A. F., 254, 262
Ouchi, W., 98, 115

Pacanowsky, M. E., 12, 20, 25,
119, 122, 137
Pace, R., 249, 261
Pace, R. W., 17, 18, 25, 68, 80,
94, 115, 202, 230
Papa, M. J., 157, 161, 167, 190,
194
Pearce, J. L., 84, 109, 116, 158,
168
Pearce, W. B., 205, 230
Pelz, D. P., 215, 230
Penley, L. E., 88, 93, 115
Perrin, P. G., 38, 51
Peterson, D., 273, 288
Pettegrew, L. S., 70, 80, 262
Planty, E., 95, 115
Pollio, H. R., 31, 32, 35, 51
Pood, E. A., 157, 161, 167
Poole, M. S., 139, 155, 157, 160,
161, 167, 251, 262
Porter, D. T., 87, 94, 115, 315,
326
Porter, L. W., 84, 109, 116, 158,
168
Post, J. E., 278, 279, 288
Prethus, R., 202, 230
Putnam, L. L., 8, 12, 14, 25, 139,
155, 156, 157, 160, 161, 167

Rainwater, L., 276, 288
Raven, B. H., 140, 166
Ray, G., 131, 137
Read, W. H., 96, 115, 219, 230
Redding, W. C., 16, 19, 26, 64,
80, 211, 230, 256, 292, 293,
299, 301, 307, 329, 330, 346
Rehder, R., 98, 115, 255, 262
Riccillo, S. C., 218, 230
Rice, R. E., 177, 186, 187, 194
Richards, W. D., 107, 115
Richetto, G. M., 61, 80, 92, 93,
95, 116, 199, 229, 316, 326
Robbins, S. P., 150, 156, 168
Robert, H. M., 253, 263
Roberts, K. H., 96, 116, 214, 230
Roethlisberger, F. L., 63, 80
Rogers, D. P., 315, 316, 319, 326
Rogers, E. M., 177, 194
Ropp, V. A., 104, 105, 114, 223,
228
Rose, R. A., 203, 205, 230
Roth, J., 251, 262
Roveda, C., 182, 188, 194
Rudolph, E., 299, 307
Ruesch, J., 41, 51
Ruffner, M., 44, 50
Russell, B., 139, 168
Russell, H. M., 19, 25, 70, 79, 83,
84, 85, 86, 87, 94, 107, 114,
205, 207, 229

Salem, P. J., 172, 187, 194
Sanborn, G. A., 42, 51
Sanders, D. H., 173, 177, 178,
179, 183, 195
Sawaya, R. N., 278, 287
Scheff, T., 206, 230

Schein, E., 154, 168, 246, 252, 263, 295, 296, 297, 299, 307, 329, 332, 337, 338, 346
Schenck-Hamlin, W. J., 38, 51
Schmuck, R. A., 338, 346
Schutz, W., 200, 230
Schwartz, R. D., 296, 307, 312, 326
Sechrest, L., 296, 307, 312, 326
Secord, P. F., 127, 137, 139, 140, 142, 168, 202, 204, 230, 236, 238, 263
Sethi, S. P., 275, 281, 282, 288
Shamo, G. W., 42, 51
Shapiro, G. L., 120, 121, 124, 136
Sheats, P., 239, 252, 261
Shelton, C., 224, 225, 230
Shepard, H. A., 17, 26, 158, 166, 330, 346
Siegel, J., 187, 194
Simon, H. A., 70, 80, 109, 115, 233, 263
Sincoff, M. Z., 316, 326
Sitkin, S. B., 147, 167
Smilowitz, M., 13, 26, 319, 326
Smircich, L., 120, 121, 137
Smith, G. L., 88, 116
Smith, R. C., 126, 127, 137, 149, 168
Smith, R. L., 92, 93, 95, 116
Snavely, B. K., 217, 223, 229
Spector, P. E., 202, 218, 220, 230
Spiker, B. K., 70, 79, 87, 88, 89, 93, 114, 115

Stech, E. L., 103, 116
Stein, L. I., 34, 51
Steiner, G., 41, 50
Steinfield, C., 195
Steinmetz, L., 202, 230
Stevens, S. S., 41, 51
Stevenson, W. B., 84, 109, 116, 158, 168
Stewart, C. J., 313, 326
Stohl, C., 256, 263
Stork, D., 110, 116
Stott, R. B., 255, 256, 262
Strauss, G., 17, 26
Sturgis, A., 253, 263
Sutton, R. I., 90, 115

Tannenbaum, A. S., 142, 168
Tapscott, D., 186, 195
Taylor, F. W., 54, 55, 57, 80
Taylor, J., 337, 346
Thierauf, R. J., 173, 174, 175, 195
Tichy, N. M., 107, 109, 116
Tjosvold, D., 142, 168
Todd, H., 202, 230
Tompkins, P. K., 6, 16, 26, 87, 92, 96, 99, 116, 127, 137
Tracy, K., 190, 194
Trenholm, S., 218, 230
Trujillo, N., 91, 116
Tubbs, S. L., 30, 42, 51
Turoff, M., 179, 194, 254, 262

Ugbah, S., 131, 137
Uttal, B., 130, 137

Van Maanen, J. W., 109, 116, 221, 230
Vergin, R. C., 179, 183, 195

Wakefield, G., 292, 307
Wallence, W., 319, 326
Walton, E., 99, 116
Walton, R. E., 158, 161, 168
Watzlawick, P., 35, 42, 51
Webb, E. J., 296, 307, 312, 326
Weber, M., 54, 56, 57, 80
Weick, K. E., 32, 51, 70, 80, 86, 103, 104, 110, 116, 188, 195, 199, 230, 235, 263
Weinberg, S. B., 32, 34, 50, 238, 260
Wenberg, J., 44, 51
Werner, E., 16, 24
West, J. M., 175, 177, 183, 195
Wheeless, L. R., 213, 230
Wheeless, V. E., 213, 230
Whisler, T., 180, 195
White, K., 220, 229
White, L. L., 16, 25, 75, 80
White, R., 240, 263
Whorf, G. L., 31, 51
Whyte, W. F., 330, 346

Wiio, O. A., 70, 80, 199, 229, 316, 326
Wilcox, J. R., 34, 50
Williams, L. C., Jr., 5, 26, 266, 271, 288
Wilmot, W., 44, 51
Wilmoth, G. H., 216, 228
Wilson, S. R., 156, 157, 167
Wiseman, G., 266, 288
Witteman, H., 199, 224, 229
Wofford, J. C., 263
Wolman, C., 243, 263
Wood, J. T., 32, 51, 132, 137
Wright, J. P., 119, 137

Yates, M. P., 8, 24, 87, 94, 115
Yoon, Y., 248, 261
Young, J. W., 219, 230

Zald, M., 158, 168
Zaleznik, A., 84, 116, 245, 263
Zawacki, R. A., 18, 25, 97, 114, 132, 137
Zima, J. P., 92, 93, 95, 116

Subject Index

Absolute information, 87
Academy of Management, 302
Acceptant interventions, 331
Action research
  in organization development,
    297
  steps in, 330
Adaptation
  and horizontal communication,
    97
  as organizational characteristic,
    18
  in organizational effectiveness,
    298
  and positive feedback, 74
Adaptors
  in body movement, 39
Administration
  Follett's theory of, 60–61
Affect displays
  in body movement, 39
Affection, 200
Agenda setting interventions,
  332–33
Ambiguity
  in language use, 32–34
  in organizational structure, 153
  strategic use of, 33–34
American Medical Association,
  278
American Motors, 73
American Society for Training
  and Development, 302
American Telephone and
  Telegraph, 274
Argumentativeness, 214–15
Assimilation Theory, 221–22
Audit. See Communication audit
Authoritarian leaders, 240
Authority-obedience leader, 241
Authority rule, 246
Automated office system, 171
Automation, 177
Average leadership style, 244
Avis Rent-a-Car, 32

Baby boomers, 132
Bargaining
  defined, 160
  distributive vs. integrative,
    161–62

Behavioral objectives, 339
Benevolent-authoritative system,
  67
Bethlehem Steel, 55, 282
Body movement
  analogy with language, 38
  categories of, 38–39
  kinesic theory, 38
Brainstorming, 254
Bureau of Labor Statistics, 6, 132

Catalytic interventions, 331
Centralization
  as a consequence of technology,
    178
  defined, 56
  vs. decentralization, 67–68
Centralized processing, 174
Channels
  and communication structure,
    91
  flexible vs. restricted, 67–68
Chrysler Corporation, 3, 33,
  73–74, 132, 276
Coaching, 338
Coalitions
  influence on organizational
    change, 130
  as network structures, 109
  in political conflict, 85, 158
Coercive power, 140
Communication
  as bilateral experience, 42
  channels of, 67–68, 91
  defined, 29
  functions of, 85–91
  interactional model of, 44
  linear model of, 43
  paradoxes in, 32, 34
  as receiver experience, 41
  rules in, 205–6
  as source experience, 41
  structure of, 91–110
  synchronic vs. diachronic, 268
  systematic distortion of, 15,
    145–46
  technological consequences for,
    175–90
  transactional model of, 44

Communication audits
  concept of, 315
  criticisms of, 319–20
  International Communication
    Association system, 316–20
  objectives of, 316
  OCD and LTT systems, 316
Communication climate
  and employee satisfaction, 70
  and participative management,
    66
  see also interpersonal climate
Communication effectiveness
  characteristics of, 12, 68
  and organizational effectiveness,
    5
Communication functions
  interpretive study of, 90–91
  types of, 85–86
  unanswered questions about,
    89–90
Communication professionals
  as consultants, 293
  demand for, 5–6
  influence of functionalism on,
    19
  occupations for, 292–93
  in public relations, 292
  in training and development,
    293
Communication structure
  definitions of, 91–92
  formal, 92–99
  informal, 99–102
  as a network, 104–10
  as a social construction, 102
Compensation and benefits
  as public communication
    subject, 273
Competition, 153
Compliance
  Barnard's theory of, 61
Compliance-gaining
  and feedback, 217
  in superior-subordinate
    communication, 217–19
Computerized accounting, 173
Computers. See Information
  processing technology
Conceptual inputs
  as intervention, 335–36

Conflict
  inevitability of, 150
  intergroup, 157–60
  interpersonal, 155–57
  management of, 154–55
  sources of, 151–54
  styles of, 155
Conflict resolution
  activities in, 155
Conformity, 237
Confrontation interventions, 331
Consensus, 246–47
Constrained decision, 268
Consultation
  and communication
    professionals, 293
  as helping activity, 293
  models of, 294–99
  organizational politics in,
    300–301
  and organization development,
    297
  and professional ethics, 301–2
Consultative system, 67
Content analysis, 320
Contingency theory, 70
Control, 57, 67–68, 200
Coordination, 3, 57
Coorientation
  states of, 206–7
  in superior-subordinate
    communication, 216–17
Country club leader, 241
Coupling
  characteristics in networks, 104,
    110
  and interdependence, 103
  loose vs. tight, 103–4
Critical theory
  described, 15–16, 143–49
  and Neomarxism, 144
  in organizational
    communication research,
    147–48
  vs. interpretivism, 149
Cultural change
  cautions regarding, 129, 132–33
  management direction in,
    129–30
  and the symbolic managers,
    130–31

Cultural variation
    in decision making, 247–48
    in use of space, 40
Culture vultures, 129
Cycles
    in group development, 252

Decentralization
    as a consequence of technology,
        178–79
    vs. centralization, 67–68
Decision-making
    and centralization, 67–68
    and culture, 247–48
    effectiveness in, 248–50
    in groups, 245–56
    models of, 253–56
    sequences, 251–52
    stages of, 250–51
Defensive communication, 212–13
Delphi, 254
Democratic leaders, 240
Democratic processes
    in organizational life, 60
Diagnosis. See organizational
    communication evaluation
Direct observation
    in organizational
        communication evaluation,
        312–13
Dissensus, 206
Distributed information, 87
Distributed processing, 175
Division of labor, 56, 59
Doctor-nurse game, 34
Documents
    use of in evaluation, 315
Double interact
    as unit of organizing, 199
Downward communication
    diffusion methods, 94
    filtering of, 94
    management theory views of, 92
    type of messages in, 93
    overload vs. inadequacy, 93–94
Dyad, 199
Dyadic communication
    theories of, 200–207

Eastern Airlines, 163–66
ECCO analysis, 323
Effective supervision
    characteristics of, 210–12
Electric theories, 60–61
Emblems
    in nonverbal communication, 38
Emergence
    in group development, 250
Employee communications. See
    internal public
    communication
ERISA, 273
Ethics
    codes of, 301–3
    in consulting, 301–3

Evaluation
    of training, 339
    see also organizational
        communication evaluation
Executive functions
    Barnard's theory of, 61
Expert power, 141
Exploitative-authoritative system,
    67
External public communication
    defined, 266
    forms of, 275
    public affairs and issues
        management, 277–82
    public relations, 276–77
External system
    in group processes, 234

Face support
    in performance feedback, 217
False consensus, 206
Fantasies, 123
Fantasy theme analysis, 123–24
Fantasy type, 123
Fatalism
    in decision situations, 268
Federal Express, 93
Feedback
    client receptivity to, 337
    and compliance-gaining, 217
    as an intervention, 336
    in interventions, 336–38
    negative, 74
    positive, 74
    in superior-subordinate
        communication, 210, 217
    and system processes, 74
Filtering
    of information, 94, 96
FIRO, 200
Fixed feature space, 39
Ford Motor Company, 11, 73, 276
Formal communication
    downward, 92–95
    horizontal, 95–96
    problems in defining, 103–4
    upward, 97–99
Function
    defined, 83
    relationship to structure, 84
    see also communication
        function
Functionalism
    contemporary form of, 16–19
    criticisms of, 19–20
    defined, 11
    living system metaphor in, 18
    machine metaphor in, 12
    traditional form of, 11–12
    view of organizational culture,
        120–21

General Motors, 73, 119, 276
Giant Food Corporation, 131,
    280–81

Grapevine communication. See
    informal communication
Group communication
    concepts in, 235
    decision process models in,
        253–56
    and effective decision making,
        248–50
    importance of procedural
        direction, 249
    influence on sense making, 256
Group-restricted codes, 34–35
Groups
    decision-making in, 245–56
    internal vs. external systems in,
        234
    maintenance roles in, 239
    norms and conformity in,
        236–37
    as organizational subsystems,
        233–34
    stages of development, 250
    task role in, 239
Groupthink, 150–51

Harvard University, 62, 64
Hawthorne studies
    attention to informal system, 99
    compliance with authority, 92
    criticism of, 64
    described, 62–64
Hierarchical structure, 56, 59
Hierarchy, 59, 71–72
Hopi Indian Language, 31
Horizontal communication
    efficiency vs. effectiveness,
        97–98
    and flexibility, 97
    management theory views of, 97
    obstacles to, 98–99
    in participative decision
        making, 97
Human communication
    functionalist views of, 11, 17–18
Human function
    in communication, 86
Human processes
    intervention in, 332
    in organizations, 4
Human relations movement
    Carnegie method, 62
    criticisms of, 64
    and the Hawthorne studies,
        62–64
Human resource development
    communication implications in,
        68
    and Maslow's need hierarchy,
        65
    and participative management,
        66
    Theory X and Theory Y, 66
Hygiene factors, 201

IBM, 3, 25, 147–48
Illustrators
    in nonverbal communication, 32

Image making
    in public relations, 276–77
    and search for meaning, 277
Impoverished leader, 241
Inclusion, 207
Indoctrination, 271
Industrial revolution, 53
Informal communication
    defined, 99
    functions of, 100
    participants in, 100
    patterns and media, 100–101
    problems in defining, 99
    relation to formal systems, 100
    role in rumor transmission, 101
    volume, speed, and reliability,
        101
Informal space
    cultural variation in, 40
Information
    absolute vs. distributed, 37
    acquisition in decision
        situations, 268–70
    defined, 30
    and meaning, 30
    methods of diffusion, 94
    overload vs. inadequacy, 93
Information adequacy
    concept of, 87
    relationship to other variables,
        88–89
Information diffusion
    defined, 87
    failures in policy, 94
Information power, 141
Information technology
    acceptance of, 184–85
    and change in organizational
        structure, 178–82
    effects on interaction, 172,
        185–89
    effects on jobs, 183–84
    effects on sense-making, 188
    influence on communication,
        172
    and the information network,
        185–89
    multimode capability, 185
    types of, 172–75
Inner perspective
    in organizational
        communication evaluation,
        311
Innovation function
    in communication, 86
Institute for Social Research, 242
Integrated data processing, 173
Interaction analysis, 321–22
Interactional model, 44
Interdependence
    in system theory, 71
Internal public communication
    concerning compensation and
        benefits, 273
    defined, 266
    effective of ERISA, 273
    effect of OSHA, 272
    media, 271
    orientation, and indoctrination,
        271–72

and promotion of morale, 274–75
role in organizational change, 273–74
safety and loss prevention through, 272–73
Internal system
in group processes, 234
International Communication Association, 88, 94, 303
Interpersonal climate, 212–13
Interpersonal needs, 200
Interpersonal relations fundamental orientation, 200
Interpretivism
as alternative to functionalism, 19
approach to organizational culture, 121–22
cultural metaphor in, 12
defined, 12
focus on meaning in, 12
methods of study, 122–29
Intervention
defined, 329
models of, 330–32
in organizational communication, 329–30
relationship to action research, 330
relationship to evaluation, 329
types in organizational communication, 332–42
Interviews
in evaluation of communication, 313, 317
Issues advocacy, 281–82
Issues management
and issues advocacy, 281–82
and organizational change, 280–81
in public communication, 277–82
tools for, 279–80

Japanese organizations
comparison to Western, 97–98
decision making, 247
use of horizontal communication, 97
use of quality circles in, 255
Jeep, 73
Job enrichment programs, 201
Junior Achievement, 272

Laissez-faire leaders, 240
Language
and experience, 31–32
as symbol system, 31
as a system of oppression, 13
Leader-member exchange, 244
Leadership
maintenance dimension, 242
sex role incongruence in, 243
styles of, 240–42
task dimension, 242

theories of, 240–45
as a trait, 240
vs. management, 244–45
Legitimate power, 141
Levels of communication, 83
Linear model, 43
Local area network, 185–90
Locus of control, 220
Loosely coupled systems, 103–4, 110

Maintenance function
in communication, 86
Maintenance roles, 239
Majority rule, 246, 253
Management information system
integrated, 173
real time, 174
Management theory. See organization theory
Matrix organization, 72
Meaning
and ambiguity, 32
defined, 30
and information, 30
in interpretivism, 12
Mechanization, 177
Mentor-protege relationships, 224–25
Metaphor
analysis of, 125–26
as basis for sense-making, 26, 125
defined, 124
types of, 125
Microcomputers, 179
Middle-of-the-road leader, 241
Minicomputers, 175
Minority coalition, 246
Models
of communication 43, 45
Modernist orientation, 14
Monitoring, 280
Monolithic consensus, 206–7
Morale and satisfaction
and public communication, 274–75
Motivation
deficiency needs, 66
drive, 66
and dyadic communication, 200–201
growth needs, 66
in human resource development, 65–66
importance in management theory, 8
managerial approach to, 68
motivator-hygiene, 201
need hierarchy, 65
Motivator-hygiene theory, 201
Motivators, 201
Mountain Bell Telephone, 274
Multisystems theory
in public communication, 268–70

NASA, 7, 98
National Science Foundation, 61
Naturalistic orientation, 14
Need hierarchy, 65
Needs assessment. See organizational communication evaluation
Negotiation. See bargaining
Network analysis
in communication audits, 318
compared to ECCO analysis, 323
limitations, 110
methods, 104–5
uses of, 108–9
Network structure
change over time, 110
properties of, 107–8
roles in, 106
New Jersey Bell Telephone, 61
Nominal group methods, 254
Nonverbal behavior, 35–40
Norms, 236–37
Northwestern University, 6

Occupational communities, 109
Occupational stress, 223
Ohio State University, 6, 242–43
Ohio University, 7
Openness, 71
Open system, 72–73
Organization
as a communication system, 3–4, 61
defined, 3
as living system, 18
as machine, 12
Organization development
defined, 297
and organizational effectiveness, 297–99
paradox in, 299
as political facilitation, 300–301
in process consultation, 297
Organizational change
facilitation of, 333
and issues management, 280–81
organization development theory of, 297–99
political dynamics in, 17
and public communication, 279
unilateral management direction in, 132
Organizational climate, 68
Organizational communication
alternative models of, 14–15
careers in, 5–6, 291–94
as cultural performance, 119
evaluation of, 309–23
field of study defined, 4–5
functions of, 85–91
influence of technology on, 172, 175–90
managerial bias in study of, 18
perspectives on, 8–15
relationship to other field, 7

role of organizational politics in, 84–85
strategies for changing, 332–42
structural-functional model of, 19, 70
structure of, 91–110
systematic distortion of, 15, 145–46
Organizational communication evaluation
defined, 309
general methods of, 312–15
perspectives on, 311
purposes of, 310
relationship to intervention, 329
specific tools for, 315–23
Organizational culture
attempting to change, 129–33
concept of, 119–20
forces influencing, 130
functionalist perspective of, 120–21
interpretivist perspective of, 121–22
methods of studying, 122–29
and workforce composition, 132
Organizational effectiveness
and communication effectiveness, 5
and motivational theory, 8
preoccupation with, 8
and quality of organizational life, 18
Organizational life
quality of, 18
Organizational order
in contemporary functionalism, 16–17
as political structure, 9–10
radical view of, 10
regulative view of, 10
Organizational politics
coalitions in, 85
in consultation, 299
impact of function and structure, 84
Organizational reality
in contemporary functionalism, 16
objective features of, 10
as a social construction, 10–11
Organizational structure. See structure
Organization theory
contingency approach to, 70
eclectic, 60–61
human relations, 62–65
human resource development, 65–70
scientific and classical, 54–60
system theory, 70–75
Orientation, 250, 271–72
OSHA, 273
Outer perspective
in organizational communication evaluation, 311

Paralanguage
  and interpretive cues, 37
  role in person perception, 38
Parliamentary procedure, 253
Participative management
  an communication climate, 66
  in human resource development, 66
  and satisfaction, 213
Participative system, 67
Personality
  and dyadic communication, 202
  types in organizations, 202–3
Pluralistic ignorance, 206
Politics. *See* Organizational politics
Power
  and communication, 143
  in competition and cooperation, 142
  in critical theory, 143–49
  and legitimation, 144
  redefining, 60–61
  reducing inequalities in, 300
  relationship to status, 140
  and social exchange, 142–43
  and structure, 144
  traditional views of, 139–43
  types of, 140–41
Prescriptive interventions, 331
Problem-facing
  in decision situations, 268–69
Process analysis, 333–34
Production function
  in communication, 85
Professional ethics, 301–3
Public affairs
  and issues management, 277–80
Public communication
  characteristics of, 266–67
  defined, 265
  external, 275–82
  internal, 271–275
  multisystems theory of, 268–70
Public relations
  and image building, 276–77
Public Service Company of New
    Mexico, 282
Purdue University, 6, 211–12

Quality circles, 255–56

Radical humanism, 13
Radical perspectives
  integrated in critical theory, 15
Radical structuralism, 13
Real time MIS, 174
Referent power, 141
Reflective thinking, 253
Reflexive comments
  analysis of, 127–29
  types of, 128

Regulators
  in body movement, 39
Reinforcement
  in group development, 250
Renaissance, 53
Renault, 73
Reward power, 140
Rhetorical vision, 123
Role
  definition of, 238
  enacted, 238
  expected, 238
  in groups, 238–39
  perceived, 238
Role conflict, 151
Romantic relationships, 224
Routine habit
  in decision situations, 268
Rules
  as basis for bureaucracy, 57
  and communicative episodes, 205
  constitutive, 205
  coorientation states in, 206, 216
  examples of in communication, 205–6
  in dyadic communication, 203–7
  regulative, 205
  as social knowledge, 203

Safety and loss prevention, 272–73
Satisfaction
  with job, 199, 211
  with superiors, 211–12
Scalar chain of command, 56, 59
Scanning, 280
Scenario writing, 280
Scientific and classical management
  comparison of theories, 57–58
  criticisms of, 59–60
  Fayol's theory, 55–56
  Taylor's scientific theory, 54–55
  Weber's bureaucratic theory, 56–57
Script analysis, 174
Self-actualization, 65–66
Self-oriented behavior
  in groups, 239, 252
Self-regulation, 18
Semifixed-feature space, 40
Serial reproduction
  and message filtering, 94
Sex discrimination, 13
Sex roles, 243
Sexual harassment, 13
Signs
  characteristics of, 35
  vs. symbols, 35
Situational theory
  of leadership, 242–43
Social exchange, 142

Social science
  as basis for organization development, 297
  in functionalism, 11
Space
  fixed-feature, 39
  informal, 40
  and proxemics, 39
  semifixed-feature, 40
Speech Communication Association, 303
Standard testing, 334–35
Status
  relationship to power, 140
Status symbols, 140
Strong culture
  characteristics of, 121
  as misleading concept, 130
Structural-functionalism, 83
Structural intervention
  in conflict management, 154
  in organizational communication, 340–42
  risks of, 341
Structure
  defined, 83
  of organizational communication, 91–92
  and power, 144
  relationship to function, 84
  as system of oppression, 13–14
Suggestion systems, 96
Superior-subordinate communication
  accuracy and distortion in, 212, 219
  argumentativeness in, 214–15
  assimilation theory in, 221–22
  compliance-gaining in, 217–18, 220
  coorientation in, 216–17
  effective of upward mobility aspirations, 219
  effect of upward influence, 215–16
  face support in, 217
  factors related to satisfaction, 211–17
  general conclusions from research on, 222–23
  importance of, 208
  interpersonal climate, 212
  locus of control in, 220
  openness and trust in, 209, 212, 219
  research on, 208–22
Superordinate goals
  in conflict management, 134
Supportive communication, 212–13
Survey questionnaires
  in evaluation of communication, 314, 317
Symbolic manager, 130–31
Symbols
  characteristics of, 31
  vs. signs, 35

System theory
  criticisms of, 75
  implications for communication, 75
  key concepts in, 71–74
  and the organismic analogy, 71
  origins of, 70
Systematic distortion, 15, 145–46

Task roles, 239
Team leaders, 242
Theory and principle interventions, 331
Theory X, 66
Theory Y, 66
Time-sharing systems, 174
Training
  careers in, 6
  as intervention, 338
  model of, 339–40
Transactional model, 44
Trend extrapolation, 279
Trend impact analysis, 280
Type Z organization, 98

Unanimity, 246
Uncertainty reduction, 86
United Auto Workers, 132
United States Postal Service, 58
University of Southern California, 6
Upward communication
  accuracy in, 96
  management receptivity to, 96
  management theory views of, 95
  token attention to, 96
  uses of, 96
Upward influence, 215–16
Upward mobility aspirations
  effects on communication, 96, 209, 219

Values
  differences in conflict, 153
Verbal behavior, 30–35

W. R. Grace Corporation, 284
Western Electric Company, 62
Wholeness, 71
Women in management, 132
Workforce composition, 132